Keeping Score

*Film and Television Music,
1988–1997*

Alvin H. Marill

The Scarecrow Press, Inc.
Lanham, Md., & London
1998

SCARECROW PRESS, INC.

Published in the United States of America
by Scarecrow Press, Inc.
4720 Boston Way
Lanham, Maryland 20706

4 Pleydell Gardens
Kent CT20 2DN, England

British Library Cataloguing in Publication Information Available

Library of Congress Cataloging-in-Publication Data

Marill, Alvin H.
  Keeping Score : film and television music, 1988–1997 / Alvin H. Marill.
      p.   cm.
  Continues: Keeping score / James L. Limbacher. 1991.
  Includes Index.
  ISBN 0-8108-3416-2
  1. Motion picture music—Bibliography.   I. Limbacher, James L.
  Keeping score.
  ML128.M7M28   1998   98-28712
  016.7815'42—dc21   CIP
                                                           MN

⊖™ The paper used in this publication meets the minimum requirements of
American National Standard for Information Sciences—Permanence of
Paper for Printed Library Materials, ANSI Z39.48–1984.
Manufactured in the United States of America.

TO MIKLOS ROZSA (1907-1995) AND HENRY MANCINI (1924-1994)
VELL AS THE TWO IRVINGS—BERLIN (1888-1989) AND CAESAR (1895-1996)

CONTENTS

INTRODUCTION

The movies keep coming—or in recent years going direct to video—and the music never stops. Well almost never.

To quote a guy named Bogart (via scriptwriters Casey Robinson and Jack Moffitt) in *Passage to Marseille* back in 1944, "funny how much more you can say with a few bars of music than a basketful of words." Those few bars were supplied, at least in this flick, by the estimable Max Steiner, who, with colleagues of the time, including Erich Wolfgang Korngold, Alfred Newman, Dimitri Tiomkin, Bernard Herrmann, and Miklos Rozsa, virtually defined the art of film composing and scoring.

These giants have passed on to that great music salon in the sky, and their mantles and batons were taken up by a talented new generation that included Alex North, David Raksin, Henry Mancini, John Williams, Elmer Bernstein, Jerry Goldsmith, Maurice Jarre, Michel Legrand, John Addison, and John Barry. In turn, these musical greats were followed by men (and now women) such as Hans Zimmer, Michael Kamen, Gabriel Yared, the Newmans (Randy, Thomas, and David), James Horner, Randy Edelman, Danny Elfman, Gary Chang, Marc Shaiman, Laura Karpman, Rachel Portman, Shirley Walker, and Nan Mishkin Schwartz.

Their lyrical scores, many still being preserved or re-created on CDs by specialty recording companies such as Varese Sarabande, Milan, Entr'Acte, Silva, and Marco Polo, as well as the more traditional Sony (Columbia), MCA, and BMG (RCA Victor), continue to enhance what moviegoers and television watchers see and hear, underpinning scene after scene, situation after situation . . . although, increasingly in the nineties, filmmakers have been spicing up their soundtracks with recordings by contemporary rock and rap performers at the expense of traditional music underscoring. Even Woody Allen, with his lifelong love of jazz and America's great composers, has opted to use the recordings of Gershwin and confreres to score his films.

In 1995, a new music tradition was begun by *Daily Variety*, which began honoring film composers with its "American Music Legend" award. The first recipient was the prolific Jerry Goldsmith, whose movie scores date back to the late 1950s with a little big-screen item called *Black Patch* and continue four decades later. The 1996 honoree was the equally prolific Elmer Bernstein, whose earliest movie score was for actor John Derek's 1951 film *Saturday's Hero,* and he, too, is still making movie music. Today, he remains the dean of active film (and sometimes television) composers.

Being a "star" composer does not mean, though, that the film score originally contracted for by the studio or the producer or the director will be the one enhancing the movie when it gets to the local multiplex. Remember Alfred Hitchcock's *Torn Curtain* (1966) and Stanley Kubrick's *2001: A Space Odyssey* (1968)?

Scores for these two originally were written by Bernard Herrmann and Alex North, respectively. They ultimately were thrown out for one reason or another, and replaced by music composed by John Addison and Richard Strauss (long dead). The discarding of Herrmann's score resulted in a permanent rupture between Hitchcock and his longtime music scorer—but then again, Hitchcock made only three more films and Herrmann threw in his musical lot with Brian De Palma and Martin Scorsese.

Henry Mancini, who scored nearly everything Blake Edwards did on film, as well as on television, from 1959 onward, originally was hired to score Hitchcock's *Frenzy* (1972), but it was Ron Goodwin's music that was finally used. Jerry Goldsmith's score for Ridley Scott's *Legend* (1985) was replaced—at least in the U.S.—by that of the Eurotech group known as Tangerine Dream. Goldsmith's, curiously, was used in the European version of the film! Elmer Bernstein's music for Walter Hill's *Last Man Standing* (1996) gave way to a score by Ry Cooder; Howard Shore's score for Ron Howard's *Ransom* (1996) was replaced by James Horner's; Michael Kamen's for Richard Donner's *Assassins* (1995) by Mark Mancina's; Randy Newman's for Wolfgang Petersen's *Air Force One* (1997) by Jerry Goldsmith's. Newman had written about seventy minutes of the score before being informed that the producers were going in another direction, so he bought it back for recycling and a possible CD retrospective of his work. (Generally, master recordings and publishing rights to the music belong to the studio that hired the composer in the first place.) Even British director Mike Figgis, who frequently scores his own films, "fired" himself, in effect, but recycled some of the music he wrote for his *The Browning Version* (1994)—composer Mark Isham's name appears in the credits—for his very different *Leaving Las Vegas* (1995).

The full-bodied, sometimes symphonic music scores remain in demand, and those who composed them—more than 7,300 individual entries—are chronicled in this updated volume that first found life in 1974 as *Film Music: From Violins to Video* and was followed by its compiler/editor James I. Limbacher in *Keeping Score: Film Music 1972-1979* and *Keeping Score: Film and Television Music 1980-1988*. The tradition and the music continue here, covering the years 1989 through 1997 (with a few titles from 1987 and 1988 that slipped by Jim and his associates).

The entries in this volume are primarily English-language theatrical and direct-to-video features and made-for-television movies and miniseries. Also included are those French, Italian and Spanish films that have made their way to the international market, together with a smattering of other foreign language movies with scores by composers who have established an international reputation.

Like its predecessors, this volume is divided into various sections: films and their composers by year; an alphabetical list of composers and their credits chronologically; and an alphabetical list of film titles. In addition, there are composer awards lists: Oscars, Emmys, Ace Awards (initially in the 1980s called CableAce), and Golden Globes, as well as a general (though not definitive) discography of original soundtracks and musical scores that can be found on CD.

For their help and inspiration in the assembling of this compilation, thanks go to good friend and researcher Jerry Vermilye, and extremely patient computer whiz Michael Weber.

And so, on the pages that follow, we continue keeping score . . .

KEY TO ABBREVIATIONS

(ABC, CBS, NBC, HBO, Showtime, and TNT refer, of course, to the television networks)

Disney-TV	Disney Channel cable network	Aut	Australian
Fam Ch	Family Channel cable network	Br	British
		Can	Canadian
Lifetime	Lifetime cable network	Dan	Danish
Syn	Syndicated television	Fr	French
USA Net	USA Network	Ger	German
		Hung	Hungarian
		Ire	Irish
BV	Buena Vista films	It	Italian
Col	Columbia Pictures	Jap	Japanese
Dream	Dreamworks	NewZea	New Zealand
Fox-TV	Fox Television	Port	Portuguese
Fox	Twentieth Century Fox Pictures	Rus	Russian
		SAfr	South African
Ind	Independent film production	Sp	Spanish
		Yugo	Yugoslavian
Par	Paramount Pictures		
Univ	Universal Pictures		
WB	Warner Bros.		

(Those joined by slashes are joint productions by two or more countries)

FILMS AND THEIR COMPOSERS BY YEAR

Film	Source/Network	Composer

1987

Film	Source/Network	Composer
Angel in Green	CBS-TV	Allyn Ferguson
Blood Vows: The Story of a Mafia Wife	NBC-TV	William Goldstein
Dangerous Affection	NBC-TV	J.A.C. Redford
Deadly Deception	CBS-TV	Duane Tatro
Dennis the Menace: The Live-Action Movie	Syn	Randy Edelman
Desperate	ABC-TV	Lee Holdridge
Different Affair, A	CBS-TV	Johnny Harris
Dirty Dozen: The Deadly Mission	NBC-TV	John Cacavas
Downpayment on Murder	NBC-TV	Laurence Rosenthal
Fight for Life	ABC-TV	Laurence Rosenthal
Ford: The Man and the Machine	Can TV	Paul Zaza
Gunsmoke: Return to Dodge	CBS-TV	Jerrold Immel
Hands of a Stranger	NBC-TV	Michel Rubini
Highwayman, The	NBC-TV	Stu Phillips
Home Fires	Showtime	Dan Kuramoto
Hoover vs. the Kennedys: The Second Civil War	Syn	Paul Hoffert
Hour of the Assassin	Ind	Fred Myrow
If It's Tuesday, This Still Must Be Belgium	NBC-TV	Ken Thorne
Impossible Spy, The	HBO	Richard Hartley
Ladies, The	NBC-TV	Morton Stevens
Laguna Heat	HBO	Patrick Williams
Long Gone	HBO	Phillip Namanworth
Long Gone	HBO	Kenny Vance
Mayflower Madam	CBS-TV	David Shire
Murder by the Book	CBS-TV	Mark Snow
Nutcracker: Money, Madness and Murder	NBC-TV	Billy Goldenberg
Perry Mason: The Case of the Lost Love	NBC-TV	Dick DeBenedictis
Perry Mason: The Case of the Murdered Madam	NBC-TV	Dick DeBenedictis
Perry Mason: The Case of the Scandalous Scoundrel	NBC-TV	Dick DeBenedictis
Perry Mason: The Case of the Sinister Spirit	NBC-TV	Dick DeBenedictis
Prison for Children	CBS-TV	Basil Poledouris
Quo Vadis?	USA/RAI-UNO	Piero Piccioni
Roman Holiday	NBC-TV	Mark Snow
Sister Margaret and the Saturday Night Ladies	CBS-TV	Gerald Alters
Stepford Children, The	NBC-TV	Joseph Conlan
Stranger in My Bed	NBC-TV	Laurence Rosenthal
Three on a Match	NBC-TV	Ian Freebairn-Smith
Three Wishes for Jamie	Syn	Paddy Moloney

U.S. Marshals: Waco & Rhinehart	ABC-TV	Tom Bahler
U.S. Marshals: Waco & Rhinehart	ABC-TV	Chris Boardman
U.S. Marshals: Waco & Rhinehart	ABC-TV	Randy Kerber
U.S. Marshals: Waco & Rhinehart	ABC-TV	Bruce Miller
U.S. Marshals: Waco & Rhinehart	ABC-TV	Joel Rosenbaum
You Ruined My Life	ABC-TV	Jonathan Tunick
Young Harry Houdini	ABC-TV	Lee Holdridge

1988

Alien From L.A.	Cannon	James Sand
Angel 3: The Final Chapter	Ind	Eric Allaman
Bad Girls From Mars	Ind	Louis Febre
Black Eagle	Ind	Terry Plumeri
Black Roses	Ind	Elliot Solomon
Blind Justice	It	Ennio Morricone
Border Heat	Ind	Chuck Cirino
Case Closed	CBS-TV	Sylvester Levay
Cinema Paradiso	It	Ennio Morricone
Counterforce	Ind	Joel Goldsmith
Dark Tower	Ind	Stacy Widelitz
Deadline: Madrid	ABC-TV	Larry Carlton
Desert Rats	NBC-TV	J. Peter Robinson
Dracula's Widow	Ind	James Campbell
Emma: Queen of the South Seas	Syn/Aut	Felicity & John Halsey
Evil in Clear River	ABC-TV	William Olvis
Expendables, The	Concorde	Jaime Fabregas
Favorite Son	BC-TV	John Morris
Friendship in Vienna, A	Disney-TV	Lee Holdridge
Goodbye, Miss 4th of July	Disney-TV	Mark Snow
Gotham	Showtime	George S. Clinton
Grand Larceny	Syn	Irwin Fisch
I'll Be Home for Christmas	NBC-TV	Jorge Calandrelli
King of the Olympics: Lives & Loves of Avery Brundage	Syn	Paul Chihara
Lawless Land, The	Concorde	Lucia Hwong
Maigret	Syn/Br	Alan Lisk
Man Against the Mob	NBC-TV	Artie Kane
Man Who Lived in the Ritz	Syn	Richard Rodney Bennett
Miracle at Beekman's Place	NBC-TV	Harry Middlebrooks
Miracle at Beekman's Place	NBC-TV	Chris Page
Misfit Brigade, The	Ind	Ole Hoyer
Moving Target	NBC-TV	Michel Rubini
Necessity	CBS-TV	Johnny Harris
Nitti	ABC-TV	Yanni
Out of the Shadows	Showtime	Dave Lawson
People Across the Lake, The	NBC-TV	Dana Kaproff
Save the Dog!	Disney-TV	J.A.C. Redford
Scandal in a Small Town	NBC-TV	Mark Snow
See You in the Morning	WB	Michael Small
Shootdown	NBC-TV	Craig Safan
Skeleton Coast	US/SAfr	Colin Shapiro
Smoke Screen	Can	Lawrence Shragge
Star Slammer: The Escape	Ind	Anthony Harris

Steal the Sky	HBO	Yanni
Stones for Ibarra	CBS-TV	Stanley Myers
Take My Daughters, Please	NBC-TV	Nan Schwartz
Taking of Flight 847: The Uli Derickson Story, The	NBC-TV	Gil Melle
Time to Remember, A	Ind	Bill Grabowski
Under the Gun	Ind	John Sterling
Unholy Matrimony	CBS-TV	Michel Rubini
Who Gets the Friends?	CBS-TV	Gary William Friedman
Winnie	NBC-TV	Bennett Salvay
Winnie	NBC-TV	W.G. Snuffy Walden
Witchcraft	Ind	Randy Miller

1989

84 Charlie Mopic	Col	Donovan
976-Evil	New Line	Thomas Chase
976-Evil	New Line	Steve Rucker
'burbs, The	Univ	Jerry Goldsmith
Abyss, The	Fox	Alan Silvestri
Action U.S.A.	Ind	Del Casher
Adventures of Baron Munchausen, The	Col	Michael Kamen
Adventures of Milo & Otis, The	Jap	Michael Boddicker
Adventures of William Tell, The	Fr	Stanislas Syrewicz
After Midnight	MGM/UA	Marc Donahue
After School	Ind	David Williams
Agatha Christie's "The Man in the Brown Suit"	CBS-TV	Arthur B. Rubinstein
Age-Old Friends	HBO	Stanley Myers
Alexa	Ind	Gregory Alper
All Dogs Go to Heaven	MGM/UA	Ralph Burns
All Dogs Go to Heaven	MGM /UA	Charles Strouse
All's Fair	Ind	Bill Myers
Always	Univ	John Williams
American Ninja 3: Blood Hunt	Cannon	George S. Clinton
Amityville: The Evil Escapes	NBC-TV	Rick Conrad
Angels of the City	Ind	John Gonzalez
Animal Behavior	Ind	Cliff Eidelman
Apartment Zero	Ind	Elia Cmiral
B.O.R.N.	Ind	William Belote
Babar: The Movie	New Line	Milan Kymlicka
Babycakes	CBS-TV	William Olvis
Back to the Future Part II	Univ	Alan Silvestri
Backtrack (aka Catchfire)	Ind	Michel Colombier
Bad Blood	Ind	Joey Mennonna
Batman	WB	Danny Elfman
Baxter	Fr	Marc Hillman
Baxter	Fr	Patrick Roffe
Baywatch: Panic at Malibu Pier	NBC-TV	Arthur B. Rubinstein
Bear, The	Col	Bill Conti
Bearskin: An Urban Fairytale	Br/Port	Michael McEvoy
Bert Rigby, You're a Fool	WB	Ralph Burns
Best of the Best	Ind	Paul Gilman
Beverly Hills Brats	Ind	Barry Goldberg

Big Man on Campus	Vestron	Joseph Vitarelli
Big Picture, The	Col	David Nichtern
Bill & Ted's Excellent Adventure	Orion	David Newman
Bionic Showdown: The Six Million Dollar Man and the Bionic Woman	NBC-TV	Bill Conti
Black Rain	Par	Hans Zimmer
Black Rainbow	Br	John Scott
Blaze	BV	Bennie Wallace
Blind Fury	TriStar	J. Peter Robinson
Blind Witness	ABC-TV	Bob Alcivar
Blood and Sand	Sp	Jesus Gluck
Blood of Heroes, The	Ind	Todd Boekelheide
Bloodfist	Concorde	Sasha Matson
Bloodhounds of Broadway	Vestron	Jonathan Sheffer
Bloodstone	Ind	Jerry J. Grant
Bye Bye Blues	Can	George Blondheim
Born on the Fourth of July	Univ	John Williams
Breakfast of Aliens	Ind	Mathew Ender
Breaking In	Goldwyn	Michael Gibbs
Breaking Point	TNT	J.A.C. Redford
Brenda Starr	New World	Johnny Mandel
Bridesmaids	CBS-TV	Paul Chihara
Bridge to Silence	CBS-TV	Fred Karlin
Brotherhood of the Rose	NBC-TV	Laurence Rosenthal
Brothers in Arms	Ind	Alan Howarth
Buying Time	MGM/UA	David Krystal
Bye Bye Baby	It	Manuel De Sica
Caddie Woodlawn	Disney-TV	Joel Hirschhorn
Caddie Woodlawn	Disney-TV	Archie Jordan
Caddie Woodlawn	Disney-TV	Al Kasha
Cage	Ind	Michael Wetherwax
Cameron's Closet	Ind	Harry Manfredini
Camille Claudel	Fr	Gabriel Yared
Cannibal Women in the Avocado Jungle of Death	Ind	Carl Dante
Captain James Cook	TNT	Jose Nieto
Carpenter, The	Ind	Pierre Bundrock
Case of the Hillside Stranglers, The	NBC-TV	Gil Melle
Cast the First Stone	NBC-TV	Ira Newborn
Casualties of War	Col	Ennio Morricone
Cat Chaser	Vestron	Chick Corea
Catacombs	Ind	Pino Donaggio
Catch Me If You Can	Ind	Tangerine Dream
Celia	Aut	Chris Neal
Chains of Gold	Ind	Trevor Jones
Chameleons	NBC-TV	David E. Kole
Champagne Charlie	Syn	Georges Garvarentz
Chances Are	TriStar	Maurice Jarre
Chattahoochee	Ind	John Keane
Checking Out	WB	Carter Burwell
Cheetah	BV	Bruce Rowland
Children of Chaos	Fr	Michel Portal
China O'Brien II	Ind	Paul F. Antonelli
China O'Brien II	Ind	David Wheatley

Chorus of Disapproval, A	Br	John Du Prez
Christian	Fr/Dan	Nikolaj Christensen
Chud II: Bud the Chud	Ind	Nicholas Pike
Class Cruise	NBC-TV	Mark Davis
Cleo/Leo	Ind	Joey Mennonna
Clownhouse	Ind	Michael Becker
Clownhouse	Ind	Thomas Richardson
Code Name Vengeance	Ind	Tim James
Cohen & Tate	Ind	Bill Conti
Cold Comfort	Can	Jeff Danna
Cold Feet	Ind	Tom Bahler
Cold Sassy Tree	TNT	Brad Fiedel
Comeback, The	CBS-TV	Craig Safan
Comedie d'Ete (Summer Interlude)	Fr	Jean-Claude Vannier
Communion	Vestron	Eric Clapton
Communion	Vestron	Allan Zavod
Connecticut Yankee in King Arthur's Court, A	NBC-TV	William Goldstein
Cook, the Thief, His Wife & Her Lover, The	Fr/Dutch	Michael Nyman
Cookie	WB	Thomas Newman
Courage Mountain	Col	Sylvester Levay
Cousins	Par	Angelo Badalamenti
Cover Girl and the Cop, The	NBC-TV	Sylvester Levay
Crack House	Cannon	Michael Piccirillo
Crime Zone	Concorde	Rick Conrad
Criminal Act	Ind	Wayne Coster
Criminal Law	Ind	Jerry Goldsmith
Cross Fire	Ind	Ron Jones
Cross of Fire	NBC-TV	William Goldstein
Cry for Help: The Tracey Thurman Story, A	NBC-TV	Nicholas Pike
Cutting Class	Ind	Jill Fraser
Cyborg	Cannon	Kevin Bassinson
Dad	Univ	James Horner
Dance of Hope	Ind	Wendy Blackstone
Dance of the Damned	Concorde	Gary Stockdale
Danger Zone II: Reaper's Revenge	Ind	Robert Etoll
Dark Holiday	NBC-TV	Paul Chihara
Dark Obsession	Br	Stanley Myers
Dark Obsession	Br	Hans Zimmer
Dark River	Turner	Lee Holdridge
Dark Side of the Moon, The	Ind	Phil Davies
Dark Side of the Moon, The	Ind	Mark Ryder
Day One	CBS-TV	Mason Daring
Dead Bang	WB	Gary Chang
Dead Calm	Aut	Graeme Revell
Dead End City	Ind	Brian Bennett
Dead Man Out	HBO	Cliff Eidelman
Dead Poets Society	BV	Maurice Jarre
Deadly Obsession	Ind	Marty Dunayer
Deadly Reactor	Ind	Brian Bennett
Deadly Silence, A	ABC-TV	Richard Gibbs
Deadly Weapon	Ind	Guy Moon
Dealers	Br	Richard Hartley
Deathmaster and the Warriors From Hell	Concorde	Israel Torres

Deep Star Six	TriStar	Harry Manfredini
Delinquents, The	Aut	Miles Goodman
Desperado: Badlands Justice	NBC-TV	Michel Colombier
Desperado: The Outlaw Wars	NBC-TV	Michel Colombier
Desperate for Love	CBS-TV	Charles Bernstein
Diamond Skulls	Br	Hans Zimmer
Dinner at Eight	TNT	Jonathan Sheffer
Disorganized Crime	BV	David Newman
Distribution of Lead, The	Ind	John Zorn
Diving In	Ind	Paul Buckmaster
Diving In	Ind	Guy Moon
Do You Know the Muffin Man?	CBS-TV	Lee Holdridge
Do the Right Thing	Univ	Bill Lee
Double Exposure	Ind	Hans Zimmer
Double Exposure	Ind	Roger Bolton
Double Your Pleasure (aka The Reluctant Angel)	NBC-TV	Tim Truman
Down Twisted	Ind	Eric Allaman
Dr. Alien	Ind	Reg Purcell
Dr. Alien	Ind	Sam Winans
Dream Breakers	CBS-TV	Glenn Paxton
Dream Date	NBC-TV	Peter Bernstein
Dream Team, The	Univ	David McHugh
Dream a Little Dream	Vestron	John William Dexter
Driving Miss Daisy	WB	Hans Zimmer
Drugstore Cowboy	Ind	Elliot Goldenthal
Dry White Season, A	MGM	Dave Grusin
Easy Wheels	Ind	John Ross
Eat a Bowl of Tea	Col	Mark Adler
Eddie and the Cruisers II: Eddie Lives!	Ind	Leon Aronson
Eddie and the Crusiers II: Eddie Lives!	Ind	Marty Simon
Edge of Sanity	Br	Frederic Talgorn
Eight Is Enough Wedding, An	NBC-TV	Billy Thorpe
Emerald City	Aut	Chris Neal
Endless Descent	Ind	Joel Goldsmith
Enemies, A Love Story	Fox	Maurice Jarre
Erik the Viking	Br	Neil Innes
Everybody's Baby: The Rescue of Jessica McClure	ABC-TV	Mark Snow
Evil Altar	Ind	George L. Briggs
Evil Altar	Ind	Bruce Lowe
Evil Below, The	Ind	Julian Laxton
Experts, The	Par	Marvin Hamlisch
Eye of the Eagle II: Inside the Enemy	Concorde	Justin Lord
Fabulous Baker Boys, The	Fox	Dave Grusin
Face of the Enemy	Ind	Esfandiar Monfaredzadeh
Fakebook	Ind	Larry Schanker
False Witness	NBC-TV	David Michael Frank
Family Business	TriStar	Cy Coleman
Far From Home	Vestron	Jonathan Elias
Farewell to the King	Orion	Basil Poledouris
Fast Food	Ind	Iris Gillon
Fat Man and Little Boy	Par	Ennio Morricone
Fear Stalk	CBS-TV	Fred Karlin

Fear, Anxiety and Depression	Goldwyn	Karyn Rachtman
Fear, Anxiety and Depression	Goldwyn	Joe Romano
Field of Dreams	Univ	James Horner
Final Days, The	ABC-TV	Cliff Eidelman
Final Notice	USA Net	Tom Scott
Finish Line	TNT	William Olvis
Fire and Rain	USA Net	Artie Kane
Fistfighter	Ind	Emiliano Redondo
Fists of Blood	Ind	Brian Beamish
Fists of Blood	Ind	Gary Hardman
Fletch Lives	Univ	Harold Faltermeyer
Fly II, The	Fox	Christopher Young
Forgotten, The	USA Net	Laurence Rosenthal
Fortress of Amerikka	Ind	David Ouimet
Francesco	Ital	Vangelis
Freeway Maniac, The	Ind	Greg Stewart
Friday the 13th Part VIII: Jason Takes Manhattan	Par	Fred Mollin
Fright Night--Part 2	Ind	Brad Fiedel
From the Dead of Night	NBC-TV	Gil Melle
Fulfillment of Mary Gray, The	CBS-TV	Gary Scott
Full Exposure: The Sex Tapes Scandals	NBC-TV	Dana Kaproff
Fun Down There	Ind	James Baker
Fun Down There	Ind	Wayne Hammond
Game, The	Ind	Julia Wilson
Get Smart, Again!	ABC-TV	Peter Rodgers Melnick
Getting It Right	Br	Colin Towns
Getting It Right	Br	Steve Tyrell
Ghostbusters II	Col	Randy Edelman
Ghosthouse	It	Piero Montanari
Gifted One, The	NBC-TV	J. Peter Robinson
Ginger Ale Afternoon	Ind	Willie Dixon
Gleaming the Cube	Fox	Jay Ferguson
Glory	TriStar	James Horner
Glory! Glory!	HBO	Christopher Dedrick
God's Will	Ind	Christopher Cameron
Gods Must Be Crazy 2, The	Col	Charles Fox
Gore Vidal's Billy the Kid	TNT	Laurence Rosenthal
Grandmother's House	Ind	Nigel Holton
Great Balls of Fire!	Orion	Jack Baran
Great Balls of Fire!	Orion	Jim McBride
Great Expectations	Disney-TV	Ken Thorne
Gross Anatomy	BV	David Newman
Gunrunner, The	New World	Rex Taylor Smith
Guts and Glory: The Rise and Fall of Oliver North	CBS-TV	Arthur B. Rubinstein
Halloween 5	Ind	John Carpenter
Halloween 5	Ind	Alan Howarth
Hardcase and Fist	Ind	Tom Tucciarone
Hardcase and Fist	Ind	Matthew Tucciarone
Harlem Nights	Par	Herbie Hancock
Haunting of Sarah Hardy, The	USA Net	Michel Rubini
Heart of Dixie	Orion	Kenny Vance
Heart of Midnight	Ind	Yanni

Heathers	NewWorld	David Newman
Heaven Becomes Hell	Ind	Jonathan Hannah
Heist, The	HBO	Arthur B. Rubinstein
Hell High	Ind	Christopher Hyans-Hart
Hell High	Ind	Rich Macar
Hell on the Battleground	Ind	Tim James
Hell on the Battleground	Ind	Mark Mancina
Hell on the Battleground	Ind	Steve McClintock
Henry V	Br	Patrick Doyle
Her Alibi	WB	Georges Delerue
Heroes Stand Alone	Concorde	Eddie Arkin
Hider in the House	Vestron	Christopher Young
High Desert Kill	USA Net	Dana Kaproff
Hijacking of the Achille Lauro, The	NBC-TV	Chris Boardman
Histoires D'Amerique	Fr/Belg	Sonia Wieder Atherton
Hit List	New Line	Garry Schyman
Hollywood Detective, The	USA Net	Arthur B. Rubinstein
Home Fires Burning	CBS-TV	Don Davis
Homer and Eddie	Ind	Eduard Artemiev
Honey, I Shrunk the Kids	BV	James Horner
Honor Bound	Ind	Mark Shreeve
Horror Show, The	MGM/UA	Harry Manfredini
House IV: The Horror Show	New Line	Harry Manfredini
How I Got Into College	Fox	Joseph Vitarelli
How to Get Ahead in Advertising	Br	David Dundas
How to Get Ahead in Advertising	Br	Rick Wentworth
Howard Beach: Making the Case for Murder	NBC-TV	Jonathan Elias
Howling V: The Rebirth	Ind	The Factory
Human Factor	Ind	Ennio Morricone
I Know My First Name Is Steven	NBC-TV	David Shire
I Love You Perfect	ABC-TV	Yanni
I Want to Go Home	Fr	John Kander
I Went to the Dance	Ind	Michael Doucet
I, Madman	Ind	Michael Hoenig
Ice House	Ind	Tony Fortuna
Ice House	Ind	Carmen Yates
Identity Crisis	Ind	E. Pearson
Immediate Family	Col	Brad Fiedel
In Country	WB	James Horner
In the Blood	Ind	Michael Case Kissel
Incident at Dark River	TNT	Lee Holdridge
Indiana Jones and the Last Crusade	Par	John Williams
Innocent Man, An	BV	Howard Shore
Iron Triangle, The	Ind	John D'Andrea
Iron Triangle, The	Ind	Michael Lloyd
Iron Triangle, The	Ind	Nick Strimple
It Had to Be You	Ind	Charles Fox
It Nearly Wasn't Christmas	Syn	Kurt Bestor
Jacknife	Ind	Bruce Broughton
Jake Spanner, Private Eye	USA Net	Jimmie Haskell
January Man, The	MGM/UA	Marvin Hamlisch
Jesus De Montreal	Can	Yves Laferriere
Jitters, The	Ind	Tom Borton
Jitters, The	Ind	Dann Linck

Johnny Handsome	TriStar	Ry Cooder
Joyriders	Br	Tony Britten
Judgment Day	Ind	Lucas Richman
Judith Krantz's "Till We Meet Again"	CBS-TV	Vladimir Cosma
Jules Verne's "Around the World in 80 Days"	NBC-TV	Billy Goldenberg
Jungle Assault	Ind	Brian Bennett
Just Another Secret	USA Net	Paul Chihara
K-9	Univ	Miles Goodman
Karate Kid III, The	Col	Bill Conti
Karen Carpenter Story, The	CBS-TV	Richard Carpenter
Kickboxer	Ind	Paul Hartzop
Kill Me Again	MGM	William Olvis
Kinjite (Forbidden Subjects)	Cannon	Greg DeBelles
Kiss Shot	CBS-TV	Steve Dorff
Kuroi Ame (Black Rain)	Jap	Toru Takemitsu
L.A. Bounty	Ind	Howard Leese
L.A. Bounty	Ind	John Sterling
L.A. Heat	Ind	John Gonzalez
L.A. Takedown	NBC-TV	Tim Truman
L.A. Vice	Ind	John Gonzalez
La Petite Veleuse (The Little Thief)	Fr	Alain Jomy
La Vie Est Rien D'Autre	Fr	Oswald D'Andrea
Lady Avenger	Ind	Jay Levy
Lady Forgets, The	CBS-TV	Walter Murphy
Lady and the Highwayman, The	CBS-TV	Laurie Johnson
Lady in a Corner	NBC-TV	David Raksin
Lean on Me	WB	Bill Conti
Lemon Sisters, The	Miramax	Howard Shore
Let It Ride	Par	Giorgio Moroder
Lethal Weapon 2	WB	Michael Kamen
Lethal Weapon 2	WB	Eric Clapton
Lethal Weapon 2	WB	David Sanborn
Leviathan	MGM/UA	Jerry Goldsmith
Licence to Kill	MGM/UA	Michael Kamen
Life Is Cheap	Ind	Mark Adler
Listen to Me	Ind	David Foster
Little Mermaid, The	BV	Alan Menken
Little Mermaid, The	BV	Howard Ashman
Little Monsters	UA	David Newman
Little White Lies	NBC-TV	Lalo Schifrin
Littlest Victims, The	CBS-TV	Joel Rosenbaum
Lo Zio Indegno (The Sleazy Uncle)	It	Stefano Marcucci
Lobster Man From Mars	Ind	Sasha Matson
Lock Up	TriStar	Bill Conti
Lonesome Dove	CBS-TV	Basil Poledouris
Long Weekend, The	Ind	Steven Fields
Look Who's Talking	TriStar	David Kitay
Lords of the Deep	Concorde	Jim Berenholtz
Lost Angels	Orion	Philippe Sarde
Love and Betrayal	CBS-TV	Charles Bernstein
Loverboy	TriStar	Michel Colombier
Luckiest Man in the World, The	Ind	Warren Vache
Luckiest Man in the World, The	Ind	Jack Gale

Mack the Knife	Ind	Kurt Weill
Magic Moments	Showtime	Alan Hawkshaw
Mahabharata, The	Br	Toshi Tsuchitori
Mahabharata, The	Br	Kim Menzer
Major League	Par	James Newton Howard
Malarek: A Street Kid Who Made It	Can	Alexandre Stank
Man Against the Mob: The Chinatown Murders	NBC-TV	Artie Kane
Manhunt: Search for the Night Stalker	NBC-TV	Sylvester Levay
Margaret Bourke-White	TNT	John Cacavas
Masque of the Red Death	Concorde	Mark Governor
Me and Him	Col	Klaus Doldinger
Meet the Hollowheads	Ind	Glenn Jordan
Mickey Spillane's Mike Hammer: Murder Takes All	CBS-TV	Ron Ramin
Midnight	Ind	Michael Wetherwax
Midnight Cop	US/Ger	Carl Carlton
Mighty Quinn, The	MGM/UA	Anne Dudley
Millennium	Fox	Eric N. Robertson
Mind Games	Ind	David Richard Campbell
Ministry of Vengeance	Concorde	Scott Roewe
Miracle Mile	Hemdale	Tangerine Dream
Misplaced	Ind	Michael Urbaniak
Miss Firecracker	Ind	David Mansfield
Money, Power, Murder	CBS-TV	Miles Goodman
Morgan's Cake	Ind	Gary Thorp
Mother's Courage: The Mary Thomas Story, A	NBC-TV	Lee Holdridge
Mother's Day	CBN	Brent Havens
Mothers, Daughters and Lovers	NBC-TV	Tom Scott
Mountains of the Moon	Carolco	Michael Small
Murder by Moonlight	CBS-TV	Trevor Jones
Murder by Night	USA Net	Paul Zaza
Murder Story	Br/Dutch	Wayne Bickerton
Murderers Among Us: The Simon Wiesenthal Story	HBO	Bill Conti
Music Box	TriStar	Philippe Sarde
Mutant on the Bounty	Ind	Tim Torrance
My Boyfriend's Back	NBC-TV	Acrobat
My Brother's Wife	ABC-TV	Laura Karpman
My Left Foot	Br	Elmer Bernstein
My Mom's a Werewolf	Ind	Barry Fasman
My Mom's a Werewolf	Ind	Dana Walden
My Name Is Bill W.	ABC-TV	Laurence Rosenthal
Mystery Train	Ind	John Lurie
Naked Lie	CBS-TV	Bob Alcivar
Nam Angels	Ind	Jaime Fabregas
Nashville Beat	TNN	Mike Post
Nasty Boys	NBC-TV	Basil Poledouris
National Lampoon's Christmas Vacation	WB	Angelo Badalamenti
Necromancer	Ind	Gary Stockdale
Necromancer	Ind	Kevin Klingler
Necromancer	Ind	Bob Mamet
Neon Empire, The	Showtime	Lalo Schifrin

Never on Tuesday	Ind	Richard Stone
New York Stories	BV	Carmine Coppola
Next of Kin	WB	Jack Nitzsche
Next of Kin	WB	Gary Chang
Nick Knight	CBS-TV	Joseph Conlan
Night Game	Ind	Pino Donaggio
Night Visitor	MGM/UA	Parmer Fuller
Night Walk	CBS-TV	Patrick Williams
Nightbreaker	TNT	Peter Bernstein
Nightlife	USA Net	Dana Kaproff
Nightmare Years, The	TNT	Vladimir Cosma
Nightmare on Elm Street 5: The Dream Child, A	New Line	Jay Ferguson
No Holds Barred	New Line	Jim Johnston
No Holds Barred	New Line	Richard Stone
No Place Like Home	CBS-TV	Charles Gross
No Return, No Surrender II	Ind	David Spear
No Safe Haven	Ind	Joel Goldsmith
Not Quite Human II	Disney-TV	Michel Rubini
Nowhere to Run	Ind	Barry Goldberg
Obsession: A Taste for Fear	Ind	Gabriele Ducros
Of Men and Angels	Ind	Eric Muhler
Offerings	Ind	Russell D. Allen
Office Party	Can	Billy Bryans
Old Gringo	Col	Lee Holdridge
On the Make	Ind	Phil Cardonna
One Man Force	Ind	David Michael Frank
One Man Force	Ind	Charles Fox
Options	Vestron	Roger Bellon
Order of the Eagle	Ind	William T. Stromberg
Original Intent	Ind	Ernie Rettino
Original Sin	NBC-TV	Lalo Schifrin
Out Cold	Ind	Michel Colombier
Out of Time	Br	Alan Parker
Out of the Dark	Ind	Paul F. Antonelli
Out of the Dark	Ind	David Wheatley
Parent Trap Hawaiian Honeymoon	NBC-TV	Joel McNeely
Parent Trap III	NBC-TV	Joel McNeely
Parenthood	Univ	Randy Newman
Parents	Ind	Jonathan Elias
Parents	Ind	Angelo Badalamenti
Paris by Night	Br	Georges Delerue
Party Incorporated	Ind	Joey Mennonna
Passion and Paradise	ABC-TV	Hagood Hardy
Penn & Teller Get Killed	WB	Paul Chihara
Penthouse, The	ABC-TV	Peter Manning Robinson
Perfect Model, The	Ind	Joe Thomas
Perfect Model, The	Ind	Steve Grissette
Perfect Witness	HBO	Brad Fiedel
Perry Mason: The Case of the All-Star Assassin	NBC-TV	Dick DeBenedictis
Perry Mason: The Case of the Lethal Lesson	NBC-TV	Dick DeBenedictis
Perry Mason: The Case of the Musical Murder	NBC-TV	Dick DeBenedictis

Personal Choice	Ind	Geoff Levin
Personal Choice	Ind	Chris Smart
Pet Sematary	Par	Elliot Goldenthal
Peter Gunn	ABC-TV	Henry Mancini
Phantom of the Mall: Eric's Revenge	Ind	Stacy Widelitz
Phantom of the Opera, The	Ind	Misha Segal
Physical Evidence	Col	Henry Mancini
Pink Cadillac	WB	Steve Dorff
Police Academy 6: City Under Siege	WB	Robert Folk
Polly	NBC-TV	Joel McNeely
Prancer	Orion	Maurice Jarre
Preppie Murder, The	ABC-TV	Chris Isaak
Preppie Murder, The	ABC-TV	Simon Rogers
Prime Target	NBC-TV	Chris Boardman
Prisoner of St. Petersburg, The	Aut/Ger	Paul Schutze
Prisoners of Inertia	Ind	William Swindler
Private Life, A	Br	Trevor Jones
Puppet Master	Ind	Richard Band
Purgatory	Ind	Julian Laxton
Queen of Hearts	Br	Michael Convertino
Quicker Than the Eye	Ind	Georges Garvarentz
Race for Glory	Ind	Jay Ferguson
Rachel Papers, The	Br	Chaz Jankel
Rage to Kill	Ind	Mark Mancina
Rage to Kill	Ind	Tim James
Rage to Kill	Ind	Steve McClintock
Rainbow, The	Vestron	Carl Davis
Red Earth, White Earth	CBS-TV	Ralph Grierson
Red King, White Knight	HBO	John Scott
Red Scorpion	Ind	Jay Chattaway
Relentless	New Line	Jay Chattaway
Renegades	Univ	Michael Kamen
Return of Sam McCloud, The	CBS-TV	Steve Dorff
Return of the Musketeers, The	Univ	Jean-Claude Petit
Return of the Swamp Thing, The	Ind	Chuck Cirino
Reunion	Fr/Ger/Br	Philippe Sarde
Revenge of Al Capone, The	NBC-TV	Craig Safan
Revenge of the Living Zombies	Ind	Erica Portnoy
Riding the Edge	Ind	Michael Gibbs
Rising Storm	Ind	Julian Laxton
Riverbend	Ind	Paul Loomis
Road House	UA	Michael Kamen
Road Raiders, The	CBS-TV	Stu Phillips
Roald Dahl's "Danny, The Champion of the World"	Disney-TV	Stanley Myers
Roe vs. Wade	NBC-TV	W. G. Snuffy Walden
Romero	Ind	Gabriel Yared
Rooftops	Ind	Michael Kamen
Rooftops	Ind	David A. Stewart
Rosalie Goes Shopping	Ger	Bob Telson
Rose Garden, The	US/Ger	Egisto Macchi
Roxanne: The Prize Pulitzer	NBC-TV	Bob Alcivar
Rude Awakening	Orion	Jonathan Elias
Runnin' Kind, The	MGM/UA	Guy Moon

Russicum (The Third Solution)	It	Renato Serio
Ryan White Story, The	ABC-TV	Mike Post
Saturday the 14th Strikes Back	Concorde	Parmer Fuller
Savage Beach	Ind	Gary Stockdale
Say Anything	Fox	Richard Gibbs
Say Anything	Fox	Anne Dudley
Say Anything	Fox	Nancy Wilson
Scandal	Br	Carl Davis
Scenes From the Class Struggle in Beverly Hills	Ind	Stanley Myers
Screwball Hotel	US/Br	Nathan Wang
Sea of Love	Univ	Trevor Jones
Season of Fear	MGM/UA	David Wolinski
Second Sight	WB	John Morris
See No Evil, Hear No Evil	TriStar	Stewart Copeland
Settle the Score	NBC-TV	Mark Snow
Severance	Ind	Daniel May
sex, lies and videotape	Ind	Cliff Martinez
Sexbomb	Ind	Leonard Marcel
Shannon's Deal	NBC-TV	Wynton Marsalis
She Knows Too Much	NBC-TV	Alf Clausen
She's Back	Vestron	Jimmie Haskell
She's Been Away	Br	Richard Hartley
She's Out of Control	Col	Alan Silvestri
She-Devil	Orion	Howard Shore
Shell Seekers, The	ABC-TV	James DiPasquale
Shirley Valentine	Par	George Hadjinassios
Shocker	Univ	William Goldstein
Sidewalk Stories	Ind	Henry Gafney
Siege of Firebase Gloria, The	Ind	Paul Shutze
Signs of Life	Ind	Howard Shore
Silence Like Glass	Ger	Anne Dudley
Silent Night, Deadly Night 3: Better Watch Out	Ind	Steve Soles
Simple Justice	Ind	Eric Turkel
Simple Justice	Ind	John Pati
Sinful Life, A	New Line	Todd Hayen
Sing	TriStar	Jay Gruska
Single Women, Married Men	CBS-TV	Johnny Mandel
Skull: A Night of Terror	Can	Phillip Strong
Slash Dance	Ind	Emilio Kauderer
Slaves of New York	TriStar	Richard Robbins
Sleepaway Camp 3: Teenage Wasteland	Ind	James Oliverio
Slipstream	Ind	Elmer Bernstein
Small Sacrifices	ABC-TV	Peter Manning Robinson
Sons	Ind	Mader
Sorry Wrong Number	USA Net	Bruce Broughton
Space Mutiny	Ind	Mark Mancina
Space Mutiny	Ind	Tim James
Speaking Parts	Can	Mychael Danna
Speed Zone	Orion	David Wheatley
Split Decisions	Ind	Basil Poledouris
Spooner	Disney-TV	Brian Banks
Spooner	Disney-TV	Anthony Marinelli

Spy	USA Net	Nan Schwartz
Squamish Fire, The	Can	Marty Simon
Star Trek V: The Final Frontier	Par	Jerry Goldsmith
Staying Together	HBO	Miles Goodman
Steel Magnolias	TriStar	Georges Delerue
Stepfather II: Make Room for Daddy	Ind	Jim Manzie
Stepfather II: Make Room for Daddy	Ind	Pat Regan
Strapless	Br	Nick Bicat
Street Justice	Lorimar	Jamii Szmadzinski
Street Justice	Ind	Paul Hertzog
Striker (Combat Force)	It	Detto Mariano
Stripped to Kill 2	Concorde	Gary Stockdale
Stuck With Each Other	NBC-TV	Mark Snow
Suffering Bastards	Ind	Dan Di Pola
Sunday's Child	Ger	Konstantin Wecker
Survival Quest	MGM/UA	Fred Myrow
Survival Quest	MGM/UA	Christopher Stone
Surviving Desire	Ind	Ned Rifle
Sweet Bird of Youth	NBC-TV	Ralph Burns
Sweetie	Aut	Martin Arminger
Swimsuit	NBC-TV	John D'Andrea
Swimsuit	NBC-TV	Michael Lloyd
Tailspin: Behind the Korean Airliner Tragedy	HBO	David Ferguson
Tainted	Ind	Hayden Wayne
Taken Away	CBS-TV	Rob Mounsey
Tales From the Crypt	HBO-TV	Ry Cooder
Tall Guy, The	Vestron	Peter Brewis
Tango & Cash	WB	Harold Faltermeyer
Tank Malling	Br	Rick Fenn
Tank Malling	Br	Nick Mason
Tap	TriStar	James Newton Howard
Tarzan in Manhattan	CBS-TV	Charles Fox
Teen Witch	Ind	Richard Elliot
Tempo Di Uccidere (The Short Cut)	It/Fr	Ennio Morricone
Terminal Force	New World	Paul Natzske
Terror Within, The	Concorde	Rick Conrad
Terror on Highway 91	CBS-TV	Artie Kane
That Summer of White Roses	Br/Yugo	Brane Zivkovic
Third Degree Burn	HBO	Charles Gross
Third Solution	It	Vangelis
Those She Left Behind	NBC-TV	Mark Snow
Three Fugitives	BV	David McHugh
Thunderboat Row	ABC-TV	Mike Post
Time Trackers	Concorde	Parmer Fuller
To Die For	Ind	Laura Perlman
To Kill a Priest	Col	Georges Delerue
Toxic Avenger Part II, The	Troma	Barrie Guard
Toxic Avenger Part III: The Last Temptation of Toxie, The	Troma	Christopher DeMarco
Trapped	USA Net	Stephen Cohn
Traveling Man	HBO	Miles Goodman
Trenchcoat in Paradise	CBS-TV	John Debney
Trial of the Incredible Hulk, The	NBC-TV	Lance Rubin

Triumph of the Spirit	Ind	Cliff Eidelman
Troop Beverly Hills	Ind	Randy Edelman
Trouble in Paradise	CBS-TV	Chris Neal
True Believer	Col	Brad Fiedel
True Blood	Ind	Scott Roewe
Turner & Hooch	BV	Charles Gross
Twist of Fate	NBC-TV	Laurence Rosenthal
Twister	Vestron	Hans Zimmer
Two Women (aka Running Away)	It	Armando Trovajoli
Two Wrongs Make a Right	Ind	Tony Byrne
UHF	Orion	John Du Prez
Unbelievable Truth, The	Ind	Jim Coleman
Uncle Buck	Univ	Ira Newborn
Unconquered	CBS-TV	Arthur B. Rubinstein
Understudy: Graveyard Shift II, The	Ind	Philip Stern
Up Your Alley	Ind	Paul Ventimiglia
Valmont	Fr/Br	Christopher Palmer
Venus Peter	Br	Jonathan Dove
Vice Academy	Ind	Alan Dermaderosian
Violent Zone	Ind	Mark Josephson
War Birds	Ind	Jerry Lambert
War of the Roses, The	Fox	David Newman
Warlock	New World	Jerry Goldsmith
We're No Angels	Par	George Fenton
Weekend at Bernie's	Fox	Andy Summers
Welcome Home	Vestron	Henry Mancini
When Harry Met Sally . . .	Col	Marc Shaiman
When He's Not a Stranger	CBS-TV	Mark Snow
When the Whales Came	Br	Christopher Gunning
When We Were Young	NBC-TV	Peter Matz
Whisper to a Scream, A	Can	Barry Fasman
Whisper to a Scream, A	Can	Dana Walden
Who's Harry Crumb?	TriStar	Michel Colombier
Wicked Stepmother	MGM/UA	Robert Folk
Wild Man	Ind	Gary Lionelli
Winter People	Col	John Scott
Wired	Ind	Basil Poledouris
Witchtrap	Ind	Dennis Michael Tenney
Wizard, The	Univ	J. Peter Robinson
Woman Obsessed, A	Ind	Joey Mennonna
Women of Brewster Place, The	ABC-TV	David Shire
Worth Winning	Fox	Patrick Williams
Yosemite: The Fate of Heaven	Ind	Todd Boekelheide
Young Einstein	Aut	Martin Arminger
Your Mother Wears Combat Boots	NBC-TV	Jeff Barry
Your Mother Wears Combat Boots	NBC-TV	Barry Fasman
Zadar! Cow From Hell	Ind	Greg Brown

1990

83 Hours 'til Dawn	CBS-TV	Gary Chang
9 ½ Ninjas	Ind	Geoffrey Leigh Tozer
Across Five Aprils	Fam Ch	Alan Dermaderosian
Across the Tracks	Ind	Joel Goldsmith

Act of Piracy	Ind	Morton Stevens
Adventures of Ford Fairlane, The	Fox	Yello
After Dark, My Sweet	Avenue	Maurice Jarre
Air America	TriStar	Charles Gross
Akira Kurosawa's Dream	Jap	Shinichiro Ikebe
Alienator	Ind	Chuck Cirino
All the Vermeers in New York	Ind	Jon A. English
Alligator Eyes	Ind	Sheila Silver
Almost an Angel	Par	Maurice Jarre
Always Remember I Love You	CBS-TV	David Shire
American Angels: Baptism of Blood, The	Par	George Hovis Hamilton
American Born	Ind	Jeff Lass
American Dream	Ind	Michael Small
Amityville Curse, The	Can/US	Milan Kymlicka
Angel of Death	CBS-TV	Harry Manfredini
Angel Town	Ind	Gil Karson
Another 48 HRS.	Par	James Horner
Any Man's Death	Ind	Jeremy Lubbock
Anything to Survive	ABC-TV	Michael Conway Baker
Appearances	NBC-TV	Joel McNeely
Arachnophobia	BV	Trevor Jones
Archie: To Riverdale and Back Again	NBC-TV	Mark Snow
Army of One	Ind	Joel Goldsmith
Avalon	TriStar	Randy Newman
Awakenings	Col	Randy Newman
Babies	NBC-TV	Misha Segal
Back Home	Disney-TV	Ilona Sekacz
Back to Back	Concorde	Rick Cox
Back to Hannibal: The Return of Tom Sawyer and Huckleberry Finn	Disney-TV	Lee Holdridge
Back to the Future Part III	Univ	Alan Silvestri
Backstreet Dreams	Ind	Bill Conti
Bad Influence	Ind	Trevor Jones
Bad Jim	Ind	Jamie Sheriff
Bangkok Hilton	TNT	Graeme Revell
Basket Case 2	Ind	Joe Renzetti
Beautiful Dreamers	Can	Lawrence Shragge
Bedroom Eyes II	Ind	Budd Carr
Berlin Conspiracy, The	Concorde	Mitko Shtelev
Bethune: The Making of a Hero	Can/Fr/China	Alan Reeves
Betsy's Wedding	BV	Bruce Broughton
Big One: The Great Los Angeles Earthquake, The	NBC-TV	David Shire
Big Slice, The	Can	Jeff Danna
Bird on a Wire	Univ	Hans Zimmer
Blind Faith	NBC-TV	Laurence Rosenthal
Blind Vengeance	USA Net	Dana Kaproff
Blood Savage	Ind	Tim Temple
Bloodmoon	Ind	Brian May
Blue Bayou	NBC-TV	Stanley Clarke
Blue Planet	IMAX	Mickey Erbe
Blue Planet	IMAX	Maribeth Solomon
Blue Steel	MGM/UA	Brad Fiedel
Body Chemistry	Concorde	Terry Plumeri

Bonfire of the Vanities, The	WB	Dave Grusin
Book of Love	New Line	Stanley Clarke
Brain Dead	Concorde	Peter Francis Rotter
Bride in Black, The	ABC-TV	Joseph Conlan
Brutal Glory	Ind	Dominic Frontiere
Bullseye!	Br	John Du Prez
Buried Alive	USA Net	Michel Colombier
Buried Alive	Ind	Frederic Talgorn
Burning Bridges	ABC-TV	Bennett Salvay
Burning Bridges	ABC-TV	W. G. Snuffy Walden
By Dawn's Early Light	HBO	Trevor Jones
Cadence	New Line	Georges Delerue
Cadillac Man	Orion	J. Peter Robinson
Caged Fury	Ind	Joe Delia
Call Me Anna	ABC-TV	Gary Sherman
Camp Cucamonga	NBC-TV	Michael Cruz
Caroline?	CBS-TV	Charles Bernstein
Cartel	Ind	Rick Krizman
Casey's Gift: For Love of a Child	NBC-TV	David McHugh
Casualty of War, A	USA Net	Paul Chihara
Challenge the Wind	Ind	Jeff Rhoades
Challenger	ABC-TV	David E. Kole
Chambre e Part (Separate Bedrooms)	Fr	Philippe Sarde
Chicago Joe and the Showgirl	Br	Hans Zimmer
Chicago Joe and the Showgirl	Br	Shirley Walker
Child in the Night	CBS-TV	Mark Snow
Child's Play 2	Univ	Graeme Revell
Children of the Bride	CBS-TV	Yanni
China Cry	Ind	Al Kasha
China Cry	Ind	Joel Hirschhorn
China Lake Murders, The	USA Net	Dana Kaproff
Chips, the War Dog	Disney-TV	David Michael Frank
Church, The	Ind	Keith Emerson
Circuitry Man	Ind	Deborah Holland
Clarence	Fam Ch	Louis Natale
Class of 1999	Ind	Michael Hoenig
Coins in the Fountain	CBS-TV	Nan Schwartz
Collision Course	Ind	Ira Newborn
Come See the Paradise	Fox	Randy Edelman
Comfort of Strangers, The	It/US	Angelo Badalamenti
Common Ground	CBS-TV	David Shire
Confessional	Syn	John Cacavas
Cool Blue	Ind	Joe Manolakakis
Corporate Affairs	Concorde	Jeff Winkless
Coupe de Ville	Univ	James Newton Howard
Court-Martial of Jackie Robinson, The	TNT	Stanley Clarke
Crash and Burn	Ind	Richard Band
Crash: The Mystery of Flight 1501	NBC-TV	Mark Snow
Crazy People	Par	Cliff Eidelman
Criminal Justice	HBO	Elliot Goldenthal
Crossing to Freedom	CBS-TV	Carl Davis
Cry in the Wild, A	Concorde	Arthur Kempel
Cry-Baby	Univ	Patrick Williams
Curiosity Kills	USA Net	Jan Hammer

Cyrano de Bergerac	Fr	Jean-Claude Petit
Daddy Nostalgia	Fr	Antoine Duhamel
Daddy's Dyin' . . . Who's Got the Will?	MGM/UA	David McHugh
Dakota Road	Br	Hans Zimmer
Dakota Road	Br	Paul Stacey
Damned River	MGM/UA	James Wesley Stemple
Dances With Wolves	Orion	John Barry
Danger Zone III: Steel Horse War	Ind	Robert Etoll
Dangerous Obsession (Mortal Sins)	Ind	Simon Boswell
Dangerous Passion	ABC-TV	Rob Mounsey
Dangerous Pursuit	USA Net	Stanley Clarke
Danielle Steel's "Fine Things"	NBC-TV	Lee Holdridge
Danielle Steel's "Kaleidoscope"	NBC-TV	Johnny Mandel
Danielle Steel's "Kaleidoscope"	NBC-TV	Dennis McCarthy
Daredreamer	Ind	Paul Speer
Daredreamer	Ind	David Lanz
Dark Avenger	CBS-TV	Sylvester Levay
Darkman	Univ	Danny Elfman
Daughter of Darkness	CBS-TV	Colin Towns
Daughter of the Streets	ABC-TV	Lee Holdridge
Days of Thunder	Par	Hans Zimmer
Dead Men Don't Lie	Ind	David Williams
Dead Reckoning	USA Net	Mark Snow
Dead Sleep	Ind	Brian May
Dead Women in Lingerie	Ind	Ciro Hurtado
Deadly Dancer	Ind	William T. Stromberg
Death Warrant	MGM/UA	Gary Chang
Death in Brunswick	Aut	Philip Judd
Death of the Incredible Hulk, The	NBC-TV	Lance Rubin
Deceptions	Showtime	Gary Scott
Decoration Day	NBC-TV	Patrick Williams
Def by Temptation	Troma	Paul Laurence
Delta Force 2	Cannon	Frederic Talgorn
Demon Wind	Ind	Bruce Wallenstein
Der Berg (The Mountain)	Ger/Swiss	Nicola Piovani
Descending Angel	HBO	James Newton Howard
Desperate Hours	MGM/UA	David Mansfield
Dick Tracy	BV	Danny Elfman
Dick Tracy	BV	Stephen Sondheim
Die Hard 2	Fox	Michael Kamen
Dimenticare Palermo	It/Fr	Ennio Morricone
Disturbed	Ind	Steven Scott Smalley
Docteur Petiot	Fr	Michel Portal
Doctor Mordrid: Master of the Unknown	Ind	Richard Band
Dog Tags	Ind	John Scott
Don Juan, Mi Querido Fantasma (Don Juan, My Love)	Sp	Bernardo Bonezzi
Donor	CBS-TV	Gary Chang
Don't Tell Her It's Me	Ind	Michael Gore
Double Revenge	Ind	Harry Manfredini
Down the Drain	Ind	Rick Krizman
Downtown	Fox	Alan Silvestri
Dreamer of Oz: The L. Frank Baum Story, The	NBC-TV	Lee Holdridge

Driving Force	Aut	Paul Schutze
Drug Wars: The Camarena Story	NBC-TV	Charles Bernstein
Drug Wars: The Camarena Story	NBC-TV	Charles Calello
Drug Wars: The Camarena Story	NBC-TV	Al Cooper
Drug Wars: The Camarena Story	NBC-TV	Ardeshir Faraj
Drug Wars: The Camarena Story	NBC-TV	Jorge Strunz
Drug Wars: The Camarena Story	NBC-TV	Warren Zevon
Duck Tales: The Movie--Treasure of the Lost Lamp	BV	David Newman
Duo Occhi Diabolici (Two Evil Eyes)	It	Pino Donaggio
Edward Scissorhands	Fox	Danny Elfman
El Diablo	HBO	William Olvis
Elliot Fauman, Ph.D.	Ind	Roger Trefousse
End of Innocence, The	Par	Michael Convertino
End of the Night	Ind	Jurgen Knieper
Endless Game, The	Showtime	Ennio Morricone
Enid Is Sleeping (aka Over Her Dead Body)	Vestron	Craig Safan
Enrapture	Ind	Joey Mennonna
Ernest Goes to Jail	BV	Bruce Arnston
Ernest Goes to Jail	BV	Kirby Shelstad
Eternity	Ind	Michel Legrand
Everybody Wins	Orion	Mark Isham
Everybody Wins	Orion	Leon Redbone
Exile	NBC-TV	Peter Bernstein
Exorcist III, The	Fox	Barry DeVorzon
Extreme Close-Up	NBC-TV	James Horner
Face of Fear, The	CBS-TV	John Debney
Face to Face	CBS-TV	Lalo Schifrin
Fall From Grace	NBC-TV	Charles Bernstein
Falling Over Backwards	Can	Milan Kymlicka
Family for Joe, A	NBC-TV	Charles Fox
Family of Spies	CBS-TV	Paul Chihara
Famine Within, The	Can	Russell Walker
Far Out Man	New Line	Jay Chattaway
Fatal Image, The	CBS-TV	Michel Colombier
Fatal Mission	Ind	Mark Winner
Fatal Skies	Ind	Daniel May
Fear	USA Net	Henry Mancini
Fellow Traveller	Br/US	Colin Towns
Final Alliance, The	Ind	Julian Laxton
Final Sanction, The	Ind	Tim James
Final Sanction, The	Ind	Steve McClintock
Fine Gold	Syn	Vladimir Horonzky
Fire Birds	BV	David Newman
First Power, The	Orion	Stewart Copeland
Flash, The	CBS-TV	Danny Elfman
Flashback	Par	Barry Goldberg
Flatliners	Col	James Newton Howard
Flying Blind	NBC-TV	Phil Marshall
Follow Your Heart	NBC-TV	Mark Snow
Fools of Fortune	Br	Hans Zimmer
Forbidden Dance, The	Col	Vladimir Horonzky
Forbidden Nights	CBS-TV	Lucia Hwong
Forgotten Prisoners: The Amnesty Files	TNT	Brad Fiedel

Fourth War, The	Ind	Bill Conti
Framed	HBO	William Olvis
Frankenhooker	Ind	Joe Renzetti
Frankenstein Unbound	Fox	Carl Davis
Freshman, The	TriStar	David Newman
Full Fathom Five	Concorde	Allan Zavod
Funny About Love	Par	Miles Goodman
Garden, The	Br	Simon Fisher Turner
Genuine Risk	Ind	Deborah Holland
Getting Lucky	Ind	Michael Paul Girard
Ghost	Par	Maurice Jarre
Ghost Dad	Univ	Henry Mancini
Ghost in Monte Carlo, A	TNT	Laurie Johnson
Ghosts Can't Do It	Ind	Junior Homrich
Girl Who Came Between Them, The	NBC-TV	Mark Snow
Girlfriend From Hell	Ind	Michael Rapp
Godfather Part III, The	Par	Nino Rota
Godfather Part III, The	Par	Carmine Coppola
Goin' to Chicago	Ind	Bob Summers
Goldeneye	Syn	Michael Berkeley
Good Cops, Bad Cops	NBC-TV	Gil Melle
Good Night Sweet Wife: A Murder in Boston	CBS-TV	Patrick Williams
Graffiti Bridge	WB	Prince
Graveyard Shift	Par	Anthony Marinelli
Graveyard Shift	Par	Brian Banks
Green Card	BV	Hans Zimmer
Gremlins 2: The New Batch	WB	Jerry Goldsmith
Grifters, The	Miramax	Elmer Bernstein
Grim Prairie Tales	Ind	Steve Dancz
Guardian, The	Univ	Jack Hues
Guess Who's Coming for Christmas?	NBC-TV	W. G. Snuffy Walden
Gumshoe Kid, The	Ind	Peter Matz
Gunsmoke: The Last Apache	CBS-TV	Bruce Rowland
Hamlet	WB	Ennio Morricone
Handmaid's Tale, The	Ind	Ryuichi Sakamoto
Hands of a Murderer	CBS-TV	Colin Towns
Hang Tough	Can	Mickey Erbe
Hang Tough	Can	Maribeth Solomon
Happy Together	Ind	Robert Folk
Hard to Kill	WB	David Michael Frank
Hardware	Br/US	Simon Boswell
Haunting of Morella, The	Concorde	Chuck Cirino
Haunting of Morella, The	Concorde	Fredric Teetsel
Havana	Univ	Dave Grusin
Heart Condition	New Line	Patrick Leonard
Heat Wave	TNT	Thomas Newman
Heaven Tonight	Aut	John Capek
Henry & June	Univ	Mark Adler
Hidden Agenda	Br	Stewart Copeland
Hiroshima: Out of the Ashes	NBC-TV	Lucia Hwong
Hitler's Daughter	USA Net	Joel McNeely
Hollywood Hot Tubs 2: Educating Crystal	Ind	John Lombardo
Home Alone	Fox	John Williams
Honeymoon Academy	Ind	Robert Folk

Horseplayer, The	Ind	Garry Schyman
Hot Spot, The	Orion	Jack Nitzsche
House Party	New Line	Marcus Miller
House of Usher, The	Ind	George S. Clinton
House of Usher, The	Ind	Gary Chang
How to Murder a Millionaire	CBS-TV	Richard Gibbs
Hunt for Red October, The	Par	Basil Poledouris
Hush-a-Bye Baby	Br	Sinead O'Connor
I Come in Peace	Ind	Jan Hammer
I Love You to Death	TriStar	James Horner
I'll Take Romance	ABC-TV	Yanni
I'm Dangerous Tonight	USA Net	Nicholas Pike
Image, The	HBO	James Newton Howard
Impulse	WB	Michel Colombier
In Defense of a Married Man	ABC-TV	Stan Getz
In the Best Interest of the Child	CBS-TV	Peter Manning Robinson
In the Line of Duty: A Cop for the Killing	NBC-TV	Mark Snow
In the Spirit	Ind	Patrick Williams
Incident, The	CBS-TV	Laurence Rosenthal
Initiation: Silent Night, Deadly Night 4	Ind	Richard Band
Instant Karma	MGM	Joel Goldsmith
Internal Affairs	Par	Brian Banks
Internal Affairs	Par	Mike Figgis
Internal Affairs	Par	Anthony Marinelli
Investigation: Inside a Terrorist Bombing, The	HBO	Shaun Davey
Jackie Collins' "Lucky/Chances"	NBC-TV	Billy Goldenberg
Jacob's Ladder	TriStar	Maurice Jarre
Jeanne, Putain du Roi (The King's Whore)	Fr	Gabriel Yared
Jekyll & Hyde	ABC-TV	John Cameron
Jetsons: The Movie	Univ	John Debney
Jezebel's Kiss	Ind	Mitchel Forman
Jobman	Ind	Joel Goldsmith
Joe Versus the Volcano	WB	Georges Delerue
Johnny Ryan	NBC-TV	Chris Boardman
Joshua's Heart	NBC-TV	Lee Holdridge
Journey of Honor	US/Jap	John Scott
Judgment	HBO	Cliff Eidelman
Jury Duty: The Comedy	ABC-TV	Ray Colcord
Keaton's Cop	Cannon	Kevin Barnes
Keaton's Cop	Cannon	David Connor
Kennedys of Massachusetts, The	ABC-TV	David Shire
Kid Who Loved Christmas, The	Syn	Stanley Clarke
Kill Crazy	Ind	David Heavener
Kill Crazy	Ind	Michael Rapp
Killer Among Us, A	NBC-TV	Gary Chang
Killing in a Small Town, A	CBS-TV	Richard Gibbs
Kindergarten Cop	Univ	Randy Edelman
King of New York	New Line	Joe Delia
Kissing Place, The	USA Net	Laurence Rosenthal
Krays, The	Br	Michael Kamen
L'Amour (Love)	Fr	Benoit Schlossberg
La Baule--Les Pins	Fr	Philippe Sarde
La Femme Nikita	Fr/It	Eric Serra

La Voce Della Luna	It/Fr	Nicola Piovani
Laker Girls	CBS-TV	Sylvester Levay
Lambada	WB	Greg DeBelles
Lantern Hill	Disney-TV	John Weisman
Laserman, The	Ind	Mason Daring
Last Best Year, The	NBC-TV	John Morris
Last Call	Ind	Michael Bishop
Last Elephant, The (aka Ivory Hunters)	TNT	Charles Bernstein
Last Flight Out	NBC-TV	Christopher Young
Last of the Finest, The	Orion	Michael Hoenig
Last of the Finest, The	Orion	Jack Nitzsche
Last Winter, The	Can	Victor Davies
Le Roman de Renard (1929-1941)	Fr	Vincent Scotto
Leatherface: Texas Chainsaw Massacre III	New Line	Jim Manzie
Leatherface: Texas Chainsaw Massacre III	New Line	Pat Regan
Legal Tender (aka Ladies Game)	Ind	William Kidd
Leona Helmsley: The Queen of Mean	CBS-TV	Dennis McCarthy
Liberty & Bash	Ind	Sasha Matson
Limit Up	Ind	John Tesh
Lisa	MGM/UA	Joe Renzetti
Listen Up	WB	Quincy Jones
Little Kidnappers, The	Disney-TV	Mark Snow
Little Vegas	Ind	Mason Daring
Living to Die	Ind	John Gonzalez
Lonely in America	Ind	Gregory Arnold
Long Walk Home, The	Miramax	George Fenton
Longtime Companion	Goldwyn	Lia Vollack
Look Who's Talking Too	TriStar	David Kitay
Lookalike, The	USA Net	Allyn Ferguson
Loose Cannons	TriStar	Paul Zaza
Lord of the Flies	Col	Philippe Sarde
Lost Capone, The	TNT	Mark Snow
Love & Murder	Can	Matthew MacCauley
Love and Hate: A Marriage Made in Hell	NBC-TV	Eric N. Robertson
Love and Lies	ABC-TV	Patrick Williams
Love at Large	Orion	Mark Isham
Love Boat: A Valentine Voyage, The	ABC-TV	Charles Fox
Love Boat: A Valentine Voyage, The	ABC-TV	Dennis McCarthy
Love Hurts	Vestron	Burt Bacharach
Love or Money	Ind	Jim Lang
Love She Sought, The	NBC-TV	Charles Bernstein
Lower Level	Ind	Terry Plumeri
Madhouse	Orion	David Newman
Magdalene	Ind	Cliff Eidelman
Magicians of the Earth	Ind	David Byrne
Maktub: The Law of the Desert	It	Ennio Morricone
Man Called Serge, A	Cannon	Chuck Cirino
Maniac Cop 2	Ind	Jay Chattaway
Marked for Death	Fox	James Newton Howard
Martians Go Home	Ind	Allan Zavod
Matter of Degrees, A	Ind	Jim Dunbar
Matters of the Heart	USA Net	Misha Segal
Max and Helen	TNT	Christopher Young
Memories of Murder	Lifetime	Joseph Conlan

Memphis Belle	WB	George Fenton
Men at Work	Ind	Stewart Copeland
Men Don't Leave	WB	Thomas Newman
Men of Respect	TriStar	Misha Segal
Menu for Murder	CBS-TV	Ron Ramin
Meridian: Kiss of the Beast	Ind	Pino Donaggio
Mermaids	Orion	Jack Nitzsche
Metropolitan	Ind	Marc Suozzo
Miami Blues	Orion	Gary Chang
Midnight Cabaret	Ind	Michel Colombier
Miller's Crossing	Fox	Carter Burwell
Milou en Mai (May Fools)	Fr	Stephane Grappelli
Mindwalk	Ind	Philip Glass
Miracle Landing	CBS-TV	Mark Snow
Misadventures of Mr. Wilt, The	Br	Anne Dudley
Misery	Col	Marc Shaiman
Mo' Better Blues	Univ	Bill Lee
Mob Boss	Ind	Don Great
Mob Boss	Ind	Chuck Cirino
Modern Love	Ind	Don Peake
Mom for Christmas, A	NBC-TV	John Farrar
Mom for Christmas, A	NBC-TV	Sean Gallery
Monk, The	Br/Sp	Anton Garcia Abril
Monster High	Ind	Richard Lyons
Montana	TNT	David McHugh
Moon 44	Ind	Joel Goldsmith
Mr. & Mrs. Bridge	Miramax	Richard Robbins
Mr. Destiny	BV	David Newman
Mr. Johnson	Ind	Georges Delerue
Murder C.O.D.	NBC-TV	Fred Karlin
Murder by Numbers	Ind	Bob Summers
Murder in Black and White	CBS-TV	Arthur B. Rubinstein
Murder in Mississippi	NBC-TV	Mason Daring
Murder in Paradise	CBS-TV	John Cacavas
Murder on Line One (Helpline)	Br/Swed	Charlie Mole
Murder Times Seven	CBS-TV	Arthur B. Rubinstein
My Blue Heaven	WB	Ira Newborn
Naked Tango	Ind	Thomas Newman
Narrow Margin	TriStar	Bruce Broughton
Nasty Hero	Ind	Ross Levinson
Navy SEALs	Orion	Sylvester Levay
Netherworld	Ind	Edgar Winter
Neverending Story II: The Next Chapter, The	WB	Robert Folk
Neverending Story II: The Next Chapter, The	WB	Giorgio Moroder
Night Angel	Ind	Cory Lerios
Night Eyes (aka Hidden Vision)	Ind	Richard Glasser
Night Life	Ind	Roger Bourland
Night of the Fox	Syn	Vladimir Cosma
Night of the Living Dead	Col	Paul McCollough
Night Visions	NBC-TV	Brad Fiedel
Nightbreed	Fox	Danny Elfman
Nightmare on the 13th Floor	USA Net	Jay Gruska
Not a Penny More, Not a Penny Less	USA Net	Michel Legrand
Nuns on the Run	Br	Yello

Nuns on the Run	Br	Yello
Nutcracker Prince, The	Can	Victor Davies
Nutcracker Prince, The	Can	Kein Gillis
Nutcracker Prince, The	Can	Jack Lenz
Old Man and the Sea, The	NBC-TV	Bruce Broughton
On Thin Ice: The Tai Babilonia Story	NBC-TV	Eric N. Robertson
One Man's War	Br	John Keane
Only One Survived	CBS-TV	Colin Towns
Operation, The	CBS-TV	Bill Conti
Opponent, The	It	Luchino Michelini
Opportunity Knocks	Univ	Miles Goodman
Opposites Attract	NBC-TV	Mark Snow
Orpheus Descending	TNT	Steve Edwards
Out of Sight, Out of Mind	Ind	Peter Rodgers Melnick
Overexposed	Concorde	Mark Governor
Pacific Heights	Fox	Hans Zimmer
Paint It Black	Vestron	Jurgen Knieper
Pair of Aces	CBS-TV	William Olvis
Parker Kane	NBC-TV	Jay Ferguson
Payback	Ind	Daryl Dragon
Pentimento	Fr	Steve Beresford
People Like Us	NBC-TV	Billy Goldenberg
Perry Mason: The Case of the Defiant Daughter	NBC-TV	Dick DeBenedictis
Perry Mason: The Case of the Desperate Deception	NBC-TV	Dick DeBenedictis
Perry Mason: The Case of the Poisoned Pen	NBC-TV	Dick DeBenedictis
Perry Mason: The Case of the Silenced Singer	NBC-TV	Dick DeBenedictis
Phantom of the Opera, The	NBC-TV	John Addison
Plot to Kill Hitler, The	CBS-TV	Laurence Rosenthal
Polly--Comin' Home	NBC-TV	Joel McNeely
Postcards From the Edge	Col	Carly Simon
Postcards From the Edge	Col	Howard Shore
Predator 2	Fox	Alan Silvestri
Presume Dangereux	Fr/It/Belg	Stelvio Cipriani
Presumed Innocent	WB	John Williams
Pretty Woman	BV	James Newton Howard
Primo Baby	Can	Amin Bhatia
Prince and the Pauper, The	BV	Nicholas Pike
Private Collections	Ind	Marty Blasick
Problem Child	Univ	Miles Goodman
Prom Night III: The Last Kiss	Can	Paul Zaza
Promise to Keep, A	NBC-TV	David Shire
Psycho IV: The Beginning	Showtime	Graeme Revell
Punisher, The	Ind	Dennis Dreith
Puppet Master II	Ind	Richard Band
Q & A	TriStar	Ruben Blades
Quest for the Mighty Sword	Ind	Carlo Maria Cordio
Quick Change	WB	Randy Edelman
Quick Change	WB	Howard Shore
Quiet Days in Clichy	Fr/It/Ger	Matthieu Chabrol
Quiet Little Neighborhood, A Perfect Little Murder	NBC-TV	Joseph Conlan

Rain Killer, The	Concorde	Terry Plumeri
Rainbow Drive	Showtime	Tangerine Dream
Red Surf	Ind	Sasha Matson
Repo Jake	Ind	John Gonzalez
Repossessed	New Line	Charles Fox
Rescuers Down Under, The	BV	Bruce Broughton
Return of SuperFly, The	Ind	Ice-T
Return of SuperFly, The	Ind	Curtis Mayfield
Return to Green Acres	CBS-TV	Dan Foliart
Return to Green Acres	CBS-TV	Vic Mizzy
Revealing Evidence	NBC-TV	James Newton Howard
Revenge	Col	Jack Nitzsche
Reversal of Fortune	WB	Mark Isham
Rich Men, Single Women	ABC-TV	Charles Fox
Ripoux Contre Ripoux (My New Partner 2)	Fr	Francis Lai
Rising Son	TNT	Gary Chang
River of Death	Cannon	Sasha Matson
Robocop 2	Orion	Leonard Rosenman
Rock Hudson	ABC-TV	Paul Chihara
Rockula	Cannon	Hilary Bercovici
Rocky V	MGM/UA	Bill Conti
Rookie, The	WB	Lennie Niehaus
Rose and the Jackal, The	TNT	Michael J. Lewis
Running Against Time	USA Net	Don Davis
Russia House, The	MGM/UA	Jerry Goldsmith
Sam and Me	Can	Mark Korven
Sandino	Ind	Joakin Bello
Santa Sangre	Ind	Simon Boswell
Satan's Princess	Ind	Norman Mamey
Schweitzer	Ind	Zane Kronje
Secret Life of Archie's Wife, The	CBS-TV	William Olvis
Secret Life of Ian Fleming, The	TNT	Carl Davis
Secret Weapon	TNT	Alan Lisk
Shadowzone	Ind	Richard Band
Shaking the Tree	Ind	David Russo
Shattered Dreams	CBS-TV	Michael Convertino
She Said No	NBC-TV	Charles Bernstein
Sheltering Sky, The	WB	Ryuichi Sakamoto
Sheltering Sky, The	WB	Richard Horowitz
Shipwrecked	Ind	Patrick Doyle
Shock 'Em Dead	Ind	Robert Decker
Shock to the System, A	Ind	Gary Chang
Short Time	Fox	Ira Newborn
Show of Force, A	Par	Georges Delerue
Sibling Rivalry	Col	Jack Elliott
Side Out	TriStar	Jeff Lorber
Silhouette	USA Net	Michel Rubini
Ski Patrol	Ind	Bruce Miller
Sky High	NBC-TV	Peter Bernstein
Sleeping Car, The	Ind	Ray Colcord
Slumber Party Massacre 3	Concorde	Jamie Sheriff
Snake Eater	Ind	John Massari
Snow Kill	USA Net	Sylvester Levay
So Proudly We Hail	CBS-TV	Gil Melle

Solar Crisis	Jap	Maurice Jarre
Somebody Has to Shoot the Picture	HBO	James Newton Howard
Son's Promise, A	ABC-TV	J.A.C. Redford
Sonny Boy	Ind	David Carradine
Sonny Boy	Ind	Carlo Maria Cordio
Soultaker	Ind	Jon McCallum
Spaced Invaders	BV	David Russo
Sparks: The Price of Passion	CBS-TV	Bob Alcivar
Spirit of '76, The	Col	David Nichtern
Spontaneous Combustion	Ind	Graeme Revell
Stanley & Iris	MGM/UA	John Williams
Stardumb	Ind	Peter Francis Rotter
State of Grace	Orion	Ennio Morricone
Steel & Lace	Ind	John Massari
Stella	BV	John Morris
Stephen King's "It"	ABC-TV	Richard Bellis
Stolen: One Husband!	CBS-TV	James DiPasquale
Storm and Sorrow	Lifetime	Gabor Presser
Story of the Beach Boys: Summer Dreams, The	ABC-TV	Jay Levy
Stranger Within, The	CBS-TV	Vladimir Horonzky
Street Asylum	Ind	Leonard Marcel
Street Hunter	Ind	Barry Fasman
Street Hunter	Ind	Dana Walden
Streets	Concorde	Aaron Davis
Strike It Rich	Br/US	Shirley Walker
Strike It Rich	Br/US	Cliff Eidelman
Sudie and Simpson	Lifetime	Michel Colombier
Sundown: The Vampire in Retreat	Vestron	Richard Stone
Sweet Revenge	US/Fr	Hubert Bougis
Sweet Revenge	TNT	Didier Vasseur
Sword of Honour	Syn	Greg Sneddon
Syngenor	Ind	Thomas Chase
Syngenor	Ind	Steve Rucker
Take, The	USA Net	David Beal
Take, The	USA Net	Michael Shrieve
Taking Care of Business	BV	Stewart Copeland
Tales From the Darkside: The Movie	Par	John Harrison
Tales From the Darkside: The Movie	Par	Chaz Jankel
Tales From the Darkside: The Movie	Par	Jim Manzie
Tales From the Darkside: The Movie	Par	Pat Regan
Tales From the Darkside: The Movie	Par	Donald A. Rubinstein
Tales of the Unknown: Warped	Ind	Vladimir Horonzky
Teenage Mutant Ninja Turtles	New Line	John Du Prez
Terminal Bliss	Cannon	Frank W. Becker
Thanksgiving Day	NBC-TV	Tom Hensley
Thanksgiving Day	NBC-TV	Alan E. Lindgren
There Were Days and Moons	Fr	Francis Lai
Think Big	Concorde	Michael Sembello
Think Big	Concorde	Hilary Bercovici
Thousand Pieces of Gold	Ind	Gary Remal Malkin
Three Men and a Little Lady	BV	James Newton Howard
Tie Me Up! Tie Me Down!	Sp	Ennio Morricone
Till There Was You	Aut	Graeme Revell

Time to Kill	Ind	Ennio Morricone
To My Daughter	NBC-TV	John D'Andrea
To My Daughter	NBC-TV	Cory Lerios
To Sleep With Anger	Ind	Stephen James Taylor
Too Much Sun	New Line	David Robbins
Too Young to Die?	NBC-TV	Charles Bernstein
Torn Apart	Ind	Peter Arnow
Torrents of Spring	Fr	Stanley Myers
Total Recall	TriStar	Jerry Goldsmith
Touch of a Stranger	Ind	Jack Alan Goga
Tragedy of Flight 103: The Inside Story, The	HBO	Carl Davis
Transylvania Twist	Concorde	Chuck Cirino
Treasure Island	TNT	Paddy Moloney
Tremors	Univ	Ernest Troost
Tune in Tomorrow . . .	Ind	Wynton Marsalis
Tusks (aka Fire in Eden)	Ind	Tom Alonso
Tutti Stanno Bene (Everybody's Fine)	It/Fr	Ennio Morricone
Twisted Obsession	Fr	Antoine Duhamel
Two Jakes, The	Par	Van Dyke Parks
Un Histoire Inventee (An Imaginary Tale)	Fr	Serge Fiori
Una Vita Scellerata (An Infamous Life)	It/Fr/Ger	Franco Battiato
Unspeakable Acts	ABC-TV	Mike Post
Urga	Fr/Rus	Eduard Artemiev
Vestige of Honor	CBS-TV	Dana Kaproff
Vietnam, Texas	Ind	Richard Stone
Vincent and Theo	Br/Fr	Gabriel Yared
Vital Signs	Fox	Miles Goodman
Voice of the Heart	Syn	Alan Parker
Voices Within: The Lives of Truddi Chase	ABC-TV	Charles Fox
Voyage of Terror: The Achille Lauro Affair	Syn	Ennio Morricone
Wait Until Spring, Bandini	WB	Angelo Badalamenti
Waiting	Aut	Martin Arminger
Watchers II	Ind	Rick Conrad
Web of Deceit	USA Net	J.A.C. Redford
Wedding Band	Syn	Steve Hunter
Weekend With Kate	Aut	Bruce Rowland
Welcome Home, Roxy Carmichael	Par	Thomas Newman
Wheels of Terror	USA Net	Jay Gruska
When Will I Be Loved?	NBC-TV	Brian Keane
When You Remember Me	ABC-TV	J. Peter Robinson
Where Pigeons Go to Die	NBC-TV	Leonard Rosenman
Where the Heart Is	BV	Peter Martin
Whispers	Ind	Fred Mollin
White Girl, The	Ind	Jimmy Lee Brown
White Girl, The	Ind	George Porter Martin
White Hunter, Black Heart	WB	Lennie Niehaus
White Palace	Univ	George Fenton
White Room	Can	Mark Korven
Why Me?	Ind	Basil Poledouris
Wild at Heart	Goldwyn	Angelo Badalamenti
Wild Orchid	Ind	Simon Goldenberg
Wild Orchid	Ind	Geoff MacCormack
Wildest Dreams	Ind	Joey Mennonna

Witchcraft II: The Temptress	Ind	Miriam Cutler
Witches, The	WB	Stanley Myers
Witching of Ben Wagner, The	Disney-TV	Kurt Bestor
Without Her Consent	NBC-TV	Mike Post
Without You I'm Nothing	Ind	Patrice Rushen
Women & Men: Stories of Seduction	HBO	Marvin Hamlisch
Working Trash	Fox-TV	Trevor Lawrence
Working Trash	Fox-TV	Bob Mithoff
World's Oldest Living Bridesmaid, The	CBS-TV	Jay Gruska
Young Guns II	Fox	Alan Silvestri
Zandalee	Ind	Pray for Rain

1991

Abraxas: Guardian of the Universe	Can	Carlos Lopes
Absolute Strangers	CBS-TV	Charles Fox
Adam Bede	Br	Richard Hartley
Addams Family, The	Par	Marc Shaiman
Adjuster, The	Can	Mychael Danna
Afraid of the Dark	Br/Fr	Richard Hartley
Aftermath: A Test of Love	CBS-TV	Leonard Rosenman
Agantuk (The Stranger)	Fr/Indian	Satyajit Ray
Alien Space Avenger	Ind	Richard Fiocca
All I Want for Christmas	Par	Bruce Broughton
Amantes (Lovers)	Sp	Jose Nieto
Ambition	Miramax	Leonard Rosenman
Ambition	Ind	Ned Rifle
American Friends	Br	Georges Delerue
American Kickboxer I	Cannon	Frank W. Becker
American Ninja 4: The Annihilation	Cannon	Nicholas Tenbroek
American Summer, An	Ind	Roger Neill
American Tail: Fievel Goes West, An	Univ	James Horner
And the Sea Will Tell	CBS-TV	Peter Manning Robinson
. . . And Then She Was Gone	NBC-TV	Peter Manning Robinson
And You Thought Your Parents Were Weird!	Ind	Randy Miller
Angel in Red (aka Uncaged)	Ind	Terry Plumeri
Anna Karamazova	Fr/Rus	Alexander Vustin
Another Pair of Aces: Three of a Kind	CBS-TV	Jay Gruska
Another You	TriStar	Charles Gross
Antonia and June	Br	Rachel Portman
Arena	Ind	Richard Band
Arrival, The	Ind	Richard Band
Art of Dying, The	Ind	John Gonzalez
Assassin of the Tsar	Br/Rus	John Altman
At Play in the Fields of the Lord	Univ	Zbigniew Preisner
Atlantis	Fr	Eric Serra
Aux Yeux du Monde (Autobus)	Fr	Gerard Torikian
Babe Ruth	NBC-TV	Steve Dorff
Baby of the Bride	CBS-TV	Jay Gruska
Backdraft	Univ	Hans Zimmer
Backfield in Motion	ABC-TV	Cliff Eidelman
Backsliding	Aut/Br	Nigel Westlake
Bad Attitudes	Fox-TV	Peter Rodgers Melnick
Ballad of the Sad Cafe, The	Ind	Richard Robbins

Bare Essentials	CBS-TV	Scott Wilk
Barocco	It	Luigi Ceccarelli
Barton Fink	Fox	Carter Burwell
Beastmaster 2: Through the Portal of Time	New Line	Robert Folk
Beauty and the Beast	BV	Howard Ashman
Beauty and the Beast	BV	Alan Menken
Bejewelled	Disney-TV	Ken Thorne
Betrayal of the Dove	Ind	Sasha Matson
Big Sweat, The	Ind	John Massari
Bikini Island	Ind	Marc David Decker
Bikini Summer	Ind	John Gonzalez
Bill & Ted's Bogus Journey	Orion	David Newman
Billy Bathgate	BV	Mark Isham
Bingo	TriStar	Richard Gibbs
Bix	US/It	Bix Beiderbecke
Black Magic Woman	Ind	Randy Miller
Black Robe	Can/Aut	Georges Delerue
Blackmail	USA Net	Joseph Conlan
Blonde Fist	Br	Alan Gill
Blood and Concrete	Ind	Vinny Golia
Blood Games	Ind	Greg Turner
Blood River	CBS-TV	William Goldstein
Blood Ties	Fox	Brad Fiedel
Bloodfist II	Concorde	Nigel Holton
Blowback	Ind	Wendy Blackstone
Body Moves	Ind	Tiromancyno
Body Parts	Par	Loek Dikker
Box Office Bunny	WB	Hummie Mann
Boys, The	ABC-TV	David Shire
Boyz N the Hood	Col	Stanley Clarke
Breathing Under Water	Aut	Elizabeth Drake
Bride of Re-Animator	Ind	Richard Band
Bridge, The	Br	Richard G. Mitchell
Bright Angel	Ind	Christopher Young
Broadway Bound	ABC-TV	David Shire
Brotherhood of the Gun	CBS-TV	Jerry Goldsmith
Brotherhood of the Gun	CBS-TV	Joel Goldsmith
Bugsy	TriStar	Ennio Morricone
Bump in the Night	CBS-TV	Gary William Friedman
Butcher's Wife, The	Par	Michael Gore
By the Sword	Ind	Bill Conti
California Casanova	Ind	Reg Powell
California Casanova	Ind	Sam Winans
Cape Fear	Univ	Elmer Bernstein
Cape Fear	Univ	Bernard Herrmann
Captive	ABC-TV	Steve Tyrell
Captive in the Land, A	US/Rus	Bill Conti
Career Opportunities	Univ	Thomas Newman
Carnal Crimes	Ind	Matthew Ross
Carnal Crimes	Ind	Jeff Fishman
Carolina Skeletons	NBC-TV	John Morris
Cast a Deadly Spell	HBO	Curt Sobel
Chaindance	Ind	Graeme Coleman
Chance of a Lifetime	NBC-TV	David McHugh

Chase, The	NBC-TV	W. G. Snuffy Walden
Cheap Shots	Ind	Jeff Beal
Chernobyl: The Final Warning	TNT	Billy Goldenberg
Chiedi la Luna (Ask for the Moon)	It	Antonio Di Pofi
Child of Darkness, Child of Light	USA Net	Jay Gruska
Child's Play 3	Univ	John D'Andrea
Child's Play 3	Univ	Cory Lerios
Children of the Night	Ind	Daniel Licht
China Moon	Orion	George Fenton
Chopper Chicks in Zombie Town	New Line	Daniel May
Christmas on Division Street	CBS-TV	George Blondheim
City of Hope	Ind	Mason Daring
City Slickers	Col	Marc Shaiman
Class Action	Fox	James Horner
Class of Nuke 'Em High Part II	Troma	Bob Mithoff
Clearcut	Can	Shane Harvey
Clearing, The	US/Rus	Tamara Kline
Closer, The	Ind	Joel Hirschhorn
Closer, The	Ind	Al Kasha
Closet Land	Univ	Richard Einhorn
Closet Land	Univ	Philip Glass
Cold Steel	Ind	David A. Jackson
Common Bonds	Ind	Graeme Coleman
Common Pursuit	BBC-TV	Ilona Sekacz
Company Business	MGM	Michael Kamen
Convicts	Ind	Peter Rodgers Melnick
Cool as Ice	Univ	Stanley Clarke
Cop-Out	Ind	Greg Turner
Count of Solar, The	Br	John Keane
Cover Up	Ind	Bruno Louchouran
Crackdown	Concorde	Terry Plumeri
Crazy from the Heart	TNT	Arthur B. Rubinstein
Crooked Hearts	MGM	Mark Isham
Crucifer of Blood, The	TNT	Carl Davis
Cry in the Wild: The Taking of Peggy Ann	NBC-TV	Sylvester Levay
Curly Sue	WB	Georges Delerue
Curse III: Blood Sacrifice, The	Ind	Julian Laxton
Curse III: Blood Sacrifice, The	Ind	Patric Van Blerk
Danielle Steel's "Changes"	NBC-TV	Lee Holdridge
Danielle Steel's "Daddy"	NBC-TV	Dennis McCarthy
Danielle Steel's "Palomino"	NBC-TV	Dominic Frontiere
Dark Backward, The	Ind	Marc David Decker
Dark Rider	Ind	Brad Scott Dish
Dark Wind, The	Ind	Michel Colombier
Darlings of the Gods	Aut	Brian May
Daughters of Privilege	NBC-TV	Patrick Williams
Daughters of the Dust	Ind	John Barnes
Daydream Believer	Aut	Todd Hunter
Daydream Believer	Aut	Johanna Pigott
Dead Again	Par	Patrick Doyle
Dead and Alive: The Race for Gus Farace	ABC-TV	Mark Snow
Dead in the Water	USA Net	Philip Giffin
Dead on the Money	TNT	Michael Minard
Dead Silence	Fox	Tim Truman

Dead Space	Ind	Daniel May
Deadlock	HBO	Richard Gibbs
Deadly	Aut	Graeme Revell
Deadly Desire	USA Net	Nan Schwartz
Deadly Game	USA Net	Tim Truman
Deadly Intentions . . . Again?	ABC-TV	J. Peter Robinson
Deadly Medicine	NBC-TV	Bob Alcivar
Deadly Surveillance	Ind	Marty Simon
Dean R. Koontz's "Servants of Twilight"	Showtime	Jim Manzie
Death Dreams	Lifetime	Gerald Gouriet
Death Has a Bad Reputation	USA Net	Paul Chihara
Death of a Schoolboy	Aut	Peter Pongo
Deceived	BV	Thomas Newman
December	Ind	Deborah Holland
December Bride	Ire	Jurgen Knieper
Deception: A Mother's Secret	NBC-TV	Peter Manning Robinson
Defending Your Life	WB	Michael Gore
Defenseless	New Line	Trevor Jones
Defenseless	New Line	Curt Sobel
Delirious	MGM	Cliff Eidelman
Delusion	Ind	Barry Adamson
Devil's Daughter, The	It	Pino Donaggio
Dillinger	ABC-TV	David McHugh
Ding et Dong: Le Film	Can	Jean-Marie Benoit
Dingo	Aut/Fr	Miles Davis
Dingo	Aut/Fr	Michel Legrand
Diplomatic Immunity	Ind	John Massari
Do or Die	Ind	Richard Lyons
Doc Hollywood	WB	Carter Burwell
Doctor, The	BV	Michael Convertino
Dogfight	WB	Mason Daring
Dollman vs. Demonic Toys	Ind	Richard Band
Dollman vs. Demonic Toys	Ind	Tony Riparetti
Don't Tell Mom the Babysitter's Dead	WB	David Newman
Don't Touch My Daughter	NBC-TV	Dana Kaproff
Double Impact	Col	Arthur Kempel
Doublecrossed	HBO	Richard Bellis
Drop Dead Fred	New Line	Randy Edelman
Drop Dead Gorgeous	USA Net	Marvin Dolgay
Drop Dead Gorgeous	USA Net	Glenn Morley
Dutch	Fox	Alan Silvestri
Dying Young	Fox	James Newton Howard
Dynasty: The Reunion	ABC-TV	Bill Conti
Dynasty: The Reunion	ABC-TV	Peter Myers
Earth Angel	ABC-TV	Kevin Klingler
Edge of Honor	Ind	William T. Stromberg
Edward II	Br	Simon Fisher Turner
El Patrullero (Highway Patrolman)	US/Mex	Zandor Schloss
Electric Moon	Br	Simeon Venkov
Eminent Domain	Ind	Zbigniew Preisner
Enchanted April	Br	Richard Rodney Bennett
Entertainers, The	ABC-TV	John D''ndrea
Entertainers, The	ABC-TV	Cory Lerios
Ernest Scared Stupid	BV	Bruce Arnston

Europa	Fr/Ger/Dan	Joachim Holbek
Europa, Europa	Fr/Ger	Zbigniew Preisner
Eve of Destruction	Orion	Philippe Sarde
Events Leading Up to My Death, The	Can	Mary Margaret O'Hara
Evil Spirits	Ind	Duane Sciaqua
Evil Toons	Ind	Chuck Cirino
Ex	Br	Jim Parker
Exposure (High Art)	Miramax	Todd Boekelheide
Exposure (High Art)	Miramax	Jurgen Knieper
Eyes of a Witness	CBS-TV	Charles Gross
Face of a Stranger	CBS-TV	Lee Holdridge
Fair Game	Ind	Giorgio Moroder
False Arrest	ABC-TV	Sylvester Levay
Fast Getaway	New Line	Bruce Rowland
Fatal Exposure	USA Net	Michel Colombier
Fatal Friendship	NBC-TV	Arthur B. Rubinstein
Father of the Bride	WB	Alan Silvestri
Favour, the Watch, and the Very Big Fish, The	Fr/Br	Vladimir Cosma
Feelin' Screwy	Ind	Chris Winfield
Femme Fatale	Ind	Parmer Fuller
Fever	HBO	Michel Colombier
Filipina Dreamgirls	Br	Simon Brint
Final Verdict	TNT	David McHugh
Finding the Way Home	ABC-TV	Lee Holdridge
Fire in the Dark	CBS-TV	Arthur Kempel
Fire! Trapped on the 37th Floor	ABC-TV	Gil Melle
Fires Within	MGM	Maurice Jarre
Firing Line, The	Ind	Marita Manuel
Fisher King, The	TriStar	George Fenton
Five Heartbeats, The	Fox	Stanley Clarke
Flea Bites	Br	Rachel Portman
Flight of Black Angel	Showtime	Rick Marvin
Flight of the Intruder	Par	Basil Poledouris
For the Boys	Fox	Dave Grusin
For the Very First Time	NBC-TV	Gregory Sill
Fourth Story	Showtime	William Olvis
Frame Up	Ind	Bob Summers
Frankenstein: The College Years	Fox-TV	Joel McNeely
Frankie and Johnny	Par	Marvin Hamlisch
Freddy's Dead: The Final Nightmare	New Line	Brian May
Fried Green Tomatoes	Univ	Thomas Newman
Futurekick	Concorde	Stan Ridgeway
FX 2: The Deadly Art of Illusion	Orion	Michael Boddicker
FX 2: The Deadly Art of Illusion	Orion	Lalo Schifrin
Gambler Returns: The Luck of the Draw, The	NBC-TV	Mark Snow
George's Island	Can	Marty Simon
Girl From Mars, The	Fam Ch	Louis Natale
Giving, The	Ind	Stephen James Taylor
Grand Canyon	Fox	James Newton Howard
Grand Isle	TNT	Elliot Goldenthal
Grass Arena, The	Br	Philip Appleby
Great Pretender, The	NBC-TV	Mike Post
Guilty Until Proven Innocent	NBC-TV	Charles Bernstein

Guilty as Charged	Ind	Steve Bartek
Guilty by Suspicion	WB	James Newton Howard
Hand That Rocks the Cradle, The	BV	Graeme Revell
Hangfire	Ind	Jim Price
Hangin' With the Homeboys	New Line	Joel Sill
Hard Promises	Col	Kenny Vance
Hard Way, The	Univ	Arthur B. Rubinstein
Harley Davidson and the Marlboro Man	MGM	Basil Poledouris
Haunted, The	Fox-TV	Richard Bellis
Haunting Fear	Troma	Chuck Cirino
He Said, She Said	Par	Miles Goodman
Hear My Song	Miramax	John Altman
Heart of Darkness: A Filmmaker's Odyssey	Ind	Todd Boekelheide
Heaven Is a Playground	New Line	Patrick O'Hearn
Held Hostage: The Sis and Jerry Levin Story	ABC-TV	Charles Fox
Hell Hath No Fury	NBC-TV	J. Peter Robinson
Her Wicked Ways	CBS-TV	Fred Karlin
Heroes of Desert Storm, The	ABC-TV	Sylvester Levay
Hi Honey I'm Dead	Fox-TV	Roger Bellon
Hit Man, The	ABC-TV	Arthur Kempel
Hitman, The	Cannon	Joel Derouin
Holidays on the River Yarra	Aut	Sam Mallet
Hollywood Boulevard II	Concorde	Mark Governor
Homicide	Ind	Alaric Jans
Hook	TriStar	John Williams
Hors la Vie	Fr/It/Belg	Nicola Piovani
Hot Shots!	Fox	Sylvester Levay
Hotel Oklahoma	Ind	Toby Fitch
House Party 2: The Pajama Jam	New Line	Vassal Benford
Howling VI: The Freaks	Ind	Patrick Gleeson
Hudson Hawk	TriStar	Michael Kamen
Hunting	Ind	John French
Hunting	Ind	David Herzog
I Dreamt I Woke Up	Br	Paddy Moloney
I Still Dream of Jeannie	NBC-TV	Ken Harrison
I'll Fly Away	NBC-TV	W. G. Snuffy Walden
If Looks Could Kill	WB	David Foster
Il Conte Max (Count Max)	It/Fr	Manuel De Sica
Il Muro di Gomma (The Invisible Wall)	Ind	Francesco De Gregori
Importance of Being Earnest, The	Ind	Roger Hamilton Spotts
Impromptu	Hemdale	John Strauss
In a Child's Name	CBS-TV	Richard Stone
In Advance of the Landing	Can	Fred Mollin
In Broad Daylight	NBC-TV	Patrick Williams
In the Line of Duty: Manhunt in the Dakotas	NBC-TV	Mark Snow
In the Nick of Time	NBC-TV	Steve Dorff
Inconvenient Woman, An	ABC-TV	Craig Safan
Indian Runner, The	Ind	Jack Nitzsche
Inner Circle, The	Col	Eduard Artemiev
Inner Sanctum	Ind	Chuck Cirino
Intimate Stranger	Ind	Jonathan Sheffer
Into the Badlands	USA Net	John Debney
Iran: Days of Crisis	TNT	Philippe Sarde
Iron & Silk	Ind	Michael Gibbs

Iron Maze	Ind	Stanley Myers
Ironclads	TNT	Allyn Ferguson
Jacquot de Nantes	Fr	Joanna Bruzdowicz
Jailbirds	CBS-TV	Ken Harrison
J'embrasse Pas (I Don't Kiss)	Fr	Philippe Sarde
JFK	WB	John Williams
Johnny Stecchino	It	Evan Lurie
Johnny Suede	Ind	Jim Farmer
Josephine Baker Story, The	HBO	Ralph Burns
Josephine Baker Story, The	HBO	Georges Delerue
Jumpin' at the Boneyard	Fox	Steve Postel
Jungle Fever	Univ	Terence Blanchard
K-9000	Fox-TV	Jan Hammer
Kafka	Miramax	Cliff Martinez
Keeping Secrets	ABC-TV	Patrick Williams
Killer's Edge, The	Ind	John Gonzalez
Killing Mind, The	Lifetime	James DiPasquale
Killing Zone, The	Ind	Jeff Lass
King Ralph	Univ	James Newton Howard
Kiss and Be Killed	Ind	Kevin Kiner
Kiss Before Dying, A	Univ	Howard Shore
Kiss Me a Killer	Ind	Nigel Holton
Knight Rider 2000	NBC-TV	Jan Hammer
L.A. Story	TriStar	Peter Rodgers Melnick
La Belle Noiseuse	Fr	Igor Stravinsky
La Chateau de Ma Mere (My Mother's Castle)	Fr	Vladimir Cosma
La Derniere Season (The Last Season)	Fr	Frederic Laperierre
La Double Vie de Veronique	Fr/Pol	Zbigniew Preisner
La Gloire de Mon Pere (My Father's Glory)	Fr	Vladimir Cosma
La Vieille qui marchait dans la mer	Fr	Philippe Sarde
L'ange	Fr	Michele Bokanowski
Last Boy Scout, The	WB	Michael Kamen
Last Hour, The	Ind	Garry Schyman
Last Prostitute, The	Lifetime	Fred Karlin
Last Riders, The	Ind	John Gonzalez
Last Romantics, The	Br	Carl Davis
Last to Go, The	ABC-TV	John Morris
Late for Dinner	Col	David Mansfield
Law Lord, The	BBC-TV	Richard Hartley
Lena's Holiday	Ind	Steve Schiff
Les Amants du Pont-Neuf	Fr	Jean-Louis Le Breton
Les Cles du Paradis (The Keys to Paradise)	Fr	Francis Lai
Let Him Have It	Br	Michael Kamen
Liar's Edge	Can	Paul Zaza
Liebestraum	TriStar	Mike Figgis
Lies Before Kisses	CBS-TV	Don Davis
Lies of the Twins	USA Net	David McHugh
Life Stinks	MGM	John Morris
Lightning Field	USA Net	J. Peter Robinson
L'Ile au Tresor (Treasure Island)	US/Fr	Jorge Arriagada
Line of Fire: The Morris Dees Story	NBC-TV	Arthur B. Rubinstein
Liquid Dreams	Ind	Ed Tomney
Little Heroes	Ind	Jon McCallum

Little Man Tate	Orion	Mark Isham
Little Noises	Ind	Kurt Hoffman
Little Noises	Ind	Fritz Van Orden
Little Piece of Heaven, A	NBC-TV	Don Davis
Little Secrets	Ind	Gene Hobson
Little Stiff, A	Ind	Kath Bloom
Livin' Large	Goldwyn	Herbie Hancock
Living a Lie	NBC-TV	Mark Snow
Locked Up: A Mother's Rage	CBS-TV	J.A.C. Redford
London Kills Me	Br	Sarah Sarhandi
London Kills Me	Br	Mark Springer
Lonely Hearts	Ind	David McHugh
Long Road Home	NBC-TV	Craig Safan
Loser	Ind	Matthew Fritz
Loser	Ind	Joey Harrow
Lost Language of Cranes, The	Br	John Pritchard
Lost Language of Cranes, The	Br	Julian Walstall
Louis L'Amour's "Conagher"	TNT	J.A.C. Redford
Love & Greed	Ind	Emilio Kauderer
Love and Curses . . . and All That Jazz	CBS-TV	Steve Tyrell
Love Kills	USA Net	Stanley Clarke
Love, Lies and Murder	NBC-TV	Charles Bernstein
Love-Moi	Can	Robert Leger
Love Without Pity	Fr	Gerard Torikian
Love Ya Tomorrow	Ind	David Chu
Lucky Day	ABC-TV	David Bell
Lucy & Desi: Before the Laughter	CBS-TV	Lee Holdridge
Lunatics: A Love Story	Ind	Joseph Lo Duca
Lune Froide (Cold Moon)	Fr	Didier Lockwood
Lune Froide (Cold Moon)	Fr	Jimi Hendrix
Madame Bovary	Fr	Matthieu Chabrol
Magic Riddle, The	Aut	Guy Gross
Man in the Moon, The	MGM	James Newton Howard
Mannequin Two: On the Move	Fox	David McHugh
March, The	BBC-TV	Richard Hartley
Marilyn and Me	ABC-TV	George Blondheim
Mark Twain and Me	Disney-TV	Laurence Rosenthal
Marla Hanson Story, The	NBC-TV	Mark Snow
Married to It	Orion	Henry Mancini
Marrying Man, The	BV	David Newman
Martial Law	Ind	Elliot Solomon
Matilda	It	Franco Piersanti
Mayrig (Mother)	Fr	Jean-Claude Petit
McBain	Ind	Christopher Franke
Mediterraneo	It	Giancarlo Bigazzi
Mediterraneo	It	Marco Falagiani
Meeting Venus	Br	Daisy Boschan
Megaville	Ind	Stacy Widelitz
Memoire Tranquee (Lapse of Memory)	Can/Fr	Alexandre Desplat
Metamorphosis: The Alien Factor	Ind	John Gray
Miracle in the Wilderness	TNT	Vladimir Horonzky
Miracle, The	Ire	Anne Dudley
Mirror, Mirror	Ind	Jimmy Lifton
Missing Pieces	Ind	Marvin Hamlisch

Mission of the Shark	CBS-TV	Craig Safan
Mississippi Masala	Ind	L. Subramaniam
Mobsters	Univ	Michael Small
Mon Pere, ce Heros	Fr	Francois Bernheim
Mortal Thoughts	Col	Mark Isham
Mother's Justice, A	NBC-TV	Richard Bellis
Motorama	Ind	Andy Summers
Mrs. Lambert Remembers Love	CBS-TV	Lee Holdridge
Murder 101	USA Net	Philip Giffin
Murder in New Hampshire: The Pamela Smart Story	CBS-TV	Gary Chang
Murder of Quality	Br	Stanley Myers
Murderous Vision	USA Net	Joe Renzetti
My Father Is Coming	Ger/US	David Van Tieghem
My Girl	Col	James Newton Howard
My Heroes Have Always Been Cowboys	Goldwyn	James Horner
My Own Private Idaho	New Line	Bill Stafford
My Son Johnny	CBS-TV	Dana Kaproff
Mystery Date	Orion	John Du Prez
N.Y.P.D. Mounted	CBS-TV	Peter Bernstein
Naked Gun 2-1/2: The Smell of Fear, The	Par	Ira Newborn
Naked Lunch	Fox	Howard Shore
Naked Obsession	Concorde	Scott Singer
Necessary Roughness	Par	Bill Conti
Never Forget	TNT	Henry Mancini
Never Leave Nevada	Ind	Ray Benson
New Jack City	WB	Michel Colombier
New Jack City	Ind	Roger Bourland
Night of the Hunter	ABC-TV	Peter Manning Robinson
Night of the Warrior	Ind	Ed Tomney
Night on Earth	Ind	Tom Waits
Nightmare in Columbia County	CBS-TV	Richard Bellis
No Contest	Can	Paul Zaza
No Secrets	Ind	Vinny Golia
Not Without My Daughter	MGM	Jerry Goldsmith
Not of This World	CBS-TV	Johnny Harris
Nothing But Trouble	WB	Michael Kamen
Nuit et Jour (Night and Day)	Fr	Marc Herouet
Object of Beauty, The	US/Br	Tom Bahler
Omen IV: The Awakening	Fox-TV	Jerry Goldsmith
Omen IV: The Awakening	Fox-TV	Jonathan Sheffer
Once Around	Univ	James Horner
One Against the Wind	CBS-TV	Lee Holdridge
One Cup of Coffee	Ind	Lee Holdridge
One False Move	Ind	Peter Haycock
One False Move	Ind	Derek Holt
One Full Moon	Br	Mark Thomas
One Good Cop	BV	David Foster
One Good Cop	BV	William Ross
One Special Victory	NBC-TV	Billy Goldenberg
Only the Lonely	Fox	Maurice Jarre
Oscar	BV	Elmer Bernstein
Other People's Money	WB	David Newman
Our Sons	ABC-TV	John Morris

Out for Justice	WB	David Michael Frank
Out of the Rain	Ind	Cengiz Yaltkaya
Paper Mask	Br	Richard Harvey
Paradise	BV	David Newman
Paris Trout	Showtime	David Shire
Payoff	Viacom	Charles Bernstein
People Under the Stairs, The	Univ	Don Peake
People Under the Stairs, The	Univ	Graeme Revell
Perfect Bride, The	USA Net	Richard Bronskill
Perfect Harmony	Disney-TV	Billy Goldenberg
Perfect Profile	Ind	Greg Krotcha
Perfect Tribute, The	ABC-TV	Lee Holdridge
Perfect Weapon, The	Par	Gary Chang
Perfectly Normal	Br/Can	Richard Gregoire
Perry Mason: The Case of the Fatal Fashion	NBC-TV	Dick DeBenedictis
Perry Mason: The Case of the Glass Coffin	NBC-TV	Dick DeBenedictis
Perry Mason: The Case of the Maligned Mobster	NBC-TV	Dick DeBenedictis
Perry Mason: The Case of the Ruthless Reporter	NBC-TV	Dick DeBenedictis
Phantasm II: Lord of the Dead	Ind	Fred Myrow
Phantasm II: Lord of the Dead	Ind	Christopher Stone
Pianist, The	Can	Andre Gagnon
Pink Lightning	Fox-TV	Steve Tyrell
Pistol: The Birth of a Legend, The	Ind	Brent Havens
Pit and the Pendulum, The	Concorde	Richard Band
Pizza Man	Ind	Daniel May
Pleasure Principle, The	Br	Sonny Southon
Pledge Night	Ind	Todd Rice
Plymouth	ABC-TV	Brad Fiedel
Point Break	Fox	Mark Isham
Poison	Ind	James Bennett
Police Story: The Freeway Killings	NBC-TV	Jerry Goldsmith
Popcorn	Can	Paul Zaza
Pope Must Diet, The	Br	Anne Dudley
Posing: Inspired by Three Real Stories	CBS-TV	Ron Ramin
Prague	Br/Fr	Jonathan Dove
Prayer of the Rollerboys	Ind	Stacy Widelitz
Prime Suspect	Granada TV	Stephen Warbeck
Prime Target	Ind	Robert Garrett
Prime Target	Ind	David Heavener
Prince	Br	Bill Connor
Prince of Tides, The	Col	James Newton Howard
Princes in Exile	Can	Normand Corbiel
Prisoner of Honor	HBO	Barry Kirsch
Prisoners of the Sun (Blood Oath)	Aut	David McHugh
Problem Child 2	Univ	David Kitay
Project: Alien	Ind	Allan Zavod
Project Eliminator	Ind	Jon McCallum
Proof	Aut	David Bridie
Prospero's Books	Br/Fr	Michael Nyman
Puppet Master III: Toulon's Revenge	Ind	Richard Band
Pure Luck	Univ	Danny Elfman
Pure Luck	Univ	Jonathan Sheffer

Queens Logic	New Line	Joe Jackson
Rage in Harlem, A	Miramax	Elmer Bernstein
Rambling Rose	New Line	Elmer Bernstein
Rape of Dr. Willis, The	CBS-TV	Mark Snow
Rapture, The	New Line	Thomas Newman
Raw Nerve	Ind	Greg Turner
Reason for Living: The Jill Ireland Story	NBC-TV	Steve Tyrell
Red Wind	USA Net	Philip Giffin
Reflecting Skin, The	Br	Nick Bicat
Regarding Henry	Par	Hans Zimmer
Return of Eliot Ness, The	NBC-TV	Lee Holdridge
Return to the Blue Lagoon	Col	Basil Poledouris
Revenge of Billy the Kid	Br	Tony Flynn
Revolution!	Ind	Tom Judson
Rhapsody in August	Jap	Shinichiro Ikebe
Rich Girl	Ind	Jay Chattaway
Ricochet	WB	Alan Silvestri
Riff-Raff	Br	Stewart Copeland
Ring of Scorpio	Aut	Martin Arminger
Robin Hood	Fox-TV	Geoffrey Burgon
Robin Hood: Prince of Thieves ̴	WB	Michael Kamen
Robot Jox	Ind	Frederic Talgorn
Rocketeer, The	BV	James Horner
Roots of Evil	Ind	Duane Sciacolla
Rover Dangerfield	WB	Rodney Dangerfield
Rover Dangerfield	WB	David Newman
Rover Dangerfield	WB	Billy Tragessar
Row of Crows, A	Ind	Robert Folk
Rubin and Ed	Ind	Fredric Murrow
Run	BV	Phil Marshall
Runaway Father	CBS-TV	James DiPasquale
Rush	MGM	Eric Clapton
Salmonberries	Ger	Bob Telson
Sarah, Plain and Tall	CBS-TV	David Shire
Scanners II: The New Order	Can	Marty Simon
Scenes From a Mall	BV	Marc Shaiman
Scissors	Ind	Alfi Kabiljo
Scorchers	Ind	Carter Burwell
Search for Signs of Intelligent Life in the Universe	Orion	Jerry Goodman
Season of Giants, A	TNT	Riz Ortolani
Secret Friends	Br	Nicholas Russell-Pavier
Seduction in Travis County, A	CBS-TV	John Debney
Seeds of Tragedy	Fox	Gerald Gouriet
Separate but Equal	ABC-TV	Carl Davis
Servants of Twilight, The	Ind	Jim Manzie
Severed Ties	Ind	Daniel Licht
Sgt. Kabukiman, N.Y.P.D.	Troma	Bob Mithoff
Shadow of a Doubt	CBS-TV	Allyn Ferguson
Shattered	MGM	Alan Silvestri
She Says She's Innocent	NBC-TV	Greg DeBelles
She Stood Alone	NBC-TV	Michael J. Lewis
Shoot First: A Cop's Vengeance	NBC-TV	W. G. Snuffy Walden
Shout	Univ	Randy Edelman

Showdown at Williams Creek	Ind	Michael Conway Baker
Showdown in Little Tokyo	WB	David Michael Frank
Shuttlecock	Br/Fr	Barry Adamson
Shuttlecock	Br/Fr	Jan Garbarek
Sidney Sheldon's "Memories of Midnight"	Syn	Ron Ramin
Silence of the Lambs, The	Orion	Howard Shore
Silent Motive	Life	Dana Kaproff
Silent Night, Deadly Night 5: The Toy Maker	Ind	Matthew Morse
Sins of the Mother	CBS-TV	Richard Gibbs
Sitter, The	Fox-TV	Laura Karpman
Sleepers	BBC-TV	David Dundas
Sleeping With The Enemy	Fox	Jerry Goldsmith
Small Dance, A	Br	Richard Harvey
Small Time	Ind	Arnold Bieber
Snakeeater II: The Drug Pusher	Ind	John Massari
Soapdish	Par	Alan Silvestri
Social Suicide	Ind	Roger Bellon
Soldier's Tale, A	Ind	John Chase
Son of the Morning Star	ABC-TV	Craig Safan
Spaulding Gray's Monster in a Box	Br	Laurie Anderson
Spotswood (aka Efficiency Expert)	Aut	Ricky Fataar
Star Trek VI: The Undiscovered Country	Par	Cliff Eidelman
Stephen King's "Sometimes They Come Back"	CBS-TV	Terry Plumeri
Stepping Out	Par	Peter Matz
Stone Cold	Col	Sylvester Levay
Stop at Nothing	Lifetime	J.A.C. Redford
Story Lady, The	NBC-TV	Lee Holdridge
Story of Boys and Girls, The	It	Riz Ortolani
Straight Out of Brooklyn	Ind	Harold Wheeler
Stranger at My Door	CBS-TV	David Bell
Stranger in the Family	ABC-TV	Michel Rubini
Strangers in Good Company	Ind	Marie Bernard
Strays	USA Net	Michel Colombier
Street Crimes	Ind	John Gonzalez
Street of No Return	Fr/Port	Karl-Heinz Schafer
Strictly Business	WB	Michel Colombier
Strip Jack Naked: Nighthawks II	Br	Adrian James Carbutt
Stroke of Midnight	Ind	Didier Vasseur
Suburban Commando	New Line	David Michael Frank
Summer My Father Grew Up, The	NBC-TV	Lee Holdridge
Sunset Strip	Ind	John Gonzalez
Super, The	Fox	Miles Goodman
Suspended Step of the Stork	Gr/Fr/It/Sp	Helena Karaindrou
Sweet Poison	USA	Jim Manzie
Sweet Talker	New Line	Peter Filleul
Sweet Talker	New Line	Richard Thompson
Switch	WB	Henry Mancini
Switched at Birth	NBC-TV	Marvin Hamlisch
Tacones Lejanos (High Heels)	Sp	Ryuichi Sakamoto
Tagget	USA Net	Michel Colombier
Taking of Beverly Hills, The	Col	Jan Hammer
Tale of the Wind, A	Fr/Dutch	Michel Portal

Talent for the Game	Par	David Newman
Talk 16	Can	Aaron Davis
Tchin Tchin (aka A Fine Romance)	Ind	Pino Donaggio
Ted and Venus	Ind	David Robbins
Teenage Mutant Ninja Turtles II: The Secret of the Ooze	New Line	John Du Prez
10 Million Dollar Getaway, The	USA Net	Peter Matz
Terminator 2: Judgment Day	TriStar	Brad Fiedel
Termini Station	Can	Mychael Danna
Terror Within II, The	Concorde	Terry Plumeri
Thelma & Louise	Pathe	Hans Zimmer
Theory of Achievement	Ind	Ned Rifle
This Gun for Hire	USA Net	Dana Kaproff
Time to Die, A	Ind	Louis Febre
Timebomb	MGM/UA	Patrick Leonard
To Cross the Rubicon	Ind	Paul Speer
To Die For 2: Son of Darkness	Ind	Mark McKenzie
To Save a Child	ABC-TV	William Olvis
Tokyo Decadence	Jap	Ryuichi Sakamoto
Total Exposure	Ind	Sasha Matson
Toy Soldiers	TriStar	Robert Folk
Trancers II: Return of Jack Deth	Ind	Phil Davies
Trancers II: Return of Jack Deth	Ind	Mark Ryder
Triple Bogey on a Par Five Hole	Ind	Michel Delory
Triple Bogey on a Par Five Hole	Ind	Anna Domino
Triple Bogey on a Par Five Hole	Ind	Mader
Triumph of the Heart: The Ricky Bell Story, A	CBS-TV	James McVay
True Colors	Par	Trevor Jones
True Identity	BV	Marc Marder
Twenty One	Br	Michael Berkeley
Twenty-One	Br	Phil Sawyer
29th Street	Fox	William Olvis
Un Coeur qui bat (Your Beating Heart)	Fr	Jean-Pierre Drouet
Unborn, The	Ind	Gary Numan
Unborn, The	Ind	Michael R. Smith
Under Suspicion	Br	Christopher Gunning
Undertow	Ind	Paata
Undying Love	Ind	Mauro J. DeTrizio
Undying Love	Ind	Dany Sciarra
Until the End of the World	Ger/Fr/Aut	Graeme Revell
Uranus	Fr	Jean-Claude Petit
US	CBS-TV	Steve Dorff
Vendetta: Secrets of a Mafia Bride	Syn	Stuart Margolin
Vendetta: Secrets of a Mafia Bride	Syn	Riz Ortolani
Vendetta: Secrets of a Mafia Bride	Syn	Bruce Ruddel
V. I. Warshawski	BV	Randy Edelman
Victim of Love	CBS-TV	Richard Shore
Voyager	Ger/Fr	Stanley Myers
Welcome to Oblivion	Concorde	Kevin Klingler
What About Bob?	BV	Miles Goodman
Whatever Happened to Baby Jane?	ABC-TV	Peter Manning Robinson
Where Angels Fear to Tread	Br	Rachel Portman

Where Sleeping Dogs Lie	TriStar	Mark Mancina
Where Sleeping Dogs Lie	TriStar	Hans Zimmer
Where the Spirits Live	Can	Buffy Sainte Marie
Whereabouts of Jenny, The	ABC-TV	Patrick Williams
Which Way Home	TNT	Bruce Rowland
White Fang	BV	Basil Poledouris
White Hot: The Mysterious Murder of Thelma Todd	NBC-TV	Mark Snow
White Lie	USA Net	Philip Giffin
White Light	Can	Paul Zaza
Whore	Ind	Michael Gibbs
Wife, Mother, Murderer: The Marie Hilley Story	ABC-TV	Mark Snow
Wild Hearts Can't Be Broken	BV	Mason Daring
Wild Texas Wind	NBC-TV	Ray Benson
Wildflower	Lifetime	Kenny Edwards
Wildflower	Lifetime	Jon Gilutin
Witchcraft III: The Kiss of Death	Ind	Miriam Cutler
Witchcraft IV: Virgin Heart	Ind	Miriam Cutler
Without Warning: The James Brady Story	HBO	Georges Delerue
Wizards of the Demon Swords	Troma	Anthony Jones
Woman Named Jackie, A	NBC-TV	Lalo Schifrin
Woman Who Sinned, The	ABC-TV	David Kurtz
Woman's Tale, A	Aut	Paul Grabowsky
Women & Men 2: Three Short Stories	HBO	Dick Hyman
Women & Men 2: Three Short Stories	HBO	Anton Sanko
Women & Men 2: Three Short Stories	HBO	Suzanne Vega
Write to Kill	Ind	Gary Scott
Writer's Block	USA Net	Nan Schwartz
Year of the Gun	Ind	Bill Conti
Yes, Virginia, There Is a Santa Claus	ABC-TV	Charles Bernstein
Young Catherine	TNT	Isaac Schwartz
Young Soul Rebels	Br	Simon Boswell

1992

1492: Conquest of Paradise	Br/Fr/Sp	Vangelis
Absence, The	Fr/Ger/Sp	Leo Marino
Aces: Iron Eagle III	New Line	Harry Manfredini
Adventures in Dinosaur City	Ind	Fredric Teetsel
Adventures in Spying	New Line	James Wesley Stemple
Affairs of the Heart	Ind	Joey Mennonna
Afterburn	HBO	Stewart Copeland
Against Her Will: An Incident in Baltimore	CBS-TV	Allyn Ferguson
Aileen Wuornos: The Selling of a Serial Killer	Br	David Bergeaud
Aladdin	BV	Howard Ashman
Aladdin	BV	Alan Menken
Aladdin	BV	Tim Rice
Alan & Naomi	Ind	Dick Hyman
Alien 3	Fox	Elliot Goldenthal
Alive	Par	James Newton Howard
All My Husbands	Fr	Johnny Caruso
All Tied Up	Ind	Bernardo Bonezzi

All-American Murder	Ind	Rod Slane
Almost Blue	Ind	Nelson G. Hinds
Amazon	Ind	Nana Vasconcelos
American Dreamers	US/Hung	Goran Bregovic
American Heart	Ind	James Newton Howard
American Heart	Ind	Tom Waits
American Me	Univ	Dennis Lambert
American Story, An	CBS-TV	Mark Snow
Amityville 1992: It's About Time	Ind	Daniel Licht
Amy Fisher: My Story	NBC-TV	Fred Mollin
Animal Behavior	Ind	Joseph Smith
Another Woman's Lipstick	Ind	George S. Clinton
Apres l'amour (Love After Love)	Fr	Serge Perathoner
Apres l'amour (Love After Love)	Fr	Yves Simon
Are You Lonesome Tonight	USA Net	J. Peter Robinson
Arizona Dream	Fr	Goran Bregovic
Armed for Action	Ind	Ron Dilulio
Army of Darkness: Evil Dead 3	Univ	Danny Elfman
Army of Darkness: Evil Dead 3	Univ	Joseph Lo Duca
Article 99	Orion	Danny Elfman
As You Like It	Br	Michael Sanvoisin
Assolto per Aver Commesso Il Fatto	It	Piero Piccioni
Babe, The	Univ	Elmer Bernstein
Baby Snatcher	CBS-TV	Paul Chihara
Back in the U.S.S.R.	Fox	Les Hooper
Back to the Streets of San Francisco	NBC-TV	Patrick Williams
Bad Behaviour	Br	John Altman
Bad Lieutenant	Ind	Joe Delia
Baraka	Ind	Michael Stearns
Basic Instinct	Carolco	Jerry Goldsmith
Basket Case 3: The Progeny	Ind	Joe Renzetti
Batman Returns	WB	Danny Elfman
Battling for Baby	CBS-TV	Mark Snow
Bebe's Kids	Par	John Barnes
Becoming Colette	US/Ger	John Scott
Bed & Breakfast	Ind	David Shire
Bed of Lies	ABC-TV	David Shire
Beethoven	Univ	Randy Edelman
Being at Home With Claude	Can	Richard Gregoire
Belle Epoque	Sp	Antoine Duhamel
Beltenebros (Prince of Shadows)	Sp	Jose Nieto
Best of the Best 2	Ind	David Michael Frank
Betty	Fr	Matthieu Chabrol
Big Girls Don't Cry . . . They Get Even	New Line	Patrick Williams
Bikini Car Wash Company 2, The	Ind	Michael R. Smith
Bikini Summer 2	Ind	Jim Halfpenny
Bitter Moon	TriStar	Vangelis
Bittersweet	Ind	Michael Raye
Black and Blue	Br	Bob Last
Black Ice	Ind	Amin Bhatia
Black Magic	Showtime	Cliff Martinez
Black to the Promised Land	Ind	Branford Marsalis
Black Velvet Gown, The	Br	Carl Davis
Blackbelt	Concorde	David & Eric Wurst

Blame It on the Bellboy	US/Br	Trevor Jones
Blast 'Em	Can	Yuri Gorbachow
Blind Man's Bluff	USA Net	Richard Bellis
Blind Vision	Ind	Shuki Levy
Blood on the Badge	Ind	Ron Dilulio
Blood Symbol	Ind	Brent Holland
Bloodfist III: Forced to Fight	Concorde	Nigel Holton
Bloodfist IV: Die Trying	Concorde	David & Eric Wurst
Blown Away	Can	Paul Zaza
Blue Black Permanent	Br	John Gray
Blue Ice	Br	Michael Kamen
Bob Roberts	Par	David Robbins
Body Chemistry II: The Voice of a Stranger	Concorde	Nigel Holton
Body Language	USA Net	Misha Segal
Body Waves	Ind	James Harry
Bodyguard, The	WB	Alan Silvestri
Bon Appetit, Mama	Ind	Mason Daring
Bonnie & Clyde: The True Story	Fox-TV	Scott Page-Pacter
Bonnie & Clyde: The True Story	Fox-TV	John Valentino
Boomerang	Par	Marcus Miller
Boris and Natasha	Showtime	David Kitay
Born Kicking	Br	Hal Lindes
Born to Ski	Ind	Ronnie Montrose
Bottom Land	Ind	Jim Young
Bound and Gagged: A Love Story	Ind	William Murphy
Boy Who Cried Bitch, The	Ind	Wendy Blackstone
Brain Donors	Par	Ira Newborn
Braindead	NewZea	Peter Dasent
Bram Stoker's Dracula	Col	Wojciech Kilar
Breaking the Rules	Miramax	David Kitay
Breaking the Silence	CBS-TV	Craig Safan
Brief History of Time, A	US/Br	Philip Glass
Broken Cord, The	ABC-TV	Laura Karpman
Brother's Keeper	Ind	Molly Mason
Brother's Keeper	Ind	Jay Unger
Buffalo Jump	Ind	Nicholas Smiley
Buffy the Vampire Slayer	Fox	Carter Burwell
Burden of Proof, The	ABC-TV	Craig Safan
Cafe Romeo	Can	Amin Bhatia
Calendar Girl, Cop, Killer? The Bambi Bembenek Story	ABC-TV	Dana Kaproff
Candyman	TriStar	Philip Glass
Canvas	Ind	Mike Hewer
Captain America	TriStar	Barry Goldberg
Captain Ron	BV	Nicholas Pike
Careful	Can	John McCulloch
Carry on Columbus	Br	John Du Prez
Cement Garden, The	Br/Ger/Fr	Edward Shearmur
Center of the Web	Ind	Greg Turner
Chain of Desire	Ind	Nathan Birnbaum
Chaplin	TriStar	John Barry
Charles & Diana: Unhappily Ever After	ABC-TV	James McVay
Charlie's Ear	Ind	Arthur Gottschalk
Child Lost Forever, A	NBC-TV	Laura Karpman

Child of Rage	CBS-TV	Gerald Gouriet
Children of the Dragon	Aut	Martin Arminger
Christmas In Connecticut	TNT	Charles Fox
Christopher Columbus: The Discovery	WB	Cliff Eidelman
Chrome Soldiers	USA Net	Steve Dorff
Cinecitta . . . Cinecitta	It	Armando Trovajoli
Citizen Cohn	HBO	Thomas Newman
City of Joy	TriStar	Ennio Morricone
Claire of the Moon	Ind	Michael Allen Harrison
Class Act	WB	Vassal Benford
Claude	Ind	Stanley Myers
Clean Machine, The	Can	Robert Marcel Lepage
Close to Eden	Ind	Eduard Artimev
Close to Eden	Ind	Jerry Bock
Clothes in the Wardrobe	BBC-TV	Stanley Myers
Code Name: Chaos	Ind	Hans Zimmer
Cold Heaven	Br	Stanley Myers
Como Agua Para Chocolat (Like Water for Chocolate)	Mex	Leo Brower
Comrades of Summer, The	HBO	William Olvis
Condition Critical	NBC-TV	Sylvester Levay
Confessions of a Suburban Girl	Br	Joseph S. Debeasi
Consenting Adults	BV	Michael Small
Conspiracy of Silence	CBS-TV	Yves Laferriere
Conte d'Hiver (A Winter's Tale)	Fr	Sebastien Erms
Contre l'Oubli (Against Oblivion)	Fr	Mino Cinelli
Cool Surface, The	Col	Dave Kopplin
Cool World	Par	Mark Isham
Coopersmith: Sweet Scent of Murder	CBS-TV	David Bell
Cormorant	BBC-TV	John Lunn
Countess Alice	BBC-TV	Ilona Sekacz
Coupable d'Innocence (Guilty of Innocence)	Fr/Pol	Jean-Claude Petit
Cousin Bobby	Ind	Anton Sanko
Crash Landing: The Rescue of Flight 232	ABC-TV	Charles Fox
Crazy in Love	TNT	Cynthia Miller
Creatures of Light	Ind	Robert Neufeld
Criminal Behavior	ABC-TV	Mike Garson
Criminal Passion	Ind	Wendy Blackstone
CrissCross	MGM	Trevor Jones
Critters 4	New Line	Peter Manning Robinson
Crossing the Bridge	BV	Peter Himmelman
Crossing, The	Aut	Martin Arminger
Cruel Doubt	NBC-TV	George S. Clinton
Crying Game, The	Miramax	Anne Dudley
Cutting Edge, The	MGM	Patrick Williams
DaVinci's War	Ind	Jeff Lass
Damage	Br/Fr	Zbigniew Preisner
Danger Island	NBC-TV	Peter Manning Robinson
Danger of Love, The	CBS-TV	Mark Snow
Danielle Steel's "Jewels"	NBC-TV	Patrick Williams
Danielle Steel's "Secrets"	NBC-TV	Arthur B. Rubinstein
Dark Horse	Ind	Roger Bellon
Day in October, A	Ind	Jens Lysdal
Day-O	NBC-TV	Lee Holdridge

Dead Ahead: The Exxon Valdez Disaster	HBO	David Ferguson
Dead Alive	NewZea	Peter Dasent
Dead Boyz Can't Fly	Ind	Rich Sanders
Dead Center (aka Crazy Joe)	Ind	Sasha Matson
Dead Romantic	BBC-TV	Richard Harvey
Deadly Bet	Ind	Louis Febre
Deadly Betrayal: The Bruce Curtis Story	NBC-TV	Louis Natale
Deadly Creatures	Miramax	Peter Dasent
Deadly Currents	Can	Stephen Price
Deadly Matrimony	NBC-TV	Lee Holdridge
Deadly Rivals	Ind	Ashley Irwin
Death Becomes Her	Univ	Alan Silvestri
Deathstalker IV: Match of Titans	Ind	Simo Lazarov
Deception	Miramax	John Barry
Deep Cover	New Line	Michel Colombier
Delicatessen	Fr	Carlos D'Alessi
Deliver Them From Evil: The Taking of Alta View	CBS-TV	Mark Snow
Delta Heat	Ind	Christopher Tyng
Demon in My View, A	Ind	Pino Donaggio
Demonic Toys	Ind	Richard Band
Desert Hawk	Ind	Roy J. Ravio
Desire and Hell at Sunset Motel	Ind	Doug Walter Castle
Desperate Choices: To Save My Child	NBC-TV	John Keane
Detour	Ind	Bill Crain
Deuce Coupe	Ind	Barry Ennis
Devlin	Showtime	John Altman
Devlin	Showtime	Minette Alton
Di Ceria dell'Untore (The Plague Tower)	It	Carlo Siliotto
Diagnosis of Murder	CBS-TV	Dick DeBenedictis
Diamond Fleece, The	USA Net	James McVay
Diary of a Hit Man	Ind	Michel Colombier
Dien Bien Phu	Fr	Georges Delerue
Diggstown	MGM	James Newton Howard
Dirty Work	USA Net	Michel Colombier
Disaster in Time	Showtime	Gerald Gouriet
Distinguished Gentleman, The	BV	Randy Edelman
Dog Bark Blue	Ind	John Massari
Doing Time on Maple Drive	Fox-TV	Laura Karpman
Dolly Dearest	Ind	Mark Snow
Donner Party, The	Ind	Brian Keane
Double Edge	CBS-TV	Gerald Gouriet
Double Edge	US/Isr	Mira J. Spektor
Double Jeopardy	Showtime	Eduard Artemiev
Double Threat	Ind	Christopher Farrell
Double Vision	Ind	Graham Sacker
Double X: The Name of the Game	Br	Raf Ravenscroft
Dr. Giggles	Univ	Brian May
Dragonfight	Ind	Bob Mithoff
Drive Like Lightning	USA Net	Jerrold Immel
Drug Wars: The Cocaine Cartel	NBC-TV	Charles Bernstein
Duel of Hearts	TNT	Laurie Johnson
Duke Ellington: Reminiscing in Tempo	Ind	Duke Ellington
Duplicates	USA Net	Dana Kaproff

Dust Devil	Br	Simon Boswell
Eight Ball	Aut	Philip Judd
El Largo Invierno (The Long Winter)	Sp	Albert Guinovart
El Maestro de Esgrima (The Fencing Master)	Sp	Jose Nieto
Elenya	Br/Ger	Simon Fisher Turner
Elizabeth R: A Year in the Life of the Queen	BBC-TV	Rachel Portman
Emma and Elvis	Ind	Wendy Blackstone
Encino Man, The	BV	J. Peter Robinson
Entangled	Ind	Jean-Francoise Fabiano
Exclusive	ABC-TV	David Michael Frank
Execution Protocol, The	Br	Robert Lockhart
Exiled in America	Ind	Jay Asher
Eye of the Storm	New Line	Christopher Franke
Eyes of the Beholder	Ind	Greg Turner
Eyes of the Eagle 3	Ind	Justin Lord
Falling Down	WB	James Newton Howard
Fatal Bond	Aut	Art Phillips
Fatal Charm	Showtime	James Donnellan
Fatal Memories	NBC-TV	Ken Wannberg
Fathers & Sons	Ind	Mason Daring
Fear Inside, The	Viacom	Michel Rubini
Fear of a Black Hat	Ind	Jim Manzie
Fear of a Black Hat	Ind	Larry Robinson
Fergie and Andrew: Behind Palace Doors	NBC-TV	Allyn Ferguson
Ferngully . . . The Last Rainforest	Fox	Alan Silvestri
Few Good Men, A	Col	Marc Shaiman
Field of Fire	Ind	Justin Lord
Final Analysis	WB	George Fenton
Final Impact	Ind	John Gonzalez
Final Shot: The Hank Gathers Story	Syn	Stanley Clarke
Finest Hour, The	Ind	Walter Christian Roth
Fixing the Shadow (aka Beyond the Law)	TriStar	John D'Andrea
Fixing the Shadow (aka Beyond the Law)	TriStar	Cory Lerios
Folks!	Fox	Michel Colombier
Fool's Fire	Ind	Elliot Goldenthal
Footstep Man, The	NewZea	Jan Preston
For Richer, For Poorer	HBO	Miles Goodman
Forever	Ind	RH Factor
Forever Young	WB	Jerry Goldsmith
Four Eyes and Six-Guns	TNT	David Shire
Frame-up II: The Cover-up	Ind	Bob Summers
Fratelli e Sorelle (Brothers and Sisters)	It	Riz Ortolani
Frauds	Aut	Guy Gross
Freddie as F.R.O.7	Br	David Dundas
Freejack	WB	Michael Boddicker
Freejack	WB	Trevor Jones
Friends and Enemies	Fr	Gary Evanoff
From the Files of Joseph Wambaugh: A Jury of One	NBC-TV	David Michael Frank
Frozen Assets	Ind	Michael Tavera
Fugitive Among Us, The	CBS-TV	Stewart Copeland
Galaxies Are Colliding	Ind	Stephen Barber
Gangsters	It	Armando Trovajoli
Gas Food Lodging	TriStar	Barry Adamson

Gas Food Lodging	TriStar	J. Mascis
Gate II	Can	George Blondheim
Getting Up and Going Home	Lifetime	James DiPasquale
Ghostwatch	Br	Philip Appleby
Giant Steps	Can	Eric Leeds
Gladiator, The	Col	Brad Fiedel
Glengarry Glen Ross	New Line	James Newton Howard
Good Fight, The	Lifetime	W. G. Snuffy Walden
Goodbye, Paradise	Ind	Stan Wentzel
Grass Roots	NBC-TV	Laurence Rosenthal
Grave Secrets: The Legacy of Hilltop Drive	CBS-TV	Patrick Williams
Greenkeeping	Aut	David Bridie
Greenkeeping	Aut	John Phillips
Grocer's Wife, The	Can	Mark Korven
Gumshoe	Ind	Peter Miller
Gun in Betty Lou's Handbag, The	BV	Richard Gibbs
Guncrazy	Ind	Ed Tomney
Gunsmoke: To the Last Man	CBS-TV	Artie Kane
Hairdresser's Husband, The	Fr	Michael Nyman
Hard Boiled	Ind	Michael Gibbs
Hard Hunted	Ind	Richard Lyons
Hard Promises	Col	George S. Clinton
Harry Bridges: A Man and His Union	Ind	Mark Adler
Harry Bridges: A Man and His Union	Ind	Pete Seeger
Hedd Wyn	Br/Welsh	John Hardy
Hellraiser III: Hell on Earth	Miramax	Randy Miller
Hellraiser III: Hell on Earth	Miramax	Christopher Young
Her Final Fury: Betty Broderick The Last Chapter	CBS-TV	Mark Snow
Hero	Col	George Fenton
Highway Heartbreaker	CBS-TV	Mark Snow
Highway to Hell	Ind	Hidden Faces
Highway to Hell	Ind	Tangerine Dream
Hit the Dutchman	US/Rus	Terry Plumeri
Hoffa	Fox	David Newman
Hold Me, Thrill Me, Kiss Me	Ind	Gerald Gouriet
Home Alone 2: Lost in New York	Fox	John Williams
Home Fires Burning	Ind	Herb Pilhofer
Homewrecker	SciFi	Dana Kaproff
Honey, I Blew Up the Kid	BV	Bruce Broughton
Honeymoon in Vegas	Col	David Newman
Honor Thy Mother	CBS-TV	Peter Manning Robinson
Horton Foote's "The Habitation of Dragons"	TNT	David Shire
House of Elliott, The	BBC-TV	Jim Parker
House of Secrets and Lies, A	CBS-TV	Billy Goldenberg
House on Sycamore Street, The	CBS-TV	Dick DeBenedictis
HouseSitter	Univ	Miles Goodman
Howards End	Br	Richard Robbins
Human Shield, The	Cannon	Robbie Patton
Hummingbird Tree, The	Br	John Keane
Hurricane Smith	Aut	Brian May
Husbands and Lovers	It	Ennio Morricone
I Don't Buy Kisses Anymore	Ind	Cobb Bussinger
I Was on Mars	Ind	Niki Reiser

Ice Runner, The	Ind	Emilio Kauderer
Il Giardino Dei Ciliegi (The Cherry Orchard)	It	Luigi Ceccarelli
Il Giardino Dei Ciliegi (The Cherry Orchard)	It	Marco Ridolfi
Il Ladro di Bambini (The Stolen Children)	It/Fr	Franco Piersanti
Illicit Behavior	USA Net	Michael Linn
Immaculate Conception	Br	Richard Harvey
In Gold We Trust	Ind	Hummie Mann
In My Daughter's Name	CBS-TV	Charles Fox
In Search of Our Fathers	Ind	Billy Childs
In Sickness and in Health	CBS-TV	William Olvis
In the Arms of a Killer	NBC-TV	Lee Holdridge
In the Best Interest of Children	NBC-TV	James DiPasquale
In the Deep Woods	NBC-TV	Sylvester Levay
In the Eyes of a Stranger	CBS-TV	Tom Bahler
In the Heat of Passion	Concorde	Ken Rarick
In the Heat of Passion	Concorde	Art Wood
In the Line of Duty: Siege at Marion	NBC-TV	Gary Chang
In the Line of Duty: Street War	NBC-TV	Mark Snow
In the Shadow of a Killer	NBC-TV	Charles Gross
In the Soup	Ind	Mader
Incident at Oglala	Ind	Jackson Browne
Incident at Oglala	Ind	John Trudell
Indecency	USA Net	Miles Goodman
Indio 2: The Revolt	Ind	Pino Donaggio
Indocine	Fr	Patrick Doyle
Innocent Blood	WB	Ira Newborn
Inside Monkey Zetterland	Ind	Rick Cox
Interceptor	HBO	Rick Marvin
Into the Sun	Ind	Randy Miller
Into the West	Br/US	Patrick Doyle
Intruders	CBS-TV	Bob Cobert
Invasion of Privacy	USA Net	Alan Dermaderosian
I.P.5: L'Ile aux Pachydermes	Fr	Gabriel Yared
JFK Assassination, The	Ind	David Wheatley
Jackie Collins' "Lady Boss"	NBC-TV	Dana Kaproff
Jamon, Jamon (Salami, Salami)	Sp	Nicola Piovani
Jennifer Eight	Par	Christopher Young
Jersey Girl	Col	Misha Segal
Jersey Girl	Col	Stephen Bedell
Jo-Jo at the Gate of Lions	Ind	Jonathan Sampson
John Lurie and the Lounge Lizards Live in Berlin	US/Jap	John Lurie
Jonathan: The Boy Nobody Wanted	NBC-TV	Misha Segal
Judas Project, The	Ind	James H. Barden
Juice	Par	Hank Shocklee
Just Another Girl on the I.R.T.	Miramax	Eric Sadler
Just Like a Woman	Br	Michael Storey
Just My Imagination	NBC-TV	David McHugh
K2	Miramax	Hans Zimmer
Keep the Change	TNT	John Keane
Keeper of the City	Showtime	Leonard Rosenman
Keys, The	NBC-TV	Dale Menten
Kickboxer III: The Art of War	Ind	Harry Manfredini
Killer Among Friends, A	CBS-TV	Richard Bellis

Killer Image	Can	Stephen Foster
Knight Moves	US/Ger	Anne Dudley
Knights	Ind	Tony Riparetti
Knowing Lisa	Ind	Stephen Webber
Kuffs	Univ	Harold Faltermeyer
L.627	Fr	Philippe Sarde
L'Amant (The Lover)	Fr/Br	Gabriel Yared
L'Angelo con la Pistola (Angel of Death)	It	Riz Ortolani
L'Envers du Decor (Portrait of Pierre Guffroy)	Fr	Philippe Sarde
L'Envers du Decor (Portrait of Pierre Guffroy)	Fr	Ennio Morricone
L'Inconnu dans la Maison (Stranger in the House)	Fr	Francis Lai
L'Ombre du doute (A Shadow of Doubt)	Fr	Reno Isaac
La Belle Histoire (The Beautiful Story)	Fr	Francis Lai
La Comiche 2 (The Comics 2)	It	Bruno Zambrini
La Contre-Allee (Both Sides of the Street)	Fr	Didier Vasseur
La Corsa dell'Innocente	It/Fr	Carlo Siliotto
La Crise (Crisis-Go-Round)	Fr	Sonia Wieder Atherton
La Fille de l'Air (The Girl in the Air)	Fr	Gabriel Yared
La Postiere (The Postmistress)	Can	Philippe McKenzie
La Sarrasine	Fr	Pierre Desrochers
La Sentinelle (The Sentinel)	Fr	Marc Sommer
La Totale! (The Jackpot!)	Fr	Vladimir Cosma
La Voix (The Voice)	Fr	Philippe Sarde
Labyrinth	Ger	Lubos Fisher
Lady Against the Odds	NBC-TV	Joel McNeely
Ladybugs	Par	Richard Gibbs
Ladykiller	USA Net	Michel Colombier
Ladykiller	USA Net	Philip Giffin
Lake Consequence	Ind	George S. Clinton
Landslide	Ind	Bob Mithoff
Laser Moon	Ind	John Standish
Last Butterfly, The	Ind	Alex North
Last Days of Chez Nous, The	Aut	Paul Grabowsky
Last Wish	ABC-TV	David Shire
Last of His Tribe, The	HBO	John Keane
Last of the Mohicans, The	Fox	Randy Edelman
Last of the Mohicans, The	Fox	Trevor Jones
Last of the Mohicans, The	Fox	Daniel Lanois
Lawnmower Man, The	New Line	Jurgen Brauninger
Laws of Gravity	Ind	Douglas Cuomo
Le Amiche del Cuore (Close Friends)	It	Nicola Piovani
Le Bal des Casse-Pieds	Fr	Vladimir Cosma
Le Cahier Vole (The Stolen Diary)	Fr	Arie Dzierlatka
Le Cri du Hibou (The Cry of the Owl)	Fr	Matthieu Chabrol
Le Grand Pardon II (Day of Atonement)	Fr	Roman Musumarra
Le Journal de Lady M	Swiss/Belg/Sp/Fr	Arie Dzierlatka
Le Petit Prince a dit	Fr/Swiss	Bruno Coulais
Le Retour de Casanova (Casanova's Return)	Fr	Bruno Coulais
Le Retour des Charlots (The Charlots Return)	Fr	Patrick Ardan
League of Their Own, A	Col	Hans Zimmer
Leap of Faith	Par	Cliff Eidelman

Leather Jackets	TriStar	Shlomo Artzi
Leaving Normal	Univ	W. G. Snuffy Walden
Legacy of Lies	USA Net	Patrick Williams
Legend of Wolf Mountain, The	Ind	Jon McCallum
Leon the Pig Farmer	Br	David A. Hughes
Leon the Pig Farmer	Br	John Murphy
Les Annees Campagne (The Country Years)	Fr	Georges Garvarentz
Let's Kill All the Lawyers	Ind	Martin Liebman
Lethal Weapon 3	WB	Michael Kamen
Lethal Weapon 3	WB	Eric Clapton
Lethal Weapon 3	WB	David Sanborn
Life in the Food Chain	Ind	Glen Roven
Life on the Edge	Ind	Mike Garson
Light Sleeper	Ind	Michael Been
Linguini Incident, The	Ind	Thomas Newman
Little Bit of Lippy, A	BBC-TV	Richard Blackford
Little Nemo: Adventures in Slumberland	Jap	Thomas Chase
Little Nemo: Adventures in Slumberland	Jap	Steve Rucker
Little Nemo: Adventures in Slumberland	Jap	Richard M. Sherman
Little Nemo: Adventures in Slumberland	Jap	Robert B. Sherman
Live Wire	HBO	Craig Safan
Live! From Death Row	Fox-TV	Don Schiff
Live! From Death Row	Fox-TV	Tully Winfield
Living End, The	Ind	Cole Coonce
Long Day Closes, The	Br	Bob Last
Long Day Closes, The	Br	Robert Lockhart
Long Roads, The	BBC-TV	John Altman
Long Shadow, The	US/Hung/Isr	Gyorgy Selmeczi
Losing Track	BBC-TV	Michael Storey
Love Can Be Murder	NBC-TV	Steven Bramson
Love Crimes	Miramax	Roger Mason
Love Crimes	Miramax	Graeme Revell
Love Field	Orion	Jerry Goldsmith
Love Potion No. 9	Fox	Jed Leiber
Loving Lulu	Ind	Kevin Klingler
Lunatic, The	Ind	Wally Badarou
Lune de Fiel (Bitter Moon)	Fr/Br	Vangelis
Mac	Ind	Richard Termini
Mad at the Moon	Ind	Gerald Gouriet
Mad Bomber in Love	Aut	Michael Roberts
Mad Dog Coll	US/Rus	Terry Plumeri
Magic Kid (aka Ninja Dragons)	Ind	Jim Halfpenny
Magical World of Chuck Jones, The	WB	Cameron Patrick
Maid for Each Other	NBC-TV	Johnny Harris
Majority Rule	Lifetime	Shirley Walker
Malcolm X	WB	Terence Blanchard
Mambo Kings, The	WB	Carlos Franzetti
Mambo Kings, The	WB	Robert Kraft
Man to Man	Br	Nigel Holland
Man Trouble	Fox	Georges Delerue
Man Upstairs, The	CBS-TV	Billy Goldenberg
Man Without a World, The	Ind	Lee Erwin
Manufacturing Consent: Noam Chomsky and the Media	Ind	Carl Schultz

Map of the Human Heart	Br/Aut/Fr/Can	Gabriel Yared
Maria's Child	BBC-TV	Philip Appleby
Mario and the Mob	ABC-TV	Robert Folk
Max et Jeremie (Max and Jeremy)	Fr	Philippe Sarde
Maximum Force	Ind	Louis Febre
Me and Veronica	TriStar	David Mansfield
Me Myself and I	Ind	Odette Springer
Meatballs 4	Ind	Steve Hunter
Medicine Man	BV	Jerry Goldsmith
Meet the Parents	Ind	Scott May
Memento Mori	Br	Georges Delerue
Memoirs of an Invisible Man	WB	Shirley Walker
Memphis	TNT	David Bell
Message From Holly, A	CBS-TV	Stewart Levin
Midnight Clear, A	Ind	Mark Isham
Midnight Fear	Ind	Steve Edwards
Midnight Ride	Cannon	Carlo Maria Cordio
Midnight's Child	Lifetime	Richard Hartley
Mighty Ducks, The	BV	David Newman
Miles From Nowhere	CBS-TV	Billy Goldenberg
Millennium: Shock of the Other	PBS	Hans Zimmer
Mind, Body & Soul	Ind	Alan Dermaderosian
Mindwarp	Ind	Mark Governor
Minister's Wife, The	Ind	Steve Edwards
Mirror Images	Ind	Joseph Smith
Miss America: Behind the Crown	NBC-TV	Billy Goldenberg
Miss Rose White	NBC-TV	Billy Goldenberg
Mistress	Ind	Galt McDermott
Mo' Money	Col	Jay Gruska
Mom and Dad Save the World	WB	Jerry Goldsmith
Moondance	Ind	Michael R. Smith
Mortal Sins	USA Net	Joseph Conlan
Mothers and Daughters	Can	Ferdnand Martel
Mother's Right: The Elizabeth Morgan Story, A	ABC-TV	James McVay
Mr. Baseball	Univ	Jerry Goldsmith
Mr. Nanny	Ind	David Johansen
Mr. Nanny	Ind	Brian Koonin
Mr. Saturday Night	Col	Marc Shaiman
Mrs. 'Arris Goes to Paris	CBS-TV	Stanley Myers
Mrs. Cage	PBS-TV	David Mansfield
Munchie	Concorde	Chuck Cirino
Muppet Christmas Carol, The	BV	Miles Goodman
Muppet Christmas Carol, The	BV	Paul Williams
Murder Without Motive: The Edmund Perry Story	NBC-TV	Ross Levinson
Murderous Affair: The Carolyn Warmus Story, A	ABC-TV	Kenny Vance
Music Tells You, The	Ind	Branford Marsalis
My Cousin Vinny	Fox	Randy Edelman
My Grandpa Is a Vampire	NewZea	Jim Manzie
My New Gun	Ind	Pat Irwin
My Sister Wife	BBC-TV	Philip Appleby
Nails	Showtime	Bill Conti

Naked Target, The	Sp	Udi Haspar
Naufraghi Sotto Costa (Shipwrecks)	It	Lamberto Macchi
Ned Blessing: The True Story of My Life	CBS-TV	David Bell
Ned Blessing: The True Story of My Life	CBS-TV	Basil Poledouris
Neil Simon's "Broadway Bound"	ABC-TV	David Shire
Nemesis	Ind	Michel Rubini
Nervous Ticks	Ind	Jay Ferguson
Newsies	BV	Jack Feldman
Newsies	BV	Alan Menken
Nickel & Dime	Ind	Stephen Bedell
Nickel & Dime	Ind	Stephen Cohn
Night and the City	Fox	James Newton Howard
Night Rhythms	Ind	Ashley Irwin
Nightman, The	NBC-TV	Gary Chang
Nightmare in the Daylight	CBS-TV	David Shire
Noises Off	BV	Phil Marshall
North of Pittsburgh	Can	Graeme Coleman
Notorious	Lifetime	Don Davis
Nottataccia (What a Night!)	It	Antonio Di Pofi
Notte di Stelle (Starry Night)	It	Luis Bacalov
Nous Deux (The Two of Us)	Fr	Michel Raffelli
Nun and the Bandit, The	Aut	Tom E. Lewis
O Pioneers!	CBS-TV	Bruce Broughton
Obsessed	ABC-TV	Lee Holdridge
October 32nd	Br	William Campbell, Jr.
October 32nd	Br	Michael O'Donnell
Of Mice and Men	MGM	Mark Isham
Off and Running	Ind	Mason Daring
Oh, What a Night	Can	Ian Thomas
Olivier, Olivier	Fr	Zbigniew Preisner
On My Own	Ind	Franco Piersanti
Once Upon a Crime	MGM	Richard Gibbs
Only You	Ind	Wendy Blackstone
Orlando	Br/Fr/It/Rus	Bob Last
Orlando	Br/Fr/It/Rus	David Motion
Orlando	Br/Fr/It/Rus	Sally Potter
Other Woman, The	Ind	Joseph Smith
Out on a Limb	Univ	Van Dyke Parks
Over the Hill	Aut	David McHugh
Overexposed	ABC-TV	Gerald Gouriet
Overkill: The Aileen Wuornos Story	CBS-TV	Dennis McCarthy
Paint Job, The	Ind	John Wesley Harding
Painting the Town	Ind	Peter Fish
Pale Blood	Ind	Jan A..P. Kaczmarek
Panama Deception, The	Ind	Chuck Wild
Part Midnight	USA Net	Steve Bartek
Partners 'n Love	Fam Ch	Louis Natale
Passed Away	BV	Richard Gibbs
Passenger 57	WB	Stanley Clarke
Passion Fish	Ind	Mason Daring
Patrick Dewaere	Fr	Patrick Dewaere
Patriot Games	Par	James Horner
Peephole	Ind	Christian Osborne
Pen Pals	US/Jap	Michael Bacon

Pensavo Fosse Amore Invece Era un Calese	It	Pino Danielle
Perfect Family	USA Net	Nicholas Pike
Perry Mason: The Case of the Fatal Framing	NBC-TV	Dick DeBenedictis
Perry Mason: The Case of the Heartbroken Bride	NBC-TV	Dick DeBenedictis
Perry Mason: The Case of the Reckless Romeo	NBC-TV	Dick DeBenedictis
Pet Semetary Two	Par	Mark Governor
Playboys, The	US/Ire	Jean-Claude Petit
Player, The	Fine Line	Thomas Newman
Poison Ivy	New Line	Aaron Davis
Power of One, The	WB	Hans Zimmer
Prelude to a Kiss	Fox	Howard Shore
President's Child, The	CBS-TV	J. Peter Robinson
Prey of the Chameleon	Showtime	Shuki Levy
Price She Paid, The	CBS-TV	Geoff Levin
Price She Paid, The	CBS-TV	Chris Many
Primary Motive	Ind	John Cale
Prime Suspect II	Granada TV	Stephen Warbeck
Private Matter, A	HBO	James Newton Howard
Project: Shadowchaser	Ind	Gary Pinder
Prom, The	Ind	Kevin Haskins
Psychic	USA Net	Milan Kymlicka
Public Eye, The	Univ	John Barry
Public Eye, The	Univ	Mark Isham
Puerto Escondido	It	Mauro Pagani
Pure Country	WB	Steve Dorff
Pushed to the Limit	Ind	Miriam Cutler
Quando Eravano Repressi (When We Were Repressed)	It	Stefano Reali
Question of Attribution, A	Br	Gerald Gouriet
Quicksand: No Escape	USA Net	Paul Chihara
Quiet Killer	CBS-TV	Marty Simon
Radio Flyer	Col	Hans Zimmer
Rage and Honor	Ind	Darryl Way
Raiders of the Sun	Concorde	Gary Earl
Raiders of the Sun	Concorde	Odette Springer
Railway Station Man, The	BBC-TV	Richard Hartley
Rain Without Thunder	Ind	Randall & Allen Lynch
Raising Cain	Univ	Pino Donaggio
Rampage	Miramax	Ennio Morricone
Rapid Fire	Fox	Christopher Young
Rebecca's Daughters	Br/Ger	Rachel Portman
Redheads	Aut	Felicity Fox
Resistance	Aut	Davood Tabrizi
Resurrected, The	Ind	Richard Band
Revenge of the Nerds III: The Next Generation	Fox-TV	Garry Schyman
Revenge on the Highway	NBC-TV	Shuki Levy
Revolver	NBC-TV	Phil Marshall
Rich in Love	MGM	Georges Delerue
Ricky e Barabba (Ricky and Barabbas)	It	Manuel De Sica
Riens du Tout (Little Nothings)	Fr	Jeff Cohen
River Runs Through It, A	Col	Mark Isham

Road to Mecca, The	Ind	Ferdi Brendgen
Road to Mecca, The	Ind	Nik Pickard
Roadside Prophets	Ind	Pray for Rain
Rock-a-Doodle	Goldwyn	Robert Folk
Romper Stomper	Aut	John Clifford White
Round Numbers	Ind	Norman Mamey
Ruby	Ind	John Scott
Run of the House	Ind	Russell Young
Runestone, The	Ind	David Newman
Running Late	Br	Richard Hartley
Running Mates	HBO	Peter Rodgers Melnick
Sacred Sex	Aut	Nick Palmer
Sarafina!	S.Afr	Hugh Masekela
Sarafina!	S.Afr	Stanley Myers
Saturday Night Special	Ind	Billy Bunrette
Saturday Night Special	Ind	Nicholas Rivera
Scanners III: The Takeover	Can	Marty Simon
Scent of a Woman	Univ	Thomas Newman
School Ties	Par	Maurice Jarre
Search for Diana	Can	Omar Khayrat
Seconds Out	Br	Stewart Copeland
Secret Passion of Robert Clayton, The	USA Net	Nicholas Pike
Secret, The	CBS-TV	Fred Karlin
Secretary, The	Ind	Ellen Mandel
Secrets	Aut	Dave Dobbyn
Seduction: Three Tales From the Inner Sanctum	ABC-TV	James DiPasquale
Seedpeople	Ind	Bob Mithoff
Seeing Red	Aut	Andrew Yencken
Sexual Advances	ABC-TV	Shirley Walker
Sexual Response	Ind	Richard Berger
Shadow of a Stranger	NBC-TV	Gary Chang
Shadows and Fog	Orion	Kurt Weill
Shame	Lifetime	David McHugh
She Woke Up	ABC-TV	Christopher Franke
Shining Through	Fox	Michael Kamen
Sidney Sheldon's "The Sands of Time"	Syn	Perry Botkin
Sidney Sheldon's "The Sands of Time"	Syn	Alberto De Almar
Silencer, The	Ind	Carole Pope
Silencer, The	Ind	Ron Sures
Silent Touch, The	Brit/Pol/Dan	Wojciech Kilar
Silent Victim	Ind	William T. Stromberg
Simple Men	Fine Line	Ned Rifle
Single White Female	Col	Howard Shore
Singles	WB	Paul Westerberg
Sins of Desire	Ind	Chuck Cirino
Sister Act	BV	Marc Shaiman
Sketch Artist	Ind	Mark Isham
Sleepwalkers	Col	Nicholas Pike
Small Kill	Ind	Mark Leggett
Snakeeater III . . . His Law	Ind	John Massari
Sneakers	Univ	James Horner
Sneakers	Univ	Branford Marsalis
Society	Ind	Phil Davies

Society	Ind	Mark Ryder
Soft Top Hard Shoulder	Br	Chris Rea
Soldier's Fortune	Ind	Chuck Cirino
Solitaire	Can	Michael Becker
Somebody's Daughter	ABC-TV	Charles Bernstein
Something to Live For: The Alison Gertz Story	ABC-TV	David Shire
South Beach	Ind	Joe Renzetti
South Central	WB	Tim Truman
Split Second	Br	Francis Haines
Split Second	Br	Steve Parsons
Stalin	HBO	Stanislas Syrewicz
Star Time	Ind	Blake Leyh
Starfire	Ind	Maurice Jarre
Stay the Night	ABC-TV	Stewart Levin
Stay Tuned	WB	Bruce Broughton
Steel Justice	NBC-TV	Frank W. Becker
Stepkids	New Line	Patrick Williams
Stickin' Together	Ind	Glynn Turman
Still Not Quite Human	Disney-TV	John Debney
Stompin' at the Savoy	CBS-TV	Harold Wheeler
Stop! Or My Mom Will Shoot	Univ	Alan Silvestri
Stormy Weathers	ABC-TV	David Bell
Storyville	Fox	Carter Burwell
Straight Talk	BV	Brad Fiedel
Stranger Among Us, A	BV	Jerry Bock
Street Wars	Ind	Yves Chicha
Street Wars	Ind	Michael Dunlap
Strictly Ballroom	Aut	David Hirschfelder
Sunstroke	USA Net	John Debney
Survive the Savage Sea	ABC-TV	Fred Karlin
Swoon	Fine Line	James Bennett
T Bone N Weasel	TNT	Steve Tyrell
Taking Back My Life: The Nancy Ziegenmeyer Story	CBS-TV	Randy Edelman
Tale of a Vampire	Br/Jap	Julian Joseph
Taste for Killing, A	USA Net	Mark Snow
Teamster Boss: The Jackie Presser Story	HBO	Brad Fiedel
Terror on Track 9	CBS-TV	Craig Safan
That Night	WB	David Newman
There Goes the Neighborhood	Par	David Bell
There's Nothing Out There	Ind	Christopher Thomas
This Is My Life	Fox	Carly Simon
3 Ninjas	BV	Rick Marvin
Those Secrets	ABC-TV	Thomas Newman
Through the Eyes of a Killer	CBS-TV	George S. Clinton
Thunderheart	TriStar	James Horner
Till Death Us Do Part	NBC-TV	George S. Clinton
Time Runner	Ind	Braun Farnon
Time Runner	Ind	Robert Smart
To Be the Best	CBS-TV	Alan Parker
To Catch a Killer	Syn	Paul Zaza
To Grandmother's House We Go	ABC-TV	Richard Bellis
To Sleep With a Vampire	Concorde	Nigel Holton

Tom and Jerry: The Movie	Turner	Leslie Bricusse
Tom and Jerry: The Movie	Turner	Henry Mancini
Tous les Matins du Monde	Fr	Jordi Savall
Town Torn Apart, A	NBC-TV	Aaron Davis
Toys	Fox	Hans Zimmer
Traces of Red	Goldwyn	Graeme Revell
Trancers III: Deth Lives	Ind	Richard Band
Trancers III: Deth Lives	Ind	Phil Davies
Trancers III: Deth Lives	Ind	Mark Ryder
Treacherous Crossing	USA Net	Curt Sobel
Tremors II: Aftershocks	Ind	Jay Ferguson
Trespass	Univ	Ry Cooder
Trial, The	Br	Carl Davis
Trial: The Price of Passion	NBC-TV	Charles Bernstein
Trip to Serendipity, A	Can	Bruce Leitl
Tuareg: The Desert Warrior	Ind	Riz Ortolani
Turn of the Screw, The	Ind	Simon Boswell
Turtle Beach	Aut	Chris Neal
Twin Peaks: Fire Walk With Me	New Line	Angelo Badalamenti
Twogether	Ind	Nigel Holton
Ultimate Desires	Ind	Braun Farnon
Ultimate Desires	Ind	Robert Smart
Ultraviolet	Ind	Ed Tomney
Un Coeur en Hiver (A Heart of Stone)	Fr	Philippe Sarde
Unbecoming Age	Ind	Jeff Lass
Under Siege	WB	Gary Chang
Under the Sun	Br	Stella Maris
Unforgiven	WB	Lennie Niehaus
Ungentlemanly Act, An	BBC-TV	Russell King
Universal Soldier	TriStar	Christopher Franke
Unlawful Entry	Fox	James Horner
Used People	Fox	Rachel Portman
Utz	Br/It/Ger	Nicola Piovani
Vagrant, The	MGM	Christopher Young
Valhalla	Ind	David M. Matthews
Van Gogh	Fr	Edith Vesperini
Vegas in Space	Ind	Bob Davis
Vent d'Est (East Wind)	Fr	Karl-Heinz Shafer
Vermont Is for Lovers	Ind	Tony Silbert
Very Polish Practice, A	Br	Carl Davis
Victor's Big Score	Ind	Stephen Snyder
Vielle Canaille (Old Rascal)	Fr	Bruno Coulais
Ville a Vendre (City for Sale)	Fr	Vladimir Cosma
Voices in the Garden	BBC-TV	Roland Romanelli
Wadeck's Mother's Friend's Son	Ind	Jonathan Sampson
Walls & Bridges	Ind	Teo Macero
Water Engine, The	TNT	Alaric Jans
Waterdance, The	Goldwyn	Michael Convertino
Waterland	Fine Line	Carter Burwell
Waxwork II: Lost in Time	Ind	Steve Schiff
Wayne's World	Par	J. Peter Robinson
We're Talkin' Serious Money	Ind	Scott Grusin
Weekend at Bernie's II	Ind	Peter Wolf

Weekend With Barbara und Ingrid, A	Ind	Steven Lovy
What She Doesn't Know	NBC-TV	Billy Goldenberg
When No One Would Listen	CBS-TV	Arthur B. Rubinstein
When the Party's Over	Ind	Joe Romano
Where Are We?: Our Trip Through America	Ind	Daniel Licht
Where the Day Takes You	Col	Mark Morgan
Whispers in the Dark	Par	Thomas Newman
White Men Can't Jump	Fox	Bennie Wallace
White Sands	WB	Patrick O'Hearn
White Trash	Ind	Fred Baker
Who Do I Gotta Kill?	Ind	Doug Katsaros
Who Killed the Baby Jesus	Ind	John Clifforth
Whole Truth, The	Ind	Bill Grabowski
Wide Sargasso Sea	Aut	Stewart Copeland
Wild Card	USA Net	W. G. Snuffy Walden
Wild Orchid 2: Two Shades of Blue	Ind	George S. Clinton
Wild West	Br	Dominic Miller
Wildlands, The	Ind	Jay Ferguson
Willing to Kill: The Texas Cheerleader Story	ABC-TV	Peter Manning Robinson
Wind	TriStar	Basil Poledouris
Winter in Lisbon, The	Sp/Fr/Port	Dizzy Gillespie
Wishman	Ind	Bob Christianson
With a Vengeance	CBS-TV	J. Peter Robinson
With Murder in Mind	CBS-TV	Misha Segal
Woman, Her Man and Her Futon, A	Ind	Joel Goldsmith
Woman Scorned: The Betty Broderick Story, A	CBS-TV	Mark Snow
Woman With a Past	NBC-TV	Don Davis
Women of Windsor, The	CBS-TV	Mickey Erbe
Women of Windsor, The	CBS-TV	Maribeth Solomon
Wuthering Heights	Br	Ryuichi Sakamoto
Year of the Comet	Col	Hummie Mann
You, Me & Marley	Br	Stephen Warbeck
You Must Remember This	PBS	Harold Wheeler
Young Indiana Jones Chronicles, The	ABC-TV	Laurence Rosenthal
Zebrahead	Ind	Taj Mahal

1993

12:01	Fox-TV	Peter Rodgers Melnick
1994 Baker Street: Sherlock Holmes Returns	CBS-TV	James DiPasquale
23h58	Fr	Laurent Cugny
A Linha do Horizonte (The Line of the Horizonte)	Fr/Port	Zbigniew Preisner
Abissinia	It	Fiorenzo Carpi
Accompanist, The	Fr	Alain Jomy
Acting on Impulse	Ind	Daniel Licht
Addams Family Values	Par	Marc Shaiman
Adrift	CBS-TV	Louis Natale
Adventures of Huck Finn, The	BV	Bill Conti
Age of Innocence, The	Col	Elmer Bernstein
Airborne	WB	Stewart Copeland
Alex	Aut/NewZea	Todd Hunter
Alex Haley's "Queen"	CBS-TV	Michael Small

Alien Intruder	Ind	Miriam Cutler
Alistair MacLean's "Death Train"	USA Net	Trevor Jones
Ambulance, The	Ind	Jay Chattaway
Ambush of Ghosts, An	Ind	Nigel Humberstone
Amityville: A New Generation	Ind	Daniel Licht
Amok	Fr	Nicola Piovani
Amongst Friends	Ind	Mick Jones
Amos & Andrew	Col	Richard Gibbs
Amy Fisher Story, The	ABC-TV	Michael Hoenig
And the Band Played On	HBO	Carter Burwell
And the Band Played On	HBO	Alan Silvestri
Angel Eyes	Ind	Chuck Cirino
Angel of Fury	Ind	Jim West
Another Stakeout	BV	Arthur B. Rubinstein
Arcade	Par	Alan Howarth
Are They Still Shooting?	Ind	Dylan Maulucci
Arthur Miller's "The American Clock"	TNT	Paul Zaza
Aspen Extreme	BV	Michael Convertino
Assassination Game	Concorde	Stephen Dimitrov
At Home With the Webbers	Ind	Anthony Guefen
Attack of the 50 Ft. Woman	HBO	Nicholas Pike
Baby of Macon, The	Br/Fr/Ger	John Blow
Baby of Macon, The	Br/Fr/Ger	Matthew Locke
Backbeat	Br	Bob Last
Backbeat	Br	Don Was
Bad Boy Bubby	Aut/It	Graham Tardif
Ballad of Little Jo, The	Ind	David Mansfield
Barbara Taylor Bradford's "Remember"	NBC-TV	David Shire
Barbarians at the Gate	HBO	Richard Gibbs
Barjo	Fr	Hugues LeBars
Based on an Untrue Story	Fox-TV	Laura Karpman
Batman: Mask of the Phantasm	WB	Shirley Walker
Beauty School	Ind	Jonathan Hannah
Bedevil	Aut	Carl Vine
Beethoven's 2nd	Univ	Randy Edelman
Benefit of the Doubt	Miramax	Hummie Mann
Benny and Joon	MGM	Rachel Portman
Better Off Dead	Lifetime	John Barnes
Between Love and Hate	ABC-TV	Charles Bernstein
Beverly Hillbillies, The	Fox	Lalo Schifrin
Beyond Suspicion	NBC-TV	Chris Boardman
Bhaji on the Beach	Br	John Altman
Bhaji on the Beach	Br	Craig Pruess
Bitter Harvest	Ind	Michael Tavera
Black Widow Murders: The Blanche Taylor Moore Story	NBC-TV	David Michael Frank
Blind Side	HBO	Brian May
Blind Spot	CBS-TV	Patrick Williams
Blindsided	USA Net	David Michael Frank
Blood In Blood Out: Bound by Honor	BV	Bill Conti
Bloodlines: Murder in the Family	NBC-TV	David Shire
Blue	Br	Simon Fisher Turner
Bodies, Rest and Motion	Ind	Michael Convertino
Body Melt	Aut	Philip Brophy

Body of Evidence	MGM/UA	Graeme Revell
Body of Influence	Ind	Ashley Irwin
Body Shot	Ind	Clif Magness
Body Snatchers	WB	Joe Delia
Boiling Point	WB	John D'Andrea
Boiling Point	WB	Cory Lerios
Bonanza: The Return	NBC-TV	Bruce Miller
Bonds of Love	CBS-TV	George S. Clinton
Bonus Malus	It	Antonio Di Pofi
Bopha!	Par	James Horner
Born to Run	Fox-TV	Simon Franglen
Born Too Soon	NBC-TV	Mark Snow
Born Yesterday	BV	George Fenton
Boxing Helena	Ind	Graeme Revell
Boys of St. Vincent, The	Can	Neil Smolar
Brain Smasher	Ind	Tony Riparetti
Broken Chain, The	TNT	Charles Fox
Broken Highway	Aut	David Faulkner
Broken Promises: Taking Emily Back	CBS-TV	Chris Boardman
Bronx Tale, A	Ind	Butch Barbella
Bronx Tale, A	Ind	Stephen Endelman
Bullion Boys, The	BBC-TV	Robert Lockhart
CB4	Univ	John Barnes
Calendar Girl	Col	Hans Zimmer
Call of the Wild	CBS-TV	Lee Holdridge
Camilla	Can/Br	John Altman
Camilla	Can/Br	Daniel Lanois
Candles in the Dark	Fam Ch	Richard Bowers
Carlito's Way	Univ	Patrick Doyle
Carnosaur	Concorde	Nigel Holton
Caro Diario (Dear Diary)	It/Fr	Nicola Piovani
Case for Murder, A	USA Net	Randy Miller
Casualties of Love: The "Long Island Lolita" Story	CBS-TV	David Michael Frank
Caught in the Act	USA Net	Arthur B. Rubinstein
Ce Que Femme Veut . . . (What a Woman Wants)	Fr	Philippe Eidel
Cemetery Club, The	BV	Elmer Bernstein
Century	Br	Michael Gibbs
Chained Heat II	Can	Bruce Curtis
Chantilly Lace	Showtime	Patrick Seymour
Children of the Corn II: The Final Sacrifice	Ind	Daniel Licht
Children of the Corn III: Urban Harvest	Ind	Daniel Licht
Christmas Reunion, A	BBC-TV	Shuki Levy
Christmas Reunion, A	BBC-TV	Stephen C. Marston
Cibel Emouvante (Wild Target)	Fr	Philippe Eidel
Class of '61	ABC-TV	John Debney
Clean, Shaven	Ind	Hahn Rowe
Cliffhanger	TriStar	Trevor Jones
Closing Numbers	Br	Barrington Pheloung
Cold Sweat	Can	Paul Zaza
Combination Platter	Ind	Brian Tibbs
Comincio Tutto per Caso (It Started by Chance)	It	Antonio Di Pofi

Complex of Fear	CBS-TV	Nan Schwartz-Mishkin
Condannato a Nozze (Condemned to Wed)	It	Antonio Di Pofi
Coneheads	Par	David Newman
Conviction of Kitty Dodds, The	CBS-TV	Craig Safan
Cool Runnings	BV	Hans Zimmer
Cooperstown	TNT	Mel Marvin
Cop and a Half	Univ	Alan Silvestri
Couples et Amants (Couples and Lovers)	Fr	Charlie Couture
Cover Girl Murders, The	USA Net	Rick Marotta
Crack Me Up	Can	Emilio Kauderer
Crime Broker	Aut	Roger Mason
Crush, The	WB	Graeme Revell
Cuisine et Dependances (Kitchen With Apartment)	Fr	Vladimir Cosma
Curacao	Showtime	Colin Towns
Cybereden	It	Giorgio Moroder
Cyborg 2	Ind	Peter Allen
Dangerous Game	MGM/UA	Joe Delia
Dangerous Woman, A	Ind	Carter Burwell
Danielle Steel's "Heartbeat"	NBC-TV	David Shire
Danielle Steel's "Message From Nam"	NBC-TV	Billy Goldenberg
Danielle Steel's "Star"	NBC-TV	Lee Holdridge
Dark Half, The	Orion	Christopher Young
Darkness Before Dawn	NBC-TV	Peter Manning Robinson
Dave	WB	James Newton Howard
Day My Parents Ran Away, The	Fox-TV	J. Peter Robinson
Day of the Dog	Aut	David Milroy
Daybreak	HBO	Michel Colombier
De eso no se habla (We Don't Want to Talk About It)	It	Nicola Piovani
De Force Avec d'Autres (Forced to Be With Others)	Fr/It	Celia Reggiani
Dead Before Dawn	ABC-TV	Sylvester Levay
Deadfall	Ind	Jim Fox
Deadly Advise	Br	Richard Harvey
Deadly Relations	ABC-TV	Philip Giffin
Death Ring	New Line	John Massari
Deep Trouble	USA Net	Arthur B. Rubinstein
Demolition Man	WB	Elliot Goldenthal
Demon Possessed	Ind	John Tatgenhorst
Dennis the Menace	WB	Jerry Goldsmith
Desperate Journey: The Allison Wilcox Story	ABC-TV	David McHugh
Desperate Motive	New Line	Parmer Fuller
Desperate Remedies	NewZea	Peter Scholes
Desperate Rescue: The Cathy Malone Story	NBC-TV	Fred Karlin
Deux Actrices (Two Can Play)	Can	Kate and Anne McGarrigle
Diana: Her True Story	NBC-TV	Ken Thorne
Diario du un Vizio (Diary of a Maniac)	It	Gato Barbieri
Digger	Can	Todd Boekelheide
Dirty Weekend	Br	David Fanshawe
Dirtysomething	BBC-TV	Simon Davison
Disappearance of Christina, The	USA Net	David Michael Frank
Disappearance of Nora, The	CBS-TV	Mark Snow

Donato and Daughter	CBS-TV	Sylvester Levay
Double Deception	NBC-TV	Gary Chang
Double Suspicion	Ind	Graeme Coleman
Double, Double, Toil and Trouble	ABC-TV	Richard Bellis
Dove Siete? Io Sono Qui	It	Pino Donaggio
Down Among the Big Boys	BBC-TV	Simon Chamberlain
Down Among the Big Boys	BBC-TV	Ray Russell
Dracula Rising	Concorde	Ed Tomney
Dragon Fire	Concorde	John Graham
Dragon: The Bruce Lee Story	Univ	Randy Edelman
Dream Lover	Ind	Christopher Young
Dust Devil: The Final Cut	US/Br	Simon Boswell
Dying to Love You	CBS-TV	Joseph Lo Duca
Dying to Remember	USA Net	Jay Gruska
Earth and the American Dream	Ind	Todd Boekelheide
Ed and His Dead Mother	Ind	Mason Daring
Eight Hundred Leagues Down the Amazon	Concorde	Jorge Tafar
El Amante Bilingue (The Bilingual Lover)	Sp	Jose Nieto
Elvis Presley	Ind	Jim Manzie
Elvis and the Colonel: The Untold Story	NBC-TV	Chris Boardman
Empty Cradle	ABC-TV	Jan A.P. Kaczmarek
Ernest Green Story, The	Disney-TV	Mason Daring
Ernest Rides Again	Ind	Bruce Arnston
Ernest Rides Again	Ind	Kirby Shelstad
Ethan Frome	Miramax	Rachel Portman
Even Cowgirls Get the Blues	New Line	k. d. lang
Even Cowgirls Get the Blues	New Line	Ben Mink
Every Breath	Ind	Nils Lofgren
Excessive Force	New Line	Charles Bernstein
Excessive Force	New Line	Alan Baumbarten
Exchange Lifeguards	Aut	John Capek
Exile and the Kingdom	Aut	David Milroy
Extreme Justice	HBO	David Michael Frank
Eye of the Stranger	Ind	Robert Garrett
Eyes of the Prey	Ind	John Garrett
Fade to Black	USA Net	Michel Colombier
Fallen Angels	Showtime	Elmer Bernstein
Family of Strangers, A	CBS-TV	Peter Manning Robinson
Family Pictures	ABC-TV	Johnny Harris
Family Prayers	Ind	Steve Tyrell
Family Torn Apart, A	NBC-TV	Gary Chang
Fanfan	Fr	Nicolas Jorelle
Far Off Place, A	BV	James Horner
Faraway, So Close!	Ger	Laurent Petitgrand
Fatal Instinct	MGM	Richard Gibbs
Fatal Justice	Ind	Jeffrey Walton
Father & Son: Dangerous Relations	NBC-TV	Mark Snow
Father Hood	BV	Patrick O'Hearn
Fausto (aka A la Mode)	Fr	Denis Barbier
Fearless	WB	Maurice Jarre
Ferie d'Agosto (August Vacation)	It	Battista Lena
Fifty/Fifty	Cannon	Peter Bernstein
Final Appeal	NBC-TV	Charles Bernstein
Final Round	Ind	Amin Bhatia

Final Round	Ind	Graeme Coleman
Fiorile	It/Fr/Ger	Nicola Piovani
Fire in the Sky	Par	Mark Isham
Fire Next Time, The	CBS-TV	Laurence Rosenthal
Firehawk	Concorde	John Graham
Firestorm: 72 Hours in Oakland	ABC-TV	Misha Segal
Firm, The	Par	Dave Grusin
Flesh and Bone	Par	Thomas Newman
Flood: Who Will Save Our Children?, The	NBC-TV	Garry McDonald
Flood: Who Will Save Our Children?, The	NBC-TV	Laurie Stone
Fly by Night	Ind	Sidney Mills
For Love and Glory	CBS-TV	John Debney
For Love or Money (aka Concierge, The)	Univ	Bruce Broughton
For the Love of My Child	NBC-TV	Joseph Julian Gonzalez
For Their Own Good	ABC-TV	J.A.C. Redford
Forced to Kill	Ind	Martin D. Bolin
Foreign Affairs	TNT	Cynthia Miller
Foreign Field, A	Br	Geoffrey Burgon
Fortress	Aut	Frederic Talgorn
Framed	Br	Nick Bicat
Frankenstein	TNT	John Cameron
Freaked	Fox	Kevin Kiner
Free Willy	WB	Basil Poledouris
Freefall	Ind	Lee Holdridge
Fresa y Chocolate (Strawberry and Chocolate)	Sp	Jose Maria Vitier
Friends	Br/Fr	Rachel Portman
Fugitive Nights: Danger in the Desert	NBC-TV	Jay Asher
Fugitive, The	WB	James Newton Howard
Full Eclipse	HBO	Gary Chang
Gadael Lenin (Leaving Lenin)	Br/Welsh	John Hardy
Genghis Cohn	BBC-TV	Carl Davis
George Balanchine's "The Nutcracker"	WB	Pyotr Ilyich Tchaikovsky
Germinal	Fr	Jean-Louis Roques
Geronimo	TNT	Patrick Williams
Geronimo: An American Legend	Col	Ry Cooder
Gettysburg	Turner	Randy Edelman
Ghost in the Machine	Fox	Graeme Revell
Ghost Mom	Fox-TV	Ian Thomas
Giovanni Falcone	It	Pino Donaggio
Good Son, The	Fox	Elmer Bernstein
Gregory K	ABC-TV	James McVay
Grief	Ind	Tom Judson
Grind	Ind	Brian Kelly
Gross Misconduct	Aut	Bruce Rowland
Groundhog Day	Col	George Fenton
Grumpy Old Men	WB	Alan Silvestri
Guilty as Sin	BV	Howard Shore
Gunsmoke: The Long Ride	CBS-TV	Artie Kane
Gypsy	CBS-TV	Jule Styne
H. P. Lovecraft's "The Unnameable II"	Ind	David Bergeaud
Hanged Man, The	Ind	Alec Bartsch
Happily Ever After	Ind	Frank W. Becker
Hard Target	Univ	Graeme Revell

Hard to Die	Ind	Chuck Cirino
Harmony Cats	Can	Graeme Coleman
Hart to Hart Returns	NBC-TV	Arthur B. Rubinstein
Harvest, The	Ind	Dave Allen
Harvest, The	Ind	Rick Boston
Hawk, The	Br	Nick Bicat
Hear No Evil	Fox	Eva Gardos
Hear No Evil	Fox	Graeme Revell
Heart and Souls	Univ	Marc Shaiman
Heart of Justice, The	TNT	Jonathan Elias
Heartbreak Kid, The	Aut	John Clifford White
Heaven & Earth	WB	Kitaro
Heidi	Disney-TV	Lee Holdridge
Hercules Returns	Aut	Philip Judd
Hexed	Col	Lance Rubin
Hit List, The	Showtime	Rick Conrad
Hitwoman: The Double Edge	Ind	Gerald Gouriet
Hocus Pocus	BV	John Debney
Home for Christmas: Little Miss Millions	Concorde	Joel Goldsmith
Home of Our Own, A	Ind	Michael Convertino
Homeward Bound: The Incredible Journey	BV	Bruce Broughton
Hostages	HBO	Richard Harvey
Hot Shots! Part Deux	Fox	Basil Poledouris
Hour of the Pig, The	Br/Fr	Alexandre Desplat
House in the Hills, A	Ind	Richard Einhorn
House in the Hills, A	Ind	Miguel Tejada-Flores
House in the Hills, A	Ind	Ken Wiederhorn
House of Cards	Miramax	James Horner
House of Secrets	NBC-TV	Anthony Marinelli
House of the Spirits, The	Ger	Hans Zimmer
Household Saints	Ind	Stephen Endelman
How U Like Me Now	Ind	Kahil El Zabar
How U Like Me Now	Ind	Chuck Webb
Huck and the King of Hearts	Ind	Chris Saranec
I Can Make You Love Me	CBS-TV	Sylvester Levay
I Giovane Mussolini (A Man Named Mussolini)	It/Sp/Ger	Nicola Piovani
I Love a Man in Uniform	Can	Ron Sures
I'll Love You Forever . . . Tonight	Ind	Robert Cairns
Ice Runner, The	Ind	Jim Goodman
Il Lungo Silenzio (The Long Silence)	It/Fr/Ger	Ennio Morricone
Il Segreto del Bosch Vecchio	It	Franco Piersanti
Il Tempo del Ritorno (Time of the Return)	It	Roberto Ciotti
In a Moment of Passion	Ind	Zbigniew Gorney
In the Company of Darkness	CBS-TV	Tim Truman
In the Line of Duty: Ambush at Waco	NBC-TV	Mark Snow
In the Line of Fire	Col	Ennio Morricone
In the Name of the Father	Br/Ire	Trevor Jones
In the Name of the Father	Br/Ire	Sinead O'Connor
In the Shadows, Someone's Watching	NBC-TV	Shuki Levy
Indecent Behavior	Ind	Randy Miller
Indecent Proposal	Par	John Barry
Indian Summer	BV	Miles Goodman
Innocent Moves	Par	James Horner

Innocent, The	Br/Ger	Gerald Gouriet
Intent to Kill	Ind	John Gonzalez
Intruso (Intruder)	Sp	Jose Nieto
Invisible: The Chronicle of Benjamin Knight	Ind	David Arkenstone
Io Speriamo Che Me La Cavo	It	D'Angio Greco
Iron Will	BV	Joel McNeely
Is That All There Is?	Br	Alan Price
It's a Wonderful Life	Ind	Melissa Etheridge
It's All True	US/Fr	Jorge Arriagada
It's Nothing Personal	NBC-TV	Tom Scott
JFK: Reckless Youth	ABC-TV	Cameron Allan
Jack Be Nimble	NewZea	Chris Neal
Jack Reed: Badge of Honor	NBC-TV	Lee Holdridge
Jack the Bear	Fox	James Horner
Jason Goes to Hell: The Final Friday	New Line	Harry Manfredini
Je M'Appelle Victor (My Name Is Victor)	Fr	Jean-Claude Vannier
Jericho Fever	USA Net	Cameron Allan
John Carpenter Presents Body Bags	Showtime	John Carpenter
John Carpenter Presents Body Bags	Showtime	Jim Lang
Jonah Who Lived in the Whale	It/Fr	Ennio Morricone
Josh and S.A.M.	Col	Thomas Newman
Journey to the Center of the Earth	NBC-TV	David Kurtz
Joy Breaker	Ind	Paul Aston
Joy Luck Club, The	BV	Rachel Portman
Judgment Day: The John List Story	CBS-TV	Craig Safan
Judgment Night	Univ	Alan Silvestri
Judith Krantz's "Torch Song"	ABC-TV	Lee Holdridge
Jurassic Park	Univ	John Williams
Just One of the Girls	Fox-TV	Amin Bhatia
Just One of the Girls	Fox-TV	Vincent Mai
Justinien Trouve, ou le Bastard de Dieu	Fr	Germinal Tenas
Kalifornia	Ind	Carter Burwell
Killer Rules	NBC-TV	Lee Holdridge
Killing Zoe	Ind	Tomandandy
King of the Hill	Ind	Cliff Martinez
Kiss of a Killer	ABC-TV	J.A.C. Redford
Kiss to Die For, A	NBC-TV	George S. Clinton
L.A. Wars	Ind	Louis Febre
La Ardilla roja (The Red Squirrel)	Sp	Alberto Iglesias
La Petite Apocalypse	Fr/It/Pol	Philippe Sarde
La Ribelle (The Rebel)	It	Carlo Crivelli
La Scorta (The Bodyguards)	It	Ennio Morricone
Labor of Love: The Arlette Schweitzer Story	CBS-TV	Fred Karlin
Lady Dragon 2	Ind	Jim West
Last Action Hero	Col	Michael Kamen
Last Hit, The	USA Net	Gary Chang
Last Light	Showtime	Jude Cole
Last Outlaw, The	HBO	Mason Daring
Last POW? The Bobby Garwood Story, The	ABC-TV	Mark Snow
Le Abre, le Maire et la Mediatheque	Fr	Sebastien Erms
Le Donne Non Vogliono Piu	It	Stefano Reali
Le Fils du Requin (The Son of the Shark)	Fr	Bruno Coulais
Le Jeune Werther (Young Werther)	Fr	Philippe Sarde
Le Mari de Leon (Leon's Husband)	Fr	Vladimir Cosma

Le Sexe de Etoiles (The Sex of the Stars)	Can	Yves Laferriere
Le Souper (The Supper)	Fr	Vladimir Cosma
Leprechaun	Ind	Kevin Kiner
L'Enfer	Fr	Matthieu Chabrol
Les Demoiselles ont eu 25 Ans	Fr	Michel Legrand
Les Demoiselles ont eu 25 Ans	Fr	Jacques Loussier
Les Marmottes (The Groundhogs)	Fr	Gabriel Yared
Les Visiteurs (The Visitors)	Fr	Eric Levi
Lethal Exposure	NBC-TV	Ken Thorne
Lettre pour L . . .	Fr	Philippe Hersant
Liar, Liar	CBS-TV	Fred Mollin
Lies and Lullabies	ABC-TV	Johnny Harris
Life With Mikey	BV	Alan Menken
Life and Times of Allen Ginsburg, The	Ind	Tom Capek
Life in the Theatre, A	TNT	David Michael Frank
Lifepod	Fox-TV	Mark Mancina
Lillian	Ind	H. Shep Williams
Linda	USA Net	David Michael Frank
Line, the Cross & the Curve, The	Br	Kate Bush
Little Buddha	Miramax	Ryuichi Sakamoto
Look Who's Talking Now	TriStar	William Ross
Lost in Africa	Ind	Garry Schyman
Lost in Yonkers	Col	Elmer Bernstein
Lotus Eaters, The	Can	John Sereda
Louis, Enfant Roi (Louis, the Child King)	Fr	Jean-Pierre Fouquey
Love and Human Remains	Can	John McCarthy
Love, Cheat & Steal	Showtime	Pray for Rain
Love, Honor & Obey: The Last Mafia Marriage	CBS-TV	Allyn Ferguson
Love in Limbo	Aut	Peter Kaldor
Love Matters	Showtime	Simon Boswell
M. Butterfly	WB	Howard Shore
Ma Saison Preferee (My Favorite Season)	Fr	Philippe Sarde
Mad Dog and Glory	Univ	Elmer Bernstein
Made in America	WB	Mark Isham
Magnificat	It	Riz Ortolani
Malice	New Line	Jerry Goldsmith
Man From Left Field, The	CBS-TV	Bobby Goldsboro
Man With Three Wives, The	CBS-TV	Mark Snow
Man Without a Face, The	WB	James Horner
Man's Best Friend	New Line	Joel Goldsmith
Maniac Cop 3: Badge of Silence	Ind	Joel Goldsmith
Mardi Gras for the Devil	Ind	Christopher Farrell
Marilyn & Bobby: Her Final Affair	USA Net	Joseph Conlan
Marked for Murder	NBC-TV	Anthony Marinelli
Masala	Can	Leslie Winston
Matinee	Univ	Jerry Goldsmith
Matter of Justice, A	NBC-TV	David Michael Frank
Mazeppa	Fr	Jean-Pierre Drouet
Me and the Kid	Orion	Bob Cobert
Men Don't Tell	CBS-TV	Cameron Allan
Menace II Society	New Line	QD III
Mercy Mission: The Rescue of Flight 771	NBC-TV	Patrick Williams
Meteor Man, The	MGM	Cliff Eidelman

Mi Vida Loca	Ind	John Taylor
Midnight Confessions	Ind	Scott Singer
Midnight Edition	Ind	Murray Attaway
Midnight Kiss	Ind	Emilio Kauderer
Midnight Witness	Ind	Graydon Hillock
Mille Bolle Blu	It	Franco Piersanti
Mina Tannenbaum	Fr	Peter Chase
Mina Tannenbaum	Fr	Emmanuelle Lemaire
Mind Twister	Ind	Peter Francis Rotter
Miracle Child	NBC-TV	Craig Safan
Miracle on I-880	NBC-TV	Lawrence Shragge
Moment of Truth: A Child Too Many	NBC-TV	Bruce Babcock
Moment of Truth: Stalking Back	NBC-TV	Bruce Babcock
Moment of Truth: Why My Daughter?	NBC-TV	Bruce Babcock
Money for Nothing	BBC-TV	John Dankworth
Money for Nothing	BV	Craig Safan
Monolith	Ind	Frank W. Becker
Morning Glory	Ind	Jonathan Elias
Mother of the Bride	CBS-TV	Bruce Miller
Mother's Revenge, A	ABC-TV	Laura Karpman
Mr. Jones	TriStar	Maurice Jarre
Mr. Wonderful	WB	Michael Gore
Mrs. Doubtfire	Fox	Howard Shore
Mrs. Lee Harvey Oswald	NBC-TV	Harald Kloser
Much Ado About Nothing	Br/US	Patrick Doyle
Murder in the Heartland	ABC-TV	Patrick Williams
Murder of Innocence	CBS-TV	Don Davis
Music of Chance, The	Ind	Phillip Johnston
Mustard Bath	Can	Rob Carroll
My Boyfriend's Back	BV	Harry Manfredini
My Forgotten Man	Aut	Anthony Marinelli
My Life	Col	John Barry
Naked	Br	Andrew Dickson
National Lampoon's Loaded Weapon I	New Line	Robert Folk
Necronomicon	Ind	Daniel Licht
Necronomicon	Ind	Joseph Lo Duca
Needful Things	Col	Patrick Doyle
Night Eyes 3	Ind	Terry Plumeri
Night Owl	Lifetime	Gil Melle
Night Owl	Ind	Mark Styles
Night Train to Venice	Ger	Alexander Bubenheim
Night Trap	Ind	Christopher Farrell
Night We Never Met, The	Miramax	Evan Lurie
Nightmare Before Christmas, The	BV	Danny Elfman
No Child of Mine	CBS-TV	Richard Bellis
No Escape, No Return	Ind	Jim Halfpenny
No Place to Hide	Cannon	Robert O. Ragland
No Worries	Aut	Patrick Seymour
No Worries	Aut	David A. Stewart
Nostradamus Kid, The	Aut	Chris Neal
Not in My Family	ABC-TV	James McVay
November Men, The	Ind	Scott Thomas Smith
Nowhere to Run	Col	Mark Isham
Nurses on the Line: The Crash of Flight 7	CBS-TV	Curt Sobel

Odd Couple: Together Again, The	CBS-TV	Charles Fox
Official Denial	SciFi	Garry McDonald
Official Denial	SciFi	Laurie Stone
Once Upon a Forest	Fox	James Horner
Only the Strong	Fox	Nigel Holton
Only the Strong	Fox	Harvey W. Mason
Only Way Out, The	ABC-TV	Gerald Gouriet
Opposite Sex . . . And How to Live With Them, The	Miramax	Ira Newborn
Ordeal in the Arctic	ABC-TV	Amin Bhatia
Ordinary Magic	Can	Mychael Danna
Other Women's Children	Lifetime	Peter Manning Robinson
Painted Desert, The	Ind	Masahiro Kawasaki
Paper Hearts	Ind	George S. Clinton
Paper Marriage	Br/Pol	Stanislas Syrewicz
Paris, France	Can	John McCarthy
Passport to Murder	NBC-TV	Charles Gross
Pelican Brief, The	WB	James Horner
Percy and Thunder	TNT	Tom Scott
Percy and Thunder	TNT	Grover Washington Jr.
Perfect Man, The	Can	George Blondheim
Perfect World, A	WB	Lennie Niehaus
Perry Mason: The Case of the Killer Kiss	NBC-TV	Dick DeBenedictis
Perry Mason: The Case of the Skin-Deep Scandal	NBC-TV	Dick DeBenedictis
Perry Mason: The Case of the Telltale Talk Show Host	NBC-TV	Dick DeBenedictis
Perry Mason Mystery: The Case of the Wicked Wives	NBC-TV	Dick DeBenedictis
Petain	Fr	Georges Garvarentz
Philadelphia	TriStar	Howard Shore
Philadelphia Experiment 2, The	Ind	Gerald Gouriet
Piano, The	Aut	Michael Nyman
Piccolo Grande Amore (Pretty Princess)	It	Simon Boswell
Pickle, The	Col	Michel Legrand
Place to Be Loved, A	CBS-TV	W.G. Snuffy Walden
Poetic Justice	Col	Stanley Clarke
Point of No Return (The Assassin)	WB	Hans Zimmer
Poisoned by Love: The Kern County Murders	CBS-TV	Steve Dorff
Portrait, The	Can	Michael Conway Baker
Portrait, The	TNT	Cynthia Miller
Positively True Adventures of the Alleged Texas Cheerleader-Murdering Mom, The	HBO	Lucy Simon
Posse	Ind	Michel Colombier
Praying Mantis	USA Net	John Debney
Precious Victims	CBS-TV	Mark Snow
Prehysteria	Ind	Richard Band
Prime Suspect III	Granada TV	Stephen Warbeck
Private Wars	Ind	Louis Febre
Program, The	BV	Michel Colombier
Project: Genesis	Ind	Andy McNeill
Prophet of Evil: The Ervil LeBaron Story	CBS-TV	Craig Safan
Public Access	Ind	John Ottman

Punk and the Princess, The	Br	Claudia Sarne
Puppet Master IV	Ind	Richard Band
Quarrel, The	Ind	William Goldstein
Quick	Ind	Robert Sprayberry
Raining Stones	Br	Stewart Copeland
Rave--Dancing to a Different Beat	Ind	Steve Deutsch
Real McCoy, The	Univ	Brad Fiedel
Reckless Kelly	Aut	Anthony Marinelli
Reckless Kelly	Aut	Yahoo Serious
Reckless Kelly	Aut	Tommy Tycho
Red Rock West	Ind	William Olvis
Regarde les hommes tomber (See How They Fall)	Fr	Alexandre Desplat
Relentless 3	New Line	Scott Grusin
Relentless: Mind of a Killer	NBC-TV	Stanley Clarke
Remains of the Day, The	Col	Richard Robbins
Remote	Ind	Richard Band
Requiem for a Handsome Bastard	Can	Jean Corriveau
Rescue Me	Cannon	Joel Hirschhorn
Rescue Me	Cannon	Al Kasha
Rescue Me	Cannon	David Waters
Return of Ironside, The	NBC-TV	John Cacavas
Return of the Living Dead 3	Ind	Barry Goldberg
Return to Lonesome Dove	CBS-TV	Ken Thorne
Rio Diablo	CBS-TV	Larry Brown
Rio Shannon	ABC-TV	Craig Safan
Rising Sun	Fox	Toru Takemitsu
River of Rage: The Taking of Maggie Keene	CBS-TV	Joseph Lo Duca
Robin Cook's "Harmful Intent"	CBS-TV	Lee Holdridge
Robin Hood: Men in Tights	Fox	Hummie Mann
RoboCop 3	Orion	Basil Poledouris
Romeo Is Bleeding	Ind	Mark Isham
Rookie of the Year	Fox	Bill Conti
Roosters	Ind	David Kitay
Royal Celebration	BBC-TV	Anne Dudley
Rubdown	USA Net	Gerald Gouriet
Ruby Cairo	Miramax	John Barry
Ruby in Paradise	Ind	Charles Engstrom
Rudy	TriStar	Jerry Goldsmith
Russian Roulette	Ind	Dan Slider
Safe	BBC-TV	Billy Bragg
Saint of Fort Washington, The	WB	James Newton Howard
Salt on Our Skin	Fr/Ger/Can	Klaus Doldinger
Sandlot, The	Fox	David Newman
Save Me	Col	Rick Marvin
Scam	Showtime	Stephen Graziano
Scattered Dreams	CBS-TV	Mark Snow
Schindler's List	Univ	John Williams
Sea Wolf, The	TNT	Charles Bernstein
Searching for Bobby Fischer	Par	James Horner
Secret Games 2: The Escort	Ind	Ashley Irwin
Secret Garden, The	WB	Zbigniew Preisner
Secret Rapture, The	Br	Richard Hartley
Seventh Coin, The	Ind	Misha Segal

Seventh Floor, The	Aut	Roger Mason
Sex, Love and Cold Hard Cash	USA Net	John Keane
Shadow of the Wolf	Can/Fr	Maurice Jarre
Shadowlands	Br	George Fenton
Shameful Secrets	ABC-TV	Laura Karpman
Shattered Trust: The Shari Karney Story	NBC-TV	Mickey Erbe
Shattered Trust: The Shari Karney Story	NBC-TV	Maribeth Solomon
Shelf Life	Ind	Andy Paley
Short Cuts	Ind	Mark Isham
Shotgun Wedding	Aut	Allan Zavod
Sidekicks	Col	David Shire
Sidekicks	Col	Alan Silvestri
Sidney Sheldon's "A Stranger in the Mirror"	ABC-TV	Amin Bhatia
Silent Cries	NBC-TV	Billy Goldenberg
Silent Tongue	Br	Patrick O'Hearn
Silver Stallion: King of the Brumbies, The	Aut	Tassos Ioannides
Sister Act 2: Back in the Habit	BV	Miles Goodman
Six Degrees of Separation	MGM/UA	Jerry Goldsmith
Skeeter	Col	David Lawrence
Skylark	CBS-TV	David Shire
Slaughter of the Innocents	Ind	Joe Renzetti
Sleepless in Seattle	TriStar	Marc Shaiman
Sliver	Par	Howard Shore
Smoke	Ind	Arnold Bieber
Smoking/No Smoking	Fr	John Pattison
Snake Eyes	Ind	Joe Delia
Snapdragon	Ind	Michael Linn
Sniper	TriStar	Gary Chang
So I Married an Axe Murderer	TriStar	Bruce Broughton
Sognando la California (California Dreaming)	It	Umberto Smalla
Sommersby	WB	Danny Elfman
Son of the Pink Panther	MGM	Henry Mancini
Son-in-Law	BV	Richard Gibbs
Sound and the Silence, The	NewZea	John Charles
Spare Me	Ind	Danny Brenner
Sparrow	It	Claudio Capponi
Sparrow	It	Alessio Vlad
Spenser: Ceremony	Lifetime	Paul Zaza
Splitting Heirs	Br	Michael Kamen
Staying Afloat	NBC-TV	Dennis McCarthy
Stefano Quantestorie	It	Sergio Conforti
Stephen King's "The Tommyknockers"	ABC-TV	Christopher Franke
Stolen Babies	Lifetime	Mason Daring
Strapped	HBO	Joe Romano
Street Knight	Cannon	David Michael Frank
Strike a Pose	Ind	Gene Ober
Striking Distance	Col	Brad Fiedel
Substitute, The	USA Net	Gerald Gouriet
Sugar Hill	Fox	Terence Blanchard
Summer House, The	Br	Stanley Myers
Super Mario Bros.	BV	Alan Silvestri
Surf Ninjas	New Line	David Kitay
Survive the Night	USA Net	Fred Mollin

Suture	Ind	Cary Berger
Sweet Killing	Fox	Jean Musy
Swing Kids	BV	James Horner
Switch, The	CBS-TV	Tangerine Dream
Sworn to Vengeance	CBS-TV	Robert Folk
Tainted Blood	USA Net	Dana Kaproff
Taking the Heat	Showtime	Patrick Williams
Tango	Fr	Angelique Nachon
Taxi Dancers	Ind	Larry Blank
Taxi Dancers	Ind	Jeffrey Silverman
Teenage Bonnie and Klepto Clyde	Ind	Terry Plumeri
Teenage Mutant Ninja Turtles III	New Line	John Du Prez
Telling Secrets	ABC-TV	Mark Snow
Temp, The	Par	Frederic Talgorn
Tempting a Married Man	Aut	Adam Lynton
Tender Loving Care	BBC-TV	Ray Singer
Test Tube Teens From the Year 2000	Ind	Reg Powell
Teste Rasate (Skinheads)	It	Eugenio Bennato
There Are No Children Here	ABC-TV	Harold Wheeler
There Was a Little Boy	CBS-TV	Anthony Marinelli
They (aka They Watch)	Showtime	Gerald Gouriet
They've Taken Our Children: The Chowchilla Kidnapping	ABC-TV	Ron Ramin
This Boy's Life	WB	Carter Burwell
This Won't Hurt a Bit!	Aut	Mario Grigorov
Three Musketeers, The	BV	Michael Kamen
Three of Hearts	New Line	Richard Gibbs
Ticks	Ind	Daniel Licht
To Dance With the White Dog	CBS-TV	Gerald Gouriet
Tombstone	BV	Bruce Broughton
Top of the World	Ind	Bruce Odland
Tout Ca . . . Pour Ca! (All That . . . for This?)	Fr	Francis Lai
Tower, The	Fox-TV	John D'Andrea
Tower, The	Fox-TV	Richard Horowitz
Tower, The	Fox-TV	Cory Lerios
Trauma	Ind	Pino Donaggio
Trial & Error	USA Net	Mickey Erbe
Trial & Error	USA Net	Maribeth Solomon
Triumph Over Disaster: The Hurricane Andrew Story	NBC-TV	Laurence Rosenthal
Trois Couleurs: Blanc	Fr/Swiss/Pol	Zbigniew Preisner
Trois Couleurs: Bleu	Fr/Swiss/Pol	Zbigniew Preisner
Tropical Heat	Ind	Del Casher
Trouble Bound	Ind	Vinny Golia
Trouble Shooters: Trapped Beneath the Earth	NBC-TV	Peter Bernstein
True Romance	WB	Mark Mancina
True Romance	WB	Hans Zimmer
Trust, The	Ind	George Burt
Trusting Beatrice	Ind	Stanley Myers
Twenty Bucks	Ind	David Robbins
Twist of the Knife, A	CBS-TV	Dick DeBenedictis
U.F.O.	Br	Clever Music
Undercover Blues	MGM	David Newman

Untamed Heart	MGM	Cliff Eidelman
Untouchables, The	Syn	Joel Goldsmith
Vanishing, The	Fox	Jerry Goldsmith
Vendetta II: The New Mafia	Syn	Stefano Mainetti
Victim of Love: The Shannon Mohr Story	NBC-TV	Gary Remal Malkin
Visions of Murder	NBC-TV	Michael Hoenig
Voyage	USA Net	Carl Davis
Wall of Silence	BBC-TV	Barrington Pheloung
Walton Thanksgiving Reunion, A	CBS-TV	Alexander Courage
Warlock: The Armagedon	Ind	Mark McKenzie
Warriors	Ind	Walter Christian Roth
Watch It	Ind	Stanley Clarke
Wax, or the Discovery of Television Among Bees	Ind	Beo Morales
Wax, or the Discovery of Television Among Bees	Ind	Brooks Williams
Wayne's World 2	Par	Carter Burwell
We're Back! A Dinosaur's Story	Univ	James Horner
What's Eating Gilbert Grape	Par	Alan Parker
What's Love Got to Do With It	BV	Stanley Clarke
When a Stranger Calls Back	Showtime	Dana Kaproff
When Love Kills: The Seduction of John Hearn	CBS-TV	Rick Marvin
When Pigs Fly	US/Ger/Jap	Joe Strummer
White Angel	Br	Harry Gregson-Williams
Who's the Man	New Line	Michael Wolff
Whose Child Is This?: The War for Baby Jessica	ABC-TV	Lawrence Shragge
Wide Eyed and Legless	BBC-TV	Colin Towns
Widows Peak	Br	Carl Davis
Wild Justice	Syn	Alan Parker
Wild Palms	ABC-TV	Ryuichi Sakamoto
Wilder Napalm	TriStar	Michael Kamen
Witchboard 2: The Devil's Doorway	Ind	Dennis Michael Tenney
Witchcraft V: Dance With the Devil	Ind	Miriam Cutler
With Hostile Intent	CBS-TV	Dana Kaproff
Without Warning: Terror in the Towers	NBC-TV	Jay Gruska
Without a Kiss Goodbye	CBS-TV	Richard Bellis
Wittgenstein	Br	Jan Latham-Koenig
Woman Who Loved Elvis, The	ABC-TV	William Olvis
Woman of Desire	US/SAfr	Rene Vedelsman
Woman on the Run: The Lawrencia Bembenek Story	NBC-TV	Peter Manning Robinson
Wrestling Ernest Hemingway	WB	Michael Convertino
Wrong Man, The	Showtime	Los Lobos
Xiyan (The Wedding Banquet)	US/Taiwan	Mader
Year in Provence, A	BBC-TV	Carl Davis
Young Americans, The	Br	David Arnold
Younger and Younger	Ger/Fr/Can	Hans Zimmer
Zelda	TNT	Patrick Williams
Zero Patience	Can	Glenn Schellenberg

3 Ninjas Kick Back	TriStar	Rick Marvin
8 Seconds	New Line	Bill Conti
A La Folie (Six Days, Six Nights)	Fr	Michael Nyman
Above the Rim	New Line	Marcus Miller
Abraham	TNT	Marco Frisina
Accidental Meeting	USA Net	Patrick Williams
Ace Ventura, Pet Detective	WB	Ira Newborn
Across the Moon	Ind	Christopher Tyng
Adventures of Priscilla, Queen of the Desert, The	Aut	Guy Gross
Against Her Will: The Carrie Buck Story	Lifetime	Mickey Erbe
Against the Wall	HBO	Gary Chang
Against Their Will: Women in Prison	ABC-TV	Al Kooper
Air Up There, The	BV	David Newman
Airheads	Fox	Carter Burwell
Alive--20 Years Later	BV	James Newton Howard
All Things Bright and Beautiful	BBC-TV	Jim Lockhart
Amateur	Ind	Ned Rifle
Amateur	Ind	Jeffrey Taylor
Amelia Earhart: The Final Flight	TNT	George S. Clinton
American Cyborg: Steel Warrior	Cannon	Blake Leyh
And Then There Was One	Lifetime	J.A.C. Redford
Andre	Par	Bruce Rowland
Angels in the Outfield	BV	Randy Edelman
Angie	BV	Jerry Goldsmith
Anni Ribelli (Laura: The Rebel Years)	It/Arg	Luis Bacalov
Another Woman	CBS-TV	David Blamires
Apex	Ind	Jim Goodwin
Armageddon: The Final Challenge	Ind	Johan Lass
Armed and Innocent	CBS-TV	Dennis McCarthy
Ascent, The	Ind	Irwin Fisch
Assault at West Point: The Court-Martial of Johnson Whittaker	Showtime	Terence Blanchard
Asterix Conquers America	Ger	Harold Faltermeyer
AstroCop	Ind	Blake Leyh
At Risk	Ind	Kevin Hedges
Ava's Magical Adventure	Ind	Mark Holden
Avalanche	Fox	Jonathan Goldsmith
Baby Brokers	NBC-TV	Anthony Marinelli
Baby's Day Out	Fox	Bruce Broughton
Babymaker: The Dr. Cecil Jacobson Story	CBS-TV	James McVay
Back in Action	Can	Varouje
Backfire!	Ind	Jeffrey Schmitt
Bad Girls	Fox	Jerry Goldsmith
Bambino Mio	Br/Fr	Stephen Warbeck
Bar Girls	Ind	Lenny Meyers
Barcelona	Ind	Tom Judson
Barcelona	Ind	Marc Suozzo
Barnabo delle Montagne	It	Stefano Caprioli
Baywatch the Movie: Forbidden Paradise	Ind	John D'Andrea
Baywatch the Movie: Forbidden Paradise	Ind	Cory Lerios
Beans of Egypt, Maine, The	Ind	Peter Manning Robinson
Beanstalk	Ind	Kevin Bassinson
Because Mommy Works	NBC-TV	Patrick Williams

Before the Rain	Fr	Anastasia
Beg!	Br	Steve Parsons
Being Human	WB	Michael Gibbs
Belle al Bar	It	Patrizio Fariselli
Bermuda Grace	NBC-TV	Hal Lindon
Betrayal of Trust	NBC-TV	Curt Sobel
Betrayed by Love	ABC-TV	George S. Clinton
Beverly Hills Cop III	Par	Nile Rodgers
Beyond Bedlam	Br	David A. Hughes
Beyond Betrayal	CBS-TV	Christopher Franke
Beyond Obsession	ABC-TV	Peter Manning Robinson
Bigfoot: The Unforgettable Encounter	Ind	Louis Febre
Bionic Ever After?	CBS-TV	Ron Ramin
Birds II: Land's End, The	Showtime	Ron Ramin
Bitter Vengeance	USA Net	David Michael Frank
Black Beauty	WB	Danny Elfman
Black Water	Ind	Gabriel Yared
Blackout	Br	Jake Williams
Blank Check	BV	Nicholas Pike
Blankman	Col	Miles Goodman
Blessing	Ind	Joseph S. Debeasi
Blind Justice	HBO	Richard Gibbs
Blindfold: Acts of Obsession	USA Net	Shuki Levy
Blink	New Line	Brad Fiedel
Blood Runner	Ind	Blake Leyh
Blown Away	MGM	Alan Silvestri
Blue Chips	Par	Jeff Beck
Blue Chips	Par	Jed Leiber
Blue Sky	Orion	Jack Nitzsche
Boca	US/Braz	Richard Feldman
Body Puzzle	It	Carlo Maria Cordio
Boulevard	Ind	Ian Thomas
Boy Meets Girl	Br	Jim Crosbie
Boy Meets Girl	Br	Geoff Southall
Brainscan	Ind	George S. Clinton
Branwen	Br	Cliff Norman
Breach of Conduct	USA	Terry Plumeri
Breaking Point	Can	Graeme Coleman
Breathing Lessons	CBS-TV	John Kander
Brilliant Disguise, A	Ind	Chris Cibelli
Broken Harvest	Ire	Patrick Cassidy
Broken Lullaby	CBS-TV	Jonathan Goldsmith
Brother Minister: The Assassination of Malcolm X	Ind	Richie Havens
Brother Minister: The Assassination of Malcolm X	Ind	Annie Lenox
Browning Version, The	Br	Mark Isham
Buddy Factor, The	Ind	Tom Heil
Burning Passion: The Margaret Mitchell Story, A	NBC-TV	Billy Goldenberg
Burning Season, The	HBO	Gary Chang
Burnt by the Sun	Fr/Rus	Eduard Artemiev
Business Affair, A	Fr/Br/Ger/Sp	Didier Vasseur
Cabin Boy	BV	Steve Bartek

Cache Cash	Fr	Vladimir Cosma
Cadafel	Br	Colin Towns
Cafe au Lait	Fr	Jean-Louis Daulne
Cage II: Arena of Death	Ind	Richard Lyons
Cagney & Lacey: The Return	CBS-TV	Dana Kaproff
Captives	Br	Colin Towns
Capture the White Flag	Ind	Gregory Nissen
Car 54, Where Are You?	Orion	Pray for Rain
Car 54, Where Are You?	Orion	Bernie Worrell
Cari Fottutissimi Amici	It	Renzo Arbore
Caroline at Midnight	Concorde	Mark Snow
Change of Place, A	CBS-TV	Brent Barkman
Change of Place, A	CBS-TV	Carl Lenox
Chase, The	Fox	Richard Gibbs
Chasers	WB	Peter Anderson
Chasers	WB	Dwight Yoakam
Chasing the River	Br	John Wetton
Cheyenne Warrior	Concorde	Arthur Kempel
Children of the Dark	CBS-TV	David Michael Frank
Child's Cry for Help, A	NBC-TV	Joseph Lo Duca
Chili's Blues	Fr/Can	Richard Gregoire
Christmas Romance, A	CBS-TV	Peter Manning Robinson
Cinder Path, The	Br	Barrington Pheloung
Cinema, de Notre Temps: Abbas Kiarostami	Fr	Georges Delerue
Circle Game, The	Can	Gordie Johnson
Circle of Friends	Br	Michael Kamen
Cisco Kid, The	TNT	Joseph Julian Gonzalez
City Slickers II: The Legend of Curly's Gold	Col	Marc Shaiman
Class of 1999: The Substitute	Ind	Andrew Keresztes
Clean Slate	MGM	Alan Silvestri
Clear and Present Danger	Par	James Horner
Clerks	Ind	Scott Angley
Client, The	WB	Howard Shore
Clifford	Orion	Richard Gibbs
Club, The	Can	Paul Zaza
Cobb	WB	Elliot Goldenthal
Color of Night	BV	Dominic Frontiere
Come Die With Me: A Mickey Spillane's Mike Hammer Mystery	CBS-TV	Ron Ramin
Come Due Coccodrilli (Like Two Crocodiles)	It/Fr	Stefano Caprioli
Companion, The	USA Net	David Shire
Con Gli Occhi Chiusi (With Closed Eyes)	It/Fr/Sp	Battista Lena
Confessions of a Hit Man	Ind	Billy Talbot
Confessions of a Sorority Girl	Showtime	Hummie Mann
Confessions: Two Faces of Evil	NBC-TV	Charles Fox
Cool and the Crazy	Showtime	Hummie Mann
Cops and Robertsons	TriStar	William Ross
Corpse Had a Familiar Face, The	CBS-TV	Patrick Williams
Corrina, Corrina	New Line	Rick Cox
Cosby Mysteries, The	NBC-TV	William H. Cosby Jr.
Cosby Mysteries, The	NBC-TV	Craig Handy
Counterfeit Contessa, The	Fox-TV	David McHugh
Country Life	Aut	Peter Best

Cowboy Way, The	Univ	David Newman
Crackerjack	Can	Peter Allen
Cracking Up	Ind	Arthur Rosen
Crew, The	Ind	Alex Wurman
Cries From the Heart	CBS-TV	James McVay
Cries Unheard: The Donna Yaklich Story	CBS-TV	Harry Manfredini
Cronos	Sp	Ian Deardon
Crooklyn	Univ	Terence Blanchard
Crow, The	Miramax	Graeme Revell
Cyborg Cop II	Ind	Bob Mithoff
D2: The Mighty Ducks	BV	J.A.C. Redford
Dallas Doll	Aut	David Hirschfelder
Dance Me Outside	Can	Mychael Danna
Dancing With Danger	USA Net	David Michael Frank
Dangerous Heart	USA Net	Philip Giffin
Dangerous Indiscretion	Ind	Richard Gibbs
Danielle Steel's "A Perfect Stranger"	NBC-TV	Lee Holdridge
Danielle Steel's "Family Album"	NBC-TV	Lee Holdridge
Danielle Steel's "Once in a Lifetime"	NBC-TV	David Shire
Dark Angel: The Ascent	Ind	Fuzzbee Morse
Dark Reflection	Fox-TV	David McHugh
Dark Side of Genius	Ind	Tom Heil
Dark Summer	Br	Clive Chin
Darker Side of Black	Br	Trevor Mathison
Darkman II: The Return of Durant	Univ	Randy Miller
Darling Family, The	Can	Mychael Danna
David's Mother	CBS-TV	David Mansfield
Day of Reckoning	NBC-TV	Garry Schyman
De Sueur et du Sang (Wonderboy)	Fr	Roland Vincent
Dead Air	USA Net	Dana Kaproff
Dead Beat	Ind	Anton Sanko
Dead Connection	Ind	Rolfe Kent
Dead Man's Revenge	USA Net	David Schwartz
Dead on Sight	Par	Harry Manfredini
Deadly Secret, The	Ind	Erik Hanson
Deadly Vows	Fox-TV	John D'Andrea
Deadly Vows	Fox-TV	Cory Lerios
Death Wish 5: The Face of Death	Ind	Terry Plumeri
Death and the Maiden	US/Fr/Br	Wojciech Kilar
Decadence	Br/Ger	Stewart Copeland
Deconstructing Sarah	USA Net	Tom Scott
Deep Red	SciFi	Gary Chang
Deficiency (Carences)	Fr	Philippe Haïm
Dellamorte Delamore (Cemetery Man)	It/Fr/Ger	Manuel De Sica
Demon Keeper	Concorde	Keith Farquarson
Demon Keeper	Concorde	Anthony Igoe
Des Feux Mal Eteints (Poorly Extinguished Fires)	Fr	Gabriel Yared
Desert Steel	Ind	Chris Caswell
Destiny in Space	Can	Mickey Erbe
Destiny in Space	Can	Maribeth Solomon
Dichiarazioni d'Amore (Declarations of Love)	It	Stefano Caprioli
Dieu Que les Femmes sont Amoureuses	Fr	Jean-Jacques Lemetre

Dinner in Purgatory	Br	David A. Hughes
Dinner in Purgatory	Br	John Murphy
Dinosaur Island	Ind	Chuck Cirino
Dirty Money	Ind	Paul Barrere
Dirty Money	Ind	Bill Payne
Disappearance of Vonnie, The	CBS-TV	Richard Bellis
Disclosure	WB	Ennio Morricone
Doc's Full Service	Ind	Chuck Pinell
Dominion	Ind	Alex Wurman
Don't Do It	Ind	Hal Lindes
Don't Get Me Started	Br/Ger	Roger Bolton
Don't Talk to Strangers	USA Net	Joseph Conlan
Doomsday Gun	HBO	Richard Harvey
Double Cross	Ind	Graeme Coleman
Double Dragon	Ind	Jay Ferguson
Dragonworld	Ind	Richard Band
Dragstrip Girl	Showtime	Hummie Mann
Dream Man	Ind	Graeme Coleman
DROP Squad	Ind	Michael Bearden
Drop Zone	Par	Hans Zimmer
Due South	CBS-TV	Jack Lenz
Due South	CBS-TV	John McCarthy
Due South	CBS-TV	Jay Semko
Dumb and Dumber	New Line	Todd Rundgren
Eat Drink Man Woman	Goldwyn	Mader
Eclipse	Can/Ger	Ernie Tollar
Ed Wood	BV	Howard Shore
Elles n'oublient pas (Love in the Strangest Way)	Fr	Jean-Marie Senia
Elles ne Pensant qua'a Ca	Fr	Jacques Davidovici
En Compagnie d'Antonin Artaud	Fr	Jean-Claude Petit
Encounters	Aut	Frank Strangio
Endless Summer II, The	Ind	Gary Hoey
Endless Summer II, The	Ind	Phil Marshall
Enemy Within, The	HBO	Joe Delia
Erotic Tales	Ger	Wendy Blackstone
Erotic Tales	Ger	David McHugh
Erotic Tales	Ger	Melvin Van Peebles
Everynight . . . Everynight	Aut	Paul Kelly
Everynight . . . Everynight	Aut	Shane O'Mara
Evolver	Ind	Christopher Tyng
Exit to Eden	Ind	Patrick Doyle
Exotica	Can	Mychael Danna
Eyes of Terror	NBC-TV	Michael Hoenig
F.T.W.	Ind	Gary Chang
Fall From Grace	CBS-TV	Gabriel Yared
Family	Br	Elvis Costello
Family	Br	John Harle
Farinelli il Castrato	Fr/It	Christopher Rousset
Fast Getaway II	Ind	David Robbins
Fatal Vows: The Alexandra O'Hara Story	CBS-TV	George S. Clinton
Father and Scout	ABC-TV	David Kitay
Fatherland	HBO	Gary Chang
Favor, The	Orion	Thomas Newman

Fearless Tiger	Ind	Varouje
Femme Fontaine: Killer Babe for the C.I.A.	Ind	Gardner Cole
Fence, The	Ind	Jeff Beal
Final Combination	Br	Rolfe Kent
Final Embrace	Concorde	Daniel Licht
Flashfire	Ind	Sylvester Levay
Flintstones, The	Univ	David Newman
Floundering	Ind	Pray for Rain
Following Her Heart	NBC-TV	Mark Snow
For the Love of Aaron	CBS-TV	Lawrence Shragge
For the Love of Nancy	ABC-TV	Dan Slider
For the Moment	Can	Victor Davies
Foreign Student	Fr	Jean-Claude Petit
Forget-Me-Not Murders, The	CBS-TV	Ken Harrison
Forrest Gump	Par	Alan Silvestri
Four Weddings and a Funeral	Br	Richard Rodney Bennett
French Silk	ABC-TV	Patrick Williams
Freres: La Roulette Roge	Fr	Yarol
Fresh	Fr	Stewart Copeland
Friend to Die For, A	NBC-TV	Chris Boardman
Fudge-a-Mania	ABC-TV	Paul Zaza
Fun	Ind	Marc Tschanz
Funny Man	Br	Steve Parsons
Gambler V: Playing for Keeps, The	CBS-TV	Larry Brown
Gambler V: Playing for Keeps, The	CBS-TV	Bob DeMarco
Gambler V: Playing for Keeps, The	CBS-TV	Edgar Struble
Genesi: La Creazione e il Diluvio	It/Ger	Ennio Morricone
Getaway, The	Univ	Mark Isham
Getting Even With Dad	MGM	Miles Goodman
Getting Gotti	CBS-TV	Patrick Williams
Getting Out	ABC-TV	Mason Daring
Ghoulies IV	TriStar	Chuck Cirino
Gift From Heaven, A	Ind	Jean-Noel Chaleat
Gift of Love, The	CBS-TV	Patrick Williams
Gino	Aut	Roger Mason
Girl in the Watermelon, The	Ind	Ana Araziz
Girls in Prison	Showtime	Hummie Mann
Glass Shield, The	Ind	Stephen James Taylor
Glitterbug	Br	Brian Eno
Go Fish	Goldwyn	Brendan Dolan
Go Fish	Goldwyn	Jennifer Sharpe
Golden Gate	Goldwyn	Elliot Goldenthal
Good King Wenceslas	Fam Ch	Charles Gross
Good Man in Africa, A	Ind	John Du Prez
Gospa	US/Yug	Nona Hendryx
Great Moments in Aviation	Br	Rachel Portman
Greedy	Univ	Randy Edelman
Green Dolphin Beat	Fox-TV	Peter Manning Robinson
Greyhounds	CBS-TV	Mike Post
Grosse Fatigue	Fr	Rene Marc Bini
Guarding Tess	TriStar	Michael Convertino
Guinevere	Lifetime	Johnny Harris
Gunmen	Miramax	John Debney
Gunsmoke: One Man's Justice	CBS-TV	Artie Kane

Guyver 2: Dark Hero, The	New Line	Les Claypool III
Hail Caesar	Ind	Roger Tallman
Handgun	Ind	Douglas Cuomo
Hans Christian Andersen's "Thumbelina"	WB	Jack Feldman
Hans Christian Andersen's "Thumbelina"	WB	Barry Manilow
Hans Christian Andersen's "Thumbelina"	WB	William Ross
Hans Christian Andersen's "Thumbelina"	WB	Bruce Sussman
Hard Evidence	Ind	Barron Abramovitch
Hard Truth, The	Ind	Daniel Licht
Hard Vice	Ind	Jeff Lass
Hart to Hart: Crimes of the Hart	NBC-TV	Arthur B. Rubinstein
Hart to Hart: Home Is Where the Hart Is	NBC-TV	Arthur B. Rubinstein
Hart to Hart: Old Friends Never Die	NBC-TV	Arthur B. Rubinstein
Harvest for the Heart	Fam Ch	Ron Halldorson
Heads	Showtime	Jonathan Goldsmith
Healer	Ind	Kamen Dranduski
Heart of Darkness	TNT	Stanley Myers
Heart of a Child	NBC-TV	Mark Snow
Heavenly Creatures	NewZea	Peter Dasent
Hell Bent	Can	Steven Hegyi
Henry & Verlin	Can	Mark Korven
Hero's Life, A	Can	Milan Kymlicka
Hidden 2, The	Ind	David McHugh
Higher Learning	Col	Stanley Clarke
Highlander III: The Sorcerer	Can/Fr/Br	J. Peter Robinson
Highway of Heartache	Can	Barbara Chamberlin
Hits!	Ind	David Lawrence
Holy Matrimony	Ind	Bruce Broughton
Honor Thy Father & Mother: The True Story of the Menendez Murders	Fox-TV	Shuki Levy
Hoop Dreams	USA Net	Ben Sidran
Hope in the Year Two	BBC-TV	Carl Davis
Hostage for a Day	Fox-TV	Ian Thomas
House Party 3	Ind	David Allen Jones
Houseguest	BV	John Debney
How the West Was Fun	ABC-TV	Richard Bellis
Hudsucker Proxy, The	WB	Carter Burwell
Human Target: Bloodfist V	Ind	David & Eric Wurst
Hush Little Baby	USA Net	Mychael Danna
Hush Little Baby	USA Net	Paul Intson
I Know My Son Is Alive	NBC-TV	Mickey Erbe
I Know My Son Is Alive	NBC-TV	Maribeth Solomon
I Like It Like That	Col	Stanley Clarke
I Like It Like That	Col	Sergio George
I Love Trouble	BV	David Newman
I Spy Returns	CBS-TV	Johnny Harris
I'll Do Anything	Col	Hans Zimmer
I.Q.	Par	Jerry Goldsmith
Ice	Ind	John Gonzalez
i.d.	Br/Ger	Will Gregory
Il Branco (The Pack)	It	Franco Piersanti
Il Mostro (The Monster)	It/Fr	Evan Lurie
Il Postino (The Postman)	It/Fr/Bel	Luis Bacalov
Il Signo Della Farfalla	It/Fr/Swiss	Carlo Crivelli

Il Toro (The Bull)	It	Ivano Fossati
Imaginary Crimes	WB	Stephen Endelman
Immortal Beloved	Br	Ludwig Van Beethoven
Improper Conduct	Ind	Alan Dermaderosian
In the Army Now	BV	Robert Folk
In the Best of Families: Marriage, Pride & Madness	CBS-TV	Don Davis
In the Cold Light of Day	BBC-TV	Philip Appleby
In the Line of Duty: The Price of Vengeance	NBC-TV	Mark Snow
Incident at Deception Ridge	USA Net	Michel Colombier
Incident in a Small Town	CBS-TV	Lee Holdridge
Indecent Behavior 2	Ind	Michel Rubini
Inkwell, The	BV	Terence Blanchard
Inner Sanctum 2	Ind	Chuck Cirino
Innocent, The	NBC-TV	Anthony Marinelli
Inside the Goldmine	Ind	Robin Lemusier
Intersection	Par	James Newton Howard
Interview With the Vampire	WB	Elliot Goldenthal
Is There Life Out There?	CBS-TV	J.A.C. Redford
It Could Happen to You	TriStar	Carter Burwell
It's Pat	BV	Mark Mothersbaugh
J'ai pas Sommiel (I Can't Sleep)	Fr/Swiss	John Pattison
Jack Reed: A Search for Justice	NBC-TV	Lee Holdridge
Jacob	TNT	Marco Frisina
Jailbreakers	Show	Hummie Mann
Jane's House	CBS-TV	David Shire
Jason's Lyric	Ind	Africa
Jason's Lyric	Ind	Matt Noble
Jeanne la Pucelle (Joan of Arc)	Fr	Jordi Savall
Jimmy Hollywood	Par	Robbie Robertson
John Jakes' "Heaven & Hell: North & South Book 3"	ABC-TV	David Bell
Jonathan Stone: Threat of Innocence	NBC	Jeff Beal
Judicial Consent	Ind	Christopher Young
Junior	Univ	James Newton Howard
Justice in a Small Town	NBC-TV	David McHugh
Kanada	Can	Earle Peach
Killer	Ind	Graeme Coleman
Killer Kid	Fr	Rene Aubry
Kim Novak Is on the Phone	It	Nicola Piovani
Kiss Goodnight, A	Ind	Chris Caswell
L'amico Immaginario (The Imaginary Friend)	It	Riccardo Fassi
L'incruste (Infiltrate)	Fr	Yarol
L'orso du Peluche (The Teddy Bear)	It/Fr	Roman Musumarra
L'uomo che Guarda (The Voyeur)	It	Riz Ortolani
L'uomo delle Stelle (The Star Man)	It	Ennio Morricone
La Bella Vita (Living It Up)	It	Claudio Cimpanelli
La Bionda (The Blonde)	It	Jurgen Knieper
La Fille de D'Artagnan (Daughter of D'Artagnan)	Fr	Philippe Sarde
La Jeune Fille du Livre	Fr	Andre Bon
La Parfum d'Yvonne	Fr	Pascale Esteve
La Prediction	Fr/Rus	Andrei Petrov

La Reine Margot (Queen Margot)	Fr/It/Ger	Goran Bregovic
La Teta I La Luna	Sp/Fr	Nicola Piovani
La Vera Vita di Antonio H.	It	Mimmo Locasciulli
La Veritable Histoire d'Artaud le Momo	Fr	Jean-Claude Petit
Ladri di Cinema (The Film Thief)	It	Luigi Ceccarelli
Lady in Waiting	Ind	Robert Ginsburg
Ladybird Ladybird	Br	George Fenton
Lakota Woman: Siege of Wounded Knee	TNT	Richard Horowitz
Lamerica	It/Fr	Franco Piersanti
Landing on the Sun, A	Br	Bill Connor
Lassie	Par	Basil Poledouris
Last Good Time, The	Goldwyn	Jonathan Tunick
Last Seduction, The	Ind	Joseph Vitarelli
Last Supper, The	Can	Nicholas Stirling
Last Tattoo, The	NewZea	John Charles
Le Cri du Coeur (The Heart's Cry)	Fr	Henri Texier
Le Fils Prefere (The Favorite Son)	Fr	Philippe Sarde
Le Secret de Jerome (Jerome's Secret)	Can	Marcel Aymar
Le Sourire (The Smile)	Fr	Pierre Boscheron
Le Sourire (The Smile)	Fr	Antoine Ouvrier
Leave of Absence	NBC-TV	Don Davis
Legend of O. B. Taggart, The	Ind	David Mansfield
Legend of O. B. Taggart, The	Ind	Larry Gatlin
Legend of O. B. Taggart, The	Ind	Randy Travis
Legends of the Fall	TriStar	James Horner
Leon (The Professional)	Fr	Eric Serra
Leprechaun 2	Ind	Jonathan Elias
Les Amoureuses	Can	Pierre Desrochers
Les Gens de la Riziere (Rice People)	Fr/Camb	Marc Marder
Les Patriotes (The Patriots)	Fr	Gerard Torikian
Lex and Rory	Ind	Frank Strangio
Liar's Club, The	Concorde	David & Eric Wurst
Liberation	Ind	Carl Davis
Lie Down With Lions	Lifetime	Carl Davis
Lies of the Heart: The Story of Laurie Kellogg	ABC-TV	Kim Schamberg
Life's Too Good	Ind	Harry Fix
Lifeforce Experiment, The	SciFi	Osvaldo Montes
Lightning Jack	Aut	Bruce Rowland
Lightning in a Bottle	Ind	Les Baxter
Lily in Winter	USA Net	David Shire
Lion King, The	BV	Elton John
Lion King, The	BV	Tim Rice
Lion King, The	BV	Hans Zimmer
Lion Strike	Ind	John Gonzalez
Lisa Theory, The	Ind	Jim Matison
Little Big League	Col	Stanley Clarke
Little Giants	WB	John Debney
Little Rascals, The	Univ	David Foster
Little Rascals, The	Univ	William Ross
Little Rascals, The	Univ	Linda Thompson
Little Women	Col	Thomas Newman
Loaded	Br/NewZea	Simon Fisher Turner
Look Me in the Eye	Br	David Chilton

Look Me in the Eye	Br	Nicholas Russell-Pavier
Love Affair	WB	Ennio Morricone
Love and a .45	Ind	Tom Verlaine
Low Down Dirty Shame, A	BV	Marcus Miller
Lucky Break	Aut	Paul Grabowsky
Lurking Fear	Ind	Jim Manzie
Lush Life	Showtime	Lennie Niehaus
M.A.N.T.I.S.	Fox-TV	Joseph Lo Duca
MacGyver: Lost Treasure of Atlantis	ABC-TV	Ken Harrison
MacGyver: Trail to Doomsday	ABC-TV	Ken Harrison
MacShayne: Final Roll of the Dice	NBC-TV	Larry Brown
MacShayne: Final Roll of the Dice	NBC-TV	Bob DeMarco
MacShayne: Final Roll of the Dice	NBC-TV	Edgar Struble
MacShayne: Winner Takes All	NBC-TV	Larry Brown
MacShayne: Winner Takes All	NBC-TV	Bob DeMarco
MacShayne: Winner Takes All	NBC-TV	Edgar Struble
Madness of King George, The	Br	George Fenton
Major League II	WB	Michel Colombier
Man of No Importance, A	Br	Julian Nott
Maniaci Sentimentali (Sentimental Maniacs)	It	Antonio Di Pofi
Mario, Maria e Mario	It/Fr	Armando Trovajoli
Mary	Aut	Douglas Stephen Rae
Mary Shelley's Frankenstein	TriStar	Patrick Doyle
Mask, The	New Line	Randy Edelman
Maverick	WB	Randy Newman
Max	Can	Graeme Coleman
Men Lie	Ind	Ernie Mannix
Men of War	BV	Gerald Gouriet
Menendez: A Killing in Beverly Hills	CBS-TV	Joseph Conlan
Mesmer	Can	Michael Nyman
Messenger	Ind	Joseph Lo Duca
Metal Skin	Aut	John Clifford White
Mi Familia (My Family)	Ind	Mark McKenzie
Miami Rhapsody	BV	Mark Isham
Middlemarch	BBC-TV	Christopher Gunning
Middlemarch	BBC-TV	Stanley Myers
Midnight Movie	Br	Christopher Gunning
Milk Money	Par	Michael Convertino
Million Dollar Babies	CBS-TV	Christopher Dedrick
Million to Juan, A	Goldwyn	Steven Johnson
Minotaur	Ind	William T. Stromberg
Miracle on 34th Street	Fox	Bruce Broughton
Mirror, Mirror 2: Raven Dance	Ind	Jimmy Lifton
Mixed Nuts	TriStar	George Fenton
Model by Day	Fox-TV	Louis Natale
Molly & Gina	Ind	Dana Walden
Moment of Truth: A Mother's Deception	NBC-TV	Laura Karpman
Moment of Truth: Broken Pledges	NBC-TV	Laura Karpman
Moment of Truth: Caught in the Crossfire	NBC-TV	Mark Snow
Moment of Truth: Cradle of Conspiracy	NBC-TV	Mark Snow
Moment of Truth: Murder or Mercy?	NBC-TV	James McVay
Moment of Truth: To Walk Again	NBC-TV	Laura Karpman
Mona Must Die	Ind	Greg O'Connor
Money to Burn	New Line	Nigel Holton

Monkey Trouble	New Line	Mark Mancina
Montparnasse-Pondichery	Fr	Vladimir Cosma
Mother's Boys	Miramax	George S. Clinton
Motorcycle Gang	Showtime	Hummie Mann
Mouvements du Desir (Desire in Motion)	Can/Swiss	Zbigniew Preisner
Mr. 247	Ind	Jan Hammer
Mr. Write	Ind	Miles Roston
Mrs. Parker and the Vicious Circle	Ind	Mark Isham
Murder Between Friends	NBC-TV	Mark Snow
Muriel's Wedding	Aut	Peter Best
Mutual Consent	Fr	Jeff Cohen
My Breast	CBS-TV	Peter Bernstein
My Father, the Hero	BV	David Newman
My Girl 2	Col	Cliff Eidelman
My Life's in Turnaround	Ind	Reed Hays
My Name Is Kate	ABC-TV	Charles Bernstein
My Summer Story (aka It Runs in the Family)	MGM	Paul Zaza
Nadja	Br	Simon Fisher Turner
Naked Gun 33-1/3: The Final Insult	Par	Ira Newborn
Naked in New York	Ind	Angelo Badalamenti
Nanook	Fr/Can	Sebastian Regnier
Natural Born Killers	WB	Trent Reznor
Natural Causes	Ind	Nathan Wang
Nell	Fox	Mark Isham
Nestore L'Ultima Corsa (Nestor's Last Trip)	It/Fr	Piero Piccioni
Neuf Mois (Nine Months)	Fr	Jacques Davidovici
Never Say Die	Ind	Adrian Levy
Never Say Die	Ind	Wendy Oldfield
Neverending Story III, The	Ger	Peter Wolf
New Age, The	WB	Mark Mothersbaugh
Next Door	Showtime	Van Dyke Parks
Next Karate Kid, The	Col	Bill Conti
Night and the Moment, The	Br/It/Fr	Ennio Morricone
Night of the Demons 2	Ind	Jim Manzie
Night Siege: Project Shadowchaser II	Ind	Steve Edwards
Nightfire	Ind	Miriam Cutler
Nina Takes a Lover	Ind	Todd Boekelheide
No Escape	Ind	Graeme Revell
Nobody's Children	Br/Fr	Jean-Claude Petit
Nobody's Fool	Par	Howard Shore
North	Col	Marc Shaiman
Nostradamus	Orion	Barrington Pheloung
Nowhere to Hide	ABC-TV	Gary Chang
Number One Fan	Ind	Robert J. Walsh
O Mary This London	Br	Stephen Warbeck
Oblivion	Ind	Pino Donaggio
Occhiopinocchio	It	Giovanni Nuti
October	Can	Richard Gregoire
Odile & Yvette at the Edge of the World	Ind	Blake Leyh
Of Love and Shadows	Ind	Jose Nieto
Oldest Living Confederate Widow Tells All	CBS-TV	Mark Snow
Oleanna	Goldwyn	Rebecca Pidgeon
Omaha (The Movie)	Ind	Andrew McPherson

On Deadly Ground	WB	Basil Poledouris
On Promised Land	Disney-TV	Mason Daring
Once Were Warriors	NewZea	Murray Grindlay
Once Were Warriors	NewZea	Murray McNabb
One More Mountain	ABC-TV	J.A.C. Redford
One Woman's Courage	NBC-TV	John Keane
One of Her Own	ABC-TV	George S. Clinton
Only You	TriStar	Rachel Portman
Out of Darkness	ABC-TV	Michel Colombier
PCU	Fox	Steve Vai
Pagemaster, The	Fox	James Horner
Paint Cans	Can	Marty Simon
Paper Boy, The	Can	Milan Kymlicka
Paper, The	Univ	Randy Newman
Parallel Lives	Showtime	Patrick Seymour
Party Girl	Ind	Anton Sanko
Passion for Justice: The Hazel Brannon Smith Story	ABC-TV	David McHugh
Passion to Kill, A	Ind	Robert Sprayberry
Past Tense	Showtime	Stephen Graziano
Past Tense	Showtime	Michael Hoenig
Paul Bowles: The Complete Insider	Ind	Paul Bowles
Peche Veniell . . . Peche Mortel . . .	Fr	Georges Rabol
Peche Veniell . . . Peche Mortel . . .	Fr	Jean-Pierre Stora
Per Amore, Solo per Amore	It	Nicola Piovani
Perez Family, The	Goldwyn	Zbigniew Preisner
Perez Family, The	Goldwyn	Alan Silvestri
Perez Family, The	Goldwyn	Arturo Sandoval
Perfect Alibi, The	Ind	Amotz Plessner
Perry Mason Mystery: The Case of the Grimacing Governor	NBC-TV	Dick DeBenedictis
Perry Mason Mystery: The Case of the Lethal Lifestyle	NBC-TV	Dick DeBenedictis
Piccoli Orrori (Little Horrors)	It	Ciro Buttari
Picture Bride	Miramax	Cliff Eidelman
Pin for the Butterfly, A	Br/Czech	Ilona Sekacz
Place for Annie, A	ABC-TV	Mark Snow
Playmaker	Orion	Mark Snow
Plughead Rewired: Circuitry Man II	Ind	Tim Kelly
Pointman	Syn	Paul Haslinger
Police Academy: Mission to Moscow	WB	Robert Folk
Pontiac Moon	Par	Randy Edelman
Porami Via (Take Me Away)	It	Paolo Lasazio
Pornographer, The	Ind	Don Schiff
Possessed by the Night	TriStar	Chuck Cirino
Postcards From America	Br	Stephen Endelman
Power of Attorney	Ind	Hal Beckett
Prehysteria 2	Ind	Richard Band
Presence, The	Ind	Peter Manning Robinson
Prestazione Straordinaria	It	Antonio Di Pofi
Priest	Br	Andy Roberts
Priez pour Nous (Pray for Us)	Fr	Raymond Alessandrini
Prince of Jutland	Fr/Br/Ger/Dan	Per Norgaard
Princess Caraboo	TriStar	Richard Hartley

Project: Genesis	Can	Claude Boux
Project Metalbeast: DNA Overload	Ind	Conrad Pope
Promise Kept: The Oksana Baiul Story, A	CBS-TV	Mark Green
Pumpkinhead 2: Blood Wings	Ind	Jim Manzie
Pumpkinhead 2: Blood Wings	Ind	Richard McHugh
Puppet Master V: The Final Chapter	Ind	Richard Band
Puppet Masters, The	BV	Colin Towns
Quiz Show	BV	Mark Isham
Race to Freedom: The Underground Railroad	Fam Ch	Christopher Dedrick
Radio Inside	Ind	Gil Goldstein
Radioland Murders	Univ	Joel McNeely
Raffle, The	Ind	Robert O. Ragland
Rapa Nui	Ind	Stewart Copeland
Rave Review	Ind	Amotz Plessner
Ray Alexander: A Taste for Justice	NBC-TV	Dick DeBenedictis
Ready to Wear (Pret-a-Porter)	Miramax	Michel Legrand
Reality Bites	Univ	Karl Wallinger
Rector's Wife	Br	Richard Hartley
Red Scorpion 2	Ind	George Blondheim
Ref, The	BV	David A. Stewart
Reflections on a Crime	Concorde	Parmer Fuller
Reform School Girl	Showtime	Hummie Mann
Relative Fear	Ind	Marty Simon
Relentless 4: Ashes to Ashes	New Line	Terry Plumeri
Renaissance Man	BV	Hans Zimmer
Return of Jafar, The	BV	Randy Petersen
Return of Jafar, The	BV	Kevin Quinn
Return of Jafar, The	BV	Mark Watters
Return of the Native, The	CBS-TV	Carl Davis
Return of Tommy Tricker	Can	Kate/Anne/Jane McGarrigle
Reunion	CBS-TV	David Shire
Revenge of the Nerds IV: Nerds in Love	Fox-TV	Garry Schyman
Revenge of the Red Baron	Concorde	Robert Randles
Richie Rich	WB	Alan Silvestri
Ride With the Wind	ABC-TV	Michel Rubini
Ring of Steel	Ind	Jeff Beal
Rise and Walk: The Dennis Byrd Story	Fox-TV	W. G. Snuffy Walden
Risk	Ind	John Paul Jones
River Wild, The	Univ	Jerry Goldsmith
Road to Wellville, The	Col	Rachel Portman
Roadracers	Showtime	Paul Boll
Roadracers	Showtime	Johnny Reno
Robin Cook's "Mortal Fear"	NBC-TV	Garry Schyman
Robot in the Family	Ind	Papo Gely
Rockford Files: I Still Love L.A., The	CBS-TV	Mike Post
Roly Poly Man, The	Aut	David Skinner
Roommates	NBC-TV	Lee Holdridge
Roseanne & Tom: Behind the Scenes	NBC-TV	Craig Safan
Roseanne: An Unauthorized Biography	Fox-TV	Scott Harper
Roswell	Showtime	Elliot Goldenthal
Rough Diamonds	Aut	Wayne Goodwin
Rough Diamonds	Aut	Mark Moffatt
Roy Cohn/Jack Smith	Ind	Michael Stahl

Royce	Showtime	Stanley Clarke
Rudyard Kipling's "The Jungle Book"	BV	Basil Poledouris
Rugged Gold	Fam Ch	Dick LeFort
Runaway Daughters	Showtime	Hummie Mann
Running Delilah	ABC-TV	Lee Holdridge
S.F.W.	Ind	Graeme Revell
Safe Passage	New Line	Mark Isham
Santa Clause, The	BV	Michael Convertino
Sarahsara (The Waterbaby)	It	Mauro Pagani
Scarlett	CBS-TV	John Morris
Scenes From the New World	Ind	Laurie Fitzgerald
Scenes From the New World	Ind	Tony Silbert
Scorned	Ind	Ronald J. Weiss
Scout, The	Fox	Bill Conti
Search and Rescue	NBC-TV	Robert Folk
Search for Grace	CBS-TV	Michael Hoenig
Season of Change	Ind	Alby Potts
Seasons of the Heart	NBC-TV	Marvin Hamlisch
Seaview Knights	Br	Oliver Davis
Second Best	Br	Simon Boswell
Second Cousin, Once Removed	Ind	Blake Leyh
Secret Sins of the Father	NBC-TV	Kenny Williams
Secret of Roan Inish, The	Ind	Mason Daring
Seduced by Evil	USA Net	George S. Clinton
Sensation	Col	Arthur Kempel
Separated by Murder	CBS-TV	Rick Marvin
Serial Mom	Ind	Basil Poledouris
Sexual Outlaws	Ind	Ashley Irwin
Shadow of Obsession	NBC-TV	Udi Harpaz
Shadow, The	Univ	Jerry Goldsmith
Shadows of Desire	CBS-TV	Mark Snow
Shaggy Dog, The	ABC-TV	Denis M. Hannigan
Shaggy Dog, The	ABC-TV	Mark Mothersbaugh
Shake, Rattle and Rock!	Showtime	Joey Altruda
Shallow Grave	Br	Simon Boswell
Shattered Image	USA Net	Noam Kaniel
Shattered Image	USA Net	Amotz Plessner
Shawshank Redemption, The	Col	Thomas Newman
She Led Two Lives	NBC-TV	Misha Segal
Shopping	Br	Barrington Pheloung
Shortcut to Paradise	Sp	Jose Nieto
Shrunken Heads	Ind	Richard Band
Signal One	Aut	Art Phillips
Silence of the Hams, The	Ind	Parmer Fuller
Silent Betrayal, A	CBS-TV	Ken Harrison
Silent Fall	WB	Stewart Copeland
Silent Witness: What a Child Saw	USA Net	Harold Wheeler
Silk Degrees	Ind	Larry Wolff
Simple Twist of Fate, A	BV	Cliff Eidelman
Sin Bin	BBC-TV	Colin Towns
Sin and Redemption	CBS-TV	David Bell
Sioux City	Ind	Christopher Lindsey
Sirens	Br/Aut	Rachel Portman
Sister My Sister	Br	Stephen Warbeck

Skallarigg	BBC-TV	Stephen Warbeck
Sleep With Me	MGM	David Lawrence
Snowbound: The Jim and Jennifer Stolpa Story	CBS-TV	Louis Natale
Sodbusters	Showtime	Louis Natale
Soft Deceit	Can	Ian Thomas
Solar Force	Ind	Don Peake
Somebody to Love	Ind	Mader
Someone Else's America	Br/Fr/Ger	Andrew Dickson
Someone Else's Child	ABC-TV	Billy Goldenberg
Someone She Knows	NBC-TV	Wendy Blackstone
Spanking the Monkey	Ind	David Carbonara
Specialist, The	WB	John Barry
Speechless	MGM	Marc Shaiman
Speed	Fox	Mark Mancina
Spenser: Pale Kings and Princes	Lifetime	Paul Zaza
Spenser: The Judas Goat	Lifetime	Brad MacDonald
Spider & Rose	Aut	Cruel Sea
Spider and the Fly, The	USA Net	Richard Bellis
Spoils of War	ABC-TV	Lawrence Shragge
Spring Awakening	CBS-TV	Lee Holdridge
Squanto: A Warrior's Tale	BV	Joel McNeely
St. Tammany Miracle, The	Ind	Jay Wiegel
Staggered	Br	Peter Brewis
Star Struck	CBS-TV	Lawrence Shragge
Star Trek Generations	Par	Dennis McCarthy
Stargate	MGM	David Arnold
State of Emergency	HBO	Robert Folk
Steel Hunter	Ind	John Gonzalez
Strangers by Night	Ind	Ashley Irwin
Street Fighter	Univ	Graeme Revell
Substitute Wife, The	NBC-TV	Mark Snow
Suite 16	Br/Belg	Walter Hus
Sum of Us, The	Aut	David Faulkner
Summertime Switch	ABC-TV	Bradley Smith
Surgeon, The (aka Exquisite Tenderness)	Ind	Christopher Franke
Surviving the Game	New Line	Stewart Copeland
Swallows Never Die in Jerusalem	Fr/Tun	Jean-Claude Petit
Swan Princess, The	New Line	Lex De Azevedo
Swan Princess, The	New Line	David Zippel
Swimming With Sharks	Ind	Tom Heil
Sword of Honor	Ind	David Rubinstein
T-Force	Ind	Louis Febre
Take Me Home Again	NBC-TV	Patrick Williams
Takeover, The	Ind	Jimmy Lifton
Tales From a Hard City	Fr/Br	Dan Carey
Talk	Aut	John Clifford White
Talking About Sex	Ind	Tim Landers
Target of Suspicion	USA Net	Eric De Marsan
Tears and Laughter: The Joan and Melissa Rivers Story	NBC-TV	Harold Wheeler
Teenage Exorcist	Ind	Chuck Cirino
Teresa's Tattoo	Ind	Andrew Keresztes
Teresa's Tattoo	Ind	Melissa Etheridge

Terminal Velocity	BV	Joel McNeely
Terror in the Night	CBS-TV	Dana Kaproff
That Eye, the Sky	Aut	David Bridie
That Eye, the Sky	Aut	John Phillips
That's Entertainment III	MGM	Marc Shaiman
Thicker Than Blood: The Larry McLinden Story	CBS-TV	Johnny Harris
Thieves Quartet	Ind	John Zorn
This Can't Be Love	CBS-TV	Peter Matz
Threesome	TriStar	Thomas Newman
Till the End of the Night	Ind	Mark Governor
Time Cop	Univ	Mark Isham
Time Is Money	Fr	Gerard Torikian
Time to Heal, A	NBC-TV	Jay Gruska
To Die For	Ind	Roger Bolton
To My Daughter With Love	NBC-TV	Branford Marsalis
To Save the Children	CBS-TV	Mickey Erbe
To Save the Children	CBS-TV	Maribeth Solomon
Tokyo Cowboy	Can	Ari Wise
Tollbooth	Ind	Adam Gorgoni
Tom & Viv	Br	Debbie Wiseman
Tonya & Nancy: The Inside Story	NBC-TV	Dennis McCarthy
Totor	Fr	Guy Boulanger
Toughguy	Ind	Sean Naidoo
Trading Mom	Ind	David Kitay
Trancers IV: Jack of Swords	Ind	Gary Fry
Trapped in Paradise	Fox	Robert Folk
Traps	Aut	Douglas Stephen Rae
Treacherous Beauties	CBS-TV	Jody Collero
Treacherous Beauties	CBS-TV	Maribeth Solomon
Trial at Fortitude Bay	Can	Simon Kendall
Trial at Fortitude Bay	Can	Al Rogers
Trial by Jury	WB	Terence Blanchard
Trick of the Eye	CBS-TV	Allyn Ferguson
Trois Couleurs: Rouge	Fr/Swiss/Pol	Zbigniew Preisner
Troll in Central Park, A	WB	Robert Folk
Troll in Central Park, A	WB	Barry Mann
True Lies	Fox	Brad Fiedel
Truman Capote's "One Christmas"	NBC-TV	Van Dyke Parks
Tryst	Ind	Tom Howard
Tutti Gli Anni, Una Volta l'Anno	It/Fr/Belg	Giovanni Venosta
Twilight Zone: Rod Serling's Lost Classics	CBS-TV	Patrick Williams
Two Fathers: Justice for the Innocent	NBC-TV	Robert Folk
Ultimate Betrayal	CBS-TV	Chris Boardman
Umbrellas	Ind	Phillip Johnston
Una Pura Formalita (A Pure Formality)	It/Fr	Ennio Morricone
Unborn II, The	Concorde	John Graham
Unconditional Love	Ind	Michael Errington
Uncovered	Br/Sp	Philippe Sarde
Under Heat	Ind	Elizabeth Swados
Undercover Cop	Ind	Randall Kent Heddon
Unforgettable Summer, An	Br/Fr	Anton Suteu
Uno a Te, Uno a Me et Uno a Raffaele	It	Jon A. English

Untamed Love	Lifetime	James DiPasquale
Unveiled	Ind	Christopher Tyng
Upstairs Neighbor, The	Ind	Bruce Langhorne
Vanya on 42nd Street	Ind	Joshua Redman
Vegas Vice	Ind	Jeff Lass
Vernon Johns Story, The	Syn	Brian Keane
Vibrations	BV	Bob Christianson
Voices From Within	NBC-TV	Cynthia Miller
Wagons East!	TriStar	Michael Small
War of the Buttons	Br/Fr	Rachel Portman
War, The	Univ	Thomas Newman
Watchers III	Concorde	Nigel Holton
Web of Deception	NBC-TV	Bob Alcivar
Wes Craven's New Nightmare	New Line	J. Peter Robinson
Whale Music	Can	George Blondheim
What Happened Was . . .	Ind	Lodovico Sorret
When a Man Loves a Woman	BV	Zbigniew Preisner
Where Are My Children?	ABC-TV	Craig Safan
While Justice Sleeps	NBC-TV	Allyn Ferguson
Whipping Boy, The	Disney-TV	Lee Holdridge
White Fang 2: The Myth of the White Wolf	BV	John Debney
White Water Mile	HBO	Pray for Rain
Why Is My Mother in My Bed?	Fr	Eric Levi
Wild Justice	Br	Mark Thomas
Windrunner	Ind	Arthur Kempel
Witch Hunt	HBO	Angelo Badalamenti
Witchcraft VI: Devil's Mistress	Ind	Miriam Cutler
With Honors	WB	Patrick Leonard
Without Consent	ABC-TV	Craig Safan
Witness to the Execution	NBC-TV	Mark Snow
Wolf	Col	Ennio Morricone
Words Upon the Window Pane	Ire	Niall Byrne
World War II: When Lions Roared	NBC-TV	John Morris
World and Time Enough	Ind	Eugene Huddleston
Wyatt Earp	WB	James Newton Howard
XXX's & OOO's	CBS-TV	Harry Stinson
Yarn Princess, The	ABC-TV	Christopher Franke
Yearling, The	CBS-TV	Lee Holdridge
Zinky Boys Go Underground	BBC-TV	Simon Boswell

1995

12 Monkeys	Univ	Paul Buckmaster
3 Ninjas Knuckle Up	TriStar	Gary Stevan Scott
3 Steps to Heaven	Br	John Eacott
93 Million Miles From the Sun	Ind	Peter Foley
A Cran (On the Edge)	Fr	Laurent Petitgrand
A Crinoline Madness	Can	Andre Duchesne
A la Campagne (Out in the Country)	Fr	Charlie Couture
Abandoned and Deceived	ABC-TV	Laura Karpman
Above Suspicion	HBO	Michael Hoenig
Ace Ventura: When Nature Calls	WB	Robert Folk
Across the Sea of Time	Col	John Barry
Acts of Love	Ind	Bruce Broughton

Addiction, The	Ind	Joe Delia
Adrenalin: Fear the Rush	Ind	Tony Riparetti
Adultere, Mode d'Emploi	Fr	Bruno Coulais
Affair, The	Br	Christopher Gunning
Alchemy	Ind	Georgia Hubley
Alchemy	Ind	Ira Kaplan
Alistair MacLean's "Night Watch"	USA Net	John Scott
All Men Are Liars	Aut	Wayne Goodwin
All Men Are Liars	Aut	Mark Moffatt
All Men Are Mortal	Br	Michael Gibbs
All Men Are Mortal	Br	Simon Fisher Turner
Almost Golden: The Jessica Savitch Story	Lifetime	David Shire
Amazing Panda Adventure, The	WB	William Ross
America's Dream	HBO	Patrice Rushen
American President, The	Col	Marc Shaiman
Among the Dead	Ind	Mark Ridlen
Android Affair, The	USA Net	Simon Boswell
Angel Baby	Aut	John Clifford White
Angela	Ind	Michael Rohatyn
Angels and Insects	US/Br	Alexander Balanescu
Angus	New Line	David Russo
Anne Frank Remembered	Br	Carl Davis
Annie: A Royal Adventure	ABC-TV	David Michael Frank
Antarctica	Sp	John Cale
Antonia's Line	Br/Belg/Dutch	Ilona Sekacz
Apollo 13	Univ	James Horner
Arabian Knight	Miramax	Robert Folk
As Good as Dead	USA Net	Patrick O'Hearn
Assassin Wore Yellow Shoes, The	It	Stefano Mainetti
Assassins	WB	Mark Mancina
At First Sight	Ind	Richard Gibbs
At the Midnight Hour	CBS-TV	Charles J. Cozens
Au Petit Marguery	Fr	Jean-Claude Nachon
August	Br	Anthony Hopkins
Avenging Angel, The	TNT	Gary Chang
Awake to Danger	NBC-TV	Charles Gross
Awfully Big Adventure, An	Br	Richard Hartley
Babe	Aut	Nigel Westlake
Baby-Sitter's Club, The	Col	David Michael Frank
Babysitter, The	Ind	Loek Dikker
Back of Beyond	Aut	Wayne Goodwin
Back of Beyond	Aut	Mark Moffatt
Backlash: Oblivion 2	Ind	Pino Donaggio
Bad Boys	Col	Mark Mancina
Bad Company	BV	Carter Burwell
Baja	Ind	Reg Powell
Ballot Measure 9	Ind	Julian Dylan Russell
Balto	Univ	James Horner
Banditi (Bandits)	It	Paolo Vivaldi
Barefoot Executive, The	ABC-TV	Philip Giffin
Basketball Diaries, The	New Line	Graeme Revell
Batman Forever	WB	Elliot Goldenthal
Beastmaster 3: The Eye of Braxus	Ind	Jan Hammer
Beauty's Revenge	NBC-TV	Chris Boardman

Behind the Blue	Can	Richard Gregoire
Betrayed: A Story of Three Women	ABC-TV	Patrick Williams
Between Love and Honor	CBS-TV	James McVay
Beyond Rangoon	Col	Hans Zimmer
Beyond the Clouds	Fr/It/Ger	Lucio Dalla
Beyond the Clouds	Fr/It/Ger	Van Morrison
Beyond the Clouds	Fr/It/Ger	Laurent Petitgrand
Beyond the Clouds	Fr/It/Ger	U2
Bidoni (Cheats)	It	Tomaso Vittorini
Big Dreams & Broken Hearts: The Dottie West Story	CBS-TV	Edgar Struble
Big Green, The	BV	Randy Edelman
Big Green, The	BV	Danny Elfman
Big Night	Ind	Gary DeMichele
Billy Madison	Univ	Randy Edelman
Billy's Holiday	Aut	Peter Cobbin
Bird of Prey	Ind	Brian Clifton
Bishop's Story, The	Ire	Roger Doyle
Black Day Blue Night	Ind	Johnny Lee Schell
Black Fox	CBS-TV	Eric N. Robertson
Black Is . . . Black Ain't	Ind	Mary Watkins
Blackwater Trail	Aut	Douglas Stephen Rae
Bleeding Hearts	Ind	Stanley Clarke
Blood & Donuts	Can	Nash the Slash
Blood for Blood	Ind	Joel Goldsmith
Blood Knot	Showtime	Michel Rubini
Bloodknot	Ind	Ian Thomas
Blue Flame	Ind	Tyler Bates
Blue in the Face	Miramax	John Lurie
Blue Juice	Ind	Simon Davison
Blue River	Fox-TV	Lawrence Shragge
Blue Skies Are a Life	Ind	Dave Reynolds
Boca a Boca (Mouth to Mouth)	Sp	Bernardo Bonezzi
Bodily Harm	Ind	Robert Sprayberry
Body Language	HBO	Colin Towns
Bonanza: Under Attack	NBC-TV	Bruce Miller
Bonjour Timothy	Can/NewZea	Daniel Scott
Born to Be Wild	WB	Mark Snow
Boston Knockout	Br	Robert Hartshorne
Boy Called Hate, A	Ind	Pray for Rain
Boys on the Side	WB	David Newman
Brady Bunch Movie, The	Par	Guy Moon
Braveheart	Par	James Horner
Breach of Trust	Ind	Graeme Coleman
Breakaway	Ind	Robert Wait
Breaking the Waves	Dan	Joachim Holbek
Bridges of Madison County, The	WB	Lennie Niehaus
Broken Trust	TNT	Richard Horowitz
Brothers in Trouble	Br	Stephen Warbeck
Brothers McMullen, The	Fox	Seamus Egan
Buccaneers, The	BBC-TV	Colin Towns
Bucchi Neri (Black Holes)	It	Pappi Corsicato
Buffalo Girls	CBS-TV	Lee Holdridge
Bulletproof Heart	Ind	Graeme Coleman

Bushwhacked	Fox	Bill Conti
Butterfly Kiss	Br	John Harle
Bye Bye Birdie	ABC-TV	Charles Strouse
Bye Bye, Love	Fox	J.A.C. Redford
Bye-Bye	Fr	Steve Shehan
Caged Hearts	Ind	Larry Wolff
Cagney & Lacey: The View Through the Glass Ceiling	CBS-TV	Ron Ramin
Cagney & Lacey: Together Again	CBS-TV	Nan Schwartz-Mishkin
Camerieri (Waiters)	It	Carlo Di Blasi
Camerieri (Waiters)	It	Paolo Rossi
Canadian Bacon	Ind	Elmer Bernstein
Candyman 2: Farewell to the Flesh	Ind	Philip Glass
Captive	Ind	Anton Sanko
Carrington	Br/Fr	Michael Nyman
Casper	Univ	James Horner
Castle Freak	Ind	Richard Band
Catwalk	Ind	Malcolm McLaren
Celluloid Closet, The	HBO	Carter Burwell
Chameleon	Ind	John Debney
Champagne Safari, The	Can	Normand Roger
Child Is Missing, A	CBS-TV	Nicholas Pike
Children of the Dust (aka A Good Day to Die)	CBS-TV	Mark Snow
Choices of the Heart: The Margaret Sanger Story	Lifetime	Jonathan Goldsmith
Christmas Box, The	CBS-TV	Richard Gibbs
Circumstances Unknown	USA Net	Joseph Conlan
Citizen X	HBO	Randy Edelman
Clockers	Univ	Terence Blanchard
Clockwork Mice	Br	David A. Hughes
Clockwork Mice	Br	John Murphy
Clueless	Par	David Kitay
Cold Comfort Farm	Br	Robert Lockhart
Coldblooded	Ind	Steve Bartek
Colony, The	USA Net	Dennis McCarthy
Colpo di Luna (Moon Shadow)	It/Fr/Dutch	Vittorio Cosma
Computer Wore Tennis Shoes, The	ABC-TV	Philip Giffin
Confidences a un Inconnu	Fr/It	Enri Lolashvili
Congo	Par	Jerry Goldsmith
Convict Cowboy	Showtime	David Bell
Copycat	WB	Christopher Young
Courtyard, The	Showtime	Mark Mothersbaugh
Cover Me	Ind	Marcus Barone
Crash	Ind	Howard Shore
Criminal	Br	Orlando Gough
Crimson Tide	BV	Hans Zimmer
Crosscut	Ind	Christopher Tyng
Crossing Guard, The	Miramax	Jack Nitzsche
Crossing Guard, The	Miramax	Joseph Vitarelli
Crossroads at Laredo	Ind	Ben Weisman
Crowfoot	CBS-TV	Ray Bunch
Crude Oasis, The	Miramax	Steven Bramson
Cry, the Beloved Country	Miramax	John Barry

Crying Freeman	Fr/Can	Patrick O'Hearn
Cure, The	Univ	Dave Grusin
Curse of the Starving Class	Showtime	John Bryant
Curse of the Starving Class	Showtime	Frank Hames
Curtis's Charm	Can	Mark Korven
Cutthroat Island	Carolco	John Debney
Cyberjack	Can/Jap	George Blondheim
Dad and Dave on Our Selection	Aut	Peter Best
Dad, the Angel and Me	Fam Ch	Stewart Levin
Dadetown	Ind	Tom Carden
Daisies in December	Showtime	Mark Thomas
Dancing in the Dark	Lifetime	Mickey Erbe
Dancing in the Dark	Lifetime	Maribeth Solomon
Dangerous Affair, A	ABC-TV	David Mansfield
Dangerous Intentions	CBS-TV	James McVay
Dangerous Minds	BV	Wendy & Lisa
Danielle Steel's "Mixed Blessings"	NBC-TV	Mark Snow
Danielle Steel's "Vanished"	NBC-TV	Francois Dompierre
Danielle Steel's "Zoya"	NBC-TV	William Goldstein
Dare to Love	ABC-TV	Ron Ramin
Darkman 3: Die Darkman Die	Ind	Randy Miller
Davy Jones' Locker	Ind	Phil Marshall
De Vliegende Hollander (The Flying Dutchman)	Dutch/Belg/Ger	Nicola Piovani
Dead by Sunset	NBC-TV	David Michael Frank
Dead Funny	Ind	Sheila Silver
Dead Man	Miramax	Neil Young
Dead Man Walking	Ind	David Robbins
Dead Presidents	BV	Danny Elfman
Dead Weekend	Showtime	Steve Hunter
Deadline for Murder: From the Files of Edna Buchanan	CBS-TV	Patrick Williams
Deadlocked: Escape From Zone 14	Fox-TV	Peter Manning Robinson
Deadly Family Secrets	NBC-TV	Nan Schwartz-Mishkin
Deadly Invasion: The Killer Bee Nightmare	Fox-TV	Garry Schyman
Deadly Love	Lifetime	Mickey Erbe
Deadly Love	Lifetime	Maribeth Solomon
Deadly Whispers	CBS-TV	Joseph Conlan
Death in Small Doses	ABC-TV	Jeff Rona
Deceived by Trust: A Moment of Truth Movie	NBC-TV	Stacy Widelitz
Degree of Guilt	NBC-TV	Craig Safan
Delinquent	Ind	Gang of Four
Delta of Venus	Ind	George S. Clinton
Denise Calls Up	Ind	Lynne Geller
Derby	ABC-TV	Paul Zaza
Desert Winds	Ind	James McVay
Desperado	Col	Los Lobos
Desperate Trail, The	TNT	Stephen Endelman
Destination Vegas	Ind	Peter Tomashek
Destiny Turns on the Radio	Ind	Steve Soles
Devil in a Blue Dress	TriStar	Elmer Bernstein
Diary of a Rapist	Fr/It/Span	Mario De Benito
Diary of a Seducer	Fr	Jean-Marie Senia

Die Hard With a Vengeance	Fox	Michael Kamen
Dillinger and Capone	Concorde	David & Eric Wurst
Disappearance of Kevin Johnson, The	Br	John Coda
Divas	Fox-TV	Stephen James Taylor
Dogfighters, The	Ind	Jimmie Haskell
Dolores Claiborne	Col	Danny Elfman
Don Juan DeMarco	New Line	Michael Kamen
Donor, The	Ind	Ronald J. Weiss
Donor Unknown	USA Net	David Bergeaud
Down Came a Blackbird	Showtime	Graeme Revell
Down, Out & Dangerous	USA Net	Mark Snow
Dr. Jekyll and Ms. Hyde	Ind	Mark McKenzie
Dracula: Dead and Loving It	Col	Hummie Mann
Dream Is a Wish Your Heart Makes, A: The Annette Funicello Story	CBS-TV	George Blondheim
Drunks	Ind	Joe Delia
Ebbie	Lifetime	Lawrence Shragge
Ecological Design: Inventing the Future	Ind	David Darling
Ed McBain's 87th Precinct	NBC-TV	Peter Bernstein
Eldorado	Can	Claude Lemothe
Element of Truth, An	CBS-TV	Billy Goldenberg
Elisa	Fr	Michel Colombier
Elisa	Fr	Serge Gainsbourg
Elisa	Fr	Zbigniew Preisner
Elle	Fr	Jorge Arriagada
Embrace of the Vampire	Ind	Joseph Williams
Empire Records	WB	Mitchell Leib
Englishman Who Went Up a Hill but Came Down a Mountain, The	Br	Stephen Endelman
Escape From Terror: The Teresa Stamper Story	NBC-TV	Philip Giffin
Escape to Witch Mountain	ABC-TV	Richard Mariun
Evil Obsession	Ind	Robert O. Ragland
Excentric Paradis	Fr	Christophe Demarthe
Excessive Force II: Force on Force	New Line	Kevin Kiner
Expect No Mercy	Can	Varouje
Expert, The	Orion	Ashley Irwin
Exquisite Tenderness	US/Ger	Christopher Franke
Eye for an Eye	Par	James Newton Howard
Eye of the Stalker: A Moment of Truth Movie	NBC-TV	Stacy Widelitz
Face on the Milk Carton, The	CBS-TV	Leonard Rosenman
Fair Game	WB	Mark Mancina
Fall of Saigon, The	Discovery	George Fenton
Fall Time	Ind	Hummie Mann
Falling From the Sky! Flight 174	ABC-TV	Ian Thomas
Falling for You	CBS-TV	Jonathan Goldsmith
Family Affair	Ind	George Duke
Family Divided, A	NBC-TV	Dana Kaproff
Family Reunion: A Relative Nightmare	ABC-TV	Robert Folk
Family of Cops	CBS-TV	Peter Manning Robinson
Far From Home: The Adventures of Yellow Dog	Fox	John Scott
Farmer & Chase	Ind	Tony Saunders

Fast	Fr	Krishna Levy
Fast Company	NBC-TV	Nicholas Pike
Father of the Bride, Part II	BV	Alan Silvestri
Fear, The	Ind	Robert O. Ragland
Feast at Midnight, A	Br	David A. Hughes
Feast at Midnight, A	Br	John Murphy
Feast of July	BV	Zbigniew Preisner
Federal Hill	Ind	David Bravo
Federal Hill	Ind	Bob Held
Feminine Touch, The	Ind	Tony Humecke
Fermo Posta Tinto Bass (P.O. Box Tinto Bass)	It	Riz Ortolani
Fiesta	Fr	Wim Mertens
Fight for Justice: The Nancy Conn Story	NBC-TV	Anthony Marinelli
Fighting for My Daughter	ABC-TV	Joseph Lo Duca
Final Cut, The	Br	Jim Parker
Fine Pena Mai (Life After Life)	It	Lamberto Coccioli
First Degree	Can	Bruce Fowler
First Knight	TriStar	Jerry Goldsmith
Fistful of Fingers, A	Br	Francois Evans
Flesh Suitcase	Ind	Mark Mothersbaugh
Flirt	US/Ger/Jap	Ned Rifle
Flirt	US/Ger/Jap	Jeffrey Taylor
Fluke	MGM/UA	Carlo Siliotto
Follow the River	ABC-TV	Ernest Troost
Forget Paris	Col	Marc Shaiman
Four Diamonds, The	Disney-TV	Phil Marshall
Four Rooms	Miramax	Combustible Edison
Four Rooms	Miramax	Esquivel
Frank and Jesse	HBO	Mark McKenzie
Frank and Ollie	BV	James Wesley Stemple
Frankie Starlight	Ind	Elmer Bernstein
Freaky Friday	ABC-TV	James McVay
Freaky Friday	ABC-TV	Lisa Harlow Stark
Free Willy 2: The Adventure Home	WB	Basil Poledouris
French Kiss	Fox	James Newton Howard
Friday	New Line	Frank Fitzpatrick
Friday	New Line	Hidden Faces
Friends at Last	CBS-TV	Mickey Erbe
Friends at Last	CBS-TV	Maribeth Solomon
From the Mixed-Up Files of Mrs Basil E. Frankweiler	ABC-TV	Ron Ramin
Full Body Massage	Showtime	Harry Gregson-Williams
Funny Bones	BV	John Altman
Gate of Heavenly Peace, The	Ind	Mark Pevsner
Gazon Maudit (French Twist)	Fr	Manuel Malou
Georgia	Ind	Steve Soles
Get Shorty	MGM/UA	John Lurie
Girl in the Cadillac	Ind	Anton Sanko
Girl With the Hungry Eyes, The	Ind	Paul Inder
Girl With the Hungry Eyes, The	Ind	Oscar O'Lochlainn
Go Now	Br	Alastair Gavin
God Drives a Pontiac	Ind	Wall of Noise
God's Army	Ind	David Williams

Gold Diggers: The Secret of Bear Mountain	Univ	Joel McNeely
Goldeneye	MGM/UA	Eric Serra
Good Old Boys, The	TNT	John McEuen
Goofy Movie, A	BV	Carter Burwell
Gordy	Miramax	Tom Bahler
Gramps	NBC-TV	Joseph Conlan
Grass Harp, The	Ind	Patrick Williams
Great Elephant Escape, The	ABC-TV	Bruce Rowland
Great Mom Swap, The	ABC-TV	David Lawrence
Grotesque, The	Br	Anne Dudley
Grumpier Old Men	WB	Alan Silvestri
Guantanamera	Sp/Cuba/Ger	Jose Nieto
Gumby: The Movie	Ind	Ozzie Ahlers
Gumby: The Movie	Ind	Marco D'Amrosio
Gumby: The Movie	Ind	Jerry Gerber
Hackers	MGM/UA	Simon Boswell
Half-Cocked	Ind	Michael Galinsky
Halloween: The Curse of Michael Myers	Ind	Alan Howarth
Hard Justice	Ind	Don Peake
Hart to Hart: Secrets of the Hart	NBC-TV	Arthur B. Rubinstein
Hart to Hart: Two Harts in ¾ Time	Fam Ch	Claude Foissy
Haunted	Br	Debbie Wiseman
Haunted World of Edward D. Wood Jr, The	Ind	Louis Febre
Haunting of Helen Walker, The	CBS-TV	Allyn Ferguson
Haut Bas Fragile (Up Down Fragile)	Fr	Francois Breant
Heading Home	Ind	Pat Irwin
Headless Body in Topless Bar	Ind	Charles P. Barnett
Headless Body in Topless Bar	Ind	Karyn Rachtman
Heartless	It	Aerosmith
Heat	WB	Elliot Goldenthal
Heaven Sent	Ind	Arlen Card
Heavy	Ind	Thurston Moore
Heavyweights	BV	J.A.C. Redford
Heidi Chronicles, The	TNT	David Shire
Hellfire	US/Rus	Vladimir Komorov
Her Deadly Rival	CBS-TV	George S. Clinton
Her Hidden Truth	NBC-TV	Patrick Williams
Here Come the Munsters	Fox-TV	Michael Skloff
Hideaway	TriStar	Trevor Jones
Holiday to Remember, A	CBS-TV	Des Jardins
Holiday to Remember, A	CBS-TV	Eric N. Robertson
Hologram Man	Ind	John Gonzalez
Homage	Ind	W. G. Snuffy Walden
Home for the Holidays	Par	Mark Isham
Horse for Danny, A	ABC-TV	Lawrence Shragge
Hotel Sorrento	Aut	Nerida Tyson-Chew
Hourglass	Ind	Chris Saranec
House	Can	Michael Timmins
House of Pain	Can	Earle Peach
How to Make an American Quilt	Univ	Thomas Newman
Hunted, The	Univ	Motofumi Yamaguchi
I Shot a Man in Vegas	Ind	Shark
If Someone Had Known	NBC-TV	Laura Karpman
Il Verificatore (The Meter Reader)	It	Peter Gordon

Il Verificatore (The Meter Reader)	It	John Martyn
Illegal in Blue	Orion	Steve Edwards
In Pursuit of Honor	HBO	John Debney
In the Bleak Midwinter	Br	Jimmy Yuill
In the Line of Duty: Hunt for Justice	NBC-TV	Mark Snow
In the Line of Duty: Kidnapped	NBC-TV	Christopher Franke
In the Mouth of Madness	New Line	John Carpenter
In the Mouth of Madness	New Line	Jim Lang
In the Name of Love: A Texas Tragedy	Fox-TV	Dennis McCarthy
In the Shadow of Evil	CBS-TV	Nicholas Pike
Incredibly True Adventures of Two Girls in Love, The	Ind	Terry Dame
Indian in the Cupboard, The	Par	Randy Edelman
Indian in the Cupboard, The	Par	Miles Goodman
Indictment: The McMartin Trial	HBO	Peter Rodgers Melnick
Infiltrator, The	Br	Hal Lindes
Inflammable	CBS-TV	Dennis McCarthy
Inner City	Fr	Base Enemy
Innocent Lies	Br/Fr	Alexandre Desplat
Innocent Sleep, The	Br	Mark Ayres
Insomnia	Ind	Amy Malina
Insomnia	Ind	Bobby Muzingo
Institute Benjamenta, The	Br	Lech Jankowski
Intimate Relations	Br/Can	Lawrence Shragge
Invaders, The	Fox-TV	Joseph Vitarelli
Io e il Re (The King and Me)	It	Antonio Di Pofi
Iron Eagle IV	Can	Paul Zaza
Irresistible Impulse	Ind	Alan Dermaderosian
It Takes Two	Ind	Ray Foote
It Takes Two	Ind	Sherman Foote
It Was Him or Us	CBS-TV	John Frizzell
Ivo the Genius	It	Patrizio Fariselli
Jack & Sarah	Br/Fr	Simon Boswell
Jack Brown, Genius	NewZea	Michael Scullion
Jade	Par	James Horner
Jake Lassiter: Justice on the Bayou	NBC-TV	Mike Post
James A. Michener's "Texas"	ABC-TV	Lee Holdridge
Jane Austen's "Pride and Prejudice"	BBC-TV	Carl Davis
Jean Seberg, American Actress	Ger/Swiss	Martial Solal
Jefferson in Paris	BV	Richard Robbins
Jeffrey	Orion	Stephen Endelman
Jeniapo	Can	Philip Glass
Jerky Boys, The	BV	Ira Newborn
Joe & Joe	Ind	Edgar Struble
Joe's Rotten World	Ind	Murielle Hamilton
Johnny Mnemonic	TriStar	Brad Fiedel
Johnny's Girl	ABC-TV	Lawrence Shragge
Johns	Ind	Charles Brown
Johns	Ind	Danny Caron
Joint Adventure	Ind	Raymond Loewy
Joseph	TNT	Marco Frisina
Journey	CBS-TV	Patrick Williams
Journey of August King, The	Miramax	Stephen Endelman
Judge Dredd	BV	Alan Silvestri

Judith Krantz's "Dazzle"	CBS-TV	Vladimir Cosma
Jumanji	TriStar	James Horner
Jungleground	Can	Varouje
Jury Duty	TriStar	David Kitay
Just Cause	WB	James Newton Howard
Kansas	ABC-TV	John Debney
Kicking and Screaming	Ind	Phil Marshall
Kid in King Arthur's Court, A	BV	J.A.C. Redford
Kidnapped	Fam Ch	Stanislas Syrewicz
Kids	Ind	Lou Barlow
Kids	Ind	John Davis
Kids of the Round Table	Can	Normand Corbiel
Killer: A Journal of Murder	Ind	Graeme Revell
Kingdom, The	Dan	Joachim Holbek
Kingfish: A Story of Huey P. Long	TNT	Patrick Williams
Kiss of Death	Fox	Trevor Jones
Kissing Miranda	Ind	John Graham
Kissinger and Nixon	TNT	Jonathan Goldsmith
Knuckleball	US/Br	Mike Hewer
Kurt Vonnegut's "Harrison Bergeron"	Showtime	Louis Natale
L'Amore Molesto	It	Steve Lacy
L'Amour Conjugal (Conjugal Duty)	Fr	Sonia Wieder Atherton
L'Annee Juliette	Fr	Caroline Petit
L'appat (The Bait)	Fr	Philippe Haim
L'uomo Proiettile (The Human Cannonball)	It	Ennio Morricone
La Ceremonie (A Judgment in Stone)	Fr/Ger	Matthieu Chabrol
La Cite des Enfantes Perdus	Fr/Sp/Ger	Angelo Badalamenti
La Fille Sueve (A Single Girl)	Fr	Kvarteto Mesta Prahi
La Fleur de mon Secret	Sp/Fr	Alberto Iglesias
La Passion Turca (Turkish Passion)	Sp	Jose Nieto
La Promesse (The Promise)	Ger/Fr	Jurgen Knieper
La Scuola (School)	It/Fr	Bill Frisell
La Seconda Volta (The Second Time)	It/Fr	Franco Piersanti
Lady Killer, The	CBS-TV	Mickey Erbe
Lady Killer, The	CBS-TV	Maribeth Solomon
Land and Freedom	Br/Sp/Ger	George Fenton
Land of Milk and Honey	Ind	Christopher Hedge
Larry McMurtry's "Streets of Laredo"	CBS-TV	David Shire
Last Gasp	Ind	Joseph Williams
Last Man Standing	Ind	Louis Febre
Last of the Dog Men	Ind	David Arnold
Last Summer in the Hamptons	Ind	Rick Baitz
Last Supper, The	Ind	Mark Mothersbaugh
Last Word, The	Showtime	Paul Buckmaster
Le Confessional (The Confessional)	Can/Br/Fr	Sasha Puttnam
Le Fabuleux Destin de Madame Petlet	Fr	Jorge Arriagada
Le Fils de Gascone (The Son of Gascone)	Fr	Angelo Zurzulo
Le Huitieme Jour (The Eighth Day)	Fr	Pierre Van Dormael
Le Hussard sur le Toit (The Horseman on the Roof)	Fr	Jean-Claude Petit
Le Petit Garcon	Fr	Philippe Sarde
Le Plus Bel Age ... (Those Were the Days...)	Fr	Alexandre Desplat
Le Roi de Paris	Fr	Quentin Damamme
Leaving Las Vegas	MGM/UA	Mike Figgis

Legacy of Sin: The William Coit Story	Fox-TV	Marty Davich
Len Deighton's "Bullet to Beijing"	Br	Rick Wakeman
Les Anges Gardiens (Guardian Angels)	Fr	Eric Levi
Les Apprentis (The Apprentices)	Fr	Philippe Eidel
Les Caprices d'un Fleuve	Fr	Rene Marc Bini
Les Enfants de Lumiere	Fr	Michel Legrand
Les Grands Ducs (The Grand Dukes)	Fr	Jean-Claude Nachon
Les Milles	Fr/Ger	Alexandre Desplat
Les Miserables	Fr	Didier Barbelivien
Les Miserables	Fr	Francis Lai
Les Miserables	Fr	Michel Legrand
Les Miserables	Fr	Philippe Sarde
Les Rendez-vous de Paris	Fr	Sebastien Erms
Les Trois Freres (Three Brothers)	Fr	Olivier Bernard
Les Trois Freres (Three Brothers)	Fr	Didier Bourdon
Les Truffes (Two Jerks and a Pig)	Fr	Benjamin Raffaelli
Letter to My Killer	USA Net	Mason Daring
Liability Crisis	Ind	Francine Trester
Lie Down With Dogs	Miramax	Jellybean Benitez
Life of Harry Dare, The	Aut	David Hirschfelder
Lisbon Story	Ger	Jurgen Knieper
Little Indian, Big City	Fr	Manu Katche
Little Lord Fauntleroy	BBC-TV	Michael Omer
Little Princess	WB	Patrick Doyle
Live Boat	Can	Sweet Dick Willie
Live Nude Girls	Ind	Anton Sanko
Live Wire: Human Timebomb	Ind	Itai Haber
Living in Oblivion	Ind	Jim Farmer
Liz: The Elizabeth Taylor Story	NBC-TV	Ken Thorne
Lo Schermo a Tre Punte	It	Ennio Morricone
Lord of Illusions	MGM/UA	Simon Boswell
Losing Isaiah	Par	Mark Isham
Lotto Land	Ind	Holmes Brothers
Love and Betrayal: The Mia Farrow Story	Fox-TV	David Michael Frank
Love and Happiness	Ind	Cameron Coulter
Loving	Br	Shaun Davey
Low Life, The	Ind	Bill Boll
Mad Dogs and Englishmen	Br	Barrie Guard
Mad Love	BV	Andy Roberts
Madame Butterfly	Fr	Giacomo Puccini
Maddening, The	Ind	Peter Manning Robinson
Madness of King George, The	Br	George Frederic Handel
Magic in the Water	TriStar	David Schwartz
Major Payne	Univ	Craig Safan
Making of Maps, The	Br	Mark Thomas
Malicious	Ind	Graeme Coleman
Mallrats	Ind	Ira Newborn
Man in the Attic, The	Showtime	Louis Natale
Man Who Wouldn't Die, The	ABC-TV	David Shire
Man With a Gun	Ind	George Blondheim
Man With the Perfect Swing, The	Ind	Paul English
Man of the House	BV	Mark Mancina
Man of the Year	Ind	Peitor Angell
Mandela	Ind	Hugh Masekela

Mandela	Ind	Cedric Samson
Mangler, The	New Line	Barrington Pheloung
Manhattan Merenge	Ind	Lalo Schifrin
Marcindo nel Buio (Marching in the Dark)	It	Pino Donaggio
Margaret's Museum	Can/Br	Milan Kymlicka
Marie de Nazareth	Fr	Olivier Llibourty
Marie-Louise	Fr	Alexandre Desplat
Martin Chuzzlewit	BBC-TV	Geoffrey Burgon
Maya Lin: A Strong Clear Vision	Ind	Charles Bernstein
Mercy	Ind	Rolfe Kent
Midwife's Tale, The	Ind	John O'Kennedy
Mighty Morphin Power Rangers: The Movie	Fox	Graeme Revell
Mirage	Ind	David Richard Campbell
Modern Affair, A	Ind	Jan Hammer
Mommy	Ind	Richard Lowry
Money Train	Col	Mark Mancina
Month by the Lake, A	Br	Nicola Piovani
Moonlight and Valentino	Ind	Howard Shore
Mortal Kombat	New Line	George S. Clinton
Mosquito	Ind	Randall & Allen Lynch
Motel	Can	Vladimir Ulman
Mother's Gift, A	CBS-TV	Lee Holdridge
Mother's Prayer, A	USA Net	Tom Scott
Mr. Holland's Opus	BV	Michael Kamen
Mrs. Munck	Showtime	Leonard Rosenman
Murder in the First	WB	Christopher Young
Murderous Intent	CBS-TV	David Shire
Mushrooms	Aut	Paul Grabowsky
Mute Witness	Br	Wilbert Hirsch
My Antonia	USA Net	David Shire
My Brother's Keeper	CBS-TV	David Shire
My Family/Mi Familia	New Line	Pepe Avila
My Mother's Courage	Ger/Br	Julian Nott
My Mother's Courage	Ger/Br	Simon Verhoeven
Naomi & Wynonna: Love Can Build a Bridge	NBC-TV	J.A.C. Redford
National Lampoon's Favorite Deadly Sins	Showtime	Adam Roth
National Lampoon's Favorite Deadly Sins	Showtime	Christopher Tyng
National Lampoon's Senior Trip	New Line	Steve Bartek
Near Room, The	Br	James Grant
Near Room, The	Br	Paul McGeechan
Nella Mischia (In the Thick of It)	It	Tiziano Popoli
Nelly & Mr. Arnaud	Fr/It/Ger	Philippe Sarde
Nemici d'Infanzia (Childhood Enemies)	It	Nicola Piovani
Neon Bible, The	Br	Robert Lockhart
Nervous Energy	Br	Stephen Warbeck
Net, The	Col	Mark Isham
Never Say Never: The Deidre Hall Story	ABC-TV	James DiPasquale
Never Talk to Strangers	Can/US	Pino Donaggio
New Jersey Drive	Ind	Wendy Blackstone
Nick of Time	Par	Arthur B. Rubinstein
Night Eyes 4: Fatal Passion	Ind	Patrick Seymour
Night of the Scarecrow	Ind	Jim Manzie

Nine Months	Fox	Hans Zimmer
Nixon	BV	John Williams
Normal Life	Ind	Robert F. McNaughton
Not Our Son	CBS-TV	Dan Foliart
Notes From Underground	Ind	Mark Governor
Nothing But the Truth	CBS-TV	Joseph Vitarelli
Nothing Personal	Br/Ire	Philip Appleby
Nothing to Lose	Ind	Chris Hajian
Now and Then	New Line	Cliff Eidelman
O. J. Simpson Story, The	Fox-TV	Harald Kloser
Old Curiosity Shop, The	Disney-TV	Mason Daring
Once in a Blue Moon	Can	Daryl Bennett
Once in a Blue Moon	Can	Jim Guttridge
One Night Stand	Concorde	David Shire
Open Season	Ind	Marvin Hamlisch
Operation Dumbo Drop	BV	David Newman
Original Sins	CBS-TV	Gary Chang
Orson Welles: The One-Man Band	Ger/Fr/Swiss	Simon Cloquet
Othello	Col	Charlie Mole
Other Mother, The: A Moment of Truth Movie	NBC-TV	Mark Snow
Other Voices, Other Rooms	Ind	Chris Hajian
Other Woman, The	CBS-TV	Peter Manning Robinson
Out of Annie's Past	USA Net	Charles Bernstein
Out of Sync	Ind	Steve Tyrell
Out There	Ind	Frankie Blue
Out There	Ind	Deborah Holland
Outbreak	WB	James Newton Howard
Outraged Fugitive	Ind	Steve Edwards
Outside the Law	Ind	Blake Leyh
Painted Hero	Ind	Rick Marotta
Palermo--Milano Solo Andata	It	Pino Donaggio
Palookaville	Ind	Rachel Portman
Panther	Ind	Stanley Clarke
Paris Was a Woman	Br	Janette Mason
Pasolini: An Italian Crime	It/Fr	Ennio Morricone
Passion of Darkly Noon, The	Br/Ger/Belg	Nick Bicat
Past the Bleachers	ABC-TV	Stewart Levin
Pebble and the Penguin, The	MGM/UA	Barry Manilow
Pebble and the Penguin, The	MGM/UA	Bruce Sussman
Pebble and the Penguin, The	MGM/UA	Mark Watters
Peggio di Cosi si Muore	It/Fr/Sp	Paolo Silvestri
Perry Mason Mystery: The Case of the Jealous Jokester	NBC-TV	Dick DeBenedictis
Personal Journey With Martin Scorsese, A	Br/US	Elmer Bernstein
Persuasion	BBC-TV	Jeremy Sams
Pharaoh's Army	Ind	Charles Ellis
Pharaoh's Army	Ind	Vince Emmett
Philosophy in the Bedroom	Ind	Robert Morgan Fisher
Phoenix and the Magic Carpet, The	Par	Alan Parker
Piano Lesson, The	CBS-TV	Dwight Andrews
Piano Lesson, The	CBS-TV	Stephen James Taylor
Picture Bride	Ind	Mark Adler
Picture Perfect	ABC-TV	Mickey Erbe

Picture Perfect	ABC-TV	Maribeth Solomon
Pie in the Sky	New Line	Michael Convertino
Place in the World, A	Ind	Emilio Kauderer
Plato's Run	Ind	Robert O. Ragland
Pocahontas	BV	Alan Menken
Poco Loco	Ind	Joel Lindheimer
Poison Ivy 2: Lily	New Line	Joseph Williams
Poliziotti (Policemen)	It/Fr	Oscar Prudente
Pompatus of Love, The	Ind	John Hill
Possession of Michael D, The	Fox-TV	John McCarthy
Powder	BV	Jerry Goldsmith
Power Within, The	Ind	Jim Halfpenny
Price of Love, The	Fox	Tim Truman
Prince for a Day	NBC-TV	Jud J. Friedman
Problem Child 3: Junior in Love	NBC-TV	David Michael Frank
Professional, The	Col	Eric Serra
Project Shadowchaser 3000	New Line	Steve Edwards
Prophecy, The	Ind	David Williams
Proteus	Br	David A. Hughes
Proteus	Br	John Murphy
Pugili (Boxers)	It	Pasquale Filasto
Pullman Paradise	Fr	Yves Cerf
Pyromaniac's Love Story, A	BV	Rachel Portman
Quick and the Dead, The	TriStar	Alan Silvestri
Raging Angels	Ind	Terry Plumeri
Ranger, the Cook and a Hole in the Sky, The	ABC-TV	Lawrence Shragge
Ray Alexander: A Menu for Murder	NBC-TV	Dick DeBenedictis
Reckless	Goldwyn	Stephen Endelman
Red Ribbon Blues	Ind	John Frizzell
Redneck	Ind	Michael Pollack
Redwood Curtain	ABC-TV	Lawrence Shragge
Remember Me	CBS-TV	Domenic Troiano
Rent-a-Kid	Viacom	Ron Ramin
Restoration	Miramax	James Newton Howard
Return of Hunter: Everyone Walks in L.A., The	NBC-TV	Joseph Conlan
Return of the Texas Chainsaw Massacre, The	Ind	Wayne Bell
Richard III	Br	Trevor Jones
Ricky Rosen's Bar Mitzvah	Ind	Ron Manus
Ricky Rosen's Bar Mitzvah	Ind	David White
Riders in the Storm	Ind	Bob DeMarco
Rigoletto	Ind	Kurt Bestor
Rob Roy	MGM/UA	Carter Burwell
Robin Cook's "Virus"	NBC-TV	Garry Schyman
Rockford Files: A Blessing in Disguise, The	CBS-TV	Pete Carpenter
Rockford Files: A Blessing in Disguise, The	CBS-TV	Mike Post
Romanzo du un Giovane Povero	It/Fr	Armando Trovajoli
Roommates	BV	Elmer Bernstein
Rough Magic	Br/It	Richard Hartley
Round Eyes in the Middle Kingdom	Ind	Todd Boekelheide
Rude	Can	Aaron Davis
Rude	Can	John Lang
Ruffian Hearts	Br	Michael Marra
Run of the Country, The	Br/Ire	Cynthia Miller

S.P.Q.R.: 2,000 and a Half Years Ago	It	Federico De Robertis
Sabrina	Par	John Williams
Sacred Hearts	Ind	Kerry Kelekovich
Safe	Ind	Ed Tomney
Sahara	Aut	Barry MacDonald
Sahara	Aut	Lawrence Stone
Saigon Baby	Br	Wolum Woolf
Saints and Sinners	Ind	Steven Miller
Saints and Sinners	Ind	Tom Varner
Saltwater Moose	Can	Paul Zaza
Salvaged Lives	Ind	Amotz Plessner
Sanctuary	Aut	Christopher Gordon
Savage Hearts	Ind	Dominic Crawford-Collins
Saved by the Light	Fox-TV	Patrick Williams
Say Yes	Fr	Philippe Sarde
Scarlet Letter, The	BV	John Barry
Scorpion Spring	Ind	Lalo Schifrin
Screamers	US/Can/Jap	Normand Corbiel
Search and Destroy	Ind	Elmer Bernstein
Season of Hope, A	CBS-TV	Ken Thorne
Secretary, The	CBS-TV	Louis Febre
Secrets	ABC-TV	Lawrence Shragge
Secrets & Lies	Br	Andrew Dickson
Seduced and Betrayed	NBC-TV	Mark Snow
See Jane Run	ABC-TV	James DiPasquale
Segreto di Stato (State Secret)	It	Pino Donaggio
Selvaggi (Savages)	It	Federico De Robertis
Sense and Sensibility	Col	Patrick Doyle
Separate Lives	Ind	William Olvis
September Songs: The Music of Kurt Weill	Ind	Kurt Weill
Serpent's Lair	Ind	Vinny Golia
Serving in Silence: The Margarethe Cammermeyer Story	NBC-TV	David Shire
Set-Up, The	Showtime	Conrad Pope
Seven	New Line	Howard Shore
Sex Is a Four-Letter Word	Aut	Frank Strangio
Shadow of a Doubt	NBC-TV	Jane Ira Bloom
Shame II: The Secret	Life	Jeff Fair
Shame II: The Secret	Lifetime	Starr Parodi
Shamrock Conspiracy, The	Syn	Ken Harrison
Sharon's Secret	USA Net	Philip Giffin
She Fought Alone	NBC-TV	Pray for Rain
She Stood Alone: The Tailhook Scandal	ABC-TV	Peter Bernstein
Shinjuku Boys	Br	Nigel Hawks
Shooter, The	US/Br/Sp	Stefano Mainetti
Shotgun Freeway: Drives Through Lost L.A.	Ind	Bob Greemore
Show, The	Ind	Stanley Clarke
Showgirls	MGM/UA	David A. Stewart
Sidney Sheldon's "Nothing Lasts Forever"	CBS-TV	Lee Holdridge
Silence of Adultery, The	Lifetime	Mickey Erbe
Silence of Adultery, The	Lifetime	Maribeth Solomon
Silver Strand	Showtime	Joseph Conlan
Simon & Simon: In Trouble Again	CBS-TV	Joseph Conlan
Sister-in-Law, The	USA Net	Richard Bellis

Sketch Artist II: Hands That See	Showtime	Tim Truman
Skin Deep	Can	Kathryn Moses
Slam Dunk Ernest	BV	Mark Adler
Slave of Dreams	Showtime	Christopher Tyng
Sleep, Baby, Sleep	ABC-TV	Don Davis
Small Faces	Br	John Keane
Smoke	Miramax	Rachel Portman
Solitaire for 2	Br	David A. Hughes
Solitaire for 2	Br	John Murphy
Solomon and Sheba	Showtime	David Kitay
Some Kind of Life	Br	David Ferguson
Something to Talk About	WB	Hans Zimmer
Sostiene Pereira (According to Pereira)	It/Fr	Ennio Morricone
Soul Survivor	Can	John McCarthy
Space Marines	Ind	Randy Miller
Species	MGM/UA	Christopher Young
Spenser: A Savage Place	Lifetime	Brad MacDonald
Sphinx, The	Can	Francois Asselin
Spike of Love	Can	Norman Orenstein
Spring Fling!	ABC-TV	Lex De Azevedo
Stand Off	Can	Jonathan Goldsmith
Star Trek: Voyager	UPN-TV	Jay Chattaway
Stars Fell on Henrietta, The	WB	David Benoit
Steal Big, Steal Little	Ind	William Olvis
Steal, The	Br	Barry Kirsch
Stephen King's "The Langoliers"	ABC-TV	Vladimir Horonzky
Stolen Innocence	CBS-TV	Joseph Conlan
Stonewall	BBC-TV	Michael Kamen
Strange Days	Fox	Graeme Revell
Stranger Beside Me, The	ABC-TV	David Mansfield
Stranger Beside Me, The	ABC-TV	Bruce Miller
Stranger in Town, A	CBS-TV	Mark Snow
Streetlife	Br	John Hardy
Stuart Saves His Family	Par	Marc Shaiman
Student Body	Ind	Alex Wurman
Sudden Death	Univ	John Debney
Sugartime	HBO	Sidney James
Surrogate, The	ABC-TV	Nicholas Pike
Suspect Device	Concorde	Christopher Lennertz
Sweet Nothing	Ind	Steven M. Stern
Tad	Fam Ch	George S. Clinton
Tails You Live, Heads You're Dead	USA Net	David Michael Frank
Taken Alive	Ind	Clif Magness
Tale of Love, A	Ind	Greg Goodman
Tales From the Crypt Presents Demon Knight	Univ	Edward Shearmur
Tales From the Crypt Presents Demon Knight	Univ	Danny Elfman
Tales From the Hood	Ind	Christopher Young
Tall Tale: The Unbelievable Adventures of Pecos Bill	BV	Randy Edelman
Tall, Dark and Deadly	USA Net	Joseph Vitarelli
Tank Girl	MGM/UA	Graeme Revell
Tarantella	Ind	Norman Moll

Tattoo Boy	Ind	Daren Bell
Tecumseh: The Last Warrior	TNT	David Shire
Temptress	Ind	Michael Stearns
Tennessee Williams' "A Streetcar Named Desire"	CBS-TV	David Mansfield
Terror in the Shadows	NBC-TV	Chris Boardman
Texas Justice	ABC-TV	Mark Snow
Texas Payback	Ind	Jim Halfpenny
Thin Ice	Br	Claire Van Kampen
Things to Do in Denver When You're Dead	Miramax	Michael Convertino
Three Wishes	Ind	Cynthia Miller
Tie That Binds, The	BV	Graeme Revell
Tie-Died: Rock 'n Roll's Most Dedicated Fans	Ind	Peter Fish
TimeMaster	Ind	Harry Manfredini
Tin Soldier, The	Showtime	Benedikt Bryden
To Die For	Col	Danny Elfman
To the Limit	Ind	Jim Halfpenny
To the Limit	Ind	Jeff Lass
To Wong Foo, Thanks for Everything! Julie Newmar	Univ	Rachel Portman
Tom Clancy's "Op Center"	NBC-TV	Patrick Williams
Tom and Huck	BV	Stephen Endelman
Tommy & the Ghost	Ind	Fred Weinberg
Tommy Boy	Par	David Newman
Tommy Boy	Par	Steve Soles
Too Pure	Ind	Stephane Meer
Total Eclipse	Br/Fr/Belg	Jan A.P. Kaczmarek
Toy Story	BV	Randy Newman
Tracks of a Killer	Ind	Barron Abramovitch
Trail of Tears	NBC-TV	Richard Marvin
Trancers V: Sudden Death	Ind	Gary Fry
Trapped in Space	SciFi	Jay Gruska
Trial by Fire	ABC-TV	Mark Snow
Trinity and Beyond	Ind	William T. Stromberg
Triplecross	Showtime	Larry Brown
Triplecross	Showtime	Daniel Stein
Truman	HBO	David Mansfield
Tunnel Vision	Aut	David Hirschfelder
Tuskegee Airmen, The	HBO	Lee Holdridge
Twilight Highway	Ind	Joe Delia
Two Bits	Miramax	Jane Musky
Two Bits & Pepper	Ind	Louis Febre
Two Deaths	Br	Hans Zimmer
Two Guys Talkin' About Girls	Ind	Richard Gibbs
Two Much (Loco de Amor)	US/Sp	Michel Camilo
Two Nudes Bathing	Br	Jocelyn West
Tyson	HBO	Stewart Copeland
Un Animal, Deux Animaux	Fr	Philippe Hersant
Un Eroe Borghese	It/Fr	Pino Donaggio
Un heros tres discret (A Self-Made Hero)	Fr	Alexandre Desplat
Uncle From Brooklyn, The	It	Joe Vitale
Under Siege 2: Dark Territory	WB	Basil Poledouris
Under the Hula Moon	Ind	Hidden Faces

Underground	Fr/Ger/Hung	Goran Bregovic
Underneath, The	Ind	Cliff Martinez
Une Femme Francaise	Fr/Br/Ger	Patrick Doyle
Unspoken Truth, The	NBC-TV	Mark Snow
Unstrung Heroes	BV	Thomas Newman
Uomini, Uomini, Uomini (Men, Men, Men)	It	Manuel De Sica
Usual Suspects, The	Ind	John Ottman
Vacant Possession	Aut	Alistair Jones
Vacanze di Natale '95	It	Manuel De Sica
Vampire in Brooklyn	Par	J. Peter Robinson
Van, The	Br	Eric Clapton
Van, The	Br	Richard Hartley
Venice Bound	Ind	Eric Kopatz
Venice Bound	Ind	James O'Brien
Viaggi di Nozze (Honeymoon Trips)	It	Fabio Liberatori
Video Fool for Love	Aut	Anthony Partos
Village of the Damned	Univ	John Carpenter
Village of the Damned	Univ	Dave Davies
Virtuosity	Par	Christopher Young
Visitors of the Night	NBC-TV	Mickey Erbe
Visitors of the Night	NBC-TV	Maribeth Solomon
Viva San Isidoro!	It	Daniele Furlanti
Voices	Br	Elliot Goldenthal
Voodoo	Ind	Keith Bilderbeck
Vow to Kill, A	USA Net	John Keane
W.E.I.R.D. World	Fox-TV	Nicholas Pike
Wacky Adventures of Dr. Boris and Nurse Shirley	Ind	Jan Castor
Waiting to Exhale	Fox	Kenneth "Babyface" Edmonds
Walk in the Clouds, A	Fox	Leo Brower
Walk in the Clouds, A	Fox	Maurice Jarre
Walking Dead, The	Ind	Gary Chang
Walton Wedding, A	CBS-TV	John Rubinstein
War Stories	NewZea	Jonathon Besser
Waterworld	Univ	James Newton Howard
Weekend in the Country, A	Ind	Patrick Williams
Welcome II the Terrordome	Br	David A. Hughes
Welcome II the Terrordome	Br	John Murphy
Welcome to the Dollhouse	Ind	Jill Wisoff
Wes Craven Presents Mind Ripper	Ind	J. Peter Robinson
West Side Waltz, The	CBS-TV	Patrick Williams
Wharf Rat, The	Showtime	Mervyn Warren
When Night Is Falling	Can	Lesley Barber
When the Darkman Calls	USA Net	David Michael Frank
When the Vows Break	Lifetime	Glenn Morley
Where's the Money, Noreen?	USA Net	Richard Bellis
While You Were Sleeping	BV	Randy Edelman
White Dwarf	Fox-TV	Stewart Copeland
White Man's Burden	Ind	Stanley Clarke
White Man's Burden	Ind	Howard Shore
White Tiger	Ind	Graeme Coleman
Whose Daughter Is She?	CBS-TV	John Frizzell

Wife, The	Ind	Lodovico Sorret
Wigstock: The Movie	Ind	Peter Fish
Wigstock: The Movie	Ind	Robert Reale
Wild Bill	MGM	Van Dyke Parks
Wild Bill: Hollywood Maverick	Turner	David Bell
Witchcraft 7: Judgment Hour	Ind	Miriam Cutler
Without Air	Ind	Kennard Ramsey
Woman of Independent Means, A	NBC-TV	Laura Karpman
Women of Spring Break, The	CBS-TV	Larry Brown
World of Jacques Demy, The	Fr	Michel Legrand
Wounded Heart	USA Net	James Legg
Young at Heart	CBS-TV	Mason Daring
Young at Hearts	Ind	Mario Grigorov
Young Poisoner's Handbook, The	Br/Ger	Rob Lane
Young Poisoner's Handbook, The	Br/Ger	Frank Strobel
Zigrail	Can	John Zorn
Zooman	Showtime	Daniel Licht

1996

101 Dalmatians	BV	Michael Kamen
2 Days in the Valley	MGM/UA	Anthony Marinelli
3	It	Manuel De Sica
40,000 Years of Dreaming	Aut	Carl Vine
A Spasso nel Tempo (Adrift in Time)	It	Manuel De Sica
Aaron Gillespie Will Make You a Star	Ind	Andrea Centazzo
Abducted: A Father's Love	NBC-TV	Joseph Conlan
Abduction of Innocence	NBC-TV	Stacy Widelitz
Abduction, The	Lifetime	Fred Mollin
Adventures of Pinocchio, The	New Line	Rachel Portman
After Jimmy	CBS-TV	Patrick Williams
Aladdin and the King of Thieves	BV	Carl Johnson
Aladdin and the King of Thieves	BV	Randy Petersen
Aladdin and the King of Thieves	BV	Kevin Quinn
Aladdin and the King of Thieves	BV	Mark Watters
Alaska	Ind	Reg Powell
Albino Alligator	Miramax	Michael Brook
All Dogs Go to Heaven 2	MGM/UA	Barry Mann
All Dogs Go to Heaven 2	MGM/UA	Mark Watters
All Dogs Go to Heaven 2	MGM/UA	Cynthia Weill
All of Them Witches	Ind	Gabriel Gonzalez
All Over Me	Ind	Miki Navazio
All She Ever Wanted	ABC-TV	James DiPasquale
All's Fair in Love & War	Ind	Gene Ober
American Beer	Can	Mark Shields
American Buffalo	Goldwyn	Thomas Newman
American Strays	Ind	John Graham
Andersonville	TNT	Gary Chang
Angel Flight Down	ABC-TV	John D'Andrea
Angel Flight Down	ABC-TV	Cory Lerios
Angel of Pennsylvania Avenue, The	Fam Ch	Simon Kendall
Angel of Pennsylvania Avenue, The	Fam Ch	Al Rogers
Angelo, Fredo and Romeo	Can	Denis Larochelle
Anna Oz	Fr/It/Swiss	Steve Turre

Apollo 11	Fam Ch	Phil Marshall
Arrival, The (aka Shockwave)	Orion	Arthur Kempel
Art of Remembrance: Simon Wiesenthal, The	Ger	John Zorn
Arthur Rimbaud	Fr/Can	Gabriel Yared
Asaltar los Cielos (Attacking the Skies)	Sp	Alberto Iglesias
Associate, The	Ind	Christopher Tyng
Asylum	Can	Alan Williams
Babysitter's Seduction, The	NBC-TV	Jan Hammer
Bachelor's Baby, A	CBS-TV	Ray Bunch
Bad Moon	WB	Daniel Licht
Bambola	It/Sp/Fr	Lucio Dalla
Bandwagon	Ind	Greg Kendall
Barb Wire	Ind	Michel Colombier
Barbara Taylor Bradford's "Everything to Gain"	CBS-TV	James DiPasquale
Basquait	Miramax	John Cale
Bastard Out of Carolina	Showtime	Van Dyke Parks
Battle Over Citizen Kane, The	Ind	Brian Keane
Beaumarchais l'insolent	Fr	Jean-Claude Petit
Beautiful Girls	Miramax	David A. Stewart
Beautiful Thing	Br	John Altman
Beavis and Butt-Head Do America	Par	John Frizzell
Bed of Roses	New Line	Michael Convertino
Before and After	BV	Howard Shore
Belly Talkers	Ind	Jack Maeby
Bermuda Triangle	ABC-TV	Louis Fagenson
Bernie	Fr	Ramon Pepin
Beyond the Call	Showtime	George S. Clinton
Bible and Gun Club, The	Ind	Shawn Patterson
Big Bully	WB	David Newman
Big Squeeze, The	Ind	Mark Mothersbaugh
Billal	Aut	Jan Preston
Bio-Dome	MGM/UA	Andrew Gross
Birdcage, The	MGM/UA	Jonathan Tunick
Bit of Scarlet, A	Br	John Eacott
Bitter Herbs and Honey	Aut	Martin Friedel
Black for Remembrance	Fr/Ger/Swiss	Gabriel Yared
Black Sheep	Par	William Ross
Blood and Wine	Fox	Michael Lorenc
Bloodhounds	USA Net	John Frizzell
Bloodhounds II	USA Net	Charles Bernstein
Blue Arrow, The	It/Swiss	Paolo Conte
Blue Rodeo	CBS-TV	Laura Karpman
Bob's Weekend	Br	Don Gould
Bob's Weekend	Br	David Mindel
Bogus	WB	Marc Shaiman
Born Free: A New Adventure	ABC-TV	David Michael Frank
Bottle Rocket	Col	Mark Mothersbaugh
Bound	Ind	Don Davis
Box of Moonlight	Ind	Jim Farmer
Box of Moonlight	Ind	John Lurie
Boy From Mercury, The	Ire/Fr/Br	Stephen McKeon
Boys	BV	Stewart Copeland

Boys Club, The	Can	Michael Timmins
Boys Next Door, The	CBS-TV	John Kander
Brassed Off	Br	Trevor Jones
Breaking Through	ABC-TV	James McVay
Breathing Room	Ind	Pat Erwin
Broken Arrow	Fox	Hans Zimmer
Broken English	NewZea	Murray Grindlay
Broken English	NewZea	Murray McNabb
Broken Giant, The	Ind	Will Oldham
Brothers of the Frontier	ABC-TV	Gene Hobson
Brother's Promise: The Dan Jansen Story, A	CBS-TV	Patrick Williams
Bruno's Waiting in the Car	It	Antonio Di Pofi
Brylcreem Boys, The	Br	Richard Hartley
Buckminster Fuller: Thinking Out Loud	Ind	Brian Keane
Bulletproof	Univ	Elmer Bernstein
Buried Secrets	NBC-TV	J. Peter Robinson
Bwana	Sp	Jose Nieto
Cable Guy, The	Col	John Ottman
Cadillac Ranch	Ind	Christopher Tyng
Cafe Society	Showtime	Raymond DeFelitta
Cagney & Lacey IV: True Convictions	CBS-TV	Ron Ramin
Calm at Sunset	CBS-TV	Ernest Troost
Canterville Ghost, The	ABC-TV	Ernest Troost
Captain Conan	Fr	Oswald D'Andrea
Captains Courageous	Fam Ch	Claude Destardins
Captains Courageous	Fam Ch	Eric N. Robertson
Captive Heart: The James Mink Story	CBS-TV	Neil Smolar
Care and Handling of Roses, The	CBS-TV	Dennis McCarthy
Care of the Spitfire Grill	Ind	James Horner
Carla's Song	Br/Ger/Sp	George Fenton
Carpool	WB	John Debney
Carried Away	Ind	Bruce Broughton
Case for Life, A	ABC-TV	Dana Kaproff
Cashing In	Ind	William Anderson
Caught	Ind	Chris Botti
Caught in the Act	Br	Simon May
Cavafy	Gr/Fr	Vangelis
Celluloide	It	Manuel De Sica
Celtic Pride	BV	Basil Poledouris
Chain Reaction	Fox	Jerry Goldsmith
Chain, The	Ind	Kendall Schmidt
Chamane	Fr/Rus	Jean-Pierre Drouet
Chamber, The	Univ	Carter Burwell
Changing Habits	Ind	David McHugh
Chasing Amy	Miramax	David Pirner
Chasing the Dragon	Lifetime	Wendy Blackstone
Chef in Love, A	Fr	Goran Bregovic
Cherokee Kid, The	HBO	Stanley Clarke
Children of the Revolution	Aut	Nigel Westlake
Christmas Every Day	Fam Ch	Billy Goldenberg
Christmas in My Hometown	CBS-TV	Dana Kaproff
Christmas Tree, The	ABC-TV	David Benoit
Citizen Ruth	Miramax	Rolfe Kent
City Hall	Col	Jerry Goldsmith

City of Industry	Ind	Stephen Endelman
Closer and Closer	Lifetime	Mickey Erbe
Closer and Closer	Lifetime	Maribeth Solomon
Co-Ed Call Girl	CBS-TV	James McVay
Cockroach That Ate Cincinnati, The	Can	Kurt Swinghammer
Code Name: Wolverine	Fox-TV	Christopher Franke
Cold Equations, the	Can	Paul Rabjohns
Cold Heart of a Killer, The	CBS-TV	Simon Kendall
Cold Heart of a Killer, The	CBS-TV	Al Rogers
Colony, The	ABC-TV	Misha Segal
Color Me Perfect	Lifetime	Nan Schwartz-Mishkin
Come mi vioi (The Way You Want Me)	It/Fr	Italo Greco
Conte d'Ete (A Summer's Tale)	Fr	Philippe Eidel
Continued Adventures of Reptile Man, The	Ind	David A. Hughes
Continued Adventures of Reptile Man, The	Ind	John Murphy
Conundrum	Showtime	Mark Snow
Cosi	Aut	Stephen Endelman
Cosmos	Can	Michael R. Smith
Cottonwood, The	Ind	Ernie Mannix
Courage Under Fire	Fox	James Horner
Couri al Verde (Penniless Hearts)	It	Daniele Silvestri
Craft, The	TriStar	Graeme Revell
Crime of the Century	HBO	John Frizzell
Critical Choices	Showtime	Patrick Seymour
Cronache del Terzo Millennio	It	Giovanna Marini
Crow 2: City of Angels, The	Miramax	Graeme Revell
Crucible, The	Fox	George Fenton
Cry in the Night, A	Can	Robert Marcel Lepage
Crying Child, The	USA Net	Shirley Walker
Curdled	Miramax	Joseph Julian Gonzalez
Cutting Loose	Ind	Ted Kuhn
D3: The Mighty Ducks	BV	J.A.C. Redford
Dallas: J.R.'s Return	CBS-TV	Jerrold Immel
Dalva	ABC-TV	Lee Holdridge
Danielle Steel's "Full Circle"	NBC-TV	Lee Holdridge
Danielle Steel's "No Greater Love"	NBC-TV	Billy Goldenberg
Danielle Steel's "Remembrance"	NBC-TV	Lee Holdridge
Danielle Steel's "The Ring"	NBC-TV	Michel Legrand
Darien Gap, The	Ind	Gareth Kear
Dark Angel	Fox-TV	Michael Wolff
Dark Breed	Ind	Louis Febre
Dating the Enemy	Aut	David Hirschfelder
Daylight	Univ	Randy Edelman
Dead Ahead	USA Net	Charles Bernstein
Dead Fire	Ind	Peter Allen
Deadly Current	Ind	Louis Natale
Deadly Pursuits	NBC-TV	John Frizzell
Deadly Voyage	HBO	John Scott
Deadly Web	NBC-TV	Stacy Widelitz
Dear God	Par	James Patrick Dunne
Dear God	Par	Jeremy Lubbock
Death Benefit	USA Net	Brian Adler
Deep Crimson	Fr/Sp/Mex	David Mansfield
Deliverance of Elaine, The	CBS-TV	Lawrence Shragge

Delphine 1--Yvan 0	Fr	Philippe Chany
Delta, The	Ind	Michael Rohatyn
Demolition High	Ind	Kevin Kiner
Demolitionist, The	Ind	Shawn Patterson
Dentist, The	Ind	Alan Howarth
Desire	Fr	Jean-Claude Petit
Devil's Food	Lifetime	Ray Colcord
Diabolique	WB	Randy Edelman
Different for Girls	Br	Stephen Warbeck
Different Kind of Christmas, A	Lifetime	Craig Safan
Dirty Laundry	Ind	James Legg
Disappearance of Finbar, The	Br/Ire/Swed	Davy Spillane
Doctor Who	Fox-TV	John Debney
Dog in the Manger, The	Sp	Jose Nieto
Don't Be a Menace to South Central	Miramax	John Barnes
Don't Look Back	HBO	Steve Soles
Double Jeopardy	CBS-TV	Arthur B. Rubinstein
Down Periscope	Fox	Randy Edelman
Dragonheart	Univ	Randy Edelman
Driftwood	Ire/Br	John Cameron
Driven	Ind	Jay Ferguson
Dunston Checks In	Fox	Miles Goodman
Dying to Be Perfect: The Ellen Hart Pena Story	ABC-TV	Dana Kaproff
Ed	Univ	Stephen Endelman
Ed McBain's 87th Precinct: Ice	NBC-TV	Joseph Conlan
Eddie	BV	Stanley Clarke
Eden	Ind	Brad Fiedel
Edie & Pen	Ind	Shawn Colvin
Emma	Br	Rachel Portman
Encino Woman	ABC-TV	David Lawrence
Enfants de Salaud	Fr/Swiss/Belg	Vincent Malone
English Patient, The	Miramax	Gabriel Yared
Entertaining Angels: The Dorothy Day Story	Ind	Bill Conti
Entertaining Angels: The Dorothy Day Story	Ind	Ashley Irwin
Eraser	WB	Alan Silvestri
Escape Clause	Showtime	Richard Marvin
Escape Clause	Showtime	Ken Thorne
Escoriandoli	It	Francesco Magnelli
Evening Star, The	Par	William Ross
Every Woman's Dream	CBS-TV	Peter Manning Robinson
Everyone Says I Love You	Miramax	Dick Hyman
Everything Relative	Ind	Frank London
Evil Has a Face	USA Net	Joseph Vitarelli
Evita	BV	Andrew Lloyd Webber
Ex, The	Can	Paul Zaza
Executive Decision	WB	Jerry Goldsmith
Extreme Measures	Col	Danny Elfman
Eyes of Asia	Fr/Ger/Port	Jorge Arriagada
Face of Evil	CBS-TV	Chris Boardman
Face to Die For, A	NBC-TV	Christopher Franke
Faithful	New Line	Phillip Johnston
Fall and Spring	Ind	Brandon Beckner
Fall Into Darkness	NBC-TV	John D'Andrea

Fall Into Darkness	NBC-TV	Cory Lerios
Fallout	Ind	Frank Ferrucci
Familia (Family)	Sp	Stephane Grappelli
Family Thing, A	MGM/UA	Charles Gross
Fan, The	TriStar	Hans Zimmer
Fantome avec Chauffeur	Fr	Wojciech Kilar
Fargo	Ind	Carter Burwell
Fear	Univ	Carter Burwell
Feeling Minnesota	Ind	Karyn Rachtman
Female Perversions	Ind	Debbie Wiseman
Festival	It	Pino Donaggio
First Kid	BV	Richard Gibbs
First Wives Club, The	Par	Marc Shaiman
Fistful of Lies	Aut	Felicity Fox
Fled	MGM/UA	Graeme Revell
Flipper	Univ	Joel McNeely
Flirting With Disaster	Miramax	Stephen Endelman
Floating Life	Aut	Davood Tabrizi
Fly Away Home	Col	Mark Isham
Follow Me Home	Ind	Cyril Neville
Follow Your Heart	It/Fr/Ger	Claudio Capponi
Follow Your Heart	It/Fr/Ger	Alessio Vlad
Fools Die Fast	Can	Grant Goodman
For Hope	ABC-TV	Peter Rodgers Melnick
For Hope	ABC-TV	Sheryl Crow
For My Daughter's Honor	CBS-TV	James McVay
For the Future: The Irvine Fertility Scandal	Lifetime	J.A.C. Redford
Forbidden Zone: Alien Abduction	Ind	Reg Powell
Forgotten Silver	NewZea	David Donaldson
Forgotten Sins	ABC-TV	Mark Snow
Foxfire	Goldwyn	Michel Colombier
Frankenstein and Me	Disney-TV	Normand Corbiel
Freeway	Ind	Danny Elfman
Frequent Flyer	ABC-TV	Johnny Harris
Friend's Betrayal, A	NBC-TV	W. G. Snuffy Walden
Frighteners, The	Univ	Danny Elfman
From Dusk Till Dawn	Ind	Graeme Revell
From the Files of "Unsolved Mysteries": Voice From the Grave	NBC-TV	Gary Remal Malkin
Fugitive X	Ind	Effrem Bergman
Funeral, The	Ind	Joe Delia
Gallivant	Br	David Burnand
Gangs in Blue	Showtime	Larry Brown
Generation X	Fox-TV	J. Peter Robinson
Get on the Bus	Col	Terence Blanchard
Getting Away With Murder	Ind	John Debney
Ghost and the Darkness, The	Par	Jerry Goldsmith
Ghosts of Mississippi	Col	Marc Shaiman
Girl 6	Ind	Prince
Glimmer Man, The	WB	Trevor Rabin
God's Lonely Man	Ind	James Fearnley
Goldy II: The Saga of the Golden Bear	Ind	Larry Bastian
Goldy II: The Saga of the Golden Bear	Ind	Jim Shaw
Gone in a Heartbeat	CBS-TV	John D'Andrea

Gone in a Heartbeat	CBS-TV	Cory Lerios
Gone in the Night	CBS-TV	Joseph Conlan
Good Doctor: The Paul Fleiss Story, The	CBS-TV	Chris Boardman
Good Luck	Ind	Tim Truman
Gotti	HBO	Mark Isham
Grace of My Heart	Ind	Larry Klein
Grand Avenue	HBO	Peter Rodgers Melnick
Grave, The	Ind	Alex Wurman
Gray's Anatomy	Ind	Cliff Martinez
Great White Hype, The	Fox	Marcus Miller
Green Plaid Shirt	Ind	Norman Moll
Gridlock	NBC-TV	Amin Bhatia
Grinders	Ind	Steven Lester
Growing Artichokes in Mimongo	It	Gian Andrea Tabacchi
Gulliver's Travels	NBC-TV	Trevor Jones
Gun for Jennifer, A	Ind	J. F. Coleman
Guy	Ind	Jeff Beal
Halfback of Notre Dame, The	Showtime	George Blondheim
Hamlet	Br	Patrick Doyle
Happy Gilmore	Univ	Mark Mothersbaugh
Hard Core Logo	Can	Shaun Tozer
Harriet the Spy	Par	Jamshied Sharafi
Harrison: Cry of the City	Syn	Ken Harrison
Hart to Hart: Harts in High Season	Fam Ch	Claude Foissy
Hart to Hart: Till Death Do Us Hart	Fam Ch	Claude Foissy
Harvest of Fire	CBS-TV	Lee Holdridge
Haunting of Lisa, The	Lifetime	Marvin Dolgay
Haunting of Lisa, The	Lifetime	Glenn Morley
Have You Seen My Son?	ABC-TV	Misha Segal
Head Above Water	US/Br	Christopher Young
Hearts Adrift	USA Net	James Legg
Heaven's Prisoners	New Line	George Fenton
Hellraiser 4: Bloodline	Ind	Daniel Licht
Her Costly Affair	NBC-TV	Michael Hoenig
Her Desperate Choice	Life	Lawrence Shragge
Her Last Chance	NBC-TV	Pray for Rain
Hidden in America	Showtime	Mason Daring
Hidden in Silence	Lifetime	Dennis McCarthy
High School High	TriStar	Ira Newborn
Hijacked: Flight 285	ABC-TV	Ian Thomas
Hit Me	Ind	Peter Manning Robinson
Hitting the Ground	Ind	Gordon Gano
Holiday Affair	USA Net	Lee Holdridge
Hollow Reed	Br	Anne Dudley
Homecoming	Showtime	W. G. Snuffy Walden
Homeward Bound II: Lost in San Francisco	BV	Bruce Broughton
Hommes Femmes: Mode d'Emploi	Fr	Francis Lai
Honey, We Shrunk Ourselves!	BV	Michael Tavera
Hostile Advances: The Kerry Ellison Story	Lifetime	Mickey Erbe
Hostile Advances: The Kerry Ellison Story	Lifetime	Maribeth Solomon
Hotel Manor Inn, The	Ind	Alan Schwartz
Hotel Paura	It/Fr	Avion Travel
Hotel de Love	Aut	Christine Woodruff
Hotel de Love	Aut	Brett Rosenberg

House Arrest	MGM/UA	Bruce Broughton
Hunchback of Notre Dame, The	BV	Alan Menken
Husband, A Wife, and a Lover, A	CBS-TV	Jonathan Goldsmith
I Crave Rock & Roll	Ind	Carmen Santa Maria
I Magi Randaci (We Three Kings)	It	Ennio Morricone
I Shot Andy Warhol	Goldwyn	John Cale
I'm Not Rappaport	Ind	Gerry Mulligan
If Looks Could Kill: From the Files of "America's Most Wanted"	Fox-TV	Harald Kloser
If Lucy Fell	TriStar	Amanda Kravat
If Lucy Fell	TriStar	Charles Pettis
If These Walls Could Talk	HBO	Cliff Eidelman
Il Caricatore (The Reel)	It	Daniele Sepe
Il Ciclone (The Cyclone)	It	Claudio Guidetti
Illtown	Ind	Brian Keane
Ilona Comes With the Rain	It/Sp	Luis Bacalov
In Cold Blood	CBS-TV	Hummie Mann
In Love and War	New Line	George Fenton
In the Blink of an Eye	ABC-TV	James McVay
In the Lake of the Woods	Fox-TV	Don Davis
In the Line of Duty: Smoke Jumpers	NBC-TV	Mark Snow
In Your Dreams	BBC-TV	Robert Lockhart
Independence Day	Fox	David Arnold
Indian Summer	Br	Peter Salem
Infinity	Ind	Bruce Broughton
Innocent Victims	ABC-TV	Charles Fox
Insulted and the Humiliated, The	It/Rus	Paul W. Mason
Intimate Betrayal	Ind	Peter Fish
Intimate Relations	Br	Lawrence Shragge
Invasion of Privacy	Ind	Angelo Badalamenti
Island of Dr. Moreau, The	New Line	Gary Chang
It Came From Outer Space II	Sci-Fi	Shirley Walker
It's My Party	MGM/UA	Basil Poledouris
Italians	It	Bruno Zambrini
Ivana Trump's "For Love Alone"	CBS-TV	Don Davis
Jack	BV	Michael Kamen
Jack Frusciante Left the Band	It	Umberto Palazzo
Jack Higgins' "On Dangerous Grounds"	Can/Br/Lux	Leon Aronson
Jack Reed: A Killer Amongst Us	NBC-TV	Lee Holdridge
Jack Reed: Death and Vengeance	NBC-TV	Peter Bernstein
James and the Giant Peach	BV	Randy Newman
Jane Austen's "Emma"	Granada TV	Dominic Muldowney
Jane Eyre	Miramax	Claudio Capponi
Jane Eyre	Miramax	Alessio Vlad
Jane Street	Ind	David Barkley
Jane Street	Ind	Dayne Kurtz
Jerry McGuire	TriStar	Nancy Wilson
Jingle All the Way	Fox	David Newman
Joe's Apartment	WB	Carter Burwell
John Carpenter's Escape From L.A.	Par	John Carpenter
John Carpenter's Escape From L.A.	Par	Shirley Walker
John Henrik Clarke: A Great and Mighty Walk	Ind	Kipper Jones
John Woo's "Once a Thief"	Fox-TV	Amin Bhatia

Joseph Conrad's "The Secret Agent"	Br	Philip Glass
Jump the Gun	Br/SAfr	Joe Nina
Juror, The	Col	James Newton Howard
Just Friends	Ind	Jim Latham
Justice for Annie: A Moment of Truth Movie	NBC-TV	Stacy Widelitz
Kama Sutra: A Tale of Love	Ind/Br/Jap	Mychael Danna
Karmina	Can	Patrick Bourgeois
Kazaam	BV	Christopher Tyng
Keeper, The	Ind	John Petersen
Kidnapping in the Family, A	ABC-TV	Andy Roberts
Kids in the Hall Brain Candy	Par	Craig Northey
Kids of Survival	Ind	Todd Boekelheide
Kidz in the Wood	NBC-TV	Richard Bellis
Kingpin	MGM/UA	Freedy Johnston
Kiss & Tell	Ind	Michael Mattioli
Kiss So Deadly, A	NBC-TV	Joseph Conlan
Kiss and Tell	ABC-TV	Tim Truman
Kissed	Can	Don MacDonald
L'age des Possibles (The Age of Potential)	Fr	Beatrice Thiriet
L'Appartement (The Apartment)	Fr/Sp/It	Peter Chase
L'arcano Incantatore (The Arcane Enchanter)	It	Pino Donaggio
L'Echappee Belle (Close Shave)	Ind	Philippe Delettrez
L'Eleve (The Pupil)	Fr	Roman Musumarra
L'enfant des Nieges (Child of the Wild)	Fr	Gerard Salesses
L'homme ideal (The Ideal Man)	Can	Francois Dompierre
La Belle Verte (Visit to a Green Planet)	Fr	Coline Serreau
La Frontiera (The Border)	It	Luis Bacalov
La Lupa (She-Wolf)	It	Ennio Morricone
La Passione	Br	Chris Rea
La Servante Aimante	Fr	Jean-Charles Capon
La Sindrome di Stendhal	It	Ennio Morricone
Land Before Time IV: Journey Though the Mists, The	Univ	James Horner
Larger Than Life	MGM/UA	Miles Goodman
Larry McMurtry's "Dead Man's Walk"	ABC-TV	David Bell
Last Dance	Ind	Mark Isham
Last Man Standing	New Line	Ry Cooder
Last of the High Kings, The	Ire/Br/Dan	Michael Convertino
Late Bloomers	Ind	Ted Pine
Late Shift, The	HBO	Ira Newborn
Lavryle Spencer's "Home Song"	CBS-TV	Ken Heller
Lawnmower Man 2: Beyond Cyberspace	New Line	Robert Folk
Layin' Low	Ind	Evan Lurie
Le Cri de la Soie (The Scream of Silk)	Fr/Swiss/Belg	Alexandre Desplat
Le Jaguar	Fr	Vladimir Cosma
Le Montreur de Boxe (The Boxing Promoter)	Fr	Alexandre Desplat
Le Polygraphe (The Lie Detector)	Fr/Can/Ger	Robert Caux
Le Sort de l'Amerique	Can	Francois Dompierre
Leading Man, The	Br	Edward Shearmur
Legend of the Ruby Silver	ABC-TV	Richard Bellis
Leopard Son, The	Br	Stewart Copeland
Les Affinites Electives	It/Fr	Carlo Crivelli
Les Victimes (Victims)	Fr	Bilondiey

Les Voleurs (Thieves)	Fr	Philippe Sarde
Level Five	Fr	Michel Krasna
Liar Liar	Univ	John Debney
Liar Liar (Theme)	Univ	James Newton Howard
Life	Aut	John Clifford White
Lifeline	USA Net	George Blondheim
Lilian's Story	Aut	Cezary Skubiszewski
Lilies	Can	Mychael Danna
Lily Dale	Showtime	Peter Rodgers Melnick
Limbic Region, The	Showtime	Gary Chang
Listen	Orion	David Davidson
Little Bigfoot	Ind	Louis Febre
Little Riders, The	Disney-TV	Lee Holdridge
Loch Ness	Br	Trevor Jones
Lone Star	Col	Mason Daring
Long Day's Journey Into Night	Can	Ron Sures
Long Kiss Goodnight, The	New Line	Alan Silvestri
Looking for Richard	Ind	Howard Shore
Loose Women	Ind	Pat Irwin
Losing Chase	Showtime	Michael Bacon
Loss of Innocence, A	CBS-TV	Mark Snow
Lost in Mississippi	Ind	Daniel Lanois
Lottery, The	NBC-TV	David Michael Frank
Love & Sex, etc.	Ind	Bob Mothersbaugh
Love Always	Ind	Jaime Valle
Love Always	Ind	Anton Sanko
Love Is All There Is	Goldwyn	Jeff Beal
Love Me, Love Me Not	Can	Andre Duchesne
Love Me, Love Me Not	Can	Rene Lussier
Love and Other Catastrophes	Aut	Oleh Witer
Love etc.	Fr	Alexandre Desplat
Lover's Knot	Ind	Laura Karpman
Luna e l'Altra	It	Carlo Siliotto
Lust and Revenge	Aut	Paul Grabowsky
Lying Eyes	NBC-TV	Dennis McCarthy
Ma Femme Me Quitte (My Woman Is Leaving Me)	Fr	Eric Levi
Ma vie sexuelle	Fr	Krishna Levy
Macadam Tribu (Macadam Tribe)	Fr	Christian Polloni
Mad Dog Time	MGM/UA	Earl Rose
Magic Island	Ind	Richard Band
Malena Is a Name From a Tango	Sp/Fr/Ger	Antoine Duhamel
Malik le Maudit (Calamity Malik)	Fr	Charles Autrand
Man Next Door, The	ABC-TV	Charles Fox
Man Who Captured Eichmann, The	TNT	Laurence Rosenthal
Manny & Lo	Ind	John Lurie
Mars Attacks!	WB	Danny Elfman
Marshal Law	Showtime	Tim Truman
Marvin's Room	Miramax	Rachel Portman
Mary & Tim	CBS-TV	Michel Colombier
Mary Reilly	TriStar	George Fenton
Maternal Instincts	USA Net	Lawrence Shragge
Matilda	TriStar	David Newman
Maximum Risk	Col	Robert Folk

Me & My Matchmaker	Ind	Mark Leggett
Memoires d'un Jeune Con	Fr	Fabien Gervaise
Mercenary	Ind	Roger Neill
Mes dix-sept Ans (I Was Seventeen)	Fr	Benoit Schlossberg
Miami Hustle	Showtime	Kevin Sepe
Michael	New Line	Randy Newman
Michael Collins	Br	Elliot Goldenthal
Microcosmos	Fr/Swiss/It	Bruno Coulais
Midsummer Night's Dream, A	Br	Howard Blake
Miniskirted Dynamo, The	Aut	Nik and Rachel Jeanes
Mirada Liquida (Liquid Gaze)	Sp	Bernardo Bonezzi
Mirror Has Two Faces, The	TriStar	Marvin Hamlisch
Mirror Has Two Faces, The	TriStar	Barbra Streisand
Mirror, Mirror	Ind	Kevin Mooney
Misery Brothers, The	Ind	Sidney James
Mission: Impossible	Par	Danny Elfman
Mission: Impossible (Theme)	Par	Lalo Schifrin
Mistaken Identity	Can	Jean Vanasse
Mistrial	HBO	Brad Fiedel
Mo'	Fr/Swiss/Hung	Jean-Pierre Mas
Mojave Moon	Ind	Johnny Caruso
Moll Flanders	MGM/UA	Mark Mancina
Mon Homme (My Man)	Fr	Henryk Gorecki
Mon Homme (My Man)	Fr	Barry White
Mondo	Fr	Alain Weber
Montana Blues	Fr	Jean-Marie Senia
Moonshine Highway	Showtime	Steve Dorff
Morrison Murders, The	USA Net	Mickey Erbe
Morrison Murders, The	USA Net	Maribeth Solomon
Moses	TNT	Marco Frisina
Mother	Par	Marc Shaiman
Mother May I Sleep With Danger?	NBC-TV	Irwin Fisch
Mother Night	Ind	Michael Convertino
Mother Trucker: The Diana Kilmury Story	TNT	Jonathan Goldsmith
Mother's Instinct, A	CBS-TV	James McVay
Mouse, The	Ind	Jonathan Edwards
Mr. and Mrs. Loving	Showtime	Branford Marsalis
Mr. Reliable: A True Story	Aut	Philip Judd
Mr. Sprechman's Boat	Ind	Christopher Tyng
Mr. Stitch	SciFi	Tomandandy
Mr. Wong	BV	Craig Safan
Mrs. Santa Claus	CBS-TV	Jerry Herman
Mrs. Winterbourne	TriStar	Patrick Doyle
Mrs. Winterbourne	Ind	Mark Watters
Mulholland Falls	MGM/UA	Dave Grusin
Multiplicity	Col	George Fenton
Munsters' Scary Little Christmas, The	Fox-TV	Christopher Stone
Muppet Treasure Island	BV	Barry Mann
Muppet Treasure Island	BV	Harry Gregson-Williams
Muppet Treasure Island	BV	Cynthia Weill
Muppet Treasure Island	BV	Hans Zimmer
Murder and Murder	Ind	Frank London
Murder at My Door	Fox-TV	Jonathan Goldsmith
My Fellow Americans	WB	William Ross

My Friend Joe	Ire/Ger	Ronan Hardiman
My Son Is Innocent	ABC-TV	Ron Ramin
My Summer Vacation	Can	Yuri Gorbachow
My Very Best Friend	CBS-TV	Patrick Williams
Mystery Science Theater 3000: The Movie	Ind	Billy Barber
Napoleon	Aut/Jap	Bill Conti
Natural Enemy	Can	Alan Reeves
Neil Simon's "Jake's Women"	CBS-TV	David Shire
Neil Simon's "London Suite"	NBC-TV	Lee Holdridge
Nenette et Boni	Fr	Tindersticks
Nerolio	It	Maria Soldatini
Never Ever	US/Br	Peter John Vettesse
Never Give Up: The Jimmy V Story	CBS-TV	Patrick Williams
Never Met Picasso	Ind	Kirstin Hersh
Never Too Late	Can	Normand Corbiel
Next Step, The	Ind	Mio Morales
Next Step, The	Ind	Brian Otto
Next Step, The	Ind	Roni Skies
Next Year . . . We'll Go to Bed by Ten	It	Roberto Ciotti
Niagaravation	Ind	Rick Howard
Niagaravation	Ind	Joe Romano
Night of the Twisters	Fam Ch	Lawrence Shragge
Night Visitors	NBC	Irwin Fisch
Nightjohn	Disney-TV	Stephen James Taylor
Ninfa Plebea	It	Ennio Morricone
No Easy Way	Ind	Mark Eitzel
No One Could Protect Her	ABC-TV	Peter Rodgers Melnick
No One Could Protect Her	ABC-TV	Bruce Miller
No One Would Tell	NBC-TV	Michael Tavera
No Way Back	US/Jap	David Williams
No Way Home	Ind	Rick Giovinazzo
No Way Home	Ind	Jeff Healey
No Way Home	Ind	Robin Ford
Norma Jean and Marilyn	HBO	Christopher Young
North Star	WB	Bruce Rowland
Not Fourteen Again	Aut	Peter Dasent
Not Me!	Can	Anne Bourne
Nutty Professor, The	Univ	David Newman
Occasional Hell, An	Ind	Anton Sanko
Ogre, The	Br/Fr/Ger	Michael Nyman
On Seventh Avenue	NBC-TV	Donald Markowitz
Once Upon a Time . . . When We Were Colored	Ind	Steve Tyrell
Once You Meet a Stranger	CBS-TV	Peter Manning Robinson
One Fine Day	Fox	James Newton Howard
One Way Out	Ind	Sean Murray
Only in America	Ind	Page McConnell
Original Gangstas	Orion	Vladimir Horonzky
Our Son, the Matchmaker	CBS-TV	Stewart Levin
Outer Limits, The	Showtime	Michael Mancina
Palla di Neve (Snowball)	It	Carlo Siliotto
Pandora's Clock	NBC-TV	Don Davis
Panic in the Sky!	Fam Ch	Todd Hayen
Paradise Lost:The Child Murders of Robin	Ind	Metallica

Hood Hill

Parklands	Aut	Richard Vella
Pasajes (Passages)	Sp	Alberto Iglesias
Passage a l'Acte (Death in Therapy)	Fr	Alexandre Desplat
Pathfinder, The	Showtime	Reg Powell
Pedale Douce (What a Drag)	Fr	Philippe Chopin
People Next Door, The	CBS-TV	David Mansfield
People vs. Larry Flynt, The	Col	Thomas Newman
Perfect Daughter, The	USA Net	Don Davis
Peter Benchley's "The Beast"	NBC-TV	Don Davis
Phantom, The	Par	David Newman
Phat Beach	Orion	Paul Stewart
Phenomenon	BV	Thomas Newman
Pianese Nunzio, 14 Anni a Maggio	It	Umberto Guarino
Pin Gods	Ind	Mark Maxwell
Pizzicata	It/Ger	Jerome Harley
Plan 10 From Outer Space	Ind	Fred Myrow
Politician's Wife, The	Br	Barrington Pheloung
Ponette	Fr	Philippe Sarde
Portrait of a Lady, The	Br/US	Wojciech Kilar
Portraits Chinois (Shadow Play)	Fr/Br	Peter Chase
Poverty and Other Delights	Can	Yves Laferriere
Power 98	Ind	Jeff Beal
Preacher's Wife, The	BV	Hans Zimmer
Precious	Miramax	Rolfe Kent
Pretty Poison	Fox-TV	Pray for Rain
Prey of the Jaguar	Ind	Jeffrey Walton
Primal Fear	Par	James Newton Howard
Primal Fear	Par	J. Peter Robinson
Princess in Love, A	CBS-TV	Peter Manning Robinson
Prisoner of Zenda Inc., The	Showtime	John Weisman
Project Grizzly	Can	Anne Bourne
Project: ALF	ABC-TV	Mark Snow
Promise to Carolyn, A	CBS-TV	Laura Karpman
Proprietor, The	WB	Richard Robbins
Prosecutors, The	NBC-TV	David Michael Frank
Pterodactyl Woman From Beverly Hills	Ind	Roy Hay
Puddle Crusier	Ind	Uncle Tupelo
Quest, The	Univ	Randy Edelman
Race Against Time: The Search for Sarah	CBS-TV	James McVay
Race the Sun	TriStar	Graeme Revell
Radiant City	ABC-TV	David Mansfield
Rage, The	Can	Paul Zaza
Rainbow	Can/Br	Alan Reeves
Ransom	BV	James Horner
Rasputin	HBO	Brad Fiedel
Ratchet	Ind	Paul Schwartz
Rattled	USA Net	Joel Goldsmith
Reasons of the Heart	USA Net	James Legg
Rebound: The Legend of Earl "The Goat" Manigault	HBO	Kevin Eubanks
Red Blooded 2	Can	Paul Zaza
Remember Me?	Br	Michael Kamen
Remember Me?	Br	Edward Shearmur

Rescuing Desire	Ind	Wendy Blackstone
Return of the Borrowers, The	BBC-TV	Howard Goodall
Rich Man's Wife, The	BV	John Frizzell
Rich Man's Wife, The	BV	James Newton Howard
Riders of the Purple Sage	TNT	Arthur Kempel
Ridicule	Fr	Antoine Duhamel
Right to Remain Silent, The	Showtime	Randy Miller
Riorno a Casa Gori (Return to Gori's House)	It	Patrizio Fariselli
Riot	Ind	Jim Halfpenny
Ripe	Ind	Anton Sanko
River Street	Aut	David Bridie
River Street	Aut	John Phillips
Road Movie	Ind	R.E.M.
Road to Galveston, The	USA Net	Stanley Clarke
Robert Rylands' Last Journey	Sp	Angel Illarramendi
Robin Cook's "Terminal"	NBC-TV	Garry Schyman
Robin of Locksley	Showtime	John Weisman
Rock, The	BV	Nick Glennie-Smith
Rock, The	BV	Hans Zimmer
Rockford Files: Friends and Foul Play, The	CBS-TV	Pete Carpenter
Rockford Files: Friends and Foul Play, The	CBS-TV	Mike Post
Rockford Files: Godfather Knows Best, The	CBS-TV	Pete Carpenter
Rockford Files: Godfather Knows Best, The	CBS-TV	Mike Post
Rockford Files: If the Frame Fits . . . , The	CBS-TV	Pete Carpenter
Rockford Files: If the Frame Fits . . . , The	CBS-TV	Mike Post
Rockford Files: Punishment and Crime, The	CBS-TV	Pete Carpenter
Rockford Files: Punishment and Crime, The	CBS-TV	Mike Post
Rolling Stones	Fr/Bulg	Jorge Arriagada
Rosamund Pilcher's "September"	Br	Richard Hartley
Roseanna's Grave (For Roseanna)	US/Br/It	Trevor Jones
Ruby Jean and Joe	Showtime	Stephen Graziano
Ruby Ridge: An American Tragedy	CBS-TV	Patrick Williams
Rumble in the Bronx	Ind	J. Peter Robinson
Run for the Dream: The Gail Devers Story	Showtime	Pete Anthony
Run for the Dream: The Gail Devers Story	Showtime	Ronnie Laws
Sabrina the Teenage Witch	Showtime	Greg DeBelles
Saint-Ex	Br	Barrington Pheloung
Samson and Delilah	TNT	Marco Frisina
Samson and Delilah (Theme)	TNT	Ennio Morricone
Santa With Muscles	Ind	James Covell
Sarah's Child	Ind	Glenn Workman
Saturday on Earth, A	Fr	Pascal Comelade
Scream	Ind	Marco Beltrami
Season in Purgatory, A	CBS-TV	Peter Manning Robinson
Secret Agent Club, The	Ind	Jan Hammer
Secret Between Friends, A: A Moment of Truth Movie	NBC-TV	Stacy Widelitz
Secret She Carried, The	NBC-TV	Jeff Fair
Secret She Carried, The	NBC-TV	Starr Parodi
Seduced by Madness: The Diane Borchardt Story	NBC-TV	Craig Safan
Seeking the Cafe Bob	Ind	Roy Hughes
Select Hotel	Fr	Jerome Coullet
Set It Off	New Line	Christopher Young

Sgt. Bilko	Univ	Alan Silvestri
Shattered Mind	NBC-TV	Kurt Wortman
She Cried No	NBC-TV	Lee Holdridge
She Woke Up Pregnant	ABC-TV	Stacy Widelitz
She's the One	Ind	Tom Petty
Sherlock Holmes: The Case of the Temporal Nexus	Ind	John Ross
Shiloh	Ind	Joel Goldsmith
Shine	Br/Aut	David Hirschfelder
Shoemaker	Can	Bill Thompson
Shooting Lily	Ind	John Massari
Shot, The	Ind	Dan Sonis
Shut Yer Mouth!	Ind	Miles Green
Silencing the Guns	Fr/Can	Guy Trepanier
Silent Lies	Ind	Phil Kimbrough
Silenzio si Nasce	It	Giancarlo Bigazzi
Sins of Silence	CBS-TV	David Bell
Sister Island	Ind	Nigel Holton
Skin White Mask	Br/Fr	Paul Gladstone-Reid
Sleepers	WB	John Williams
Sling Blade	Miramax	Daniel Lanois
Sling Blade	Miramax	Hughes Winborne
Small Time	Ind	Vinny Golia
Smalltime	Br	Gavin Clarke
Solo	Col	Christopher Franke
Some Mother's Son	Br	Bill Whelan
Somebody Is Waiting	Br	Elia Cmiral
Sophie and the Moonhanger	Lifetime	Charles Bernstein
Sortez des Rangs (Fall Out)	Fr	Jean-Philippe Goude
Soul of the Game	HBO	Lee Holdridge
Space Jam	WB	James Newton Howard
Space Truckers	US/Ire	Colin Towns
Special Effects	Ind	Christopher Stone
Special Report: Journey to Mars	CBS-TV	Mark Snow
Spitfire Grill, The	Ind	James Horner
Spy Hard	BV	Bill Conti
Squillo (Call Girl)	It	Pino Donaggio
Stand Against Fear: A Moment of Truth Movie	NBC-TV	Stacy Widelitz
Star Command	UPN	Lee Holdridge
Star Trek: First Contact	Par	Jerry Goldsmith
Starlight	Can	Michael Conway Baker
Stealing Beauty	Br/It/Fr	Richard Hartley
Stella Does Tricks	Br	Nick Bicat
Step Toward Tomorrow, A	CBS-TV	Ron Ramin
Stepford Husbands, The	CBS-TV	Dana Kaproff
Stephen King's "Thinner"	Par	Daniel Licht
Steve Martini's "Undue Influence"	CBS-TV	Jeff Beal
Sticks and Stones	Ind	Hummie Mann
Still Waters Run Deep	Fr	Beatrice Thiriet
Stolen Hearts	WB	Nick Glennie-Smith
Stolen Hearts	WB	Paddy Moloney
Stolen Memories: Secrets From the Rose Garden	Fam Ch	Paul Zaza

Storia d'Amore con i Crampi	It	Tony Esposito
Strange Blues of Cowboy Red, The	Can	John Hopkins
Strange Blues of Cowboy Red, The	Can	Les Vaughan
Stranger to Love, A	CBS-TV	Laura Karpman
Street Corner Justice	Ind	K. Alexander Wilkinson
Striptease	Col	Howard Shore
Stupids, The	New Line	Christopher Stone
Substance of Fire, The	Miramax	Joseph Vitarelli
Substitute, The	Orion	Gary Chang
Sudden Terror: The Hijacking of School Bus 17	ABC-TV	Brian Adler
Suddenly	ABC-TV	David Mansfield
Summer of Ben Tyler, The	CBS-TV	Van Dyke Parks
Summer of Fear	CBS-TV	Mark Snow
Sun the Moon and the Stars, The	Ire	Noel Eccles
Sunchaser, The	WB	Maurice Jarre
Sunset Park	Ind	Kay Gee
Sunset Park	Ind	Miles Goodman
Surviving Piccaso	WB	Richard Robbins
Susanna	Sp	Javier Navarrete
Swann	Can/Br	Richard Rodney Bennett
Sweet Angel Mine	Can/Br	Daniel Lanois
Sweet Angel Mine	Can/Br	John McCarthy
Sweet Dreams	ABC-TV	Pray for Rain
Sweet Temptation	CBS-TV	Mark Snow
Swingers	Miramax	Justin Reinhardt
Switchblade Sisters	Miramax	Chuck Day
Switchblade Sisters	Miramax	Medusa
Switchblade Sisters	Miramax	Richard Person
Tabu: Dernier Voyage	Fr	Yves Roche
Tales From the Crypt: Bordello of Blood	Univ	Chris Boardman
Talk to Me	Ind	David McLary
Talk to Me	ABC-TV	Peter Manning Robinson
Tangled Web, A	CBS-TV	Chris Walden
That Thing You Do	Fox	Howard Shore
Theodore Rex	New Line	Robert Folk
Theremin: An Electronic Odyssey	Orion	Hal Wilner
Thin Line Between Love and Hate, A	New Line	Roger Troutman
Things I Never Told You	US/Sp	Alfonso Vilalonga
Thorn Birds: The Missing Years, The	CBS-TV	Garry McDonald
Thorn Birds: The Missing Years, The	CBS-TV	Lawrence Stone
Thrill	NBC-TV	Michael Hoenig
Tiera (Earth)	Sp	Alberto Iglesias
'Til Christmas	Ind	Pat Irwin
Time to Kill, A	WB	Elliot Goldenthal
Timeless	Ind	Joseph Hart Sr.
Timepiece	CBS-TV	Eric Colvin
Timepiece	CBS-TV	Richard Gibbs
Tin Cup	WB	William Ross
Tire a Part (Limited Edition)	Fr	Jean-Philippe Goude
Titanic	CBS-TV	Lennie Niehaus
To Brave Alaska	ABC-TV	Louis Natale
To Face Her Past	CBS-TV	Peter Manning Robinson
To Gillian on Her 37th Birthday	Col	James Horner

To Love, Honor and Deceive	ABC-TV	Brian Adler
To Sir With Love II	CBS-TV	Trevor Lawrence
To the Ends of Time	SciFi	Eckhart Seeber
Tornado!	Fox-TV	Garry Schyman
Trees Lounge	Ind	Evan Lurie
Trigger Effect, The	Ind	James Newton Howard
Trilogy of Terror II	USA Net	Bob Cobert
Trois Vies et un Suele Mort	Fr	Jorge Arriagada
Trojan Eddie	Br	John Keane
Troublesome Creek: A Midwestern	Ind	Sheldon Mirowitz
True American, A	Ind	Leroy Schuler
True Blue	Br	Stanislas Syrewicz
Truth About Cats and Dogs, The	Fox	Howard Shore
Tu Nombre Envenena Mis Suenos	Sp	Jose Nieto
Turbulence	MGM/UA	Shirley Walker
Turning April	Aut	Lesley Barber
Twelfth Night	Br	Shaun Davey
Twisted	Ind	Q Lazzarus
Twisted Desire	NBC-TV	Gary Chang
Twister	WB/Univ	Mark Mancina
Two Dads and a Mom	Fr	Denis Lefdup
Two If by Sea	WB	Nick Glennie-Smith
Two If by Sea	WB	Paddy Moloney
Two Mothers for Zachary	ABC-TV	Peter Rodgers Melnick
Ultimate Lie, The	NBC-TV	Peter Bernstein
Un Caso d'Amore (Love Case)	It	Stefano Arnaldi
Un Divan a New York (A Couch in New York)	Fr	Sonia Wieder Atherton
Un Ete a la Goulette	Fr/Belg	Jean-Marie Senia
Under the Bridge	Ind	Jimmy Weinstein
Undertow	Showtime	John Frizzell
Unexpected Family, An	USA Net	Tom Scott
Unfinished Affair, An	ABC-TV	Lee Holdridge
Unforgettable	MGM/UA	Christopher Young
Unforgivable	CBS-TV	Roger Bellon
Unhook the Stars	Miramax	Steven Hufsteter
Uninvited, The	CBS-TV	Wendy Blackstone
Unlikely Angel	CBS-TV	Ray Bunch
Unlikely Angel	CBS-TV	Dolly Parton
Uomini senza Donna (Men Without Women)	It	Sergio Cammariere
Up Close and Personal	BV	Thomas Newman
Very Brady Sequel, A	Par	Guy Moon
Vesna va Veloce (Vesna Goes Fast)	It/Fr	Jan Garbarek
Visions	Ind	John Ross
Vitte Strozzate (Strangled Lives)	It/Fr/Belg	Ennio Morricone
Vivid	Can	Guy Zerafa
Waiting for Guffman	Ind	Christopher Guest
Waiting for Guffman	Ind	Michael McKean
Waiting for Guffman	Ind	Harry Shearer
Waiting for Michelangelo	Can/Swiss	Claude Destardins
Waiting for Michelangelo	Can/Swiss	Eric N. Robertson
Walking and Talking	Miramax	Billy Bragg
War at Home, The	BV	Basil Poledouris

Warriors of Virtue	US/China	Don Davis
Watermelon Woman, The	Ind	Bill Coleman
Wavelength	Par	Michael Storey
We the Jury	USA Net	Jonathan Goldsmith
Wedding Bell Blues	Ind	Paul Christian Gordon
Welcomes Says the Angel	Ind	Nels Cline
Welcomes Says the Angel	Ind	George Lockwood
What I Have Written	Aut	David Bridie
What I Have Written	Aut	John Phillips
What Kind of Mother Are You?	NBC-TV	Lawrence Shragge
What Love Sees	CBS-TV	Allyn Ferguson
When Saturday Comes	Br	Anne Dudley
Where Truth Lies	Ind	David & Eric Wurst
White Squall	BV	Jeff Rona
White Squall	BV	Hans Zimmer
Whole Wide World, The	Ind	Harry Gregson-Williams
Whole in the Moon, The	NewZea/Can	Daniel Scott
Wild America	WB	J.A.C. Redford
William Shakespeare's Romeo + Juliet	Fox	Craig Armstrong
William Shakespeare's Romeo + Juliet	Fox	Nelle Hooper
Wind in the Willow, The	Br	Colin Towns
Winner, The	Ind	Pray for Rain
Winner, The	Ind	Zandor Schloss
Wiseguy	ABC-TV	Walter Murphy
Wiseguy	ABC-TV	Mike Post
Within the Rock	Can	Tony Fennell
Within the Rock	Can	Rod Gammons
Without Evidence	Ind	Franco Piersanti
Woman Undone	Showtime	Daniel Licht
Woman's Guide to Adultery, A	Ind	Daemion Barry
Wrong Woman, The	CBS-TV	Marty Simon
X,Y	Fr/Belg	Jacques Davidovici
Yesterday's Target	Showtime	Todd Hayen
Zarkorr! The Invader	Ind	Richard Band
Zone 39	Aut	Burkhard Dailwitz

1997

100 Proof	Ind	Michael Mosier
100 Proof	Ind	George Nicholas
12 Angry Men	Showtime	Kenyon Hopkins
12 Angry Men	Showtime	Charlie Haden
20,000 Leagues Under the Sea	CBS-TV	John Scott
4 Little Girls	Ind	Terence Blanchard
6th Man, The	BV	Marcus Miller
8 Heads in a Duffel Bag	Orion	Andrew Gross
A Ciegas (Blinded)	Sp	Mario De Benito
A,B,C . . . Manhattan	Ind	Eric A. Hammer
Aaron's Magic Village	Fr/Ger/Isr	Michel Legrand
Absolute Power	Col	Lennie Niehaus
Absolute Truth, The	CBS-TV	Brahm Wenger
Accident, The: A Moment of Truth Movie	NBC-TV	Stacy Widelitz
Addicted to Love	WB	Rachel Portman
Advocate's Devil, The	ABC-TV	David Mansfield

Affliction	Ind	Michael Brook
AfterGlow	Br	Mark Isham
Air Bud	BV	Brahm Wenger
Air Force One	Col	Jerry Goldsmith
Al Limite (To the Limit)	Fr/Sp	Mario De Benito
Alibi	ABC-TV	Don Davis
Alien Resurrection	Fox	John Frizzell
Alive & Kicking	Ind	Peter Salem
All Lies End in Murder	ABC-TV	Lawrence Shragge
All the Winters That Have Been	CBS-TV	Peter Manning Robinson
Allie & Me	Ind	Mark Chait
Altri Domini (Other Men)	It	Gianni Coscia
Always Say Goodbye	Ind	Randall Willis
American Perfekt	Ind	Simon Boswell
American Werewolf in Paris, An	Br/Dutch	Wilbert Hirsch
Amistad	Dream	John Williams
Amor de Hombre (Manly Love)	Sp	Jose Manuel Pagan
Amour et Confusions	Fr	Jacques Davidovici
Anaconda	Col	Randy Edelman
Anastasia	Fox	David Newman
Angels in the Endzone	ABC-TV	Frederic Talgorn
Anna Karenina	WB	Sir Georg Solti
Another Nine & a Half Weeks	Ind	Stephen Parsons
Any Mother's Son	Lifetime	Pray for Rain
Any Place but Home	USA Net	Dennis McCarthy
Apostle, The	Ind	David Mansfield
Arguing the World	Ind	Adam Guettel
Arlette	Fr	William Sheller
Arresting Gena	Ind	Pat Irwin
Artemisia	Fr/It/Ger	Krishna Levy
As Good As It Gets	TriStar	Hans Zimmer
Assassin(s)	Fr	Carter Burwell
Assault on Devil's Island	Can	John D'Andrea
Assault on Devil's Island	Can	Cory Lerios
Assault on Dome 4	Ind	Peter Waldman
Assignment, The	Can	Normand Corbeil
Assistant, The	Can	Lawrence Shragge
Asteroid	NBC-TV	Shirley Walker
Austin Powers: International Man of Mystery	New Line	George S. Clinton
B.A.P.S.	New Line	Stanley Clarke
Bad Manners	Ind	Ira Newborn
Bad to the Bone	ABC-TV	Joseph Conlan
Badge of Betrayal	ABC-TV	Stacy Widelitz
Barbara Taylor Bradford's "Love in Another Town"	CBS-TV	Lawrence Shragge
Barbecue: A Love Story	Can	Darden Smith
Barracuda	Fr/Ger/Belg	Philippe Haim
Bat Out of Hell	Fr	Laurent Coq
Bat Out of Hell	Fr	Benjamin Raffaelli
Batman & Robin	WB	Elliot Goldenthal
Bean	Br	Howard Goodall
Beautician and the Beast, The	Par	Cliff Eidelman
Before Women Had Wings	ABC-TV	Anton Sanko
Bella Mafia	CBS-TV	Joseph Vitarelli

Bent	Br	Philip Glass
Beverly Hills Family Robinson	ABC-TV	Phil Marshall
Beverly Hills Ninja	TriStar	George S. Clinton
Beyond the Garden	Sp	Nicola Piovani
Big Empty, The	Ind	Jean-Michel Michenaud
Bitter End, The	Ind	Wendy Blackstone
Black & White & Red All Over	Ind	David Steele
Blackout, The	US/Fr	Joe Delia
Blackrock	Aut	Steve Kilbey
Bliss	Sony	Jan A. P. Kaczmarek
Blood Oranges, The	Ind	Angelo Badalamenti
Boogie Nights	New Line	Michael Penn
Booty Call	Col	Robert Folk
Born Into Exile	NBC-TV	Dana Kaproff
Borrowed Hearts	CBS-TV	John Weisman
Borrowers, The	Br	Harry Gregson-Williams
Boxer, The	Br/Ire	Gavin Friday
Boxer, The	Br/Ire	Maurice Roycroft
Boxer, The	Br/Ire	Maurice Seezer
Boys Life 2	Ind	Robert Folk
Boys Life 2	Ind	Danny Troob
Brave, The	Ind	Iggy Pop
Breach of Faith: A Family of Cops II	CBS-TV	Peter Manning Robinson
Breakdown	Par	Basil Poledouris
Breaking Up	WB	Mark Mothersbaugh
Breaking the Surface	USA Net	Richard Bellis
Breast Men	HBO	Dennis McCarthy
Bridge of Time	ABC-TV	Irwin Fisch
Bring Me the Head of Mavis Davis	Br	Christopher Tyng
Brokers	Ind	Josh Kramon
Brooklyn State of Mind, A	Can	Paul Zaza
Brother's Kiss, A	Ind	Frank London
Buddy	Col	Elmer Bernstein
Buffalo Soldiers	TNT	Joel McNeely
Bullet	Aut	Randall Poster
Bumping the Odds	Br	Michael Conn
Buried Alive II	USA Net	Michel Colombier
Butch Camp	Ind	Conrad Pope
C'est Pour la Bonne Cause	Fr	Jean-Marie Senia
Call to Remember, A	Starz!	Sam Winans
Cameleon	Br	Mark Thomas
Camere da Letto (Bedrooms)	It	Nicola Piovani
Can't You Hear the Wind Howl?	Ind	Robert Johnson
Career Girls	Br	Marianne Jean-Baptiste
Career Girls	Br	Tony Remy
Carne Tremula (Live Flesh)	Sp/Fr	Alberto Iglesias
Castle, The	Aut	Craig Harnath
Cats Don't Dance	WB	Steve Goldstein
Child's Wish, A	CBS-TV	Stacy Widelitz
Childhood Sweetheart?	CBS-TV	Patrick Williams
Chile Obstinate Memory	Can/Fr	Robert Marcel Lepage
Chinese Box	Fr/Jap/US	Graeme Revell
Christmas List, The	Fam Ch	Brahm Wenger
Christmas Memory, A	CBS-TV	Lee Holdridge

Climb, The	Fr/NewZea	Greco Casadeus
Clockwatchers	Ind	Mader
Cloned	NBC-TV	Mark Snow
Close to Danger	ABC-TV	Cameron Allan
Clover	USA Net	Lawrence Shragge
Clubbed to Death	Fr/Port	Philippe Cohen-Solal
Cold Around the Heart	Fox	Mason Daring
Colin Fitz	Ind	Pat Irwin
Color of Justice	Showtime	Michel Colombier
Colors Straight Up	Ind	John Barnes
Colors Straight Up	Ind	Joseph Julian Gonzalez
Commandments	Ind	Joseph Vitarelli
Con Air	Touchstone	Mark Mancina
Con Air	Touchstone	Trevor Rabin
Conspiracy Theory	WB	Carter Burwell
Contact	WB	Alan Silvestri
Contagious	USA Net	Stephen Graziano
Convictions	Lifetime	Billy Goldenberg
Cop Land	Miramax	Howard Shore
Country Justice	CBS-TV	James McVay
Courting Courtney	Ind	Daniel Gold
Critical Care	Ind	Michael Convertino
Crowned and Dangerous	ABC-TV	Jeff Fair
Crowned and Dangerous	ABC-TV	Starr Parodi
Cube	Ind	Mark Korven
Dancing on the Moon	Can	Milan Kymlicka
Dangerous Ground	New Line	Stanley Clarke
Dante's Peak	Univ	John Frizzell
Dante's Peak	Univ	James Newton Howard
Darklands	Br	David A. Hughes
Darklands	Br	John Murphy
Das Lieben Ist Eine Baustelle	Ger	Jurgen Knieper
Das Lieben Ist Eine Baustelle	Ger	Christian Steyer
David	TNT	Carlo Siliotto
De Que Se Rien Las Mujeres?	Sp	Joan Vivres
Dead by Midnight	ABC-TV	Mason Daring
Dead Man's Gun	Showtime	Terry Frewer
Dead Silence	HBO	Jonathan Goldsmith
Deadly Vision, A	ABC-TV	Chris Walden
Dean Koontz's "Intensity"	Fox-TV	George S. Clinton
Death in Granada	Sp	Mark McKenzie
Deep Family Secrets	CBS-TV	Chris Boardman
Def Jam's How to Be a Player	Ind	Darren Floyd
Defenders, The: Playback	Showtime	Mark Isham
Deja Vu	Ind	Gail Schoen
Deli, The	Ind	Ernie Mannix
Der Unfisch (The Unfish)	Aut/Ger	Harald Kloser
Designated Mourner, The	Br	Richard Hartley
Detention: Siege at Johnson High	ABC-TV	Brian Adler
Devil's Advocate, The	WB	James Newton Howard
Devil's Child, The	ABC-TV	Christopher Franke
Devil's Own, The	Col	James Horner
Diana and Me	Aut	Brett Rosenberg
Didier	Fr	Philippe Chany

Dinner at Fred's	Can	Carlos Lopes
Dinner, The	Ind	Kevin Eubanks
Directors on Directors	It/US	Alessandro Molinari
Directors on Directors	It/US	Carlo Siliotto
Disappearance of Garcia Lorca, The	Sp	Mark McKenzie
Ditchdigger's Daughters, The	Fam Ch	Phil Marshall
Divided by Hate	USA Net	Joseph Conlan
Doberman	Fr	Schyzomaniac
Dog's Best Friend	Disney-TV	David Lawrence
Dogtown	Ind	Steve Stevens
Doing Time for Patsy Cline	Aut	Peter Best
Don King: Only in America	HBO	Anthony Marinelli
Donnie Brasco	TriStar	Patrick Doyle
Doomsday Rock	Fam Ch	Brian Trenchard-Smith
Double Team	Col	Gary Chang
Downtime	Br	Simon Boswell
Dream With the Fishes	Ind	Tito Larriva
Drive, She Said	Can	Dennis Burke
Drive, The	Can	John Hamilton
Dukes of Hazzard, The: Reunion!	CBS-TV	Steve Wariner
Dying to Belong	NBC-TV	Michael Tavera
Echo	ABC-TV	Peter Manning Robinson
Ed McBain's 87th Precinct: Heatwave	NBC-TV	Patrick Williams
Edge, The	Fox	Jerry Goldsmith
Education of Little Tree, The	Par	Mark Isham
Eight Days a Week	Ind	Kevin Bassinson
El Amior Perjudica Seriamente La Salud	Sp/Fr	Bernardo Bonezzi
El Che	Fr/Sp	Jorge Arriagada
El Color de las Nubes	Sp	Sebastian Marine
El Imposter	Arg	Nicola Piovani
Ellen Foster	CBS-TV	John Morris
Elmore Leonard's "Gold Coast"	Showtime	Peter Harris
Elvis Meets Nixon	Showtime	Larry Brown
End of Summer	Showtime	Patrick Seymour
End of Violence, The	US/Fr	Ry Cooder
Eve's Bayou	Ind	Terence Blanchard
Event Horizon	Par	Michael Kamen
Every 9 Seconds	NBC-TV	Peter Rodgers Melnick
Excess Baggage	Col	John Lurie
Excuse Me, Darling, but Lucas Loved Me	Sp	Manuel Villalta
Eye of God	Ind	David Van Tieghem
Facciamo Fiesta (Let's Fiesta)	It	Paolo Vivaldi
Face	Br	Andy Roberts
Face Down	Ind	Joe Lovano
Face Down	Ind	Gunther Schiller
Face/Off	Par	John Powell
Fairy Tale: A True Story	Par	Zbigniew Preisner
Fakin' Da Funk	Ind	Charles Gross
Fall	Ind	Amanda Kavat
Fast, Cheap & Out of Control	Ind	Caleb Sampson
Fathers' Day	WB	James Newton Howard
Father's Day	Ger	Peter Wolf
Fear and Learning at Hoover Elementary	Ind	Vinny Golia
Fever Pitch	Br	Neil McColl

Film	Studio	Composer
Fierce Creatures	Univ	Jerry Goldsmith
Fifth Element, The	Fr	Eric Serra
Fight in the Fields, The	Ind	Pete Sears
Final Descent	CBS-TV	David Benoit
Finalmente Soli	It	Germano Mazzocchetti
Fire Down Below	WB	Nick Glennie-Smith
Fire Down Below	WB	Mark Mansbridge
Firelight	US/Br	Christopher Gunning
Fireworks	It	Claudio Guidetti
. . . First Do No Harm	ABC-TV	Hummie Mann
First Love, Last Rites	Ind	Nathan Larson
First Love, Last Rites	Ind	Craig Weldren
First Strike	US/Hong	J. Peter Robinson
First Time Felon	HBO	Joseph Vitarelli
Fish Tale Soup	Can	David Bradstreet
Five Desperate Hours	NBC-TV	Marty Davich
Flash	ABC-TV	Bruce Rowland
Floating	Ind	David Mansfield
Flood: A River's Rampage	Fam Ch	Irwin Fisch
Flubber	BV	Danny Elfman
Follow the Bitch	Ind	Dane Davis
Follow Your Heart	Ind	Harry Manfredini
Food of Love	Br/Fr	Adrian Johnston
Fools Rush In	Col	Alan Silvestri
For Richer or Poorer	Univ	Randy Edelman
Forbidden Territory: Stanley's Search for Livingstone	ABC-TV	Mark Adler
Foreign Body, A (Sinon, Oui)	Fr/Can	Catherine Ringer
Foreign Body, A (Sinon, Oui)	Fr/Can	Archie Shepp
Frank Capra's American Dream	TriStar	John Hodian
Fratelli Coltelli (Knife Brothers)	It	Antonio Di Pofi
Free Willy 3: The Rescue	WB	Cliff Eidelman
Friends 'til the End	NBC-TV	Christophe Beck
From Today Until Tomorrow	Fr/Ger	Arnold Schoenberg
Full Monty, The	Br	Anne Dudley
Full Tilt Boogie	Ind	Dominic Kelly
Further Gesture, A	Br/Ger/Ire/Jap	John Keane
G.I. Jane	BV	Trevor Jones
Gambler, The	Br/Dutch/Hung	Brian Lock
Gambler, The	Br/Dutch/Hung	Gerard Schurmann
Game, The	Ind	Howard Shore
Gang Related	Orion	Mickey Hart
Garden of Redemption, The	Showtime	John Altman
Gattaca	Col	Michael Nyman
Genealogies d'un Crime	Fr	Jorge Arriagada
George B.	Ind	David Reynolds
George Wallace	TNT	Gary Chang
George of the Jungle	BV	Marc Shaiman
Gerrie & Louise	Can	Jonathan Goldsmith
Get to the Heart: The Barbara Mandrell Story	CBS-TV	Dennis McCarthy
Ghosts	Ind	Nicholas Pike
Gingerbread Man, The	Ind	Mark Isham
Girl With Brains in Her Feet, The	Br	Rob Lane
Glam	Ind	Geoffrey Moore

Go for Gold!	Ger/Sp/Fr	Mick Harvey
Going All the Way	Ind	Tomandandy
Going Ballistic	Sp/Fr	Juan Sueiro
Gold in the Streets	Br	Kila
Good Burger	Par	Stewart Copeland
Good Will Hunting	Miramax	Danny Elfman
Goodbye America	Ind	Roy Hay
Gravesend	Ind	Bill Laswell
Great Expectations	Fox	Patrick Doyle
Gridlock'd	Ind	Stewart Copeland
Grizzly Mountain	Ind	Jon McCallum
Grosse Pointe Blank	BV	Joe Strummer
Gun, a Car, a Blonde, A	Ind	Harry Manfredini
Guy Maddin: Waiting for Twilight	Can	Jeff Gilman
Hacks	Ind	Anthony Marinelli
Hanging Garden, The	Can	John Roby
Hantises (Hauntings)	Fr	Alfred Schnittke
Hayseed	Can	Robert Scott
Hazlo por Mi (Do It for Me)	Sp	Juan Carlos Cuello
Headhunter's Sister, The	Ind	Michael Montes
Heart Full of Rain	CBS-TV	Patrick Williams
Heart of Fire	CBS-TV	George S. Clinton
Heartless	USA Net	Mike De Martino
Heaven's Burning	Aut	Michael Atkinson
Heaven's Burning	Aut	Graeme Koehne
Henry Fool	Ind	Hal Hartley
Henry: Portrait of a Serial Killer 2	Ind	Robert F. McNaughton
Hercules	BV	Alan Menken
High Stakes	Lifetime	Joseph Conlan
High Voltage	Ind	Steve Edwards
Hijacking Hollywood	Ind	Erik Lundmark
Hired Heart, The	Lifetime	Ralph Grierson
Holiday in Your Heart	ABC-TV	Michael Tavera
Home Alone 3	Fox	Nick Glennie-Smith
Home Before Dark	Ind	Jeanine Cowen
Home Invasion	NBC-TV	Patrick Williams
Hoodlum	MGM/UA	Elmer Bernstein
Hope	TNT	Dave Grusin
Horsey	Can	Hellenkeller
Horton Foote's "Alone"	Showtime	David Shire
Hostile Waters	HBO	David Ferguson
House of America	Br/Dutch	John Cale
House of Frankenstein	NBC-TV	Don Davis
House of Yes, The	Miramax	Rolfe Kent
House of Yes, The	Miramax	Jeff Rona
How I Spent My Summer Vacation	Ind	Johnny Barrow
Hudson River Blues	Ind	Charlie Barnett
Hugo Pool	Ind	Danilo Perez
Hunchback, The	TNT	Edward Shearmur
I Know What You Did Last Summer	Col	John Debney
I Love You, I Love You Not	Ind	Mark Berger
I Love You, I Love You Not	Ind	Gil Goldstein
I Love You . . . Don't Touch Me!	Ind	Jane Ford
I Went Down	Ire/Br	Dario Marianelli

I'll Be Home for Christmas	CBS-TV	Geoff Levin
Ice Storm, The	Fox	Mychael Danna
Il Carniere (The Gamebag)	It	Pino Donaggio
Il Principe di Homburg	It	Carlo Crivelli
Il Sindaco (The Mayor)	It	Antonio Di Pofi
Il Vaggio della Sposa (The Bride's Journey)	It	Germano Mazzocchetti
Imax Nutcracker, The	Ind	Pyotr Ilyich Tchaikovsky
In & Out	Par	Marc Shaiman
In Amor de Sorciere (Witch Way Love)	Fr	Jean-Felix Lalanne
In Barca a Verla Contromano	It	Mauro Pagani
In His Father's Shoes	Showtime	John Weisman
In the Company of Men	Ind	Karel Roessingn
In the Company of Men	Ind	Ken Williams
In the Gloaming	HBO	Dave Grusin
In the Line of Duty: Blaze of Glory	NBC-TV	John D'Andrea
In the Line of Duty: Blaze of Glory	NBC-TV	Cory Lerios
In the Presence of Mine Enemies	Showtime	Dead Can Dance
Incognito	WB	John Ottman
Indefensible: The Truth About Edward Brannigan	CBS-TV	Dana Kaproff
Informant, The	Ire/US	Shane MacGowan
Inside/Out	Ind	J. K. Eareckson
Inspirations	Ind	Patrick Seymour
Into Thin Air: Death on Everest	ABC-TV	Lee Holdridge
Into the Arms of Danger: A Moment of Truth Movie	NBC-TV	Stacy Widelitz
Inventing the Abbotts	Fox	Michael Kamen
Island on Bird Street, The	Br/Dan/Ger	Zbigniew Preisner
Isle of Lesbos	Ind	Jeff B. Harmon
Jack London's "The Call of the Wild"	Fam Ch	Alan Reeves
Jackal, The	Univ	Carter Burwell
James Gang, The	Br/Can	Bernard Butler
Jitters	Lifetime	Peter Rodgers Melnick
Joe Torre: Curveballs Along the Way	Showtime	John Weisman
Joe's So Mean to Josephine	Can	Ron Sures
Joe's Wedding	Can	Mark Korven
Joey	Aut	Roger Mason
John Grisham's "The Rainmaker"	Par	Elmer Bernstein
Journey of the Heart	CBS-TV	Roger Kellaway
Journey to the Beginning of the World	Fr/Port	Emmanuel Nunes
Jules Verne's "20,000 Leagues Under the Sea"	ABC-TV	Mark Snow
Julian Po	Ind	Patrick Williams
Jungle 2 Jungle	BV	Michael Convertino
K	Fr	Philippe Sarde
Keep the Aspidistra Flying	Br	Mike Batt
Keeping the Promise	CBS-TV	Peter Manning Robinson
Ken Follett's "The Third Twin"	CBS-TV	Don Davis
Keys to Tulsa	Ind	Stephen Endelman
Kicked in the Head	Ind	Stephen Endelman
Killing Mr. Griffin	NBC-TV	Christophe Beck
Kini & Adams	Fr	Wally Badarou
Kiss Me, Guido	Ind	Randall Poster
Kiss the Girls	Par	Mark Isham

Kissing a Fool	Ind	Joseph Williams
Kitchen Party	Can	Shaun Tozer
Knots Landing: Back to the Cul-De-Sac	CBS-TV	Jerrold Immel
Kull the Conqueror	Univ	Joel Goldsmith
Kundun	BV	Philip Glass
L'appartamento (The Apartment)	It	Carlo Crivelli
L'autre Cote de la Mer	Fr	Beatrice Thiriet
L.A. Confidential	WB	Jerry Goldsmith
L.A. Johns	Fox-TV	Barry Goldberg
La Buena Estella (Lucky Star)	Sp/Fr/It	Eva Gancedo
La Cible (The Target)	Fr/Swiss/Sp	Christian Gaubert
La Comtesse de Baton Rouge	Can	Michel Cusson
La Conciergerie (The Haven)	Can	Jean-Marie Benoit
La Divine Poursuite	Fr	Quentin Damamme
La Femme de Chambre du Titanic	Sp/Fr/It	Alberto Iglesias
La Grande Quercia (The Wide Oak)	It	Fabrizio Siciliano
La Herida Luminosa	Sp	Manuel Balboa
La Medaglia (The Medal)	It	Alessandro Molinari
La Terza Luna	Swiss/It/Fr	Pino Donaggio
La Tregua (The Truce)	It/Fr/Ger/Swiss	Luis Bacalov
La Verite si je Mens	Fr	Gerard Presgurvic
La Vie de Jesus	Fr	Richard Cuvillier
La Vita e Bella (Life Is Beautiful)	Fr	Nicola Piovani
Last Bus Home, The	Ire	Cathal Coughlan
Last Days of Frankie the Fly, The	Ind	George S. Clinton
Last Stand at Saber River	TNT	David Shire
Last Time I Committed Suicide, The	Ind	Tyler Bates
Latin Boys Go to Hell	US/Ger/Sp/Jap	Ari Gold
Latin Boys Go to Hell	US/Ger/Sp/Jap	John Zorn
Lawn Dogs	Br	Trevor Jones
Lay of the Land, The	Can	Jeff Lass
Le Acrobate (The Acrobats)	It/Swiss	Giovanni Venosta
Le Bossu (On Guard!)	Fr/It/Ger	Philippe Sarde
Le Jour et La Nuit (Day and Night)	Fr/Sp/Can/Belg	Maurice Jarre
Le Mani Forti (The Gray Zone)	It	Dario Lucantoni
Le Pari (The Bet)	Fr	Jean-Christophe Prudhomme
Le Plus Beau Metier du Monde	Fr	Vladimir Cosma
Le Siege de l'ame (The Seat of the Soul)	Can	Francois Dompierre
Le Venere de Willendorf	It	Savio Riccardi
Leave It to Beaver	Univ	Randy Edelman
Legend of the Lost Tomb	Ind	Kevin Kiner
Lena's Dreams	Ind	Don Braden
Les Boys (The Boys)	Can	Normand Corbeil
Les Couleurs du Diable	Fr/It	Michel Portal
Les Palmes de M. Schutz (Pierre and Marie)	Fr	Vladimir Cosma
Les Randonneurs (The Hikers)	Fr	Philippe Eidel
Les Soeurs Soleil (The Sun Sisters)	Fr	Eric Levi
Lesser Evil, The	Ind	Don Davis
Let Me Call You Sweetheart	Fam Ch	Domenic Troiano
Let's Stick Together	Br	Jim Meacock
Levitation	Ind	Leonard Rosenman
Lewis & Clark & George	Ind	Ben Vaughn
Liar	Ind	Harry Gregson-Williams

Licensed to Kill	Ind	Miriam Cutler
Lies He Told	ABC-TV	Jeff Beal
Life Apart: Hasidism in America, A	Ind	Yale Storm
Life During Wartime	Ind	Christophe Beck
Life Is a Bluff	Ger	Gunter Moll
Life Less Ordinary, A	Br	David Arnold
Lifebreath	Ind	Michael Kessler
Lift	Ind	Dan & Kristi Lawrence
Little Bird	Sp	Alejandro Masso
Little Boy Blue	Ind	Stewart Copeland
Little City	Miramax	Mader
Little Girls in Pretty Boxes	Lifetime	Jeff Fair
Little Girls in Pretty Boxes	Lifetime	Starr Parodi
Locusts, The	Orion	Carter Burwell
Lolita	Br/Fr	Ennio Morricone
Long Way Home, The	Ind	Lee Holdridge
Lost Highway	Ind	Angelo Badalamenti
Lost Treasure of Dos Santos	Fam Ch	Fred Karlin
Lost World: Jurassic Park, The	Univ	John Williams
Louisa May Alcott's "The Inheritance"	CBS-TV	Christopher Franke
Love Bug, The	ABC-TV	Shirley Walker
Love God	Ind	Tracy McKnight
Love Jones	New Line	Darryl Jones
Love and Death on Long Island	Br/Can	Richard Grassby-Lewis
Love! Valour! Compassion!	Ind	Harold Wheeler
Love's Deadly Triangle: The Texas Cadet Murder	NBC-TV	Dennis McCarthy
Love, Math and Sex	Fr/Belg/Swiss	Bernard Lubat
Love-Struck	Fam Ch	Joseph Conlan
Loved	Ind	David Baerwald
Lovelife	Ind	Adam Fields
Lovemaster, The	Ind	Michael Skloff
Lover Girl	Ind	Mark Kilian
Lucie Aubrac	Fr	Philippe Sarde
"M" Word, The	Ind	Jon Wolfson
Ma vie en rose	Fr/Br/Belg	Dominique Declan
Macbeth	Scot	Richard Cherns
Mad City	WB	Thomas Newman
Made Men	Ind	Chris Hajian
Major Crime	Can	Jonathan Goldsmith
Maker, The	Ind	Paul Buckmaster
Man Who Knew Too Little, The	WB	Christopher Young
Mandela and deKlerk	Showtime	Cedric Gradus-Samson
Marcello Mastroianni: I Remember, Yes I Remember	It	Armando Trovajoli
Marianna Ucria	It/Fr	Franco Piersanti
Marie Baie des Anges	Fr	Carlo Crivelli
Mario Puzo's "The Last Don"	CBS-TV	Angelo Badalamenti
Mario Puzo's "The Last Don"	CBS-TV	Roger Bellon
Marion	Fr	Anne-Marie Fijal
Marquise	Fr/It/Sp/Swiss	Jordi Savall
Married to a Stranger	Fam Ch	Paul Zaza
Mary Jane's Not a Virgin Anymore	Ind	Rama Kolesnikow
Masterminds	Col	Anthony Marinelli

Match Made in Heaven, A	CBS-TV	Don Davis
Matchbox Circus Train	Ind	Mike DeMartino
Matchmaker, The	Ire/Br/US	John Altman
Matusalem II	Can	Milan Kymlicka
McHale's Navy	Univ	Dennis McCarthy
Medusa's Child	ABC-TV	Louis Febre
Meet Wally Sparks	Ind	Michel Colombier
Melanie Darrow	USA Net	Dick DeBenedictis
Member of the Wedding, The	USA Net	Laurence Rosenthal
Men	Ind	Mark Mothersbaugh
Men in Black	Col	Danny Elfman
Men With Guns	Sony	Mason Daring
Messieurs Les Enfants (Men Will Be Boys)	Fr/Sp	Jean-Claude Petit
Metro	BV	Steve Porcaro
Metroland	Br/Fr	Mark Knopfler
Midnight in the Garden of Good and Evil	WB	Lennie Niehaus
Midwife's Tale, A	Ind	Todd Boekelhide
Mill on the Floss, The	Br	John Scott
Mimic	Ind	Marco Beltrami
Miracle in the Woods	CBS-TV	Ernest Troost
Misbegotten	Can	Paul Zaza
Miss Evers' Boys	HBO	Charles Bernstein
Mojo	Br	Murray Gold
Money Talks	New Line	Lalo Schifrin
Monk Dawson	Br	Mark Jensen
Mordburo	Fr/Belg/It	Krishna Levy
Morella	Ind	Carl Schurtz
Mortal Kombat 2 Annihilation	New Line	George S. Clinton
Most Wanted	New Line	Paul Buckmaster
Mother Knows Best	ABC-TV	Patrick Williams
Mother Teresa: In the Name of God's Poor	Fam Ch	Irwin Fisch
Mouse Hunt	Dream	Alan Silvestri
Moving In Moving Out	Ind	Andrew Hollander
Mr. Magoo	BV	Michael Tavera
Mr. Nice Guy	New Line	J. Peter Robinson
Mr. Vincent	Ind	Chris Hajian
Mr. Vincent	Ind	Steven Louis Infante
Mrs. Brown	Br	Stephen Warbeck
Mrs. Dalloway	Br	Ilona Sekacz
Ms. Scrooge	USA Net	David Shire
Murder Live	NBC-TV	Gary Chang
Murder at 1600	WB	Christopher Young
Murder in My Mind	CBS-TV	Michel Colombier
My Best Friend's Wedding	TriStar	James Newton Howard
My Brother Jack	Ind	Gregory Alper
My Stepson, My Lover	USA Net	Joseph Conlan
Myth of Fingerprints, The	Ind	David Bridie
Myth of Fingerprints, The	Ind	John Phillips
National Lampoon's "Dad's Week Off"	Par	Mark Bonilla
National Lampoon's "The Don's Analyst"	Par	Mader
Neil Simon's "The Sunshine Boys"	CBS-TV	Irwin Fisch
Nevada	Ind	Robert Perry
Niagara Niagara	Ind	Michael Timmins
Niagara Niagara	Ind	Jeff Bird

Nick & Rachel	Ind	Margaret Hetherman
Nick and Jane	Ind	Marc Suozzo
Night Falls on Manhattan	Par	Mark Isham
Night Orchid	Ind	C. C. Adcock
Night Sins	CBS-TV	Mark Snow
NightScream	NBC-TV	Garry Schyman
Nightmare Come True, A	CBS-TV	Jeff Fair
Nightmare Come True, A	CBS-TV	Starr Parodi
Nil by Mouth	Br	Eric Clapton
Nirvana	It/Fr	Federico De Robertis
Nirvana	It/Fr	Mauro Pagani
North End, The	Ind	Adam Steinberg
North Shore Fish	Showtime	Donald Markowitz
Northern Lights	Disney-TV	Patrick Seymour
Not in This Town	USA Net	Don Davis
Nothing Sacred	Ind	Gary Stockdale
Nothing to Lose	BV	Robert Folk
Ocean Tribe	Ind	Sean Murray
Odyssey, The	NBC-TV	Eduard Artemiev
Office Killer	Ind	Evan Lurie
Old Man Dogs	Ind	Michael Huggins
Oliver Twist	ABC-TV	Van Dyke Parks
On Connait la Chanson (Same Old Song)	Fr/Swiss/Belg	Bruno Fontaine
On the 2nd Day of Christmas	Lifetime	David Bergeaud
On the Edge of Innocence	NBC-TV	Dana Kaproff
One Dog Day	Ind	Kilgore Trout
One Night Stand	New Line	Mike Figgis
Only Thrill, The	Ind	Peter Rodgers Melnick
Operation Condor	Ind	Stephen Endelman
Oranges Ameres (Bitter Oranges)	Fr/It/Sp	Alain Jomy
Orgazmo	Ind	Paul Robb
Oscar and Lucinda	US/Aut	Thomas Newman
Our God's Brother	It/Ger/Pol	Wojciech Kilar
Our Mother's Murder	USA Net	Joseph Conlan
Out of Nowhere	ABC-TV	Richard Bellis
Out to Sea	Fox	David Newman
Pale Saints	Can	Michael Theriault
Pale Saints	Can	Ian Thomas
Paperback Romance	Aut	Paul Grabowsky
Paradise Road	Aut/US	Ross Edwards
Parting Shots	Br	Chris Rea
Passion in the Desert	Ind	Jose Nieto
Path to Paradise	HBO	Mitchell Froom
Paws	Aut/Br	Mario Millo
Payback	ABC-TV	Mark Snow
Peacemaker, The	Dream	Hans Zimmer
Perdita Durango	Sp/Mex	Simon Boswell
Perfect Body	NBC-TV	Pray for Rain
Perfect Crime	USA Net	Joseph Conlan
Perfect Moment	Ind	Michael Whalen
Perfect Mother, The	CBS-TV	Mark Snow
Pest, The	TriStar	Kevin Kiner
Photographing Fairies	Br	Simon Boswell
Picture Perfect	Fox	Carter Burwell

Pippi Longstocking	Can/Ger/Swiss	Anders Berglund
Planet of Junior Brown, The	Ind	Christopher Dedrick
Plato's Run	Ind	Robert O. Ragland
Playing God	BV	Richard Hartley
Port Djema	Fr/It/Greek	Sanjay Mishra
Postman, The	WB	James Newton Howard
Postmortem	Ind	Tony Riparetti
Prayer in the Dark, A	USA Net	David Michael Frank
Preaching to the Perverted	Br	Maya & Magnus Fiennes
Prefontaine	BV	Mason Daring
Price of Heaven, The	CBS-TV	Mark Snow
Price of Kissing, The	Ind	Phil Marshall
Prince, The	Ind	David Michael Frank
Prison of Secrets	Lifetime	Nan Schwartz-Mishkin
Private Parts	Par	Van Dyke Parks
Pronto	Showtime	John Altman
Pur Boy	Br	Neil McColl
Purgatory County	Ind	Mike Mariconda
Quadrille	Fr	Bertrand Burgalat
Quicksilver Highway	Fox-TV	Mark Mothersbaugh
Quiet Days in Hollywood	Ger	Harald Kloser
Quiet Room, The	Aut	Graham Tardif
Raising the Ashes	Ind	Gary Remal Malkin
Real Blonde, The	Par	Jim Farmer
Red Corner	MGM	Thomas Newman
Regeneration	Br/Can	Mychael Danna
Relic, The	Par	John Debney
Reluctant Angel	Can	Ben Johannsen
Reluctant Angel	Can	Geoff Bennett
Rescuers: Stories of Courage: Two Women	Showtime	Hummie Mann
Resurrection Man	Br	Gary Burns
Resurrection Man	Br	David Holmes
Retroactive	Orion	Tim Truman
Revenge of the Woman in Black, The	Fr/Can	Milan Kymlicka
Rhinoceros Hunting in Budpest	Br/Fr	John Cale
Rhodes	BBC-TV	Alan Parker
Rhyme & Reason	Miramax	Benedikt Bryden
Rien ne va plus	Fr/Swiss	Matthieu Chabrol
Right Connections, The	Showtime	Michel Colombier
Riot	Showtime	Luke Cresswell
Riot	Showtime	Steve McNicholas
Ripper, The	Aut	Mason Daring
Road Ends	Ind	David Mansfield
Road to Graceland, The	Ind	Stephen Endelman
Road to Nhill	Aut	Elizabeth Drake
Robert Ludlum's "The Apocalypse Watch"	ABC-TV	Ken Thorne
Robin Cook's "Invasion"	NBC-TV	Don Davis
Rocketman	BV	Michael Tavera
Rockford Files: Murder and Misdemeanors, The	CBS-TV	Mike Post
Rockford Files: Murder and Misdemeanors, The	CBS-TV	Pete Carpenter
Rodgers and Hammerstein's "Cinderella"	ABC-TV	Richard Rodgers
Romance and Rejection	Br	Howard J. Davidson

Romy and Michele's High School Reunion	BV	Steve Bartek
Ronnie & Julie	Showtime	Daryl Bennett
Ronnie & Julie	Showtime	Jim Guttridge
Rose Hill	CBS-TV	Steve Dorff
Rosewood	WB	John Williams
Rossini: or the Fatal Question, Who Slept With Who	Ger	Dario Farina
Rough Riders	TNT	Elmer Bernstein
Rough Riders	TNT	Peter Bernstein
Rudyard Kipling's "The Second Jungle Book"	TriStar	John Scott
Runaway Car	Fox-TV	J. Peter Robinson
Running Time	Ind	Joseph Lo Duca
Saint, The	Par	Graeme Revell
Sand Trap	Ind	Bennett Salvay
Santa Fe	Ind	Mark Governor
Santo Stefano	It	Nicola Piovani
Sarabande	Can	Johann Sebastian Bach
Saraka Bo	Fr	Jean-Claude Petit
Scottish Tale, The	Ind	Ed Bogas
Scream 2	Miramax	Marco Beltrami
Sea Wolf, The	Can	Roger Neill
Second Civil War, The	HBO	Hummie Mann
Secret Life of Algernon, The	Can	Graeme Coleman
Secret, The	NBC-TV	Brian Adler
Seduction in a Small Town	ABC-TV	Richard Bellis
Selena	WB	Dave Grusin
Serpent's Kiss, The	Fr/Br/Sp	Goran Bregovic
Setting Son, The	Ind	Eric Colvin
Seven Years in Tibet	TriStar	John Williams
Shadow Conspiracy	BV	Bruce Broughton
Shampoo Horns	Sp	Angel Illarramendi
She's So Lovely	Miramax	Joseph Vitarelli
Shooting Fish	Br	Stanislas Syrewicz
Shopping for Fangs	Can/US	Steven Pranoto
Shot in the Foot	Fr	Christopher Defays
Shot in the Foot	Fr	Olivier Defays
Sick (The Life and Death of Bob Flanagan, Supermasochist)	Ind	Blake Leyh
Simple Wish, A	Univ	Bruce Broughton
Sins of the Mind	USA Net	David Bergeaud
Sisters and Other Strangers	CBS-TV	Patrick Williams
Six Gestures	Can	Johann Sebastian Bach
Six Ways to Sunday	Ind	Theodore Shapiro
Slab Boys, The	Br	Jack Bruce
Slaves to the Underground	Ind	Mike Martt
Sleeping With the Devil	CBS-TV	Chris Boardman
Sleepwalking Killer, The	NBC-TV	Gary Remal Malkin
Sliding Doors	US/Br	David Hirschfelder
Small Hours, The	Ind	Harald Kloser
Smile Like Yours, A	Par	William Ross
Smilla's Sense of Snow	Ger/Swed/Dan	Harry Gregson-Williams
Smilla's Sense of Snow	Ger/Swed/Dan	Hans Zimmer
Snake Skin Jacket	Ind	John Adair

Snide & Prejudice	Ind	Allan Zavod
Snow White: A Tale of Terror	Ind	John Ottman
Soleil (Sun)	Fr/Ger/It	Vladimir Cosma
Something Borrowed, Something Blue	CBS-TV	Nan Schwartz-Mishkin
Somewhere in the City	Ind	John Cale
Soul Food	Fox	Wendy Melvoin
Souler Opposite, The	Ind	Peter Himmelman
Soulmates	Ind	David Russo
Spanish Prisoner, The	Ind	Carter Burwell
Sparkler	Ind	David Russo
Spawn	New Line	Graeme Revell
Speed 2: Cruise Control	Fox	Mark Mancina
Spice World	Br	Paul Newcastle
Sprung	Ind	Stanley Clarke
Stag	Can	Paul Zaza
Stand-Ins	Ind	Bill Elliott
Starship Troopers	TriStar	Basil Poledouris
States of Control	Ind	Richard Termini
Steaming Milk	Ind	Miles Roston
Steel	WB	Mervyn Warren
Steel Chariots	Fox-TV	John D'Andrea
Steel Chariots	Fox-TV	Cory Lerios
Stephen King's "The Shining"	ABC-TV	Nicholas Pike
Stepsister, The	USA Net	Peter Manning Robinson
Stiff Upper Lips	Br	David A. Hughes
Stiff Upper Lips	Br	John Murphy
Still Breathing	Ind	Paul Mills
Stir	Ind	Keith Bilderbeck
Stolen Women	CBS-TV	Dana Kaproff
Stranger in My Home	CBS-TV	Marco Beltrami
Strong Island Boys	Ind	Joshua Sitron
Sub Down	Ind	Stefano Mainetti
Subway Stories	HBO	Mecca Bodega
Suicide Kings	Ind	Tim Simonec
Sunday	Ind	Nossiter
Survival on the Mountain	NBC-TV	Jonathan Goldsmith
Swan Princess: Escape From Castle Mountain, The	Ind	Lex De Azevedo
Sweet Hereafter, The	Can	Mychael Danna
Sweet Jane	Ind	Walter Werzowa
Sweetest Gift, The	Showtime	Lawrence Shragge
Sweethearts	Ind	Carl Schurtz
Swept From the Sea	Br	John Barry
Switchback	Par	Basil Poledouris
Tale of Sweeney Todd	Br	Richard Rodney Bennett
Talos the Mummy	Ind	Stefano Mainetti
Tango Lesson, The	Br	Sally Potter
Tano da Mortre	It	Nino D'Angelo
Tell Me No Secrets	ABC-TV	Christopher Franke
Telling Lies in America	Can	Nicholas Pike
Tempete dans un verre d'eau	Fr	Jonathan Sampson
Tesstimone a Rischio (Witness in Danger)	It	Franco Piersanti
Thank God He Met Lizzie	Aut	Martin Arminger
That Darn Cat	Disney-TV	Richard Kendall Gibbs

That Old Feeling	Univ	Patrick Williams
Their Second Chance	Lifetime	Craig Safan
This World, Then the Fireworks	Orion	Pete Rugolo
Thousand Acres, A	BV	Richard Hartley
Thousand Men and a Baby, A	CBS-TV	David Michael Frank
Thousand Wonders of the Universe, The	Can/Fr	Mick Morris
Three Lives of Karen, The	USA Net	Pray for Rain
Thrill Ride: The Science of Fun	Ind	Michael Stearns
Tichborne Claimant, The	Br	Nicholas Hooper
Ticket, The	USA Net	Charles Bernstein
Tidal Wave: No Escape	ABC-TV	Bruce Rowland
Ties to Rachel	Ind	Ben Wilborn
'Til There Was You	Par	Terence Blanchard
'Til There Was You	Par	Miles Goodman
Time to Say Goodbye?	Lifetime	Peter Rodgers Melnick
Titanic	Par	James Horner
To Dance With Olivia	CBS-TV	David Shire
Tomorrow Never Dies	MGM/UA	David Arnold
Tonka	Fr/It	Gabriel Yared
Too Close to Home	CBS-TV	Jonathan Goldsmith
Too Much Sleep	Ind	Michael Tooney
Toothless	ABC-TV	David Michael Frank
Top of the World	Ind	Robert O. Ragland
Tortilla y Cinema	Fr/Sp	Bruno Bertoli
Touch	MGM/UA	David Grohl
Touched by Evil	ABC-TV	Dan Slider
Tower of Terror	ABC-TV	Louis Febre
Tram a la Malvarrosa	Sp	Antoine Duhamel
Transatlantique	Fr/Port	Jorge Arriagada
Traveller	Ind	Andy Paley
Trial and Error	New Line	Phil Marshall
Tricks	Showtime	Patrick Seymour
Trouble on the Corner	Ind	Robert Een
Trucks	USA Net	Michael Richard Plowman
True Love and Chaos	Aut	David Bowers
True Love and Chaos	Aut	Martin Lubran
True Women	CBS-TV	Bruce Broughton
Truth or Consequences, N.M.	Sony	Jude Cole
Turbo: A Power Rangers Movie	Fox	Shuki Levy
TwentyFourSeven	Br	Boo Hewerdine
TwentyFourSeven	Br	Neil McColl
Twilight of the Golds, The	Showtime	Lee Holdridge
Twilight of the Ice Nymphs, The	Can	John McCulloch
Twin Town	Br	Mark Thomas
Two Came Back	ABC-TV	Michael Tavera
Two Voices	Lifetime	J.A.C. Redford
U-Turn	TriStar	Ennio Morricone
Ugly, The	NewZea	Victoria Kelly
Ulee's Gold	Orion	Charles Engstrom
Un Frere	Fr	Philippe Sarde
Under Wraps	Disney-TV	David Michael Frank
Under the Lighthouse Dancing	Ind	Nerida Tyson-Chew
Under the Skin	Br	Ilona Sekacz
Undertaker's Wedding, The	Can	Varouje

Underworld	Ind	Anthony Marinelli
Univers'l	Ind	Gregory Ives
Unwed Father	ABC-TV	Mark Mothersbaugh
Up 'n' Under	Br	Mark Thomas
Up on the Roof	Br	Alan Parker
Vacation in Hell	It	Fabrizio Siciliano
Vanishing Point	Fox-TV	James Verboort
Vegas Vacation	WB	Joel McNeely
Victory	Br/Fr/Ger	Richard Hartley
Violet's Visit	Aut	Paul Anthony Smith
Voice of the Children	Ind	Peter Fish
Volcano	Fox	Alan Silvestri
Volcano: Fire on the Mountain	ABC-TV	David Michael Frank
Wag the Dog	New Line	Mark Knopfler
Walton Easter, A	CBS-TV	Patrick Williams
Washington Square	BV	Jan A.P. Kaczmarek
Watermelon Woman, The	Ind	Paul Shapiro
Wax Mask	It/Fr	Maurizio Abeni
Weapons of Mass Distraction	HBO	Don Davis
Welcome to Sarajevo	Br/US	Adrian Johnston
Welcome to Woop Woop	Aut/Br	Stewart Copeland
Well, The	Aut	Stephen Rae
Western	Fr	Bernardo Sandoval
Westing Game, The	Ind	Parmer Fuller
What Happened to Bobby Earl?	CBS-TV	David Bell
What the Deaf Man Heard	CBS-TV	J.A.C. Redford
When Danger Follows You Home	USA Net	Charles Bernstein
When Innocence Is Lost	Lifetime	Dennis McCarthy
When Secrets Kill	ABC-TV	Richard Hartley
When Time Expires	Ind	Todd Hayen
When the Cradle Falls	CBS-TV	Joseph Conlan
While My Pretty One Sleeps	Fam Ch	Domenic Troiano
Wild America	WB	Joel McNeely
Wilde	Br	Debbie Wiseman
Wildly Available	Ind	Porter Jordan
William Faulkner's "Old Man"	CBS-TV	Lawrence Shragge
Wind in the Willows, The	Br	John Du Prez
Wind in the Willows, The	Br	Terry Jones
Wings of the Dove, The	Br	Edward Shearmur
Wings of the Dove, The	Br	Gabriel Yared
Winter Guest, The	Br	Michael Kamen
Wishmaster	Ind	Harry Manfredini
Woodlanders, The	Br	George Fenton
Wounded	Ind	Ross Vannelli
Wright Brothers, The	Ind	Jim England
XXL	Fr	Goran Beregovic
Zeus and Roxanne	MGM	Bruce Rowland

COMPOSERS AND THEIR FILMS

ABENI, MAURIZIO
Wax Mask (1997)

ABRAMOVITCH, BARRON
Hard Evidence (1994)
Tracks of a Killer (1995)

ABRIL, ANTON GARCIA
Monk, The (1990)

ACROBAT
My Boyfriend's Back (1989)

ADAIR, JOHN
Snake Skin Jacket (1997)

ADAMSON, BARRY
Delusion (1991)
Shuttlecock (1991)
Gas Food Lodging (1992)

ADCOCK, C. C.
Night Orchid (1997)

ADDISON, JOHN
Phantom of the Opera, The (1990)

ADLER, BRIAN
Death Benefit (1996)
Sudden Terror: The Hijacking of School
Bus 17(1996)
To Love, Honor and Deceive (1996)
Detention: Siege at Johnson High (1997)
Secret, The (1997)

ADLER, MARK
Eat a Bowl of Tea (1989)
Life Is Cheap (1989)
Henry & June (1990)
Harry Bridges: A Man and His Union
(1992)
Picture Bride (1995)
Slam Dunk Ernest (1995)
Forbidden Territory: Stanley's Search for
Livingstone (1997)

AEROSMITH
Heartless (1995)

AFRICA
Jason's Lyric (1994)

AHLERS, OZZIE
Gumby: The Movie (1995)

ALCIVAR, BOB
Blind Witness (1989)
Naked Lie (1989)
Roxanne: The Prize Pulitzer (1989)
Sparks: The Price of Passion (1990)
Deadly Medicine (1991)
Web of Deception (1994)

ALESSANDRINI, RAYMOND
Priez pour Nous (Pray for Us) (1994)

ALLAMAN, ERIC
Angel 3: The Final Chapter (1988)
Down Twisted (1989)

ALLAN, CAMERON
Jericho Fever (1993)
JFK: Reckless Youth (1993)
Men Don't Tell (1993)
Close to Danger (1997)

ALLEN, DAVE
Harvest, The (1993)

ALLEN, PETER
Cyborg 2 (1993)
Crackerjack (1994)
Dead Fire (1996)

ALLEN, RUSSELL D.
Offerings (1989)

ALONSO, TOM
Tusks (aka Fire in Eden) (1990)

ALPER, GREGORY
  Alexa (1989)
  My Brother Jack (1997)

ALTERS, GERALD
  Sister Margaret and the Saturday Night
    Ladies (1987)

ALTMAN, JOHN
  Assassin of the Tsar (1991)
  Hear My Song (1991)
  Long Roads, The (1992)
  Bad Behaviour (1992)
  Devlin (1992)
  Bhaji on the Beach (1993)
  Camilla (1993)
  Funny Bones (1995)
  Beautiful Thing (1996)
  Garden of Redemption, The (1997)
  Matchmaker, The (1997)
  Pronto (1997)

ALTON, MINETTE
  Devlin (1992)

ALTRUDA, JOEY
  Shake, Rattle and Rock! (1994)

ANASTASIA
  Before the Rain (1994)

ANDERSON, LAURIE
  Spaulding Gray's Monster in a Box
    (1991)

ANDERSON, PETER
  Chasers (1994)

ANDERSON, WILLIAM
  Cashing In (1996)

ANDREWS, DWIGHT
  Piano Lesson, The (1995)

ANGELL, PEITOR
  Man of the Year (1995)

ANGLEY, SCOTT
  Clerks (1994)

ANTHONY, PETE
  Run for the Dream: The Gail Devers
    Story (1996)

ANTONELLI, PAUL F.
  China O'Brien II (1989)
  Out of the Dark (1989)

APPLEBY, PHILIP
  Grass Arena, The (1991)
  Ghostwatch (1992)
  Maria's Child (1992)
  My Sister Wife (1992)
  In the Cold Light of Day (1994)
  Nothing Personal (1995)

ARAZIZ, ANA
  Girl in the Watermelon, The (1994)

ARBORE, RENZO
  Cari Fottutissimi Amici (1994)

ARDAN, PATRICK
  Le Retour des Charlots (The Charlots
    Return) (1992)

ARKENSTONE, DAVID
  Invisible: The Chronicle of Benjamin
    Knight (1993)

ARKIN, EDDIE
  Heroes Stand Alone (1989)

ARMINGER, MARTIN
  Sweetie (1989)
  Young Einstein (1989)
  Waiting (1990)
  Ring of Scorpio (1991)
  Children of the Dragon (1992)
  Crossing, The (1992)
  Thank God He Met Lizzie (1997)

ARMSTRONG, CRAIG
  William Shakespeare's Romeo + Juliet
    (1996)

ARNALDI, STEFANO
  Un Caso d'Amore (Love Case) (1996)

ARNOLD, DAVID
  Young Americans, The (1993)
  Stargate (1994)
  Last of the Dog Men (1995)
  Independence Day (1996)
  Life Less Ordinary, A (1997)
  Tomorrow Never Dies (1997)

ARNOLD, GREGORY
  Lonely in America (1990)

ARNOW, PETER
  Torn Apart (1990)

ARNSTON, BRUCE
  Ernest Goes to Jail (1990)
  Ernest Scared Stupid (1991)
  Ernest Rides Again (1993)

ARONSON, LEON
  Eddie and the Cruisers: Eddie Lives!
    (1989)
  Jack Higgins' "On Dangerous Grounds"
    (1996)

ARRIAGADA, JORGE
  L'Ile au Tresor (Treasure Island) (1991)
  It's All True (1993)
  Elle (1995)
  Le Fabuleux Destin de Madame Petlet
    (1995)
  Eyes of Asia (1996)
  Rolling Stones (1996)
  Trois Vies et un Suele Mort (1996)
  El Che (1997)
  Genealogies d'un Crime (1997)
  Transatlantique (1997)

ARTEMIEV, EDUARD
  Homer and Eddie (1989)
  Urga (1990)
  Inner Circle, The (1991)
  Close to Eden (1992)
  Double Jeopardy (1992)
  Burnt by the Sun (1994)
  Odyssey, The (1997)

ARTZI, SHLOMO
  Leather Jackets (1992)

ASHER, JAY
  Exiled in America (1992)
  Fugitive Nights: Danger in the Desert
    (1993)

ASHMAN, HOWARD
  Little Mermaid, The (1989)
  Beauty and the Beast (1991)
  Aladdin (1992)

ASSELIN, FRANCOIS

Sphinx, The (1995)

ASTON, PAUL
  Joy Breaker (1993)

ATHERTON, SONIA WIEDER
  Histoires D'Amerique (1989)
  La Crise (Crisis-Go-Round) (1992)
  L'Amour Conjugal (Conjugal Duty)
    (1995)
  Un Divan a New York (A Couch in New
    York) (1996)

ATKINSON, MICHAEL
  Heaven's Burning (1997)

ATTAWAY, MURRAY
  Midnight Edition (1993)

AUBRY, RENE
  Killer Kid (1994)

AUTRAND, CHARLES
  Malik le Maudit (Calamity Malik) (1996)

AVILA, PEPE
  My Family/Mi Familia (1995)

AYMAR, MARCEL
  Le Secret de Jerome (Jerome's Secret)
    (1994)

AYRES, MARK
  Innocent Sleep, The (1995)

BABCOCK, BRUCE
  Moment of Truth: Stalking Back (1993)
  Moment of Truth: A Child Too Many
    (1993)
  Moment of Truth: Why My Daughter?
    (1993)

BACALOV, LUIS
  Notte di Stelle (Starry Night) (1992)
  Anni Ribelli (Laura: The Rebel Years)
    (1994)
  Il Postino (The Postman) (1994)
  Ilona Comes With the Rain (1996)
  La Frontiera (The Border) (1996)
  La Tregua (The Truce) (1997)

BACH, JOHANN SEBASTIAN
  Sarabande (1997)

Six Gestures (1997)

BACHARACH, BURT
Love Hurts (1990)

BACON, MICHAEL
Pen Pals (1992)
Losing Chase (1996)

BADALAMENTI, ANGELO
Cousins (1989)
National Lampoon's Christmas Vacation
(1989)
Parents (1989)
Comfort of Strangers, The (1990)
Wild at Heart (1990)
Wait Until Spring, Bandini (1990)
Twin Peaks: Fire Walk With Me (1992)
Witch Hunt (1994)
Naked in New York (1994)
La Cite des Enfantes Perdus (1995)
Invasion of Privacy (1996)
Lost Highway (1997)
Blood Oranges, The (1997)
Mario Puzo's "The Last Don" (1997)

BADAROU, WALLY
Lunatic, The (1992)
Kini & Adams (1997)

BAERWALD, DAVID
Loved (1997)

BAHLER, TOM
U.S. Marshals: Waco & Rhinehart
(1987)
Cold Feet (1989)
Object of Beauty, The (1991)
In the Eyes of a Stranger (1992)
Gordy (1995)

BAITZ, RICK
Last Summer in the Hamptons (1995)

BAKER, FRED
White Trash (1992)

BAKER, JAMES
Fun Down There (1989)

BAKER, MICHAEL CONWAY
Anything to Survive (1990)
Showdown at Williams Creek (1991)

Portrait, The (1993)
Starlight (1996)

BALANESCU, ALEXANDER
Angels and Insects (1995)

BALBOA, MANUEL
La Herida Luminosa (1997)

BAND, RICHARD
Puppet Master (1989)
Crash and Burn (1990)
Doctor Mordrid: Master of the Unknown
(1990)
Initiation: Silent Night, Deadly Night 4
(1990)
Puppet Master II (1990)
Shadowzone (1990)
Arena (1991)
Arrival, The (1991)
Bride of Re-Animator (1991)
Dollman vs. Demonic Toys (1991)
Pit and the Pendulum, The (1991)
Puppet Master III: Toulon's Revenge
(1991)
Demonic Toys (1992)
Resurrected, The (1992)
Trancers III: Deth Lives (1992)
Prehysteria (1993)
Puppet Master IV (1993)
Remote (1993)
Dragonworld (1994)
Prehysteria 2 (1994)
Puppet Master V: The Final Chapter
(1994)
Shrunken Heads (1994)
Castle Freak (1995)
Magic Island (1996)
Zarkorr! The Invader (1996)

BANKS, BRIAN
Spooner (1989)
Graveyard Shift (1990)
Internal Affairs (1990)

BARAN, JACK
Great Balls of Fire! (1989)

BARBELIVIEN, DIDIER
Les Miserables (1995)

BARBELLA, BUTCH
Bronx Tale, A (1993)

BARBER, BILLY
  Mystery Science Theater 3000: The
    Movie (1996)

BARBER, LESLEY
  When Night Is Falling (1995)
  Turning April (1996)

BARBER, STEPHEN
  Galaxies Are Colliding (1992)

BARBIER, DENIS
  Fausto (aka A la Mode) (1993)

BARBIERI, GATO
  Diario du un Vizio (Diary of a Maniac)
    (1993)

BARDEN, JAMES H.
  Judas Project, The (1992)

BARKLEY, DAVID
  Jane Street (1996)

BARKMAN, BRENT
  Change of Place, A (1994)

BARLOW, LOU
  kids (1995)

BARNES, JOHN
  Daughters of the Dust (1991)
  Bebe's Kids (1992)
  CB4 (1993)
  Better Off Dead (1993)
  Don't Be a Menace to South Central
    (1996)
  Colors Straight Up (1997)

BARNES, KEVIN
  Keaton's Cop (1990)

BARNETT, CHARLIE
  Hudson River Blues (1997)

BARNETT, CHARLES P.
  Headless Body in Topless Bar (1995)

BARONE, MARCUS
  Cover Me (1995)

BARRERE, PAUL
  Dirty Money (1994)

BARROW, JOHNNY
  How I Spent My Summer Vacation
    (1997)

BARRY, DAEMION
  Woman's Guide to Adultery, A (1996)

BARRY, JEFF
  Your Mother Wears Combat Boots
    (1989)

BARRY, JOHN
  Dances With Wolves (1990)
  Chaplin (1992)
  Deception (1992)
  Public Eye, The (1992)
  Indecent Proposal (1993)
  My Life (1993)
  Ruby Cairo (1993)
  Specialist, The (1994)
  Across the Sea of Time (1995)
  Cry, the Beloved Country (1995)
  Scarlet Letter, The (1995)
  Swept From the Sea (1997)

BARTEK, STEVE
  Guilty as Charged (1991)
  Part Midnight (1992)
  Cabin Boy (1994)
  Coldblooded (1995)
  National Lampoon's Senior Trip (1995)
  Romy and Michele's High School
    Reunion (1997)

BARTSCH, ALEC
  Hanged Man, The (1993)

BASE ENEMY
  Inner City (1995)

BASSINSON, KEVIN
  Cyborg (1989)
  Beanstalk (1994)
  Eight Days a Week (1997)

BASTIAN, LARRY
  Goldy II: The Saga of the Golden Bear
    (1996)

BATES, TYLER
  Blue Flame (1995)
  Last Time I Committed Suicide, The
    (1997)

BATT, MIKE
    Keep the Aspidistra Flying (1997)

BATTIATO, FRANCO
    Una Vita Scellerata (An Infamous Life)
        (1990)

BAUMBARTEN, ALAN
    Excessive Force (1993)

BAXTER, LES
    Lightning in a Bottle (1994)

BEAL, DAVID
    Take, The (1990)

BEAL, JEFF
    Cheap Shots (1991)
    Fence, The (1994)
    Jonathan Stone: Threat of Innocence
        (1994)
    Ring of Steel (1994)
    Guy (1996)
    Love Is All There Is (1996)
    Power 98 (1996)
    Steve Martini's "Undue Influence"
        (1996)
    Lies He Told (1997)

BEAMISH, BRIAN
    Fists of Blood (1989)

BEARDEN, MICHAEL
    DROP Squad (1994)

BECK, CHRISTOPHE
    Friends 'til the End (1997)
    Killing Mr. Griffin (1997)
    Life During Wartime (1997)

BECK, JEFF
    Blue Chips (1994)

BECKER, FRANK W.
    Terminal Bliss (1990)
    American Kickboxer I (1991)
    Steel Justice (1992)
    Happily Ever After (1993)
    Monolith (1993)

BECKER, MICHAEL
    Clownhouse (1989)
    Solitaire (1992)

BECKETT, HAL
    Power of Attorney (1994)

BECKNER, BRANDON
    Fall and Spring (1996)

BEDELL, STEPHEN
    Jersey Girl (1992)
    Nickel & Dime (1992)

BEEN, MICHAEL
    Light Sleeper (1992)

BEIDERBECKE, BIX
    Bix (1991)

BELL, DAREN
    Tattoo Boy (1995)

BELL, DAVID
    Lucky Day (1991)
    Stranger at My Door (1991)
    Coopersmith: Sweet Scent of Murder
        (1992)
    Memphis (1992)
    Ned Blessing: The True Story of My Life
        (1992)
    Stormy Weathers (1992)
    There Goes the Neighborhood (1992)
    John Jakes' "Heaven & Hell: North &
        South Book 3" (1994)
    Sin and Redemption (1994)
    Convict Cowboy (1995)
    Wild Bill: Hollywood Maverick (1995)
    Larry McMurtry's "Dead Man's Walk"
        (1996)
    Sins of Silence (1996)
    What Happened to Bobby Earl? (1997)

BELL, WAYNE
    Return of the Texas Chainsaw Massacre,
        The (1995)

BELLIS, RICHARD
    Stephen King's "It" (1990)
    Doublecrossed (1991)
    Haunted, The (1991)
    Mother's Justice, A (1991)
    Nightmare in Columbia County (1991)
    Blind Man's Bluff (1992)
    Killer Among Friends, A (1992)
    To Grandmother's House We Go (1992)
    Double, Double, Toil and Trouble (1993)

No Child of Mine (1993)
Without a Kiss Goodbye (1993)
Disappearance of Vonnie, The (1994)
How the West Was Fun (1994)
Spider and the Fly, The (1994)
Sister-in-Law, The (1995)
Where's the Money, Noreen? (1995)
Kidz in the Wood (1996)
Legend of the Ruby Silver (1996)
Breaking the Surface (1997)
Out of Nowhere (1997)
Seduction in a Small Town (1997)

BELLO, JOAKIN
   Sandino (1990)

BELLON, ROGER
   Options (1989)
   Hi Honey I'm Dead (1991)
   Social Suicide (1991)
   Dark Horse (1992)
   Unforgivable (1996)
   Mario Puzo's "The Last Don" (1997)

BELOTE, WILLIAM
   B.O.R.N. (1989)

BELTRAMI, MARCO
   Scream (1996)
   Mimic (1997)
   Scream 2 (1997)
   Stranger in My Home (1997)

BENFORD, VASSAL
   House Party 2: The Pajama Jam (1991)
   Class Act (1992)

BENITEZ, JELLYBEAN
   Lie Down With Dogs (1995)

BENNATO, EUGENIO
   Teste Rasate (Skinheads) (1993)

BENNETT, BRIAN
   Dead End City (1989)
   Deadly Reactor (1989)
   Jungle Assault (1989)

BENNETT, DARYL
   Once in a Blue Moon (1995)
   Ronnie & Julie (1997)

BENNETT, GEOFF

Reluctant Angel (1997)

BENNETT, JAMES
   Poison (1991)
   Swoon (1992)

BENNETT, RICHARD RODNEY
   Man Who Lived in the Ritz (1988)
   Enchanted April (1991)
   Four Weddings and a Funeral (1994)
   Swann (1996)
   Tale of Sweeney Todd (1997)

BENOIT, DAVID
   Stars Fell on Henrietta, The (1995)
   Christmas Tree, The (1996)
   Final Descent (1997)

BENOIT, JEAN-MARIE
   Ding et Dong: Le Film (1991)
   La Conciergerie (The Haven) (1997)

BENSON, RAY
   Never Leave Nevada (1991)
   Wild Texas Wind (1991)

BERCOVICI, HILARY
   Rockula (1990)
   Think Big (1990)

BEREGOVIC, GORAN
   XXL (1997)

BERENHOLTZ, JIM
   Lords of the Deep (1989)

BERESFORD, STEVE
   Pentimento (1990)

BERGEAUD, DAVID
   Aileen Wuornos: The Selling of a Serial
      Killer (1992)
   H. P. Lovecraft's "The Unnamable II"
      (1993)
   Donor Unknown (1995)
   On the 2nd Day of Christmas (1997)
   Sins of the Mind (1997)

BERGER, CARY
   Suture (1993)

BERGER, MARK
   I Love You, I Love You Not (1997)

BERGER, RICHARD
Sexual Response (1992)

BERGLUND, ANDERS
Pippi Longstocking (1997)

BERGMAN, EFFREM
Fugitive X (1996)

BERKELEY, MICHAEL
Goldeneye (1990)
Twenty One (1991)

BERNARD, MARIE
Strangers in Good Company (1991)

BERNARD, OLIVIER
Les Trois Freres (Three Brothers) (1995)

BERNHEIM, FRANCOIS
Mon Pere, ce Heros (1991)

BERNSTEIN, CHARLES
Desperate for Love (1989)
Love and Betrayal (1989)
Caroline? (1990)
Drug Wars: The Camarena Story (1990)
Fall From Grace (1990)
Last Elephant, The (aka Ivory Hunters)
    (1990)
Love She Sought, The (1990)
She Said No (1990)
Too Young to Die? (1990)
Guilty Until Proven Innocent (1991)
Love, Lies and Murder (1991)
Payoff (1991)
Yes, Virginia, There Is a Santa Claus
    (1991)
Drug Wars: The Cocaine Cartel (1992)
Somebody's Daughter (1992)
Trial: The Price of Passion (1992)
Between Love and Hate (1993)
Excessive Force (1993)
Final Appeal (1993)
Sea Wolf, The (1993)
My Name Is Kate (1994)
Maya Lin: A Strong Clear Vision (1995)
Out of Annie's Past (1995)
Bloodhounds II (1996)
Dead Ahead (1996)
Sophie and the Moonhanger (1996)
Miss Evers' Boys (1997)
Ticket, The (1997)

When Danger Follows You Home (1997)

BERNSTEIN, ELMER
My Left Foot (1989)
Slipstream (1989)
Grifters, The (1990)
Cape Fear (1991)
Oscar (1991)
Rage in Harlem, A (1991)
Rambling Rose (1991)
Babe, The (1992)
Age of Innocence, The (1993)
Cemetery Club, The (1993)
Fallen Angels (1993)
Good Son, The (1993)
Lost in Yonkers (1993)
Mad Dog and Glory (1993)
Canadian Bacon (1995)
Devil in a Blue Dress (1995)
Frankie Starlight (1995)
Personal Journey With Martin Scorsese,
    A (1995)
Roommates (1995)
Search and Destroy (1995)
Bulletproof (1996)
Buddy (1997)
Hoodlum (1997)
John Grisham's "The Rainmaker" (1997)
Rough Riders (1997)

BERNSTEIN, PETER
Dream Date (1989)
Nightbreaker (1989)
Exile (1990)
Sky High (1990)
N.Y.P.D. Mounted (1991)
Fifty/Fifty (1993)
Trouble Shooters: Trapped Beneath the
    Earth (1993)
My Breast (1994)
Ed McBain's 87th Precinct (1995)
She Stood Alone: The Tailhook Scandal
    (1995)
Jack Reed: Death and Vengeance (1996)
Ultimate Lie, The (1996)
Rough Riders (1997)

BERTOLI, BRUNO
Tortilla y Cinema (1997)

BESSER, JONATHON
War Stories (1995)

BEST, PETER
  Country Life (1994)
  Muriel's Wedding (1994)
  Dad and Dave on Our Selection (1995)
  Doing Time for Patsy Cline (1997)

BESTOR, KURT
  It Nearly Wasn't Christmas (1989)
  Witching of Ben Wagner, The (1990)
  Rigoletto (1995)

BHATIA, AMIN
  Primo Baby (1990)
  Black Ice (1992)
  Cafe Romeo (1992)
  Final Round (1993)
  Just One of the Girls (1993)
  Ordeal in the Arctic (1993)
  Sidney Sheldon's "A Stranger in the
    Mirror" (1993)
  Gridlock (1996)
  John Woo's "Once a Thief" (1996)

BICAT, NICK
  Strapless (1989)
  Reflecting Skin, The (1991)
  Framed (1993)
  Hawk, The (1993)
  Passion of Darkly Noon, The (1995)
  Stella Does Tricks (1996)

BICKERTON, WAYNE
  Murder Story (1989)

BIEBER, ARNOLD
  Small Time (1991)
  Smoke (1993)

BIGAZZI, GIANCARLO
  Mediterraneo (1991)
  Silenzio si Nasce (1996)

BILDERBECK, KEITH
  Voodoo (1995)
  Stir (1997)

BILONDIEY
  Les Victimes (Victims) (1996)

BINI, RENE MARC
  Grosse Fatigue (1994)
  Les Caprices d'un Fleuve (1995)

BIRD, JEFF
  Niagara Niagara (1997)

BIRNBAUM, NATHAN
  Chain of Desire (1992)

BISHOP, MICHAEL
  Last Call (1990)

BLACKFORD, RICHARD
  Little Bit of Lippy, A (1992)

BLACKSTONE, WENDY
  Dance of Hope (1989)
  Blowback (1991)
  Boy Who Cried Bitch, The (1992)
  Criminal Passion (1992)
  Emma and Elvis (1992)
  Only You (1992)
  Erotic Tales (1994)
  Someone She Knows (1994)
  New Jersey Drive (1995)
  Chasing the Dragon (1996)
  Rescuing Desire (1996)
  Uninvited, The (1996)
  Bitter End, The (1997)

BLADES, RUBEN
  Q & A (1990)

BLAKE, HOWARD
  Midsummer Night's Dream, A (1996)

BLAMIRES, DAVID
  Another Woman (1994)

BLANCHARD, TERENCE
  Jungle Fever (1991)
  Malcolm X (1992)
  Sugar Hill (1993)
  Assault at West Point: The Court-Martial
    of Johnson Whittaker (1994)
  Crooklyn (1994)
  Inkwell, The (1994)
  Trial by Jury (1994)
  Clockers (1995)
  Get on the Bus (1996)
  4 Little Girls (1997)
  Eve's Bayou (1997)
  'Til There Was You (1997)

BLANK, LARRY
  Taxi Dancers (1993)

BLASICK, MARTY
  Private Collections (1990)

BLONDHEIM, GEORGE
  Blye Bye Blues (1989)
  Christmas on Division Street (1991)
  Marilyn and Me (1991)
  Gate II (1992)
  Perfect Man, The (1993)
  Red Scorpion 2 (1994)
  Whale Music (1994)
  Cyberjack (1995)
  Man With a Gun (1995)
  Dream Is a Wish Your Heart Makes, A
    (1995)
  Halfback of Notre Dame, The (1996)
  Lifeline (1996)

BLOOM, JANE IRA
  Shadow of a Doubt (1995)

BLOOM, KATH
  Little Stiff, A (1991)

BLOW, JOHN
  Baby of Macon, The (1993)

BLUE, FRANKIE
  Out There (1995)

BOARDMAN, CHRIS
  U.S. Marshals: Waco & Rhinehart
    (1987)
  Hijacking of the Achille Lauro, The
    (1989)
  Prime Target (1989)
  Johnny Ryan (1990)
  Beyond Suspicion (1993)
  Broken Promises: Taking Emily Back
    (1993)
  Elvis and the Colonel: The Untold Story
    (1993)
  Friend to Die For, A (1994)
  Ultimate Betrayal (1994)
  Beauty's Revenge (1995)
  Terror in the Shadows (1995)
  Face of Evil (1996)
  Good Doctor: The Paul Fleiss Story, The
    (1996)
  Tales From the Crypt: Bordello of Blood
    (1996)
  Deep Family Secrets (1997)
  Sleeping With the Devil (1997)

BOCK, JERRY
  Close to Eden (1992)
  Stranger Among Us, A (1992)

BODDICKER, MICHAEL
  Adventures of Milo & Otis, The (1989)
  FX 2: The Deadly Art of Illusion (1991)
  Freejack (1992)

BODEGA, MECCA
  Subway Stories (1997)

BOEKELHEIDE, TODD
  Blood of Heroes, The (1989)
  Yosemite: The Fate of Heaven (1989)
  Exposure (1991)
  Heart of Darkness: A Filmmaker's
    Odyssey (1991)
  Digger (1993)
  Earth and the American Dream (1993)
  Nina Takes a Lover (1994)
  Round Eyes in the Middle Kingdom
    (1995)
  Kids of Survival (1996)
  Midwife's Tale, A (1997)

BOGAS, ED
  Scottish Tale, The (1997)

BOKANOWSKI, MICHELE
  L'ange (1991)

BOLIN, MARTIN D.
  Forced to Kill (1993)

BOLL, BILL
  Low Life, The (1995)

BOLL, PAUL
  Roadracers (1994)

BOLTON, ROGER
  Double Exposure (1989)
  Don't Get Me Started (1994)
  To Die For (1994)

BON, ANDRE
  La Jeune Fille du Livre (1994)

BONEZZI, BERNARDO
  Don Juan, Mi Querido Fantasma (Don
    Juan, My Love) (1990)
  All Tied Up (1992)

Boca a Boca (Mouth to Mouth) (1995)
Mirada Liquida (Liquid Gaze) (1996)
El Amor Perjudica Seriamente La Salud
  (1997)

BONILLA, MARK
  National Lampoon's "Dad's Week Off"
    (1997)

BORTON, TOM
  Jitters, The (1989)

BOSCHAN, DAISY
  Meeting Venus (1991)

BOSCHERON, PIERRE
  Le Sourire (The Smile) (1994)

BOSTON, RICK
  Harvest, The (1993)

BOSWELL, SIMON
  Dangerous Obsession (Mortal Sins)
    (1990)
  Hardware (1990)
  Santa Sangre (1990)
  Young Soul Rebels (1991)
  Dust Devil (1992)
  Turn of the Screw, The (1992)
  Dust Devil: The Final Cut (1993)
  Love Matters (1993)
  Piccolo Grande Amore (Pretty Princess)
    (1993)
  Second Best (1994)
  Shallow Grave (1994)
  Zinky Boys Go Underground (1994)
  Android Affair, The (1995)
  Hackers (1995)
  Jack & Sarah (1995)
  Lord of Illusions (1995)
  American Perfekt (1997)
  Downtime (1997)
  Perdita Durango (1997)
  Photographing Fairies (1997)

BOTKIN, PERRY
  Sidney Sheldon's "Windmills of the
    Gods" (1988)
  Sidney Sheldon's "The Sands of Time"
    (1992)

BOTTI, CHRIS
  Caught (1996)

BOUGIS, HUBERT
  Sweet Revenge (1990)

BOULANGER, GUY
  Totor (1994)

BOURDON, DIDIER
  Les Trois Freres (Three Brothers) (1995)

BOURGEOIS, PATRICK
  Karmina (1996)

BOURLAND, ROGER
  Night Life (1990)
  New Jack City (1991)

BOURNE, ANNE
  Not Me! (1996)
  Project Grizzly (1996)

BOUX, CLAUDE
  Project: Genesis (1994)

BOWERS, DAVID
  True Love and Chaos (1997)

BOWERS, RICHARD
  Candles in the Dark (1993)

BOWLES, PAUL
  Paul Bowles: The Complete Insider
    (1994)

BRADEN, DON
  Lena's Dreams (1997)

BRADSTREET, DAVID
  Fish Tale Soup (1997)

BRAGG, BILLY
  Safe (1993)
  Walking and Talking (1996)

BRAMSON, STEVEN
  Love Can Be Murder (1992)
  Crude Oasis, The (1995)

BRAUNINGER, JURGEN
  Lawnmower Man, The (1992)

BRAVO, DAVID
  Federal Hill (1995)

BREANT, FRANCOIS
  Haut Bas Fragile (Up Down Fragile)
    (1995)

BREGOVIC, GORAN
  American Dreamers (1992)
  Arizona Dream (1992)
  La Reine Margot (Queen Margot) (1994)
  Underground (1995)
  Chef in Love, A (1996)
  Serpent's Kiss, The (1997)

BRENDGEN, FERDI
  Road to Mecca, The (1992)

BRENNER, DANNY
  Spare Me (1993)

BREWIS, PETER
  Tall Guy, The (1989)
  Staggered (1994)

BRICUSSE, LESLIE
  Tom and Jerry: The Movie (1992)

BRIDIE, DAVID
  Proof (1991)
  Greenkeeping (1992)
  That Eye, the Sky (1994)
  What I Have Written (1996)
  River Street (1996)
  Myth of Fingerprints, The (1997)

BRIGGS, GEORGE L.
  Evil Altar (1989)

BRINT, SIMON
  Filipina Dreamgirls (1991)

BRITTEN, TONY
  Joyriders (1989)

BRONSKILL, RICHARD
  Perfect Bride, The (1991)

BROOK, MICHAEL
  Albino Alligator (1996)
  Affliction (1997)

BROPHY, PHILIP
  Body Melt (1993)

BROUGHTON, BRUCE

Jacknife (1989)
Sorry Wrong Number (1989)
Betsy's Wedding (1990)
Narrow Margin (1990)
Old Man and the Sea, The (1990)
Rescuers Down Under, The (1990)
All I Want for Christmas (1991)
Honey, I Blew Up the Kid (1992)
O Pioneers! (1992)
Stay Tuned (1992)
Homeward Bound: The Incredible
  Journey (1993)
For Love or Money (aka Concierge, The)
  (1993)
So I Married an Axe Murderer (1993)
Tombstone (1993)
Baby's Day Out (1994)
Holy Matrimony (1994)
Miracle on 34th Street (1994)
Acts of Love (1995)
Carried Away (1996)
Homeward Bound II: Lost in San
  Francisco (1996)
House Arrest (1996)
  Infinity (1996)
Shadow Conspiracy (1997)
Simple Wish, A (1997)
True Women (1997)

BROWER, LEO
  Como Agua Para Chocolat (Like Water
    for Chocolate (1992)
  Walk in the Clouds, A (1995)

BROWN, CHARLES
  Johns (1995)

BROWN, GREG
  Zadar! Cow From Hell (1989)

BROWN, JIMMY LEE
  White Girl, The (1990)

BROWN, LARRY
  Rio Diablo (1993)
  Gambler V: Playing for Keeps, The
    (1994)
  MacShayne: Final Roll of the Dice
    (1994)
  MacShayne: Winner Takes All (1994)
  Women of Spring Break, The (1995)
  Triplecross (1995)
  Gangs in Blue (1996)

Elvis Meets Nixon (1997)

BROWNE, JACKSON
  Incident at Oglala (1992)

BRUCE, JACK
  Slab Boys, The (1997)

BRUZDOWICZ, JOANNA
  Jacquot de Nantes (1991)

BRYANS, BILLY
  Office Party (1989)

BRYANT, JOHN
  Curse of the Starving Class (1995)

BRYDEN, BENEDIKT
  Tin Soldier, The (1995)
  Rhyme & Reason (1997)

BUBENHEIM, ALEXANDER
  Night Train to Venice (1993)

BUCKMASTER, PAUL
  Diving In (1989)
  12 Monkeys (1995)
  Last Word, The (1995)
  Maker, The (1997)
  Most Wanted (1997)

BUNCH, RAY
  Crowfoot (1995)
  Bachelor's Baby, A (1996)
  Unlikely Angel (1996)

BUNDROCK, PIERRE
  Carpenter, The (1989)

BUNRETTE, BILLY
  Saturday Night Special (1992)

BURGALAT, BERTRAND
  Quadrille (1997)

BURGON, GEOFFREY
  Robin Hood (1991)
  Foreign Field, A (1993)
  Martin Chuzzlewit (1995)

BURKE, DENNIS
  Drive, She Said (1997)

BURNAND, DAVID
  Gallivant (1996)

BURNS, GARY
  Resurrection Man (1997)

BURNS, RALPH
  All Dogs Go to Heaven (1989)
  Bert Rigby, You're a Fool (1989)
  Sweet Bird of Youth (1989)
  Josephine Baker Story, The (1991)

BURT, GEORGE
  Trust, The (1993)

BURWELL, CARTER
  Checking Out (1989)
  Miller's Crossing (1990)
  Barton Fink (1991)
  Doc Hollywood (1991)
  Scorchers (1991)
  Buffy the Vampire Slayer (1992)
  Storyville (1992)
  Waterland (1992)
  And the Band Played On (1993)
  Dangerous Woman, A (1993)
  Kalifornia (1993)
  This Boy's Life (1993)
  Wayne's World 2 (1993)
  Airheads (1994)
  Hudsucker Proxy, The (1994)
  It Could Happen to You (1994)
  Bad Company (1995)
  Celluloid Closet, The (1995)
  Goofy Movie, A (1995)
  Rob Roy (1995)
  Chamber, The (1996)
  Fargo (1996)
  Fear (1996)
  Joe's Apartment (1996)
  Assassin(s) (1997)
  Conspiracy Theory (1997)
  Jackal, The (1997)
  Locusts, The (1997)
  Picture Perfect (1997)
  Spanish Prisoner, The (1997)

BUSH, KATE
  Line, the Cross & the Curve, The (1993)

BUSSINGER, COBB
  I Don't Buy Kisses Anymore (1992)

BUTLER, BERNARD
James Gang, The (1997)

BUTTARI, CIRO
Piccoli Orrori (Little Horrors) (1994)

BYRNE, DAVID
Magicians of the Earth (1990)

BYRNE, NIALL
Words Upon the Window Pane (1994)

BYRNE, TONY
Two Wrongs Make a Right (1989)

CACAVAS, JOHN
Dirty Dozen: The Deadly Mission (1987)
Dirty Dozen: The Fatal Mission, The
  (1988)
Margaret Bourke-White (1989)
Confessional (1990)
Murder in Paradise (1990)
Return of Ironside, The (1993)

CAIRNS, ROBERT
I'll Love You Forever . . . Tonight
  (1993)

CALANDRELLI, JORGE
I'll Be Home for Christmas (1988)

CALE, JOHN
Primary Motive (1992)
Antarctica (1995)
I Shot Andy Warhol (1996)
Basquait (1996)
House of America (1997)
Somewhere in the City (1997)
Rhinoceros Hunting in Budpest (1997)

CALELLO, CHARLES
Drug Wars: The Camarena Story (1990)

CAMERON, CHRISTOPHER
God's Will (1989)

CAMERON, JOHN
Jekyll & Hyde (1990)
Frankenstein (1993)
Driftwood (1996)

CAMILO, MICHEL
Two Much (Loco de Amor) (1995)

CAMMARIERE, SERGIO
Uomini senza Donna (Men Without
  Women) (1996)

CAMPBELL, DAVID RICHARD
Mind Games (1989)
Mirage (1995)

CAMPBELL, JAMES
Dracula's Widow (1988)

CAMPBELL, WILLIAM JR.
October 32nd (1992)

CAPEK, JOHN
Heaven Tonight (1990)
Exchange Lifeguards (1993)

CAPEK, TOM
Life and Times of Allen Ginsburg, The
  (1993)

CAPON, JEAN-CHARLES
La Servante Aimante (1996)

CAPPONI, CLAUDIO
Sparrow (1993)
Follow Your Heart (1996)
Jane Eyre (1996)

CAPRIOLI, STEFANO
Barnabo delle Montagne (1994)
Come Due Coccodrilli (Like Two
  Crocodiles) (1994)
Dichiarazioni d'Amore (Declarations of
  Love) (1994)

CARBONARA, DAVID
Spanking the Monkey (1994)

CARBUTT, ADRIAN JAMES
Strip Jack Naked: Nighthawks II (1991)

CARD, ARLEN
Heaven Sent (1995)

CARDEN, TOM
Dadetown (1995)

CARDONNA, PHIL
On the Make (1989)

CAREY, DAN
Tales From a Hard City (1994)

CARLTON, CARL
Midnight Cop (1989)

CARLTON, LARRY
Deadline: Madrid (1988)

CARON, DANNY
Johns (1995)

CARPENTER, JOHN
Halloween 5 (1989)
John Carpenter Presents Body Bags
(1993)
In the Mouth of Madness (1995)
Village of the Damned (1995)
John Carpenter's Escape From L.A.
(1996)

CARPENTER, PETE
Rockford Files: A Blessing in Disguise,
The (1995)
Rockford Files: Friends and Foul Play,
The (1996)
Rockford Files: Godfather Knows Best,
The (1996)
Rockford Files: If the Frame Fits . . . ,
The (1996)
Rockford Files: Punishment and Crime,
The (1996)
Rockford Files: Murder and
Misdemeanors, The (1997)

CARPENTER, RICHARD
Karen Carpenter Story, The (1989)

CARPI, FIORENZO
Abissinia (1993)

CARR, BUDD
Bedroom Eyes II (1990)

CARRADINE, DAVID
Sonny Boy (1990)

CARROLL, ROB
Mustard Bath (1993)

CARUSO, JOHNNY
All My Husbands (1992)
Mojave Moon (1996)

CASADEUS, GRECO
Climb, The (1997)

CASHER, DEL
Action U.S.A. (1989)
Tropical Heat (1993)

CASSIDY, PATRICK
Broken Harvest (1994)

CASTLE, DOUG WALTER
Desire and Hell at Sunset Motel (1992)

CASTOR, JAN
Wacky Adventures of Dr. Boris and
Nurse Shirley (1995)

CASWELL, CHRIS
Desert Steel (1994)
Kiss Goodnight, A (1994)

CAUX, ROBERT
Le Polygraphe (The Lie Detector) (1996)

CECCARELLI, LUIGI
Barocco (1991)
Il Giardino Dei Ciliegi (The Cherry
Orchard) (1992)
Ladri di Cinema (The Film Thief) (1994)

CENTAZZO, ANDREA
Aaron Gillespie Will Make You a Star
(1996)

CERF, YVES
Pullman Paradise (1995)

CHABROL, MATTHIEU
Quiet Days in Clichy (1990)
Madame Bovary (1991)
Betty (1992)
Le Cri du Hibou (The Cry of the Owl)
(1992)
L'Enfer (1993)
La Ceremonie (A Judgment in Stone)
(1995)
Rien ne va plus (1997)

CHAIT, MARK
Allie & Me (1997)

CHALEAT, JEAN-NOEL
Gift From Heaven, A (1994)

CHAMBERLAIN, SIMON
Down Among the Big Boys (1993)

CHAMBERLIN, BARBARA
Highway of Heartache (1994)

CHANG, GARY
Dead Bang (1989)
Next of Kin (1989)
83 Hours 'til Dawn (1990)
Death Warrant (1990)
Donor (1990)
House of Usher, The (1990)
Killer Among Us, A (1990)
Miami Blues (1990)
Rising Son (1990)
Shock to the System, A (1990)
Murder in New Hampshire: The Pamela
    Smart Story (1991)
Perfect Weapon, The (1991)
In the Line of Duty: Siege at Marion
    (1992)
Nightman, The (1992)
Shadow of a Stranger (1992)
Under Siege (1992)
Double Deception (1993)
Family Torn Apart, A (1993)
Full Eclipse (1993)
Last Hit, The (1993)
Sniper (1993)
Against the Wall (1994)
Burning Season, The (1994)
Deep Red (1994)
Fatherland (1994)
F.T.W. (1994)
Nowhere to Hide (1994)
Avenging Angel, The (1995)
Original Sins (1995)
Walking Dead, The (1995)
Andersonville (1996)
Island of Dr. Moreau, The (1996)
Limbic Region, The (1996)
Substitute, The (1996)
Twisted Desire (1996)
Double Team (1997)
George Wallace (1997)
Murder Live (1997)

CHANY, PHILIPPE
Delphine 1--Yvan 0 (1996)
Didier (1997)

CHARLES, JOHN

Sound and the Silence, The (1993)
Last Tattoo, The (1994)

CHASE, JOHN
Soldier's Tale, A (1991)

CHASE, PETER
Mina Tannenbaum (1993)
L'Appartement (The Apartment) (1996)
Portraits Chinois (Shadow Play) (1996)

CHASE, THOMAS
976-Evil (1989)
Syngenor (1990)
Little Nemo: Adventures in Slumberland
    (1992)

CHATTAWAY, JAY
Red Scorpion (1989)
Relentless (1989)
Far Out Man (1990)
Maniac Cop 2 (1990)
Rich Girl (1991)
Ambulance, The (1993)
Star Trek: Voyager (1995)

CHERNS, RICHARD
Macbeth (1997)

CHICHA, YVES
Street Wars (1992)

CHIHARA, PAUL
King of the Olympics: Lives & Loves
    Avery Brundage (1988)
Bridesmaids (1989)
Dark Holiday (1989)
Just Another Secret (1989)
Penn & Teller Get Killed (1989)
Casualty of War, A (1990)
Family of Spies (1990)
Rock Hudson (1990)
Death Has a Bad Reputation (1991)
Baby Snatcher (1992)
Quicksand: No Escape (1992)

CHILDS, BILLY
In Search of Our Fathers (1992)

CHILTON, DAVID
Look Me in the Eye (1994)

CHIN, CLIVE
  Dark Summer (1994)

CHOPIN, PHILIPPE
  Pedale Douce (What a Drag) (1996)

CHRISTENSEN, NIKOLAJ
  Christian (1989)

CHRISTIANSON, BOB
  Wishman (1992)
  Vibrations (1994)

CHU, DAVID
  Love Ya Tomorrow (1991)

CIBELLI, CHRIS
  Brilliant Disguise, A (1994)

CIMPANELLI, CLAUDIO
  La Bella Vita (Living It Up) (1994)

CINELLI, MINO
  Contre l'Oubli (Against Oblivion) (1992)

CIOTTI, ROBERTO
  Il Tempo del Ritorno (Time of the
    Return) (1993)
  Next Year . . . We'll Go to Bed by Ten
    (1996)

CIPRIANI, STELVIO
  Presume Dangereux (1990)

CIRINO, CHUCK
  Border Heat (1988)
  Return of the Swamp Thing, The (1989)
  Alienator (1990)
  Haunting of Morella, The (1990)
  Man Called Serge, A (1990)
  Mob Boss (1990)
  Transylvania Twist (1990)
  Evil Toons (1991)
  Haunting Fear (1991)
  Inner Sanctum (1991)
  Munchie (1992)
  Sins of Desire (1992)
  Soldier's Fortune (1992)
  Angel Eyes (1993)
  Hard to Die (1993)
  Dinosaur Island (1994)
  Ghoulies IV (1994)
  Inner Sanctum 2 (1994)

Possessed by the Night (1994)
  Teenage Exorcist (1994)

CLAPTON, ERIC
  Communion (1989)
  Lethal Weapon 2 (1989)
  Rush (1991)
  Lethal Weapon 3 (1992)
  Van, The (1995)
  Nil by Mouth (1997)

CLARKE, GAVIN
  Smalltime (1996)

CLARKE, STANLEY
  Out on the Edge (1989)
  Blue Bayou (1990)
  Book of Love (1990)
  Dangerous Pursuit (1990)
  Court-Martial of Jackie Robinson, The
    (1990)
  Kid Who Loved Christmas, The (1990)
  Boyz N the Hood (1991)
  Cool as Ice (1991)
  Five Heartbeats, The (1991)
  Love Kills (1991)
  Final Shot: The Hank Gathers Story
    (1992)
  Passenger 57 (1992)
  Poetic Justice (1993)
  Relentless: Mind of a Killer (1993)
  Watch It (1993)
  What's Love Got to Do With It (1993)
  Higher Learning (1994)
  I Like It Like That (1994)
  Little Big League (1994)
  Royce (1994)
  Bleeding Hearts (1995)
  Panther (1995)
  Show, The (1995)
  White Man's Burden (1995)
  Cherokee Kid, The (1996)
  Eddie (1996)
  Road to Galveston, The (1996)
  B.A.P.S. (1997)
  Dangerous Ground (1997)
  Sprung (1997)

CLAUSEN, ALF
  She Knows Too Much (1989)

CLAYPOOL III, LES
  Guyver 2: Dark Hero, The (1994)

CLEVER MUSIC
  U.F.O. (1993)

CLIFFORTH, JOHN
  Who Killed the Baby Jesus (1992)

CLIFTON, BRIAN
  Bird of Prey (1995)

CLINE, NELS
  Welcome Says the Angel (1996)

CLINTON, GEORGE S.
  Gotham (1988)
  American Ninja 3: Blood Hunt (1989)
  House of Usher, The (1990)
  Another Woman's Lipstick (1992)
  Cruel Doubt (1992)
  Hard Promises (1992)
  Lake Consequence (1992)
  Through the Eyes of a Killer (1992)
  Till Death Us Do Part (1992)
  Wild Orchid 2: Two Shades of Blue
    (1992)
  Bonds of Love (1993)
  Kiss to Die For, A (1993)
  Paper Hearts (1993)
  Amelia Earhart: The Final Flight (1994)
  Betrayed by Love (1994)
  Brainscan (1994)
  Fatal Vows: The Alexandra O'Hara
    Story (1994)
  Mother's Boys (1994)
  One of Her Own (1994)
  Seduced by Evil (1994)
  Delta of Venus (1995)
  Her Deadly Rival (1995)
  Mortal Kombat (1995)
  Tad (1995)
  Beyond the Call (1996)
  Austin Powers: International Man of
    Mystery (1997)
  Beverly Hills Ninja (1997)
  Dean Koontz's "Intensity" (1997)
  Heart of Fire (1997)
  Last Days of Frankie the Fly, The (1997)
  Mortal Kombat 2 Annihilation (1997)

CLOQUET, SIMON
  Orson Welles: The One-Man Band
    (1995)

CMIRAL, ELIA
  Apartment Zero (1989)
  Somebody Is Waiting (1996)

COBBIN, PETER
  Billy's Holiday (1995)

COBERT, BOB
  Intruders (1992)
  Me and the Kid (1993)
  Trilogy of Terror II (1996)

COCCIOLI, LAMBERTO
  Fine Pena Mai (Life After Life) (1995)

CODA, JOHN
  Disappearance of Kevin Johnson, The
    (1995)

COHEN, JEFF
  Riens du Tout (Little Nothings) (1992)
  Mutual Consent (1994)

COHEN-SOLAL, PHILIPPE
  Clubbed to Death (1997)

COHN, STEPHEN
  Trapped (1989)
  Nickel & Dime (1992)

COLCORD, RAY
  Jury Duty: The Comedy (1990)
  Sleeping Car, The (1990)
  Devil's Food (1996)

COLE, GARDNER
  Femme Fontaine: Killer Babe for the
    C.I.A. (1994)

COLE, JUDE
  Last Light (1993)
  Truth or Consequences, N.M. (1997)

COLEMAN, BILL
  Watermelon Woman, The (1996)

COLEMAN, CY
  Family Business (1989)

COLEMAN, GRAEME
  Chaindance (1991)
  Common Bonds (1991)
  North of Pittsburgh (1992)

Double Suspicion (1993)
Final Round (1993)
Harmony Cats (1993)
Breaking Point (1994)
Double Cross (1994)
Dream Man (1994)
Killer (1994)
Max (1994)
Breach of Trust (1995)
Bulletproof Heart (1995)
Malicious (1995)
White Tiger (1995)
Secret Life of Algernon, The (1997)

COLEMAN, J. F.
Gun for Jennifer, A (1996)

COLEMAN, JIM
Unbelievable Truth, The (1989)

COLLERO, JODY
Treacherous Beauties (1994)

COLOMBIER, MICHEL
Backtrack (aka Catchfire) (1989)
Desperado: Badlands Justice (1989)
Desperado: The Outlaw Wars (1989)
Loverboy (1989)
Out Cold (1989)
Who's Harry Crumb? (1989)
Buried Alive (1990)
Fatal Image, The (1990)
Impulse (1990)
Midnight Cabaret (1990)
Sudie and Simpson (1990)
Dark Wind, The (1991)
Fatal Exposure (1991)
Fever (1991)
New Jack City (1991)
Strays (1991)
Strictly Business (1991)
Tagget (1991)
Deep Cover (1992)
Diary of a Hit Man (1992)
Dirty Work (1992)
Folks! (1992)
Ladykiller (1992)
Daybreak (1993)
Fade to Black (1993)
Posse (1993)
Program, The (1993)
Incident at Deception Ridge (1994)
Major League II (1994)

Out of Darkness (1994)
Elisa (1995)
Barb Wire (1996)
Foxfire (1996)
Mary & Tim (1996)
Buried Alive II (1997)
Color of Justice (1997)
Meet Wally Sparks (1997)
Murder in My Mind (1997)
Right Connections, The (1997)

COLVIN, ERIC
Timepiece (1996)
Setting Son, The (1997)

COLVIN, SHAWN
Edie & Pen (1996)

COMBUSTIBLE EDISON
Four Rooms (1995)

COMELADE, PASCAL
Saturday on Earth, A (1996)

CONFORTI, SERGIO
Stefano Quantestorie (1993)

CONLAN, JOSEPH
Stepford Children, The (1987)
Nick Knight (1989)
Bride in Black, The (1990)
Memories of Murder (1990)
Quiet Little Neighborhood, A Perfect
    Little Murder (1990)
Blackmail (1991)
Mortal Sins (1992)
Marilyn & Bobby: Her Final Affair
    (1993)
Don't Talk to Strangers (1994)
Menendez: A Killing in Beverly Hills
    (1994)
Circumstances Unknown (1995)
Deadly Whispers (1995)
Gramps (1995)
Return of Hunter: Everyone Walks in
    L.A., The (1995)
Silver Strand (1995)
Simon & Simon: In Trouble Again
    (1995)
Stolen Innocence (1995)
Abducted: A Father's Love (1996)
Ed McBain's 87th Precinct: Ice (1996)
Gone in the Night (1996)

Kiss So Deadly, A (1996)
Bad to the Bone (1997)
Divided by Hate (1997)
High Stakes (1997)
Love-Struck (1997)
My Stepson, My Lover (1997)
Our Mother's Murder (1997)
Perfect Crime (1997)
When the Cradle Falls (1997)

CONN, MICHAEL
Bumping the Odds (1997)

CONNOR, BILL
Prince (1991)
Landing on the Sun, A (1994)

CONNOR, DAVID
Keaton's Cop (1990)

CONRAD, RICK
Amityville: The Evil Escapes (1989)
Crime Zone (1989)
Terror Within, The (1989)
Watchers II (1990)
Hit List, The (1993)

CONTE, PAOLO
Blue Arrow, The (1996)

CONTI, BILL
Bear, The (1989)
Bionic Showdown: The Six Million
    Dollar Man and the Bionic Woman
    (1989)
Cohen & Tate (1989)
Karate Kid III, The (1989)
Lean on Me (1989)
Lock Up (1989)
Murderers Among Us: The Simon
    Wiesenthal Story (1989)
Backstreet Dreams (1990)
Fourth War, The (1990)
Operation, The (1990)
Rocky V (1990)
By the Sword (1991)
Captive in the Land, A (1991)
Dynasty: The Reunion (1991)
Necessary Roughness (1991)
Year of the Gun (1991)
Nails (1992)
Adventures of Huck Finn, The (1993)

Blood In Blood Out: Bound by Honor
    (1993)
Rookie of the Year (1993)
8 Seconds (1994)
Next Karate Kid, The (1994)
Scout, The (1994)
Bushwhacked (1995)
Entertaining Angels: The Dorothy Day
    Story (1996)
Napoleon (1996)
Spy Hard (1996)

CONVERTINO, MICHAEL
Queen of Hearts (1989)
End of Innocence, The (1990)
Shattered Dreams (1990)
Doctor, The (1991)
Waterdance, The (1992)
Aspen Extreme (1993)
Bodies, Rest and Motion (1993)
Home of Our Own, A (1993)
Wrestling Ernest Hemingway (1993)
Guarding Tess (1994)
Milk Money (1994)
Santa Clause, The (1994)
Pie in the Sky (1995)
Things to Do in Denver When You're
    Dead (1995)
Bed of Roses (1996)
Last of the High Kings, The (1996)
Mother Night (1996)
Critical Care (1997)
Jungle 2 Jungle (1997)

COODER, RY
Johnny Handsome (1989)
Tales From the Crypt (1989)
Trespass (1992)
Geronimo: An American Legend (1993)
Last Man Standing (1996)
End of Violence, The (1997)

COONCE, COLE
Living End, The (1992)

COOPER, AL
Drug Wars: The Camarena Story (1990)

COPELAND, STEWART
See No Evil, Hear No Evil (1989)
First Power, The (1990)
Hidden Agenda (1990)
Men at Work (1990)

Taking Care of Business (1990)
Riff-Raff (1991)
Afterburn (1992)
Fugitive Among Us, The (1992)
Seconds Out (1992)
Wide Sargasso Sea (1992)
Airborne (1993)
Raining Stones (1993)
Decadence (1994)
Fresh (1994)
Rapa Nui (1994)
Silent Fall (1994)
Surviving the Game (1994)
Tyson (1995)
White Dwarf (1995)
Boys (1996)
Leopard Son, The (1996)
Good Burger (1997)
Gridlock'd (1997)
Little Boy Blue (1997)
Welcome to Woop Woop (1997)

COPPOLA, CARMINE
New York Stories (1989)
Godfather Part III, The (1990)

COQ, LAURENT
Bat Out of Hell (1997)

CORBIEL, NORMAND
Princes in Exile (1991)
Kids of the Round Table (1995)
Screamers (1995)
Frankenstein and Me (1996)
Never Too Late (1996)
Assignment, The (1997)
Les Boys (The Boys) (1997)

CORDIO, CARLO MARIA
Quest for the Mighty Sword (1990)
Sonny Boy (1990)
Midnight Ride (1992)
Body Puzzle (1994)

COREA, CHICK
Cat Chaser (1989)

CORRIVEAU, JEAN
Requiem for a Handsome Bastard (1993)

CORSICATO, PAPPI
Bucchi Neri (Black Holes) (1995)

COSBY, WILLIAM H. JR.
Cosby Mysteries, The (1994)

COSCIA, GIANNI
Altri Domini (Other Men) (1997)

COSMA, VITTORIO
Colpo di Luna (Moon Shadow) (1995)

COSMA, VLADIMIR
Judith Krantz's "Till We Meet Again"
    (1989)
Nightmare Years, The (1989)
Night of the Fox (1990)
Favour, the Watch, and the Very Big
    Fish, The (1991)
La Chateau de Ma Mere (My Mother's
    Castle) (1991)
La Gloire de Mon Pere (My Father's
    Glory) (1991)
La Totale! (The Jackpot!) (1992)
Le Bal des Casse-Pieds (1992)
Ville a Vendre (City for Sale) (1992)
Cuisine et Dependances (Kitchen With
    Apartment) (1993)
Le Mari de Leon (Leon's Husband)
    (1993)
Le Souper (The Supper) (1993)
Cache Cash (1994)
Montparnasse-Pondichery (1994)
Judith Krantz's "Dazzle" (1995)
Le Jaguar (1996)
Le Plus Beau Metier du Monde (1997)
Les Palmes de M. Schutz (Pierre and
    Marie) (1997)
Soleil (Sun) (1997)

COSTELLO, ELVIS
Family (1994)

COSTER, WAYNE
Criminal Act (1989)

COUGHLAN, CATHAL
Last Bus Home, The (1997)

COULAIS, BRUNO
Le Petit Prince a dit (1992)
Le Retour de Casanova (Casanova's
    Return) (1992)
Vielle Canaille (Old Rascal) (1992)
Le Fils du Requin (The Son of the Shark)
    (1993)

Adultere, Mode d'Emploi (1995)
Microcosmos (1996)

COULLET, JEROME
Select Hotel (1996)

COULTER, CAMERON
Love and Happiness (1995)

COURAGE, ALEXANDER
Walton Thanksgiving Reunion, A (1993)

COUTURE, CHARLIE
Couples et Amants (Couples and Lovers)
(1993)
A la Campagne (Out in the Country)
(1995)

COVELL, JAMES
Santa With Muscles (1996)

COWEN, JEANINE
Home Before Dark (1997)

COX, RICK
Back to Back (1990)
Inside Monkey Zetterland (1992)
Corrina, Corrina (1994)

COZENS, CHARLES J.
At the Midnight Hour (1995)

CRAIN, BILL
Detour (1992)

CRAWFORD-COLLINS, DOMINIC
Savage Hearts (1995)

CRESSWELL, LUKE
Riot (1997)

CRIVELLI, CARLO
La Ribelle (The Rebel) (1993)
Il Signo Della Farfalla (1994)
Les Affinites Electives (1996)
Il Principe di Homburg (1997)
L'appartamento (The Apartment) (1997)
Marie Baie des Anges (1997)

CROSBIE, JIM
Boy Meets Girl (1994)

CROW, SHERYL

For Hope (1996)

CRUEL SEA
Spider & Rose (1994)

CRUZ, MICHAEL
Camp Cucamonga (1990)

CUELLO, JUAN CARLOS
Hazlo por Mi (Do It for Me) (1997)

CUGNY, LAURENT
23h58 (1993)

CUOMO, DOUGLAS
Laws of Gravity (1992)
Handgun (1994)

CURTIS, BRUCE
Chained Heat II (1993)

CUSSON, MICHEL
La Comtesse de Baton Rouge (1997)

CUTLER, MIRIAM
Witchcraft II: The Temptress (1990)
Witchcraft III: The Kiss of Death (1991)
Witchcraft IV: Virgin Heart (1991)
Pushed to the Limit (1992)
Alien Intruder (1993)
Witchcraft V: Dance With the Devil
(1993)
Nightfire (1994)
Witchcraft VI: Devil's Mistress (1994)
Witchcraft 7: Judgment Hour (1995)
Licensed to Kill (1997)

CUVILLIER, RICHARD
La Vie de Jesus (1997)

D'ALESSI, CARLOS
Delicatessen (1992)

D'AMROSIO, MARCO
Gumby: The Movie (1995)

D'ANDREA, JOHN
Iron Triangle, The (1989)
Swimsuit (1989)
To My Daughter (1990)
Child's Play 3 (1991)
Entertainers, The (1991)

Fixing the Shadow (aka Beyond the
   Law) (1992)
Boiling Point (1993)
Tower, The (1993)
 Baywatch the Movie: Forbidden
   Paradise (1994)
 Deadly Vows (1994)
Angel Flight Down (1996)
Fall Into Darkness (1996)
Gone in a Heartbeat (1996)
Assault on Devil's Island (1997)
In the Line of Duty: Blaze of Glory
   (1997)
Steel Chariots (1997)

D'ANDREA, OSWALD
   La Vie Est Rien D'Autre (1989)
   Captain Conan (1996)

D'ANGELO, NINO
   Tano da Mortre (1997)

DAILWITZ, BURKHARD
   Zone 39 (1996)

DALLA, LUCIO
   Beyond the Clouds (1995)
   Bambola (1996)

DAMAMME, QUENTIN
   Le Roi de Paris (1995)
   La Divine Poursuite (1997)

DAME, TERRY
   Incredibly True Adventures of Two Girls
      in Love, The (1995)

DANCZ, STEVE
   Grim Prairie Tales (1990)

DANGERFIELD, RODNEY
   Rover Dangerfield (1991)

DANIELLE, PINO
   Pensavo Fosse Amore Invece Era un
      Calese (1992)

DANKWORTH, JOHN
   Money for Nothing (1993)

DANNA, JEFF
   Cold Comfort (1989)
   Big Slice, The (1990)

DANNA, MYCHAEL
   Speaking Parts (1989)
   Adjuster, The (1991)
   Termini Station (1991)
   Ordinary Magic (1993)
   Darling Family, The (1994)
   Dance Me Outside (1994)
   Exotica (1994)
   Hush Little Baby (1994)
   Kama Sutra: A Tale of Love (1996)
   Lilies (1996)
   Ice Storm, The (1997)
   Regeneration (1997)
   Sweet Hereafter, The (1997)

DANTE, CARL
   Cannibal Women in the Avocado Jungle
      of Death (1989)

DARING, MASON
   Day One (1989)
   Laserman, The (1990)
   Little Vegas (1990)
   Murder in Mississippi (1990)
   City of Hope (1991)
   Dogfight (1991)
   Wild Hearts Can't Be Broken (1991)
   Bon Appetit, Mama (1992)
   Fathers & Sons (1992)
   Off and Running (1992)
   Passion Fish (1992)
   Ed and His Dead Mother (1993)
   Ernest Green Story, The (1993)
   Last Outlaw, The (1993)
   Stolen Babies (1993)
   Getting Out (1994)
   On Promised Land (1994)
   Secret of Roan Inish, The (1994)
   Letter to My Killer (1995)
   Old Curiosity Shop, The (1995)
   Young at Heart (1995)
   Lone Star (1996)
   Hidden in America (1996)
   Cold Around the Heart (1997)
   Dead by Midnight (1997)
   Men With Guns (1997)
   Prefontaine (1997)
   Ripper, The (1997)

DARLING, DAVID
   Ecological Design: Inventing the Future
      (1995)

DASENT, PETER
  Braindead (1992)
  Dead Alive (1992)
  Deadly Creatures (1992)
  Heavenly Creatures (1994)
  Not Fourteen Again (1996)

DAULNE, JEAN-LOUIS
  Cafe au Lait (1994)

DAVEY, SHAUN
  Investigation: Inside a Terrorist
    Bombing, The (1990)
  Loving (1995)
  Twelfth Night (1996)

DAVICH, MARTY
  Legacy of Sin: The William Coit Story
    (1995)
  Five Desperate Hours (1997)

DAVIDOVICI, JACQUES
  Elles ne Pensant qua'a Ca (1994)
  Neuf Mois (Nine Months) (1994)
  X, Y (1996)
  Amour et Confusions (1997)

DAVIDSON, DAVID
  Listen (1996)

DAVIDSON, HOWARD J.
  Romance and Rejection (1997)

DAVIES, DAVE
  Village of the Damned (1995)

DAVIES, PHIL
  Dark Side of the Moon, The (1989)
  Trancers II: Return of Jack Deth (1991)
  Trancers III: Deth Lives (1992)
  Society (1992)

DAVIES, VICTOR
  Last Winter, The (1990)
  Nutcracker Prince, The (1990)
  For the Moment (1994)

DAVIS, AARON
  Streets (1990)
  Talk 16 (1991)
  Poison Ivy (1992)
  Town Torn Apart, A (1992)
  Rude (1995)

DAVIS, BOB
  Vegas in Space (1992)

DAVIS, CARL
  Rainbow, The (1989)
  Scandal (1989)
  Crossing to Freedom (1990)
  Frankenstein Unbound (1990)
  Secret Life of Ian Fleming, The (1990)
  Tragedy of Flight 103: The Inside Story,
    The (1990)
  Crucifer of Blood, The (1991)
  Last Romantics, The (1991)
  Separate but Equal (1991)
  Black Velvet Gown, The (1992)
  Trial, The (1992)
  Very Polish Practice, A (1992)
  Genghis Cohn (1993)
  Widows Peak (1993)
  Voyage (1993)
  Year in Provence, A (1993)
  Hope in the Year Two (1994)
  Liberation (1994)
  Lie Down With Lions (1994)
  Return of the Native, The (1994)
  Anne Frank Remembered (1995)
  Jane Austen's "Pride and Prejudice"
    (1995)

DAVIS, DANE
  Follow the Bitch (1997)

DAVIS, DON
  Home Fires Burning (1989)
  Running Against Time (1990)
  Lies Before Kisses (1991)
  Little Piece of Heaven, A (1991)
  Notorious (1992)
  Woman With a Past (1992)
  Murder of Innocence (1993)
  In the Best of Families: Marriage, Pride
    & Madness (1994)
  Leave of Absence (1994)
  Sleep, Baby, Sleep (1995)
  Bound (1996)
  In the Lake of the Woods (1996)
  Ivana Trump's "For Love Alone" (1996)
  Pandora's Clock (1996)
  Perfect Daughter, The (1996)
  Peter Benchley's "The Beast" (1996)
  Warriors of Virtue (1996)
  Alibi (1997)
  House of Frankenstein (1997)

Ken Follett's "The Third Twin" (1997)
Lesser Evil, The (1997)
Match Made in Heaven, A (1997)
Not in This Town (1997)
Robin Cook's "Invasion" (1997)
Weapons of Mass Distraction (1997)

DAVIS, JOHN
kids (1995)

DAVIS, MARK
Class Cruise (1989)

DAVIS, MILES
Dingo (1991)

DAVIS, OLIVER
Seaview Knights (1994)

DAVISON, SIMON
Dirtysomething (1993)
Blue Juice (1995)

DAY, CHUCK
Switchblade Sisters (1996)

De ALMAR, ALBERTO
Sidney Sheldon's "The Sands of Time"
(1992)

De AZEVEDO, LEX
Swan Princess, The (1994)
Spring Fling! (1995)
Swan Princess: Escape From Castle
Mountain, The (1997)

DeBELLES, GREG
Kinjite (Forbidden Subjects) (1989)
Lambada (1990)
She Says She's Innocent (1991)
Sabrina the Teenage Witch (1996)

De BENEDICTIS, DICK
Perry Mason: The Case of the Lost Love
(1987)
Perry Mason: The Case of the Murdered
Madam (1987)
Perry Mason: The Case of the
Scandalous Scoundrel (1987)
Perry Mason: The Case of the Sinister
Spirit (1987)
Perry Mason: The Case of the Avenging
Ace (1988)

Perry Mason: The Case of the Lady in
the Lake (1988)
Perry Mason: The Case of the All-Star
Assassin (1989)
Perry Mason: The Case of the Lethal
Lesson (1989)
Perry Mason: The Case of the Musical
Murder (1989)
Perry Mason: The Case of the Defiant
Daughter (1990)
Perry Mason: The Case of the Desperate
Deception (1990)
Perry Mason: The Case of the Poisoned
Pen (1990)
Perry Mason: The Case of the Silenced
Singer (1990)
Perry Mason: The Case of the Fatal
Fashion (1991)
Perry Mason: The Case of the Glass
Coffin (1991)
Perry Mason: The Case of the Maligned
Mobster (1991)
Perry Mason: The Case of the Ruthless
Reporter (1991)
Diagnosis of Murder (1992)
House on Sycamore Street, The (1992)
Perry Mason: The Case of the Fatal
Framing (1992)
Perry Mason: The Case of the
Heartbroken Bride (1992)
Perry Mason: The Case of the Reckless
Romeo (1992)
Perry Mason: The Case of the Killer Kiss
(1993)
Perry Mason: The Case of the Skin-Deep
Scandal (1993)
Perry Mason: The Case of the Telltale
Talk Show Host (1993)
Perry Mason Mystery: The Case of the
Wicked Wives (1993)
Twist of the Knife, A (1993)
Perry Mason Mystery: The Case of the
Grimacing Governor (1994)
Perry Mason Mystery: The Case of the
Lethal Lifestyle (1994)
Ray Alexander: A Taste for Justice
(1994)
Perry Mason Mystery: The Case of the
Jealous Jokester (1995)
Ray Alexander: A Menu for Murder
(1995)
Melanie Darrow (1997)

De BENITO, MARIO
  Diary of a Rapist (1995)
  A Ciegas (Blinded) (1997)
  Al Limite (To the Limit) (1997)

De GREGORI, FRANCESCO
  Il Muro di Gomma (The Invisible Wall)
    (1991)

De MARSAN, ERIC
  Target of Suspicion (1994)

De MARTINO, MIKE
  Heartless (1997)

DeMARCO, BOB
  Gambler V: Playing for Keeps, The
    (1994)
  MacShayne: Winner Takes All (1994)
  MacShayne: Final Roll of the Dice
    (1994)
  Riders in the Storm (1995)

DeMARCO, CHRISTOPHER
  Toxic Avenger Part III, The (1989)

DeMARTINO, MIKE
  Matchbox Circus Train (1997)

DeMICHELE, GARY
  Big Night (1995)

De ROBERTIS, FEDERICO
  S.P.Q.R.: 2,000 and a Half Years Ago
    (1995)
  Selvaggi (Savages) (1995)
  Nirvana (1997)

De SICA, MANUEL
  Bye Bye Baby (1989)
  Il Conte Max (Count Max) (1991)
  Ricky e Barabba (Ricky and Barabbas)
    (1992)
  Dellamorte Delamore (Cemetery Man)
    (1994)
  Uomini, Uomini, Uomini (Men, Men,
    Men) (1995)
  Vacanze di Natale '95 (1995)
  3 (1996)
  A Spasso nel Tempo (Adrift in Time)
    (1996)
  Celluloide (1996)

DeFELITTA, RAYMOND
  Cafe Society (1996)

DeVORZON, BARRY
  Exorcist III, The (1990)

DEAD CAN DANCE
  In the Presence of Mine Enemies (1997)

DEARDON, IAN
  Cronos (1994)

DEBEASI, JOSEPH S.
  Confessions of a Suburban Girl (1992)
  Blessing (1994)

DEBNEY, JOHN
  Trenchcoat in Paradise (1989)
  Face of Fear, The (1990)
  Jetsons: The Movie (1990)
  Into the Badlands (1991)
  Seduction in Travis County, A (1991)
  Still Not Quite Human (1992)
  Sunstroke (1992)
  Class of '61 (1993)
  For Love and Glory (1993)
  Hocus Pocus (1993)
  Praying Mantis (1993)
  Gunmen (1994)
  Houseguest (1994)
  Little Giants (1994)
  White Fang 2: The Myth of the White
    Wolf (1994)
  Chameleon (1995)
  Cutthroat Island (1995)
  In Pursuit of Honor (1995)
  Kansas (1995)
  Sudden Death (1995)
  Carpool (1996)
  Doctor Who (1996)
  Getting Away With Murder (1996)
  Liar Liar (1996)
  I Know What You Did Last Summer
    (1997)
  Relic, The (1997)

DECKER, MARC DAVID
  Bikini Island (1991)
  Dark Backward, The (1991)

DECKER, ROBERT
  Shock 'Em Dead (1990)

DECLAN, DOMINIQUE
Ma vie en rose (1997)

DEDRICK, CHRISTOPHER
Glory! Glory! (1989)
Million Dollar Babies (1994)
Race to Freedom: The Underground
Railroad (1994)
Planet of Junior Brown, The (1997)

DEFAYS, CHRISTOPHER
Shot in the Foot (1997)

DEFAYS, OLIVIER
Shot in the Foot (1997)

DELERUE, GEORGES
Her Alibi (1989)
Paris by Night (1989)
Steel Magnolias (1989)
To Kill a Priest (1989)
Cadence (1990)
Joe Versus the Volcano (1990)
Mr. Johnson (1990)
Show of Force, A (1990)
American Friends (1991)
Black Robe (1991)
Curly Sue (1991)
Josephine Baker Story, The (1991)
Without Warning: The James Brady
Story (1991)
Dien Bien Phu (1992)
Man Trouble (1992)
Memento Mori (1992)
Rich in Love (1992)
Cinema, de Notre Temps: Abbas
Kiarostami (1994)

DELETTREZ, PHILIPPE
L'Echappee Belle (Close Shave) (1996)

DELIA, JOE
Caged Fury (1990)
King of New York (1990)
Bad Lieutenant (1992)
Body Snatchers (1993)
Dangerous Game (1993)
Snake Eyes (1993)
Enemy Within, The (1994)
Addiction, The (1995)
Drunks (1995)
Twilight Highway (1995)
Funeral, The (1996)

Blackout, The (1997)

DELORY, MICHEL
Triple Bogey on a Par Five Hole (1991)

DEMARTHE, CHRISTOPHE
Excentric Paradis (1995)

DERMADEROSIAN, ALAN
Vice Academy (1989)
Across Five Aprils (1990)
Invasion of Privacy (1992)
Mind, Body & Soul (1992)
Improper Conduct (1994)
Irresistible Impulse (1995)

DEROUIN, JOEL
Hitman, The (1991)

DESPLAT, ALEXANDRE
Memoire Tranquee (Laps of Memory)
(1991)
Hour of the Pig, The (1993)
Regarde les hommes tomber (See How
They Fall) (1993)
Innocent Lies (1995)
Le Plus Bel Age . . . (Those Were the
Days . . .) (1995)
Les Milles (1995)
Marie-Louise (1995)
Un heros tres discret (A Self-Made Hero)
(1995)
Le Cri de la Soie (The Scream of Silk)
(1996)
Le Montreur de Boxe (The Boxing
Promoter) (1996)
Love etc. (1996)
Passage a l'Acte (Death in Therapy)
(1996)

DESROCHERS, PIERRE
La Sarrasine (1992)
Les Amoureuses (1994)

DESTARDINS, CLAUDE
Captains Courageous (1996)
Waiting for Michelangelo (1996)

DETRIZIO, MAURO J.
Undying Love (1991)

DEUTSCH, STEVE
  Rave--Dancing to a Different Beat
    (1993)

DEWAERE, PATRICK
  Patrick Dewaere (1992)

DEXTER, JOHN WILLIAM
  Dream a Little Dream (1989)

Di BLASI, CARLO
  Camerieri (Waiters) (1995)

DiLULIO, RON
  Armed for Action (1992)
  Blood on the Badge (1992)

Di POFI, ANTONIO
  Chiedi la Luna (Ask for the Moon)
    (1991)
  Nottataccia (What a Night!) (1992)
  Bonus Malus (1993)
  Comincio Tutto per Caso (It Started by
    Chance) (1993)
  Condannato a Nozze (Condemned to
    Wed) (1993)
  Maniaci Sentimentali (Sentimental
    Maniacs) (1994)
  Prestazione Straordinaria (1994)
  Io e il Re (The King and Me) (1995)
  Bruno's Waiting in the Car (1996)
  Fratelli Coltelli (Knife Brothers) (1997)
  Il Sindaco (The Mayor) (1997)

Di POLA, DAN
  Suffering Bastards (1989)

DiPASQUALE, JAMES
  Shell Seekers, The (1989)
  Stolen: One Husband! (1990)
  Killing Mind, The (1991)
  Runaway Father (1991)
  In the Best Interest of the Children
    (1992)
  Getting Up and Going Home (1992)
  Seduction: Three Tales From the Inner
    Sanctum (1992)
  1994 Baker Street: Sherlock Holmes
    Returns (1993)
  Untamed Love (1994)
  Never Say Never: The Deidre Hall Story
    (1995)
  See Jane Run (1995)

All She Ever Wanted (1996)
Barbara Taylor Bradford's "Everything
  to Gain" (1996)

DICKSON, ANDREW
  Naked (1993)
  Someone Else's America (1994)
  Secrets & Lies (1995)

DIKKER, LOEK
  Body Parts (1991)
  Babysitter, The (1995)

DIMITROV, STEPHEN
  Assassination Game (1993)

DISH, BRAD SCOTT
  Dark Rider (1991)

DIXON, WILLIE
  Ginger Ale Afternoon (1989)

DOBBYN, DAVE
  Secrets (1992)

DOENBERG, DAVE
  Gummo (1997)

DOLAN, BRENDAN
  Go Fish (1994)

DOLDINGER, KLAUS
  Me and Him (1989)
  Salt on Our Skin (1993)

DOLGAY, MARVIN
  Drop Dead Gorgeous (1991)
  Haunting of Lisa, The (1996)

DOMINO, ANNA
  Triple Bogey on a Par Five Hole (1991)

DOMPIERRE, FRANCOIS
  Danielle Steel's "Vanished" (1995)
  Le Sort de l'Amerique (1996)
  L'homme ideal (The Ideal Man) (1996)
  Le Siege de l'ame (The Seat of the Soul)
    (1997)

DONAGGIO, PINO
  Catacombs (1989)
  Night Games (1989)

Duo Occhi Diabolici (Two Evil Eyes)
(1990)
Meridian: Kiss of the Beast (1990)
Devil's Daughter, The (1991)
Tchin Tchin (aka A Fine Romance)
(1991)
Demon in My View, A (1992)
Indio 2: The Revolt (1992)
Raising Cain (1992)
Dove Siete? Io Sono Qui (1993)
Giovanni Falcone (1993)
Trauma (1993)
Oblivion (1994)
Backlash: Oblivion 2 (1995)
Marcindo nel Buio (Marching in the
Dark) (1995)
Never Talk to Strangers (1995)
Palermo--Milano Solo Andata (1995)
Segreto di Stato (State Secret) (1995)
Un Eroe Borghese (1995)
L'arcano Incantatore (The Arcane
Enchanter) (1996)
Festival (1996)
Squillo (Call Girl) (1996)
Il Carniere (The Gamebag) (1997)
La Terza Luna (1997)

DONAHUE, MARC
After Midnight (1989)

DONALDSON, DAVID
Forgotten Silver (1996)

DONNELLAN, JAMES
Fatal Charm (1992)

DONOVAN
84 Charlie Mopic (1989)

DORFF, STEVE
Kiss Shot (1989)
Pink Cadillac (1989)
Return of Sam McCloud, The (1989)
Babe Ruth (1991)
In the Nick of Time (1991)
US (1991)
Chrome Soldiers (1992)
Pure Country (1992)
Poisoned by Love: The Kern County
Murders (1993)
Moonshine Highway (1996)
Rose Hill (1997)

DOUCET, MICHAEL
I Went to the Dance (1989)

DOVE, JONATHAN
Venus Peter (1989)
Prague (1991)

DOYLE, PATRICK
Henry V (1989)
Shipwrecked (1990)
Dead Again (1991)
Indocine (1992)
Into the West (1992)
Carlito's Way (1993)
Much Ado About Nothing (1993)
Needful Things (1993)
Exit to Eden (1994)
Little Princess (1995)
Mary Shelley's Frankenstein (1994)
Sense and Sensibility (1995)
Une Femme Francaise (1995)
Hamlet (1996)
Mrs. Winterbourne (1996)
Donnie Brasco (1997)
Great Expectations (1997)

DOYLE, ROGER
Bishop's Story, The (1995)

DRAGON, DARYL
Payback (1990)

DRAKE, ELIZABETH
Breathing Under Water (1991)
Road to Nhill (1997)

DRANDUSKI, KAMEN
Healer (1994)

DREITH, DENNIS
Punisher, The (1990)

DROUET, JEAN-PIERRE
Un Coeur qui bat (Your Beating Heart)
(1991)
Mazeppa (1993)
Chamane (1996)

Du PREZ, JOHN
Chorus of Disapproval, A (1989)
UHF (1989)
Bullseye! (1990)
Teenage Mutant Ninja Turtles (1990)

Mystery Date (1991)
Teenage Mutant Ninja Turtles II: The
    Secret of the Ooze (1991)
Carry on Columbus (1992)
Teenage Mutant Ninja Turtles III (1993)
Good Man in Africa, A (1994)
Wind in the Willows, The (1997)

DUCHESNE, ANDRE
A Crinoline Madness (1995)
Love Me, Love Me Not (1996)

DUCROS, GABRIELE
Obsession: A Taste for Fear (1989)

DUDLEY, ANNE
Mighty Quinn, The (1989)
Say Anything (1989)
Silence Like Glass (1989)
Misadventures of Mr. Wilt, The (1990)
Miracle, The (1991)
Pope Must Diet, The (1991)
Crying Game, The (1992)
Knight Moves (1992)
Royal Celebration (1993)
Grotesque, The (1995)
Hollow Reed (1996)
When Saturday Comes (1996)
Full Monty, The (1997)

DUHAMEL, ANTOINE
Daddy Nostalgia (1990)
Twisted Obsession (1990)
Belle Epoque (1992)
Malena Is a Name From a Tango (1996)
Ridicule (1996)
Tram a la Malvarrosa (1997)

DUKE, GEORGE
Family Affair (1995)

DUNAYER, MARTY
Deadly Obsession (1989)

DUNBAR, JIM
Matter of Degrees, A (1990)

DUNDAS, DAVID
How to Get Ahead in Advertising (1989)
Sleepers (1991)
Freddie as F.R.O.7 (1992)

DUNLAP, MICHAEL

Street Wars (1992)

DUNNE, JAMES PATRICK
Dear God (1996)

DZIERLATKA, ARIE
Le Cahier Vole (The Stolen Diary)
    (1992)
Le Journal de Lady M (1992)

EACOTT, JOHN
3 Steps to Heaven (1995)
Bit of Scarlet, A (1996)

EARECKSON, J. K.
Inside/Out (1997)

EARL, GARY
Raiders of the Sun (1992)

ECCLES, NOEL
Sun the Moon and the Stars, The (1996)

EDELMAN, RANDY
Dennis the Menace: The Live-Action
    Movie (1987)
Ghostbusters II (1989)
Troop Beverly Hills (1989)
Come See the Paradise (1990)
Kindergarten Cop (1990)
Quick Change (1990)
Drop Dead Fred (1991)
Shout (1991)
V. I. Warshawski (1991)
Beethoven (1992)
Distinguished Gentleman, The (1992)
Last of the Mohicans, The (1992)
My Cousin Vinny (1992)
Taking Back My Life: The Nancy
    Ziegenmeyer Story (1992)
Beethoven's 2nd (1993)
Dragon: The Bruce Lee Story (1993)
Gettysburg (1993)
Angels in the Outfield (1994)
Greedy (1994)
Mask, The (1994)
Pontiac Moon (1994)
Big Green, The (1995)
Billy Madison (1995)
Citizen X (1995)
Indian in the Cupboard, The (1995)
Tall Tale: The Unbelievable Adventures
    of Pecos Bill (1995)

While You Were Sleeping (1995)
Daylight (1996)
Diabolique (1996)
Down Periscope (1996)
Dragonheart (1996)
Quest, The (1996)
Anaconda (1997)
For Richer or Poorer (1997)
Leave It to Beaver (1997)

EDMONDS, KENNETH "BABYFACE"
Waiting to Exhale (1995)

EDWARDS, JONATHAN
Mouse, The (1996)

EDWARDS, KENNY
Wildflower (1991)

EDWARDS, ROSS
Paradise Road (1997)

EDWARDS, STEVE
Orpheus Descending (1990)
Minister's Wife, The (1992)
Midnight Fear (1992)
Night Siege: Project Shadowchaser II
    (1994)
Outraged Fugitive (1995)
Project Shadowchaser 3000 (1995)
Illegal in Blue (1995)
High Voltage (1997)

EEN, ROBERT
Trouble on the Corner (1997)

EGAN, SEAMUS
Brothers McMullen, The (1995)

EIDEL, PHILIPPE
Ce Que Femme Veut . . . (What a
    Woman Wants) (1993)
Cibel Emouvante (Wild Target) (1993)
Les Apprentis (The Apprentices) (1995)
Conte d'Ete (A Summer's Tale) (1996)
Un air de famille (1996)
Les Randonneurs (The Hikers) (1997)

EIDELMAN, CLIFF
Animal Behavior (1989)
Dead Man Out (1989)
Final Days, The (1989)
Triumph of the Spirit (1989)

Crazy People (1990)
Judgment (1990)
Magdalene (1990)
Strike It Rich (1990)
Backfield in Motion (1991)
Delirious (1991)
Star Trek VI: The Undiscovered Country
    (1991)
Christopher Columbus: The Discovery
    (1992)
Leap of Faith (1992)
Meteor Man, The (1993)
Untamed Heart (1993)
My Girl 2 (1994)
Picture Bride (1994)
Simple Twist of Fate, A (1994)
Now and Then (1995)
If These Walls Could Talk (1996)
Beautician and the Beast, The (1997)
Free Willy 3: The Rescue (1997)

EINHORN, RICHARD
Closet Land (1991)
House in the Hills, A (1993)

EITZEL, MARK
No Easy Way (1996)

EL ZABAR, KAHIL
How U Like Me Now (1993)

ELFMAN, DANNY
Batman (1989)
Darkman (1990)
Dick Tracy (1990)
Edward Scissorhands (1990)
Flash, The (1990)
Nightbreed (1990)
Pure Luck (1991)
Army of Darkness: Evil Dead 3 (1992)
Article 99 (1992)
Batman Returns (1992)
Nightmare Before Christmas, The (1993)
Sommersby (1993)
Black Beauty (1994)
Big Green, The (1995)
Dead Presidents (1995)
Dolores Claiborne (1995)
Tales From the Crypt Presents Demon
    Knight (1995)
To Die For (1995)
Extreme Measures (1996)
Freeway (1996)

Frighteners, The (1996)
Mars Attacks! (1996)
Mission: Impossible (1996)
Flubber (1997)
Good Will Hunting (1997)
Men in Black (1997)

ELIAS, JONATHAN
Far From Home (1989)
Howard Beach: Making the Case for
    Murder (1989)
Parents (1989)
Rude Awakening (1989)
Heart of Justice, The (1993)
Morning Glory (1993)
Leprechaun 2 (1994)

ELLINGTON, DUKE
Duke Ellington: Reminiscing in Tempo
    (1992)

ELLIOT, RICHARD
Teen Witch (1989)

ELLIOTT, BILL
Stand-Ins (1997)

ELLIOTT, JACK
Sibling Rivalry (1990)

ELLIS, CHARLES
Pharaoh's Army (1995)

EMERSON, KEITH
Church, The (1990)

EMMETT, VINCE
Pharaoh's Army (1995)

ENDELMAN, STEPHEN
Bronx Tale, A (1993)
Household Saints (1993)
Imaginary Crimes (1994)
Postcards From America (1994)
Desperate Trail, The (1995)
Englishman Who Went Up a Hill, but
    Came Down a Mountain, The (1995)
Jeffrey (1995)
Journey of August King, The (1995)
Reckless (1995)
Tom and Huck (1995)
City of Industry (1996)
Cosi (1996)

Ed (1996)
Flirting With Disaster (1996)
Keys to Tulsa (1997)
Kicked in the Head (1997)
Operation Condor (1997)
Road to Graceland, The (1997)

ENDER, MATHEW
Breakfast of Aliens (1989)

ENGLAND, JIM
Wright Brothers, The (1997)

ENGLISH, JON A.
All the Vermeers in New York (1990)
Uno a Te, Uno a Me et Uno a Raffaele
    (1994)

ENGLISH, PAUL
Man With the Perfect Swing, The (1995)

ENGSTROM, CHARLES
Ruby in Paradise (1993)
Ulee's Gold (1997)

ENNIS, BARRY
Deuce Coupe (1992)

ENO, BRIAN
Glitterbug (1994)

ERBE, MICKEY
Blue Planet (1990)
Hang Tough (1990)
Women of Windsor, The (1992)
Shattered Trust: The Shari Karney Story
    (1993)
Trial & Error (1993)
Against Her Will: The Carrie Buck Story
    (1994)
Destiny in Space (1994)
I Know My Son Is Alive (1994)
To Save the Children (1994)
Dancing in the Dark (1995)
Deadly Love (1995)
Friends at Last (1995)
Lady Killer, The (1995)
Picture Perfect (1995)
Silence of Adultery, The (1995)
Visitors of the Night (1995)
Closer and Closer (1996)
Hostile Advances: The Kerry Ellison
    Story (1996)

Morrison Murders, The (1996)

ERMS, SEBASTIEN
Conte d'Hiver (A Winter's Tale) (1992)
Le Abre, le Maire et la Mediatheque
(1993)
Les Rendez-vous de Paris (1995)

ERRINGTON, MICHAEL
Unconditional Love (1994)

ERWIN, LEE
Man Without a World, The (1992)

ERWIN, PAT
Breathing Room (1996)

ESPOSITO, TONY
Storia d'Amore con i Crampi (1996)

ESQUIVEL
Four Rooms (1995)

ESTEVE, PASCALE
La Parfum d'Yvonne (1994)

ETHERIDGE, MELISSA
It's a Wonderful Life (1993)
Teresa's Tattoo (1994)

ETOLL, ROBERT
Danger Zone II: Reaper's Revenge
(1989)
Danger Zone III: Steel Horse War (1990)

EUBANKS, KEVIN
Rebound: The Legend of Earl "The
Goat" Manigault (1996)
Dinner, The (1997)

EVANOFF, GARY
Friends and Enemies (1992)

EVANS, FRANCOIS
Fistful of Fingers, A (1995)

FABIANO, JEAN-FRANCOISE
Entangled (1992)

FABREGAS, JAIME
Expendables, The (1988)
Nam Angels (1989)

FACTORY, THE
Howling V: The Rebirth (1989)

FAGENSON, LOUIS
Bermuda Triangle (1996)

FAIR, JEFF EDEN
Shame II: The Secret (1995)
Secret She Carried, The (1996)
Crowned and Dangerous (1997)
Little Girls in Pretty Boxes (1997)
Nightmare Come True, A (1997)

FALAGIANI, MARCO
Mediterraneo (1991)

FALTERMEYER, HAROLD
Fletch Lives (1989)
Tango & Cash (1989)
Kuffs (1992)
Asterix Conquers America (1994)

FANSHAWE, DAVID
Dirty Weekend (1993)

FARAJ, ARDESHIR
Drug Wars: The Camarena Story (1990)

FARINA, DARIO
Rossini: or the Fatal Question, Who
Slept With Who (1997)

FARISELLI, PATRIZIO
Belle al Bar (1994)
Ivo the Genius (1995)
Riorno a Casa Gori (Return to Gori's
House) (1996)

FARMER, JIM
Johnny Suede (1991)
Living in Oblivion (1995)
Box of Moonlight (1996)
Real Blonde, The (1997)

FARNON, BRAUN
Time Runner (1992)
Ultimate Desires (1992)

FARQUARSON, KEITH
Demon Keeper (1994)

FARRAR, JOHN
Mom for Christmas, A (1990)

FARRELL, CHRISTOPHER
Double Threat (1992)
Mardi Gras for the Devil (1993)
Night Trap (1993)

FASMAN, BARRY
My Mom's a Werewolf (1989)
Whisper to a Scream, A (1989)
Your Mother Wears Combat Boots
(1989)
Street Hunter (1990)

FASSI, RICCARDO
L'amico Immaginario (The Imaginary
Friend) (1994)

FATAAR, RICKY
Spotswood (aka Efficiency Expert)
(1991)

FAULKNER, DAVID
Broken Highway (1993)
Sum of Us, The (1994)

FEARNLEY, JAMES
God's Lonely Man (1996)

FEBRE, LOUIS
Bad Girls From Mars (1988)
Time to Die, A (1991)
Deadly Bet (1992)
Maximum Force (1992)
L.A. Wars (1993)
Private Wars (1993)
Bigfoot: The Unforgettable Encounter
(1994)
T-Force (1994)
Haunted World of Edward D. Wood Jr.,
The (1995)
Last Man Standing (1995)
Secretary, The (1995)
Two Bits & Pepper (1995)
Dark Breed (1996)
Little Bigfoot (1996)
Medusa's Child (1997)
Tower of Terror (1997)

FELDMAN, JACK
Newsies (1992)
Hans Christian Andersen's
"Thumbelina" (1994)

FELDMAN, RICHARD

Boca (1994)

FENN, RICK
Tank Malling (1989)

FENNELL, TONY
Within the Rock (1996)

FENTON, GEORGE
We're No Angels (1989)
Long Walk Home, The (1990)
Memphis Belle (1990)
White Palace (1990)
Fisher King, The (1991)
China Moon (1991)
Final Analysis (1992)
Hero (1992)
Born Yesterday (1993)
Groundhog Day (1993)
Shadowlands (1993)
Ladybird Ladybird (1994)
Madness of King George, The (1994)
Mixed Nuts (1994)
Fall of Saigon, The (1995)
Land and Freedom (1995)
Carla's Song (1996)
Crucible, The (1996)
Heaven's Prisoners (1996)
In Love and War (1996)
Mary Reilly (1996)
Multiplicity (1996)
Woodlanders, The (1997)

FERGUSON, ALLYN
Angel in Green (1987)
Lookalike, The (1990)
Ironclads (1991)
Shadow of a Doubt (1991)
Against Her Will: An Incident in
Baltimore (1992)
Fergie and Andrew: Behind Palace
Doors (1992)
Love, Honor & Obey: The Last Mafia
Marriage (1993)
Trick of the Eye (1994)
While Justice Sleeps (1994)
Haunting of Helen Walker, The (1995)
What Love Sees (1996)

FERGUSON, DAVID
Tailspin: Behind the Korean Airliner
Tragedy (1989)

Dead Ahead: The Exxon Valdez Disaster (1992)
Some Kind of Life (1995)
Hostile Waters (1997)

FERGUSON, JAY
Gleaming the Cube (1989)
Nightmare on Elm Street 5: The Dream Child, A (1989)
Race for Glory (1989)
Parker Kane (1990)
Nervous Ticks (1992)
Tremors II: Aftershocks (1992)
Wildlands, The (1992)
Double Dragon (1994)
Driven (1996)

FERRUCCI, FRANK
Fallout (1996)

FIEDEL, BRAD
Cold Sassy Tree (1989)
Fright Night--Part 2 (1989)
Immediate Family (1989)
Perfect Witness (1989)
True Believer (1989)
Blue Steel (1990)
Forgotten Prisoners: The Amnesty Files (1990)
Night Visions (1990)
Blood Ties (1991)
Plymouth (1991)
Terminator 2: Judgment Day (1991)
Gladiator, The (1992)
Straight Talk (1992)
Teamster Boss: The Jackie Presser Story (1992)
Real McCoy, The (1993)
Striking Distance (1993)
Blink (1994)
True Lies (1994)
Johnny Mnemonic (1995)
Eden (1996)
Mistrial (1996)
Rasputin (1996)

FIELDS, ADAM
Lovelife (1997)

FIELDS, STEVEN
Long Weekend, The (O'Despair) (1989)

FIENNES, MAYA & MAGNUS

Preaching to the Perverted (1997)

FIGGIS, MIKE
Internal Affairs (1990)
Liebestraum (1991)
Leaving Las Vegas (1995)
One Night Stand (1997)

FIJAL, ANNE-MARIE
Marion (1997)

FILASTO, PASQUALE
Pugili (Boxers) (1995)

FILLEUL, PETER
Sweet Talker (1991)

FIOCCA, RICHARD
Alien Space Avenger (1991)

FIORI, SERGE
Un Histoire Inventee (An Imaginary Tale) (1990)

FISCH, IRWIN
Grand Larceny (1988)
Ascent, The (1994)
Mother May I Sleep With Danger? (1996)
Night Visitors (1996)
Bridge of Time (1997)
Flood: A River's Rampage (1997)
Mother Teresa: In the Name of God's Poor (1997)
Neil Simon's "The Sunshine Boys" (1997)

FISH, PETER
Painting the Town (1992)
Tie-Died: Rock 'n Roll's Most Dedicated Fans (1995)
Wigstock: The Movie (1995)
Intimate Betrayal (1996)
Voice of the Children (1997)

FISHER, LUBOS
Labyrinth (1992)

FISHER, ROBERT MORGAN
Philosophy in the Bedroom (1995)

FISHMAN, JEFF
Carnal Crimes (1991)

FITCH, TOBY
Hotel Oklahoma (1991)

FITZGERALD, LAURIE
Scenes From the New World (1994)

FITZPATRICK, FRANK
Friday (1995)

FIX, HARRY
Life's Too Good (1994)

FLINTER. JASON
Big Swap, The (1997)

FLOYD, DARREN
Def Jam's How to Be a Player (1997)

FLYNN, TONY
Revenge of Billy the Kid (1991)

FOISSY, CLAUDE
Hart to Hart: Two Harts in 3/4 Time
(1995)
Hart to Hart: Harts in High Season
(1996)
Hart to Hart: Till Death Do Us Hart
(1996)

FOLEY, PETER
93 Million Miles From the Sun (1995)

FOLIART, DAN
Return to Green Acres (1990)
Not Our Son (1995)

FOLK, ROBERT
Police Academy 6: City Under Siege
(1989)
Wicked Stepmother (1989)
Happy Together (1990)
Honeymoon Academy (1990)
Neverending Story II: The Next Chapter,
The (1990)
Beastmaster 2: Through the Portal of
Time (1991)
Row of Crows, A (1991)
Toy Soldiers (1991)
Mario and the Mob (1992)
Rock-a-Doodle (1992)
National Lampoon's Loaded Weapon I
(1993)
Sworn to Vengeance (1993)

In the Army Now (1994)
Police Academy: Mission to Moscow
(1994)
Search and Rescue (1994)
State of Emergency (1994)
Trapped in Paradise (1994)
Troll in Central Park, A (1994)
Two Fathers: Justice for the Innocent
(1994)
Ace Ventura: When Nature Calls (1995)
Arabian Knight (1995)
Family Reunion: A Relative Nightmare
(1995)
Lawnmower Man 2: Beyond Cyberspace
(1996)
Maximum Risk (1996)
Theodore Rex (1996)
Booty Call (1997)
Boys Life 2 (1997)
Nothing to Lose (1997)

FONTAINE, BRUNO
On Connait la Chanson (Same Old Song)
(1997)

FOOTE, RAY
It Takes Two (1995)

FOOTE, SHERMAN
It Takes Two (1995)

FORD, JANE
I Love You . . . Don't Touch Me! (1997)

FORD, ROBIN
No Way Home (1996)

FORMAN, MITCHEL
Jezebel's Kiss (1990)

FORTUNA, TONY
Ice House (1989)

FOSSATI, IVANO
Il Toro (The Bull) (1994)

FOSTER, DAVID
Listen to Me (1989)
If Looks Could Kill (1991)
One Good Cop (1991)
Little Rascals, The (1994)

FOSTER, STEPHEN
  Killer Image (1992)

FOUQUEY, JEAN-PIERRE
  Louis, Enfant Roi (Louis, the Child
    King) (1993)

FOWLER, BRUCE
  First Degree (1995)

FOX, CHARLES
  Gods Must Be Crazy 2, The (1989)
  It Had to Be You (1989)
  One Man Force (1989)
  Tarzan in Manhattan (1989)
  Family for Joe, A (1990)
  Love Boat: A Valentine Voyage, The
    (1990)
  Repossessed (1990)
  Rich Men, Single Women (1990)
  Voices Within: The Lives of Truddi
    Chase (1990)
  Absolute Strangers (1991)
  Held Hostage: The Sis and Jerry Levin
    Story (1991)
  Crash Landing: The Rescue of Flight 232
    (1992)
  Christmas in Connecticut (1992)
  In My Daughter's Name (1992)
  Broken Chain, The (1993)
  Odd Couple: Together Again, The (1993)
  Confessions: Two Faces of Evil (1994)
  Innocent Victims (1996)
  Man Next Door, The (1996)

FOX, FELICITY
  Redheads (1992)
  Fistful of Lies (1996)

FOX, JIM
  Deadfall (1993)

FRANGLEN, SIMON
  Born to Run (1993)

FRANK, DAVID MICHAEL
  False Witness (1989)
  One Man Force (1989)
  Hard to Kill (1990)
  Chips, the War Dog (1990)
  Out for Justice (1991)
  Showdown in Little Tokyo (1991)
  Suburban Commando (1991)

  Best of the Best 2 (1992)
  Exclusive (1992)
  From the Files of Joseph Wambaugh: A
    Jury of One (1992)
  Blindsided (1993)
  Black Widow Murders: The Blanche
    Taylor Moore Story (1993)
  Casualties of Love: The "Long Island
    Lolita" Story (1993)
  Disappearance of Christina, The (1993)
  Extreme Justice (1993)
  Linda (1993)
  Life in the Theatre, A (1993)
  Matter of Justice, A (1993)
  Street Knight (1993)
  Bitter Vengeance (1994)
  Children of the Dark (1994)
  Dancing With Danger (1994)
  Annie: A Royal Adventure (1995)
  Baby-Sitter's Club, The (1995)
  Dead by Sunset (1995)
  Love and Betrayal: The Mia Farrow
    Story (1995)
  Problem Child 3: Junior in Love (1995)
  Tails You Live, Heads You're Dead
    (1995)
  When the Darkman Calls (1995)
  Born Free: A New Adventure (1996)
  Lottery, The (1996)
  Prosecutors, The (1996)
  Prayer in the Dark, A (1997)
  Prince, The (1997)
  Thousand Men and a Baby, A (1997)
  Toothless (1997)
  Under Wraps (1997)
  Volcano: Fire on the Mountain (1997)

FRANKE, CHRISTOPHER
  McBain (1991)
  Eye of the Storm (1992)
  She Woke Up (1992)
  Universal Soldier (1992)
  Stephen King's "The Tommyknockers"
    (1993)
  Beyond Betrayal (1994)
  Surgeon, The (aka Exquisite Tenderness)
    (1994)
  Yarn Princess, The (1994)
  Exquisite Tenderness (1995)
  In the Line of Duty: Kidnapped (1995)
  Code Name: Wolverine (1996)
  Face to Die For, A (1996)
  Solo (1996)

Devil's Child, The (1997)
Louisa May Alcott's "The Inheritance"
   (1997)
Tell Me No Secrets (1997)

FRANZETTI, CARLOS
   Mambo Kings, The (1992)

FRASER, JILL
   Cutting Class (1989)

FREEBAIRN-SMITH, IAN
   Three on a Match (1987)

FRENCH, JOHN
   Hunting (1991)

FREWER, TERRY
   Dead Man's Gun (1997)

FRIDAY, GAVIN
   Boxer, The (1997)

FRIEDEL, MARTIN
   Bitter Herbs and Honey (1996)

FRIEDMAN, GARY WILLIAM
   Who Gets the Friends? (1988)
   Bump in the Night (1991)

FRIEDMAN, JUD J.
   Prince for a Day (1995)

FRISELL, BILL
   La Scuola (School) (1995)

FRISINA, MARCO
   Abraham (1994)
   Jacob (1994)
   Joseph (1995)
   Moses (1996)
   Samson and Delilah (1996)

FRITZ, MATTHEW
   Loser (1991)

FRIZZELL, JOHN
   It Was Him or Us (1995)
   Red Ribbon Blues (1995)
   Whose Daughter Is She? (1995)
   Beavis and Butt-Head Do America
      (1996)
   Bloodhounds (1996)

Crime of the Century (1996)
Deadly Pursuits (1996)
Rich Man's Wife, The (1996)
Undertow (1996)
Alien Resurrection (1997)
Dante's Peak (1997)

FRONTIERE, DOMINIC
   Brutal Glory (1990)
   Danielle Steel's "Palomino" (1991)
   Color of Night (1994)

FROOM, MITCHELL
   Path to Paradise (1997)

FRY, GARY
   Trancers IV: Jack of Swords (1994)
   Trancers V: Sudden Death (1995)

FULLER, PARMER
   Night Visitor (1989)
   Saturday the 14th Strikes Back (1989)
   Time Trackers (1989)
   Femme Fatale (1991)
   Desperate Motive (1993)
   Reflections on a Crime (1994)
   Silence of the Hams, The (1994)
   Westing Game, The (1997)

FURLANTI, DANIELE
   Viva San Isidoro! (1995)

GAFNEY, HENRY
   Sidewalk Stories (1989)

GAGNON, ANDRE
   Pianist, The (1991)

GAINSBOURG, SERGE
   Elisa (1995)

GALE, JACK
   Luckiest Man in the World, The (1989)

GALINSKY, MICHAEL
   Half-Cocked (1995)

GALLERY, SEAN
   Mom for Christmas, A (1990)

GAMMONS, ROD
   Within the Rock (1996)

GANCEDO, EVA
La Buena Estella (Lucky Star) (1997)

GANG OF FOUR
Delinquent (1995)

GANO, GORDON
Hitting the Ground (1996)

GARBAREK, JAN
Shuttlecock (1991)
Vesna va Veloce (Vesna Goes Fast)
(1996)

GARDOS, EVA
Hear No Evil (1993)

GARRETT, JOHN
Eyes of the Prey (1993)

GARRETT, ROBERT
Prime Target (1991)
Eye of the Stranger (1993)

GARSON, MIKE
Criminal Behavior (1992)
Life on the Edge (1992)

GARVARENTZ, GEORGES
Champagne Charlie (1989)
Quicker Than the Eye (1989)
Les Annees Campagne (The Country
Years) (1992)
Petain (1993)

GATLIN, LARRY
Legend of O. B. Taggart, The (1994)

GAUBERT, CHRISTIAN
La Cible (The Target) (1997)

GAVIN, ALASTAIR
Go Now (1995)

GEE, KAY
Sunset Park (1996)

GELLER, LYNNE
Denise Calls Up (1995)

GELY, PAPO
Robot in the Family (1994)

GEORGE, SERGIO
I Like It Like That (1994)

GERBER, JERRY
Gumby: The Movie (1995)

GERVAISE, FABIEN
Memoires d'un Jeune Con (1996)

GETZ, STAN
In Defense of a Married Man (1990)

GIBBS, MICHAEL
Breaking In (1989)
Riding the Edge (1989)
Iron & Silk (1991)
Whore (1991)
Hard Boiled (1992)
Century (1993)
Being Human (1994)
All Men Are Mortal (1995)

GIBBS, RICHARD [KENDALL]
Deadly Silence, A (1989)
Say Anything (1989)
How to Murder a Millionaire (1990)
Killing in a Small Town, A (1990)
Bingo (1991)
Deadlock (1991)
Sins of the Mother (1991)
Gun in Betty Lou's Handbag, The (1992)
Ladybugs (1992)
Once Upon a Crime (1992)
Passed Away (1992)
Amos & Andrew (1993)
Barbarians at the Gate (1993)
Fatal Instinct (1993)
Son-in-Law (1993)
Three of Hearts (1993)
Blind Justice (1994)
Chase, The (1994)
Clifford (1994)
Dangerous Indiscretion (1994)
At First Sight (1995)
Christmas Box, The (1995)
Two Guys Talkin' About Girls (1995)
First Kid (1996)
Timepiece (1996)
That Darn Cat (1997)

GIFFIN, PHILIP
Dead in the Water (1991)
Murder 101 (1991)

Red Wind (1991)
White Lie (1991)
Ladykiller (1992)
Deadly Relations (1993)
Dangerous Heart (1994)
Barefoot Executive, The (1995)
Computer Wore Tennis Shoes, The
    (1995)
Escape From Terror: The Teresa Stamper
    Story (1995)
Sharon's Secret (1995)

GILL, ALAN
    Blonde Fist (1991)

GILLESPIE, DIZZY
    Winter in Lisbon, The (1992)

GILLIS, KEIN
    Nutcracker Prince, The (1990)

GILLON, IRIS
    Fast Food (1989)

GILMAN, JEFF
    Guy Maddin: Waiting for Twilight
        (1997)

GILMAN, PAUL
    Best of the Best (1989)

GILUTIN, JON
    Wildflower (1991)

GINSBURG, ROBERT
    Lady in Waiting (1994)

GIOVINAZZO, RICK
    No Way Home (1996)

GIRARD, MICHAEL PAUL
    Getting Lucky (1990)

GLADSTONE-REID, PAUL
    Skin White Mask (1996)

GLASS, PHILIP
    Mindwalk (1990)
    Closet Land (1991)
    Brief History of Time, A (1992)
    Candyman (1992)
    Candyman 2: Farewell to the Flesh
        (1995)

Jeniapo (1995)
Bent (1997)
Joseph Conrad's "The Secret Agent"
    (1996)
Kundun (1997)

GLASSER, RICHARD
    Night Eyes (aka Hidden Vision) (1990)

GLEESON, PATRICK
    Howling VI: The Freaks (1991)

GLENNIE-SMITH, NICK
    Rock, The (1996)
    Stolen Hearts (1996)
    Two If by Sea (1996)
    Fire Down Below (1997)
    Home Alone 3 (1997)

GLUCK, JESUS
    Blood and Sand (1989)

GOGA, JACK ALAN
    Touch of a Stranger (1990)

GOLD, ARI
    Latin Boys Go to Hell (1997)

GOLD, DANIEL
    Courting Courtney (1997)

GOLD, MURRAY
    Mojo (1997)

GOLDBERG, BARRY
    Beverly Hills Brats (1989)
    Nowhere to Run (1989)
    Flashback (1990)
    Captain America (1992)
    Return of the Living Dead 3 (1993)
    L.A. Johns (1997)

GOLDENBERG, BILLY
    Nutcracker: Money, Madness and
        Murder (1987)
    Jules Verne's "Around the World in 80
        Days"(1989)
    Jackie Collins' "Lucky/Chances" (1990)
    People Like Us (1990)
    Perfect Harmony (1991)
    Chernobyl: The Final Warning (1991)
    One Special Victory (1991)
    House of Secrets and Lies, A (1992)

Man Upstairs, The (1992)
Miles From Nowhere (1992)
Miss America: Behind the Crown (1992)
Miss Rose White (1992)
What She Doesn't Know (1992)
Danielle Steel's "Message From
   Nam"(1993)
Silent Cries (1993)
Burning Passion: The Margaret Mitchell
   Story, A (1994)
Someone Else's Child (1994)
Element of Truth, An (1995)
Christmas Every Day (1996)
Danielle Steel's "No Greater Love"
   (1996)
Convictions (1997)

GOLDENBERG, SIMON
   Wild Orchid (1990)

GOLDENTHAL, ELLIOT
   Drugstore Cowboy (1989)
   Pet Semetary (1989)
   Criminal Justice (1990)
   Grand Isle (1991)
   Alien 3 (1992)
   Fool's Fire (1992)
   Demolition Man (1993)
   Cobb (1994)
   Golden Gate (1994)
   Interview With the Vampire (1994)
   Roswell (1994)
   Batman Forever (1995)
   Heat (1995)
   Voices (1995)
   Michael Collins (1996)
   Time to Kill, A (1996)
   Batman & Robin (1997)
   Butcher Boy, The (1997)

GOLDSBORO, BOBBY
   Man From Left Field, The (1993)

GOLDSMITH, JERRY
   'burbs, The (1989)
   Criminal Law (1989)
   Leviathan (1989)
   Star Trek V: The Final Frontier (1989)
   Warlock (1989)
   Gremlins 2: The New Batch (1990)
   Russia House, The (1990)
   Total Recall (1990)
   Brotherhood of the Gun (1991)

Not Without My Daughter (1991)
Omen IV: The Awakening, The (1991)
Police Story: The Freeway Killings
   (1991)
Sleeping With the Enemy (1991)
Basic Instinct (1992)
Forever Young (1992)
Love Field (1992)
Medicine Man (1992)
Mom and Dad Save the World (1992)
Mr. Baseball (1992)
Dennis the Menace (1993)
Malice (1993)
Matinee (1993)
Rudy (1993)
Six Degrees of Separation (1993)
Vanishing, The (1993)
Angie (1994)
Bad Girls (1994)
I.Q. (1994)
River Wild, The (1994)
Shadow, The (1994)
Congo (1995)
First Knight (1995)
Powder (1995)
Chain Reaction (1996)
City Hall (1996)
Executive Decision (1996)
Ghost and the Darkness, The (1996)
Star Trek: First Contact (1996)
Air Force One (1997)
Edge, The (1997)
Fierce Creatures (1997)
L.A. Confidential (1997)

GOLDSMITH, JOEL
   Counterforce (1988)
   Endless Descent (1989)
   No Safe Haven (1989)
   Across the Tracks (1990)
   Army of One (1990)
   Instant Karma (1990)
   Jobman (1990)
   Moon 44 (1990)
   Brotherhood of the Gun (1991)
   Woman, Her Man and Her Futon, A
      (1992)
   Home for Christmas: Little Miss
      Millions (1993)
   Maniac Cop 3: Badge of Silence (1993)
   Man's Best Friend (1993)
   Untouchables, The (1993)
   Blood for Blood (1995)

Rattled (1996)
Shiloh (1996)
Kull the Conqueror (1997)

GOLDSMITH, JONATHAN
  Avalanche (1994)
  Broken Lullaby (1994)
  Heads (1994)
  Choices of the Heart: The Margaret
    Sanger Story (1995)
  Falling for You (1995)
  Kissinger and Nixon (1995)
  Stand Off (1995)
  Husband, A Wife, and a Lover, A (1996)
  Mother Trucker: The Diana Kilmury
    Story (1996)
  Murder at My Door (1996)
  We the Jury (1996)
  Dead Silence (1997)
  Gerrie & Louise (1997)
  Major Crime (1997)
  Survival on the Mountain (1997)
  Too Close to Home (1997)

GOLDSTEIN, GIL
  Radio Inside (1994)
  I Love You, I Love You Not (1997)

GOLDSTEIN, STEVE
  Cats Don't Dance (1997)

GOLDSTEIN, WILLIAM
  Blood Vows: The Story of a Mafia Wife
    (1987)
  Connecticut Yankee in King Arthur's
    Court, A (1989)
  Cross of Fire (1989)
  Shocker (1989)
  Blood River (1991)
  Quarrel, The (1993)
  Danielle Steel's "Zoya" (1995)

GOLIA, VINNY
  Blood and Concrete (1991)
  No Secrets (1991)
  Trouble Bound (1993)
  Serpent's Lair (1995)
  Small Time (1996)
  Fear and Learning at Hoover Elementary
    (1997)

GONZALEZ, GABRIEL
  All of Them Witches (1996)

GONZALEZ, JOHN
  Angels of the City (1989)
  L.A. Heat (1989)
  L.A. Vice (1989)
  Living to Die (1990)
  Repo Jake (1990)
  Art of Dying, The (1991)
  Bikini Summer (1991)
  Killer's Edge, The (1991)
  Last Riders, The (1991)
  Street Crimes (1991)
  Sunset Strip (1991)
  Final Impact (1992)
  Intent to Kill (1993)
  Ice (1994)
  Lion Strike (1994)
  Steel Hunter (1994)
  Hologram Man (1995)

GONZALEZ, JOSEPH JULIAN
  For the Love of My Child (1993)
  Cisco Kid, The (1994)
  Curdled (1996)
  Colors Straight Up (1997)

GOODALL, HOWARD
  Return of the Borrowers, The (1996)
  Bean (1997)

GOODMAN, GRANT
  Fools Die Fast (1996)

GOODMAN, GREG
  Tale of Love, A (1995)

GOODMAN, JERRY
  Search for Signs of Intelligent Life in the
    Universe, The (1991)

GOODMAN, JIM
  Ice Runner, The (1993)

GOODMAN, MILES
  Delinquents, The (1989)
  K-9 (1989)
  Money, Power, Murder (1989)
  Staying Together (1989)
  Traveling Man (1989)
  Funny About Love (1990)
  Opportunity Knocks (1990)
  Problem Child (1990)
  Vital Signs (1990)
  He Said, She Said (1991)

Super, The (1991)
What About Bob? (1991)
For Richer, For Poorer (1992)
HouseSitter (1992)
Indecency (1992)
Muppet Christmas Carol, The (1992)
Indian Summer (1993)
Sister Act 2: Back in the Habit (1993)
Blankman (1994)
Getting Even With Dad (1994)
Indian in the Cupboard, The (1995)
Dunston Checks In (1996)
Larger Than Life (1996)
Sunset Park (1996)
'Til There Was You (1997)

GOODWIN, JIM
Apex (1994)

GOODWIN, WAYNE
Rough Diamonds (1994)
All Men Are Liars (1995)
Back of Beyond (1995)

GORBACHOW, YURI
Blast 'Em (1992)
My Summer Vacation (1996)

GORDON, CHRISTOPHER
Sanctuary (1995)

GORDON, PAUL CHRISTIAN
Wedding Bell Blues (1996)

GORDON, PETER
Il Verificatore (The Meter Reader)
(1995)

GORE, MICHAEL
Don't Tell Her It's Me (1990)
Butcher's Wife, The (1991)
Defending Your Life (1991)
Mr. Wonderful (1993)

GORECKI, HENRYK
Mon Homme (My Man) (1996)

GORGONI, ADAM
Tollbooth (1994)

GORNEY, ZBIGNIEW
In a Moment of Passion (1993)

GOTTSCHALK, ARTHUR
Charlie's Ear (1992)

GOUDE, JEAN-PHILIPPE
Sortez des Rangs (Fall Out) (1996)
Tire a Part (Limited Edition) (1996)

GOUGH, ORLANDO
Criminal (1995)

GOULD, DON
Bob's Weekend (1996)

GOURIET, GERALD
Death Dreams (1991)
Seeds of Tragedy (1991)
Child of Rage (1992)
Disaster in Time (1992)
Double Edge (1992)
Hold Me, Thrill Me, Kiss Me (1992)
Mad at the Moon (1992)
Overexposed (1992)
Question of Attribution, A (1992)
Hitwoman: The Double Edge (1993)
Innocent, The (1993)
Only Way Out, The (1993)
Philadelphia Experiment 2, The (1993)
Substitute, The (1993)
They (aka They Watch) (1993)
To Dance With the White Dog (1993)
Men of War (1994)

GOVERNOR, MARK
Masque of the Red Death (1989)
Overexposed (1990)
Hollywood Boulevard II (1991)
Mindwarp (1992)
Pet Sematary Two (1992)
Till the End of the Night (1994)
Notes From Underground (1995)
Santa Fe (1997)

GRABOWSKI, BILL
Time to Remember, A (1988)
Whole Truth, The (1992)

GRABOWSKY, PAUL
Woman's Tale, A (1991)
Last Days of Chez Nous, The (1992)
Lucky Break (1994)
Mushrooms (1995)
Lust and Revenge (1996)
Paperback Romance (1997)

GRADUS-SAMSON, CEDRIC
Mandela and deKlerk (1997)

GRAHAM, JOHN
Dragon Fire (1993)
Firehawk (1993)
Unborn II, The (1994)
Kissing Miranda (1995)
American Strays (1996)

GRANT, JAMES
Near Room, The (1995)

GRANT, JERRY J.
Bloodstone (1989)

GRAPPELLI, STEPHANE
Milou en Mai (May Fools) (1990)
Familia (Family) (1996)

GRASSBY-LEWIS, RICHARD
Love and Death on Long Island (1997)

GRAY, BRIAN
Middleton's Changling (1997)

GRAY, JOHN
Metamorphosis: The Alien Factor (1991)
Blue Black Permanent (1992)

GRAZIANO, STEPHEN
Scam (1993)
Past Tense (1994)
Ruby Jean and Joe (1996)
Contagious (1997)

GREAT, DON
Mob Boss (1990)

GRECO, D'ANGIO
Io Speriamo Che Me La Cavo (1993)

GRECO, ITALO
Come mi vioi (The Way You Want Me)
(1996)

GREEMORE, BOB
Shotgun Freeway: Drives Through Lost
L.A. (1995)

GREEN, MARK
Promise Kept: The Oksana Baiul Story,
A (1994)

GREEN, MILES
Shut Yer Mouth! (1996)

GREGOIRE, RICHARD
Perfectly Normal (1991)
Being at Home With Claude (1992)
Chili's Blues (1994)
October (1994)
Behind the Blue (1995)

GREGORY, WILL
i.d. (1994)

GREGSON-WILLIAMS, HARRY
White Angel (1993)
Full Body Massage (1995)
Muppet Treasure Island (1996)
Whole Wide World, The (1996)
Borrowers, The (1997)
Liar (1997)
Smilla's Sense of Snow (1997)

GRIERSON, RALPH
Red Earth, White Earth (1989)
Hired Heart, The (1997)

GRIGOROV, MARIO
This Won't Hurt a Bit! (1993)
Young at Hearts (1995)

GRINDLAY, MURRAY
Once Were Warriors (1994)
Broken English (1996)

GRISSETTE, STEVE
Perfect Model, The (1989)

GROHL, DAVID
Touch (1997)

GROSS, ANDREW
Bio-Dome (1996)
8 Heads in a Duffel Bag (1997)

GROSS, CHARLES
No Place Like Home (1989)
Third Degree Burn (1989)
Turner & Hooch (1989)
Air America (1990)
Another You (1991)
Eyes of a Witness (1991)
In the Shadow of a Killer (1992)
Passport to Murder (1993)

Good King Wenceslas (1994)
Awake to Danger (1995)
Family Thing, A (1996)
Fakin' Da Funk (1997)

GROSS, GUY
Magic Riddle, The (1991)
Frauds (1992)
Adventures of Priscilla, Queen of the
Desert, The (1994)

GRUSIN, DAVE
Dry White Season, A (1989)
Fabulous Baker Boys, The (1989)
Bonfire of the Vanities, The (1990)
Havana (1990)
For the Boys (1991)
Firm, The (1993)
Cure, The (1995)
Mulholland Falls (1996)
Hope (1997)
In the Gloaming (1997)
Selena (1997)

GRUSIN, SCOTT
We're Talkin' Serious Money (1992)
Relentless 3 (1993)

GRUSKA, JAY
Sing (1989)
Nightmare on the 13th Floor (1990)
Wheels of Terror (1990)
World's Oldest Living Bridesmaid, The
(1990)
Another Pair of Aces: Three of a Kind
(1991)
Baby of the Bride (1991)
Child of Darkness, Child of Light (1991)
Mo' Money (1992)
Dying to Remember (1993)
Without Warning: Terror in the Towers
(1993)
Time to Heal, A (1994)
Trapped in Space (1995)

GUARD, BARRIE
Toxic Avenger, Part II (1989)
Mad Dogs and Englishmen (1995)

GUARINO, UMBERTO
Pianese Nunzio, 14 Anni a Maggio
(1996)

GUEFEN, ANTHONY
At Home With the Webbers (1993)

GUEST, CHRISTOPHER
Waiting for Guffman (1996)

GUETTEL, ADAM
Arguing the World (1997)

GUIDETTI, CLAUDIO
Il Ciclone (The Cyclone) (1996)
Fireworks (1997)

GUINOVART, ALBERT
El Largo Invierno (The Long Winter)
(1992)

GUNNING, CHRISTOPHER
When the Whales Came (1989)
Under Suspicion (1991)
Middlemarch (1994)
Midnight Movie (1994)
Affair, The (1995)
Firelight (1997)

GUTTRIDGE, JIM
Once in a Blue Moon (1995)
Ronnie & Julie (1997)

HABER, ITAI
Live Wire: Human Timebomb (1995)

HADEN, CHARLIE
12 Angry Men (1997)

HADJINASSIOS, GEORGE
Shirley Valentine (1989)

HAIM, PHILIPPE
Deficiency (Carences) (1994)
L'appat (The Bait) (1995)
Barracuda (1997)

HAINES, FRANCIS
Split Second (1992)

HAJIAN, CHRIS
Nothing to Lose (1995)
Other Voices, Other Rooms (1995)
Made Men (1997)
Mr. Vincent (1997)

HALFPENNY, JIM
  Bikini Summer 2 (1992)
  Magic Kid (aka Ninja Dragons) (1992)
  No Escape, No Return (1993)
  Power Within, The (1995)
  Texas Payback (1995)
  To the Limit (1995)
  Riot (1996)

HALLDORSON, RON
  Harvest for the Heart (1994)

HALSEY, FELICITY & JOHN
  Emma: Queen of the South Seas (1988)

HAMES, FRANK
  Curse of the Starving Class (1995)

HAMILTON, GEORGE HOVIS
  American Angels: Baptism of Blood,
    The (1990)

HAMILTON, JOHN
  Drive, The (1997)

HAMILTON, MURIELLE
  Joe's Rotten World (1995)

HAMLISCH, MARVIN
  Experts, The (1989)
  January Man, The (1989)
  Women & Men: Stories of Seduction
    (1990)
  Frankie and Johnny (1991)
  Missing Pieces (1991)
  Switched at Birth (1991)
  Seasons of the Heart (1994)
  Open Season (1995)
  Mirror Has Two Faces, The (1996)

HAMMER, ERIC A.
  A,B,C . . . Manhattan (1997)

HAMMER, JAN
  Curiosity Kills (1990)
  I Come in Peace (1990)
  K-9000 (1991)
  Knight Rider 2000 (1991)
  Taking of Beverly Hills, The (1991)
  Mr. 247 (1994)
  Beastmaster 3: The Eye of Braxus (1995)
  Modern Affair, A (1995)
  Babysitter's Seduction, The (1996)

Secret Agent Club, The (1996)

HAMMOND, WAYNE
  Fun Down There (1989)

HANCOCK, HERBIE
  Harlem Nights (1989)
  Livin' Large (1991)

HANDEL, GEORGE FREDERIC
  Madness of King George, The (1995)

HANDY, CRAIG
  Cosby Mysteries, The (1994)

HANNAH, JONATHAN
  Heaven Becomes Hell (1989)
  Beauty School (1993)

HANNIGAN, DENIS M.
  Shaggy Dog, The (1994)

HANSON, ERIK
  Deadly Secret, The (1994)

HARDIMAN, RONAN
  My Friend Joe (1996)

HARDING, JOHN WESLEY
  Paint Job, The (1992)

HARDMAN, GARY
  Fists of Blood (1989)

HARDY, HAGOOD
  Passion and Paradise (1989)

HARDY, JOHN
  Hedd Wyn (1992)
  Gadael Lenin (Leaving Lenin) (1993)
  Streetlife (1995)

HARLE, JOHN
  Family (1994)
  Butterfly Kiss (1995)

HARLEY, JEROME
  Pizzicata (1996)

HARMON, JEFF B.
  Isle of Lesbos (1997)

HARNATH, CRAIG
Castle, The (1997)

HARPAZ, UDI
Shadow of Obsession (1994)

HARPER, SCOTT
Roseanne: An Unauthorized Biography
(1994)

HARRIS, ANTHONY
Star Slammer: The Escape (1988)

HARRIS, JOHNNY
Different Affair, A (1987)
Necessity (1988)
Not of This World (1991)
Maid for Each Other (1992)
Family Pictures (1993)
Lies and Lullabies (1993)
Guinevere (1994)
I Spy Returns (1994)
Thicker Than Blood: The Larry
McLinden Story (1994)
Frequent Flyer (1996)

HARRIS, PETER
Elmore Leonard's "Gold Coast" (1997)

HARRISON, JOHN
Tales From the Darkside: The Movie
(1990)

HARRISON, KEN
I Still Dream of Jeannie (1991)
Jailbirds (1991)
Forget-Me-Not Murders, The (1994)
MacGyver: Lost Treasure of Atlantis
(1994)
MacGyver: Trail to Doomsday (1994)
Silent Betrayal, A (1994)
Shamrock Conspiracy, The (1995)
Harrison: Cry of the City (1996)

HARRISON, MICHAEL ALLEN
Claire of the Moon (1992)

HARROW, JOEY
Loser (1991)

HARRY, JAMES
Body Waves (1992)

HART, MICKEY
Gang Related (1997)

HART, JOSEPH SR.
Timeless (1996)

HARTLEY, HAL
Henry Fool (1997)

HARTLEY, RICHARD
Impossible Spy, The (1987)
Dealers (1989)
She's Been Away (1989)
Adam Bede (1991)
Afraid of the Dark (1991)
Law Lord, The (1991)
March, The (1991)
Midnight's Child (1992)
Railway Station Man, The (1992)
Running Late (1992)
Secret Rapture, The (1993)
Princess Caraboo (1994)
Rector's Wife (1994)
Awfully Big Adventure, An (1995)
Rough Magic (1995)
Van, The (1995)
Brylcreem Boys, The (1996)
Rosamund Pilcher's "September" (1996)
Stealing Beauty (1996)
Designated Mourner, The (1997)
Playing God (1997)
Thousand Acres, A (1997)
Victory (1997)
When Secrets Kill (1997)

HARTSHORNE, ROBERT
Boston Knockout (1995)

HARTZOP, PAUL
Kickboxer (1989)

HARVEY, MICK
Go for Gold! (1997)

HARVEY, RICHARD
Paper Mask (1991)
Small Dance, A (1991)
Dead Romantic (1992)
Immaculate Conception (1992)
Deadly Advise (1993)
Hostages (1993)
Doomsday Gun (1994)

HARVEY, SHANE
  Clearcut (1991)

HASKELL, JIMMIE
  Jake Spanner, Private Eye (1989)
  She's Back (1989)
  Dogfighters, The (1995)

HASKINS, KEVIN
  Prom, The (1992)

HASLINGER, PAUL
  Pointman (1994)

HASPAR, UDI
  Naked Target, The (1992)

HAVENS, BRENT
  Mother's Day (1989)
  Pistol: The Birth of a Legend, The (1991)

HAVENS, RICHIE
  Brother Minister: The Assassination of
    Malcolm X (1994)

HAWKS, NIGEL
  Shinjuku Boys (1995)

HAWKSHAW, ALAN
  Magic Moments (1989)

HAY, ROY
  Pterodactyl Woman From Beverly Hills
    (1996)
  Goodbye America (1997)

HAYCOCK, PETER
  One False Move (1991)

HAYEN, TODD
  Sinful Life, A (1989)
  Panic in the Sky! (1996)
  Yesterday's Target (1996)
  When Time Expires (1997)

HAYS, REED
  My Life's in Turnaround (1994)

HEALEY, JEFF
  No Way Home (1996)

HEAVENER, DAVID
  Kill Crazy (1990)

Prime Target (1991)

HEDDON, RANDALL KENT
  Undercover Cop (1994)

HEDGE, CHRISTOPHER
  Land of Milk and Honey (1995)

HEDGES, KEVIN
  At Risk (1994)

HEGYI, STEVEN
  Hell Bent (1994)

HEIL, TOM
  Buddy Factor, The (1994)
  Dark Side of Genius (1994)
  Swimming With Sharks (1994)

HELD, BOB
  Federal Hill (1995)

HELLENKELLER
  Horsey (1997)

HELLER, KEN
  Lavryle Spencer's Home Song (1996)

HENDRIX, JIMI
  Lune Froide (Cold Moon) (1991)

HENDRYX, NONA
  Gospa (1994)

HENSLEY, TOM
  Thanksgiving Day (1990)

HERMAN, JERRY
  Mrs. Santa Claus (1996)

HEROUET, MARC
  Nuit et Jour (Night and Day) (1991)

HERRMANN, BERNARD
  Cape Fear (1991)

HERSANT, PHILIPPE
  Lettre pour L . . . (1993)
  Un Animal, Deux Animaux (1995)

HERSH, KIRSTIN
  Never Met Picasso (1996)

HERTZOG, PAUL
Street Justice (1989)

HERZOG, DAVID
Hunting (1991)

HETHERMAN, MARGARET
Nick & Rachel (1997)

HEWER, MIKE
Canvas (1992)
Knuckleball (1995)

HEWERDINE, BOO
TwentyFourSeven (1997)

HIDDEN FACES
Highway to Hell (1992)
Friday (1995)
Under the Hula Moon (1995)

HIGGINS, KENNETH
Hemingway (1988)

HILER, JOHN DAVID
Out on Bail (1989)

HILL, JOHN
Pompatus of Love, The (1995)

HILLMAN, MARC
Baxter (1989)

HILLOCK, GRAYDON
Midnight Witness (1993)

HIMMELMAN, PETER
Crossing the Bridge (1992)
Souler Opposite, The (1997)

HINDS, NELSON G.
Almost Blue (1992)

HIRSCH, WILBERT
Mute Witness (1995)
American Werewolf in Paris, An (1997)

HIRSCHFELDER, DAVID
Strictly Ballroom (1992)
Dallas Doll (1994)
Life of Harry Dare, The (1995)
Tunnel Vision (1995)
Dating the Enemy (1996)

Shine (1996)
Sliding Doors (1997)

HIRSCHHORN, JOEL
Caddie Woodlawn (1989)
China Cry (1990)
Closer, The (1991)
Rescue Me (1993)

HOBSON, GENE
Little Secrets (1991)
Brothers of the Frontier (1996)

HODIAN, JOHN
Frank Capra's American Dream (1997)

HOENIG, MICHAEL
I, Madman (1989)
Class of 1999 (1990)
Last of the Finest, The (1990)
Amy Fisher Story, The (1993)
Visions of Murder (1993)
Eyes of Terror (1994)
Past Tense (1994)
Search for Grace (1994)
Above Suspicion (1995)
Her Costly Affair (1996)
Thrill (1996)

HOEY, GARY
Endless Summer II, The (1994)

HOFFERT, PAUL
Hoover vs. The Kennedys: The Second
Civil War (1987)

HOFFMAN, KURT
Little Noises (1991)

HOLBEK, JOACHIM
Europa (1991)
Breaking the Waves (1995)
Kingdom, The (1995)

HOLDEN, MARK
Ava's Magical Adventure (1994)

HOLDRIDGE, LEE
Desperate (1987)
Young Harry Houdini (1987)
Friendship in Vienna, A (1988)
Dark River (1989)
Do You Know the Muffin Man? (1989)

Mother's Courage: The Mary Thomas
    Story, A (1989)
Incident at Dark River (1989)
Old Gringo (1989)
Back to Hannibal: The Return of Tom
    Sawyer and Huckleberry Finn (1990)
Danielle Steel's "Fine Things" (1990)
Daughter of the Streets (1990)
Dreamer of Oz: The L. Frank Baum
    Story, The (1990)
Joshua's Heart (1990)
Danielle Steel's "Changes" (1991)
Face of a Stranger (1991)
Finding the Way Home (1991)
Lucy & Desi: Before the Laughter (1991)
Mrs. Lambert Remembers Love (1991)
One Against the Wind (1991)
One Cup of Coffee (1991)
Perfect Tribute, The (1991)
Return of Eliot Ness, The (1991)
Story Lady, The (1991)
Summer My Father Grew Up, The
    (1991)
Day-O (1992)
Deadly Matrimony (1992)
In the Arms of a Killer (1992)
Obsessed (1992)
Call of the Wild (1993)
Danielle Steel's "Star" (1993)
Freefall (1993)
Heidi (1993)
Jack Reed: Badge of Honor (1993)
Judith Krantz's "Torch Song" (1993)
Killer Rules (1993)
Robin Cook's "Harmful Intent" (1993)
Danielle Steel's "A Perfect Stranger"
    (1994)
Danielle Steel's "Family Album" (1994)
Incident in a Small Town (1994)
Jack Reed: A Search for Justice (1994)
Roommates (1994)
Running Delilah (1994)
Spring Awakening (1994)
Whipping Boy, The (1994)
Yearling, The (1994)
Buffalo Girls (1995)
James A. Michener's "Texas" (1995)
Mother's Gift, A (1995)
Sidney Sheldon's "Nothing Lasts
    Forever" (1995)
Tuskegee Airmen, The (1995)
Dalva (1996)
Danielle Steel's "Full Circle" (1996)

Danielle Steel's "Remembrance" (1996)
Harvest of Fire (1996)
Holiday Affair (1996)
Jack Reed: A Killer Amongst Us (1996)
Little Riders, The (1996)
Neil Simon's "London Suite" (1996)
She Cried No (1996)
Soul of the Game (1996)
Star Command (1996)
Unfinished Affair, An (1996)
Christmas Memory, A (1997)
Into Thin Air: Death on Everest (1997)
Long Way Home, The (1997)
Twilight of the Golds, The (1997)

HOLLAND, BRENT
    Blood Symbol (1992)

HOLLAND, DEBORAH
    Circuitry Man (1990)
    Genuine Risk (1990)
    December (1991)
    Out There (1995)

HOLLAND, NIGEL
    Man to Man (1992)

HOLLANDER, ANDREW
    Moving In Moving Out (1997)

HOLMES, DAVID
    Resurrection Man (1997)

HOLMES BROTHERS
    Lotto Land (1995)

HOLT, DEREK
    One False Move (1991)

HOLTON, NIGEL
    Grandmother's House (1989)
    Bloodfist II (1991)
    Kiss Me a Killer (1991)
    Bloodfist III: Forced to Fight (1992)
    Body Chemistry II: The Voice of a
        Stranger (1992)
    To Sleep With a Vampire (1992)
    Twogether (1992)
    Carnosaur (1993)
    Only the Strong (1993)
    Money to Burn (1994)
    Watchers III (1994)
    Sister Island (1996)

HOMRICH, JUNIOR
Ghosts Can't Do It (1990)

HOOPER, LES
Back in the U.S.S.R. (1992)

HOOPER, NELLE
William Shakespeare's Romeo + Juliet
(1996)

HOOPER, NICHOLAS
Tichborne Claimant, The (1997)

HOPKINS, ANTHONY
August (1995)

HOPKINS, JOHN
Strange Blues of Cowboy Red, The
(1996)

HOPKINS, KENYON
12 Angry Men (1997)

HORNER, JAMES
Dad (1989)
Field of Dreams (1989)
Glory (1989)
Honey, I Shrunk the Kids (1989)
In Country (1989)
Another 48 HRS. (1990)
Extreme Close-Up (1990)
I Love You to Death (1990)
American Tail: Fievel Goes West, An
(1991)
Class Action (1991)
My Heroes Have Always Been Cowboys
(1991)
Once Around (1991)
Rocketeer, The (1991)
Patriot Games (1992)
Sneakers (1992)
Thunderheart (1992)
Unlawful Entry (1992)
Bopha! (1993)
Far Off Place, A (1993)
House of Cards (1993)
Innocent Moves (1993)
Jack the Bear (1993)
Man Without a Face, The (1993)
Once Upon a Forest (1993)
Pelican Brief, The (1993)
Searching for Bobby Fischer (1993)
Swing Kids (1993)

We're Back! A Dinosaur's Story (1993)
Clear and Present Danger (1994)
Legends of the Fall (1994)
Pagemaster, The (1994)
Apollo 13 (1995)
Balto (1995)
Braveheart (1995)
Casper (1995)
Jade (1995)
Jumanji (1995)
Care of the Spitfire Grill (1996)
Courage Under Fire (1996)
Land Before Time IV: Journey Though
the Mists, The (1996)
Ransom (1996)
Spitfire Grill, The (1996)
To Gillian on Her 37th Birthday (1996)
Devil's Own, The (1997)
Titanic (1997)

HORONZKY, VLADIMIR
Fine Gold (1990)
Forbidden Dance, The (1990)
Stranger Within, The (1990)
Tales of the Unknown: Warped (1990)
Miracle in the Wilderness (1991)
Stephen King's "The Langoliers" (1995)
Original Gangstas (1996)

HOROWITZ, RICHARD
Sheltering Sky, The (1990)
Tower, The (1993)
Lakota Woman: Siege of Wounded Knee
(1994)
Broken Trust (1995)

HOWARD, JAMES NEWTON
Major League (1989)
Package, The (1989)
Tap (1989)
Coupe de Ville (1990)
Descending Angel (1990)
Flatliners (1990)
Image, The (1990)
Marked for Death (1990)
Pretty Woman (1990)
Revealing Evidence (1990)
Somebody Has to Shoot the Picture
(1990)
Three Men and a Little Lady (1990)
Dying Young (1991)
Grand Canyon (1991)
Guilty by Suspicion (1991)

King Ralph (1991)
Man in the Moon, The (1991)
My Girl (1991)
Prince of Tides, The (1991)
Alive (1992)
American Heart (1992)
Diggstown (1992)
Falling Down (1992)
Glengarry Glen Ross (1992)
Night and the City (1992)
Private Matter, A (1992)
Dave (1993)
Fugitive, The (1993)
Saint of Fort Washington, The (1993)
Alive--20 Years Later (1994)
Intersection (1994)
Junior (1994)
Wyatt Earp (1994)
Eye for an Eye (1995)
French Kiss (1995)
Just Cause (1995)
Outbreak (1995)
Restoration (1995)
Waterworld (1995)
Juror, The (1996)
Liar Liar (Theme) (1996)
One Fine Day (1996)
Primal Fear (1996)
Rich Man's Wife, The (1996)
Space Jam (1996)
Trigger Effect, The (1996)
Dante's Peak (1997)
Devil's Advocate, The (1997)
Fathers' Day (1997)
My Best Friend's Wedding (1997)
Postman, The (1997)

HOWARD, RICK
Niagaravation (1996)

HOWARD, TOM
Tryst (1994)

HOWARTH, ALAN
Brothers in Arms (1989)
Halloween 5 (1989)
Arcade (1993)
Halloween: The Curse of Michael Myers
(1995)
Dentist, The (1996)

HOYER, OLE
Misfit Brigade, The (1988)

HUBLEY, GEORGIA
Alchemy (1995)

HUDDLESTON, EUGENE
World and Time Enough (1994)

HUES, JACK
Guardian, The (1990)

HUFSTETER, STEVEN
Unhook the Stars (1996)

HUGGINS, MICHAEL
Old Man Dogs (1997)

HUGHES, DAVID A.
Leon the Pig Farmer (1992)
Beyond Bedlam (1994)
Dinner in Purgatory (1994)
Clockwork Mice (1995)
Feast at Midnight, A (1995)
Proteus (1995)
Solitaire for 2 (1995)
Welcome II the Terrordome (1995)
Continued Adventures of Reptile Man,
The (1996)
Darklands (1997)
Stiff Upper Lips (1997)

HUGHES, ROY
Seeking the Cafe Bob (1996)

HUMBERSTONE, NIGEL
Ambush of Ghosts, An (1993)

HUMECKE, TONY
Feminine Touch, The (1995)

HUNTER, STEVE
Wedding Band (1990)
Meatballs 4 (1992)
Dead Weekend (1995)

HUNTER, TODD
Daydream Believer (1991)
Alex (1993)

HURTADO, CIRO
Dead Women in Lingerie (1990)

HUS, WALTER
Suite 16 (1994)

HWONG, LUCIA
  Lawless Land, The (1988)
  Forbidden Nights (1990)
  Hiroshima: Out of the Ashes (1990)

HYANS-HART, CHRISTOPHER
  Hell High (1989)

HYMAN, DICK
  Women & Men 2: Three Short Stories
    (1991)
  Alan & Naomi (1992)
  Everyone Says I Love You (1996)

ICE-T
  Return of Superfly (1990)

IGLESIAS, ALBERTO
  La ardilla roja (The Red Squirrel) (1993)
  La Fleur de mon Secret (1995)
  Asaltar los Cielos (Attacking the Skies)
    (1996)
  Pasajes (Passages) (1996)
  Tiera (Earth) (1996)
  Carne Tremula (Live Flesh) (1997)
  La Femme de Chambre du Titanic (1997)

IGOE, ANTHONY
  Demon Keeper (1994)

IKEBE, SHINICHIRO
  Akira Kurosawa's Dream (1990)
  Rhapsody in August (1991)

ILLARRAMENDI, ANGEL
  Robert Rylands' Last Journey (1996)
  Shampoo Horns (1997)

IMMEL, JERROLD
  Gunsmoke: Return to Dodge (1987)
  Outside Woman, The (1989)
  Drive Like Lightning (1992)
  Dallas: J.R.'s Return (1996)
  Knots Landing: Back to the Cul-De-Sac
    (1997)

INDER, PAUL
  Girl With the Hungry Eyes, The (1995)

INFANTE, STEVEN LOUIS
  Mr. Vincent (1997)

INNES, NEIL

Erik the Viking (1989)

INTSON, PAUL
  Hush Little Baby (1994)

IOANNIDES, TASSOS
  Silver Stallion: King of the Brumbies,
    The (1993)

IRWIN, ASHLEY
  Deadly Rivals (1992)
  Night Rhythms (1992)
  Body of Influence (1993)
  Secret Games 2: The Escort (1993)
  Sexual Outlaws (1994)
  Strangers by Night (1994)
  Expert, The (1995)
  Entertaining Angels: The Dorothy Day
    Story (1996)

IRWIN, PAT
  My New Gun (1992)
  Heading Home (1995)
  Loose Women (1996)
  'Til Christmas (1996)
  Arresting Gena (1997)
  Colin Fitz (1997)

ISAAC, RENO
  L'Ombre du doute (A Shadow of Doubt)
    (1992)

ISAAK, CHRIS
  Preppie Murder, The (1989)

ISHAM, MARK
  Everybody Wins (1990)
  Love at Large (1990)
  Reversal of Fortune (1990)
  Billy Bathgate (1991)
  Crooked Hearts (1991)
  Little Man Tate (1991)
  Mortal Thoughts (1991)
  Point Break (1991)
  Cool World (1992)
  Midnight Clear, A (1992)
  Of Mice and Men (1992)
  Public Eye, The (1992)
  River Runs Through It, A (1992)
  Sketch Artist (1992)
  Fire in the Sky (1993)
  Made in America (1993)
  Nowhere to Run (1993)

Romeo Is Bleeding (1993)
Short Cuts (1993)
Browning Version, The (1994)
Getaway, The (1994)
Miami Rhapsody (1994)
Mrs. Parker and the Vicious Circle
   (1994)
Nell (1994)
Quiz Show (1994)
Safe Passage (1994)
Time Cop (1994)
Home for the Holidays (1995)
Losing Isaiah (1995)
Net, The (1995)
Fly Away Home (1996)
Gotti (1996)
AfterGlow (1997)
Defenders, The: Playback (1997)
Education of Little Tree, The (1997)
Gingerbread Man, The (1997)
Last Dance (1996)
Kiss the Girls (1997)
Night Falls on Manhattan (1997)

IVES, GREGORY
   Univers'l (1997)

JACKSON, DAVID A.
   Cold Steel (1991)

JACKSON, JOE
   Queens Logic (1991)

JAMES, SIDNEY
   Sugartime (1995)
   Misery Brothers, The (1996)

JAMES, TIM
   Code Name Vengeance (1989)
   Hell on the Battleground (1989)
   Rage to Kill (1989)
   Space Mutiny (1989)
   Final Sanction, The (1990)

JANKEL, CHAZ
   Rachel Papers, The (1989)
   Tales From the Darkside: The Movie
      (1990)

JANKOWSKI, LECH
   Institute Benjamenta, The (1995)

JANS, ALARIC

Homicide (1991)
Water Engine, The (1992)

JARDINS, DES
   Holiday to Remember, A (1995)

JARRE, MAURICE
   Chances Are (1989)
   Dead Poets Society (1989)
   Enemies, A Love Story (1989)
   Prancer (1989)
   After Dark, My Sweet (1990)
   Almost an Angel (1990)
   Ghost (1990)
   Jacob's Ladder (1990)
   Solar Crisis (1990)
   Fires Within (1991)
   Only the Lonely (1991)
   School Ties (1992)
   Starfire (1992)
   Fearless (1993)
   Mr. Jones (1993)
   Shadow of the Wolf (1993)
   Walk in the Clouds, A (1995)
   Sunchaser, The (1996)
   Le Jour et La Nuit (Day and Night)
      (1997)

JEAN-BAPTISTE, MARIANNE
   Career Girls (1997)

JEANES, NIK AND RACHEL
   Miniskirted Dynamo, The (1996)

JENSEN, MARK
   Monk Dawson (1997)

JOHANNSEN, BEN
   Reluctant Angel (1997)

JOHANSEN, DAVID
   Mr. Nanny (1992)

JOHN, ELTON
   Lion King, The (1994)

JOHNSON, CARL
   Aladdin and the King of Thieves (1996)

JOHNSON, CRAIG
   Big Swap, The (1997)

JOHNSON, GORDIE
  Circle Game, The (1994)

JOHNSON, LAURIE
  Lady and the Highwayman, The (1989)
  Ghost in Monte Carlo, A (1990)
  Duel of Hearts (1992)

JOHNSON, ROBERT
  Can't You Hear the Wind Howl? (1997)

JOHNSON, STEVEN
  Million to Juan, A (1994)

JOHNSTON, ADRIAN
  Food of Love (1997)
  Welcome to Sarajevo (1997)

JOHNSTON, FREEDY
  Kingpin (1996)

JOHNSTON, JIM
  No Holds Barred (1989)

JOHNSTON, PHILLIP
  Music of Chance, The (1993)
  Umbrellas (1994)
  Faithful (1996)

JOMY, ALAIN
  La Petite Veleuse (The Little Thief)
    (1989)
  Accompanist, The (1993)
  Oranges Ameres (Bitter Oranges) (1997)

JONES, ALISTAIR
  Vacant Possession (1995)

JONES, ANTHONY
  Wizards of the Demon Swords (1991)

JONES, DARRYL
  Love Jones (1997)

JONES, DAVID ALLEN
  House Party 3 (1994)

JONES, JOHN PAUL
  Risk (1994)

JONES, KIPPER
  John Henrik Clarke: A Great and Mighty
    Walk (1996)

JONES, MICK
  Amongst Friends (1993)

JONES, QUINCY
  Listen Up (1990)

JONES, RON
  Cross Fire (1989)

JONES, TERRY
  Wind in the Willows, The (1997)

JONES, TREVOR
  Chains of Gold (1989)
  Murder by Moonlight (1989)
  Private Life, A (1989)
  Sea of Love (1989)
  Arachnophobia (1990)
  Bad Influence (1990)
  By Dawn's Early Light (1990)
  Defenseless (1991)
  True Colors (1991)
  Blame It on the Bellboy (1992)
  CrissCross (1992)
  Freejack (1992)
  Last of the Mohicans, The (1992)
  Alistair MacLean's "Death Train" (1993)
  Cliffhanger (1993)
  In the Name of the Father (1993)
  Hideaway (1995)
  Kiss of Death (1995)
  Richard III (1995)
  Brassed Off (1996)
  Dark City (1996)
  Gulliver's Travels (1996)
  Loch Ness (1996)
  Roseanna's Grave (For Roseanna) (1996)
  G.I. Jane (1997)
  Lawn Dogs (1997)

JORDAN, ARCHIE
  Caddie Woodlawn (1989)

JORDAN, GLENN
  Meet the Hollowheads (1989)

JORDAN, PORTER
  Wildly Available (1997)

JORELLE, NICOLAS
  Fanfan (1993)

JOSEPH, JULIAN
  Tale of a Vampire (1992)

JOSEPHSON, MARK
  Violent Zone (1989)

JUDD, PHILIP
  Death in Brunswick (1990)
  Eight Ball (1992)
  Hercules Returns (1993)
  Mr. Reliable: A True Story (1996)

JUDSON, TOM
  Revolution! (1991)
  Grief (1993)
  Barcelona (1994)

KABILJO, ALFI
  Scissors (1991)

KACZMAREK, JAN A. P.
  Pale Blood (1992)
  Empty Cradle (1993)
  Total Eclipse (1995)
  Bliss (1997)
  Washington Square (1997)

KALDOR, PETER
  Love in Limbo (1993)

KAMEN, MICHAEL
  Adventures of Baron Munchausen, The
    (1989)
  Lethal Weapon 2 (1989)
  Licence to Kill (1989)
  Renegades (1989)
  Road House (1989)
  Rooftops (1989)
  Die Hard 2 (1990)
  Krays, The (1990)
  Company Business (1991)
  Hudson Hawk (1991)
  Last Boy Scout, The (1991)
  Let Him Have It (1991)
  Nothing but Trouble (1991)
  Robin Hood: Prince of Thieves (1991)
  Blue Ice (1992)
  Lethal Weapon 3 (1992)
  Shining Through (1992)
  Last Action Hero (1993)
  Splitting Heirs (1993)
  Three Musketeers, The (1993)
  Wilder Napalm (1993)

Circle of Friends (1994)
Don Juan DeMarco (1995)
Die Hard With a Vengeance (1995)
Mr. Holland's Opus (1995)
Stonewall (1995)
Jack (1996)
101 Dalmations (1996)
Remember Me? (1996)
Event Horizon (1997)
Inventing the Abbotts (1997)
Winter Guest, The (1997)

KANDER, JOHN
  I Want to Go Home (1989)
  Breathing Lessons (1994)
  Boys Next Door, The (1996)

KANE, ARTIE
  Man Against the Mob (1988)
  Fire and Rain (1989)
  Man Against the Mob: The Chinatown
    Murders (1989)
  Terror on Highway 91 (1989)
  Gunsmoke: To the Last Man (1992)
  Gunsmoke: The Long Ride (1993)
  Gunsmoke: One Man's Justice (1994)

KANIEL, NOAM
  Shattered Image (1994)

KAPLAN, IRA
  Alchemy (1995)

KAPROFF, DANA
  People Across the Lake, The (1988)
  Full Exposure: The Sex Tapes Scandal
    (1989)
  High Desert Kill (1989)
  Nightlife (1989)
  Blind Vengeance (1990)
  China Lake Murders, The (1990)
  Vestige of Honor (1990)
  Don't Touch My Daughter (1991)
  My Son Johnny (1991)
  Silent Motive (1991)
  This Gun for Hire (1991)
  Calendar Girl, Cop, Killer? The Bambi
    Bembenek Story (1992)
  Duplicates (1992)
  Homewrecker (1992)
  Jackie Collins' "Lady Boss" (1992)
  Tainted Blood (1993)
  When a Stranger Calls Back (1993)

With Hostile Intent (1993)
Cagney & Lacey: The Return (1994)
Dead Air (1994)
Terror in the Night (1994)
Family Divided, A (1995)
Case for Life, A (1996)
Christmas in My Hometown (1996)
Dying to Be Perfect: The Ellen Hart Pena
    Story (1996)
Stepford Husbands, The (1996)
Born Into Exile (1997)
Indefensible: The Truth About Edward
    Brannigan (1997)
On the Edge of Innocence (1997)
Stolen Women (1997)

KARAINDROU, HELENA
  Suspended Step of the Stork (1991)

KARLIN, FRED
  Bridge to Silence (1989)
  Fear Stalk (1989)
  Murder C.O.D. (1990)
  Her Wicked Ways (1991)
  Last Prostitute, The (1991)
  Secret, The (1992)
  Survive the Savage Sea (1992)
  Desperate Rescue: The Cathy Malone
      Story (1993)
  Labor of Love: The Arlette Schweitzer
      Story (1993)
  Lost Treasure of Dos Santos (1997)

KARPMAN, LAURA
  My Brother's Wife (1989)
  Sitter, The (1991)
  Broken Cord, The (1992)
  Child Lost Forever, A (1992)
  Doing Time on Maple Drive (1992)
  Based on an Untrue Story (1993)
  Mother's Revenge, A (1993)
  Shameful Secrets (1993)
  Moment of Truth: A Mother's Deception
      (1994)
  Moment of Truth: Broken Pledges (1994)
  Moment of Truth: To Walk Again (1994)
  Abandoned and Deceived (1995)
  If Someone Had Known (1995)
  Woman of Independent Means, A (1995)
  Blue Rodeo (1996)
  Lover's Knot (1996)
  Promise to Carolyn, A (1996)
  Stranger to Love, A (1996)

KARSON, GIL
  Angel Town (1990)

KASHA, AL
  Caddie Woodlawn (1989)
  China Cry (1990)
  Closer, The (1991)
  Rescue Me (1993)

KATCHE, MANU
  Little Indian, Big City (1995)

KATSAROS, DOUG
  Who Do I Gotta Kill? (1992)

KAUDERER, EMILIO
  Slash Dance (1989)
  Love & Greed (1991)
  Ice Runner, The (1992)
  Crack Me Up (1993)
  Midnight Kiss (1993)
  Place in the World, A (1995)

KAVAT, AMANDA
  Fall (1997)

KAWASAKI, MASAHIRO
  Painted Desert, The (1993)

KEANE, BRIAN
  When Will I Be Loved? (1990)
  Donner Party, The (1992)
  Vernon Johns Story, The (1994)
  Battle Over Citizen Kane, The (1996)
  Buckminster Fuller: Thinking Out Loud
      (1996)
  Illtown (1996)

KEANE, JOHN
  Chattahoochee (1989)
  One Man's War (1990)
  Count of Solar, The (1991)
  Desperate Choices: To Save My Child
      (1992)
  Hummingbird Tree, The (1992)
  Keep the Change (1992)
  Last of His Tribe, The (1992)
  Sex, Love and Cold Hard Cash (1993)
  One Woman's Courage (1994)
  Small Faces (1995)
  Vow to Kill, A (1995)
  Trojan Eddie (1996)
  Further Gesture, A (1997)

KEAR, GARETH
Darien Gap, The (1996)

KELEKOVICH, KERRY
Sacred Hearts (1995)

KELLAWAY, ROGER
Journey of the Heart (1997)

KELLY, BRIAN
Grind (1993)

KELLY, DOMINIC
Full Tilt Boogie (1997)

KELLY, PAUL
Everynight . . . Everynight (1994)

KELLY, TIM
Plughead Rewired: Circuitry Man II
(1994)

KELLY, VICTORIA
Ugly, The (1997)

KEMPEL, ARTHUR
Cry in the Wild, A (1990)
Double Impact (1991)
Fire in the Dark (1991)
Hit Man, The (1991)
Cheyenne Warrior (1994)
Sensation (1994)
Windrunner (1994)
Arrival, The (aka Shockwave) (1996)
Riders of the Purple Sage (1996)

KENDALL, GREG
Bandwagon (1996)

KENDALL, SIMON
Trial at Fortitude Bay (1994)
Angel of Pennsylvania Avenue, The
(1996)
Cold Heart of a Killer, The (1996)

KENT, ROLFE
Dead Connection (1994)
Final Combination (1994)
Mercy (1995)
Citizen Ruth (1996)
Precious (1996)
House of Yes, The (1997)

KERBER, RANDY
U.S. Marshals: Waco & Rhinehart
(1987)

KERESZTES, ANDREW
Class of 1999: The Substitute (1994)
Teresa's Tattoo (1994)

KESSLER, MICHAEL
Lifebreath (1997)

KHAYRAT, OMAR
Search for Diana (1992)

KIDD, WILLIAM
Legal Tender (aka Ladies Game) (1990)

KILA
Gold in the Streets (1997)

KILAR, WOJCIECH
Bram Stoker's Dracula (1992)
Silent Touch, The (1992)
Death and the Maiden (1994)
Fantome avec Chauffeur (1996)
Portrait of a Lady, The (1996)
Our God's Brother (1997)

KILBEY, STEVE
Blackrock (1997)

KILIAN, MARK
Lover Girl (1997)

KIMBROUGH, PHIL
Silent Lies (1996)

KINER, KEVIN
Kiss and Be Killed (1991)
Freaked (1993)
Leprechaun (1993)
Excessive Force II: Force on Force
(1995)
Demolition High (1996)
Legend of the Lost Tomb (1997)
Pest, The (1997)

KING, RUSSELL
Ungentlemanly Act, An (1992)

KIRSCH, BARRY
Prisoner of Honor (1991)

Steal, The (1995)

KISSEL, MICHAEL CASE
In the Blood (1989)

KITARO
Heaven & Earth (1993)

KITAY, DAVID
Look Who's Talking (1989)
Look Who's Talking Too (1990)
Problem Child 2 (1991)
Boris and Natasha (1992)
Breaking the Rules (1992)
Roosters (1993)
Surf Ninjas (1993)
Father and Scout (1994)
Trading Mom (1994)
Clueless (1995)
Jury Duty (1995)
Solomon and Sheba (1995)

KLEIN, LARRY
Grace of My Heart (1996)

KLINE, TAMARA
Clearing, The (1991)

KLINGLER, KEVIN
Necromancer (1989)
Earth Angel (1991)
Welcome to Oblivion (1991)
Loving Lulu (1992)

KLOSER, HARALD
Mrs. Lee Harvey Oswald (1993)
O. J. Simpson Story, The (1995)
If Looks Could Kill: From the Files of
    America's Most Wanted (1996)
Der Unfisch (The Unfish) (1997)
Quiet Days in Hollywood (1997)
Small Hours, The (1997)

KNIEPER, JURGEN
End of the Night (1990)
Paint It Black (1990)
December Bride (1991)
Exposure (High Art) (1991)
La Bionda (The Blonde) (1994)
La Promesse (The Promise) (1995)
Lisbon Story (1995)
Das Lieben Ist Eine Baustelle (1997)

KNOPFLER, MARK
Metroland (1997)
Wag the Dog (1997)

KOEHNE, GRAEME
Heaven's Burning (1997)

KOLE, DAVID E.
Challenger (1989)
Chameleons (1990)

KOLESNIKOW, RAMA
Mary Jane's Not a Virgin Anymore
    (1997)

KOMOROV, VLADIMIR
Hellfire (1995)

KOONIN, BRIAN
Mr. Nanny (1992)

KOOPER, AL
Against Their Will: Women in Prison
    (1994)

KOPATZ, ERIC
Venice Bound (1995)

KOPPLIN, DAVE
Cool Surface, The (1992)

KORVEN, MARK
Sam and Me (1990)
White Room (1990)
Grocer's Wife, The (1992)
Henry & Verlin (1994)
Curtis's Charm (1995)
Cube (1997)
Joe's Wedding (1997)

KRAFT, ROBERT
Mambo Kings, The (1992)

KRAMON, JOSH
Brokers (1997)

KRASNA, MICHEL
Level Five (1996)

KRAVAT, AMANDA
If Lucy Fell (1996)

KRIZMAN, RICK
Cartel (1990)
Down the Drain (1990)

KRONJE, ZANE
Schweitzer (1990)

KROTCHA, GREG
Perfect Profile (1991)

KRYSTAL, DAVID
Buying Time (1989)

KUHN, TED
Cutting Loose (1996)

KURAMOTO, DAN
Home Fires (1987)

KURTZ, DAVID
Woman Who Sinned, The (1991)
Journey to the Center of the Earth (1993)

KURTZ, DAYNE
Jane Street (1996)

KYMLICKA, MILAN
Babar: The Movie (1989)
Amityville Curse, The (1990)
Falling Over Backwards (1990)
Psychic (1992)
Hero's Life, A (1994)
Paper Boy, The (1994)
Margaret's Museum (1995)
Dancing on the Moon (1997)
Matusalem II (1997)
Revenge of the Woman in Black, The
(1997)

LACY, STEVE
L'Amore Molesto (1995)

LAFERRIERE, YVES
Jesus De Montreal (1989)
Conspiracy of Silence (1992)
Le Sexe de Etoiles (The Sex of the Stars)
(1993)
Poverty and Other Delights (1996)

LAI, FRANCIS
Ripoux Contre Ripoux (My New Partner
2) (1990)
There Were Days and Moons (1990)

Les Cles du Paradis (The Keys to
Paradise) (1991)
La Belle Histoire (The Beautiful Story)
(1992)
L'Inconnu dans la Maison (Stranger in
the House) (1992)
Tout Ca . . . Pour Ca! (All That . . . for
This?) (1993)
Les Miserables (1995)
Hommes Femmes: Mode d'Emploi
(1996)

LALANNE, JEAN-FELIX
In Amor de Sorciere (Witch Way Love)
(1997)

LAMBERT, DENNIS
American Me (1992)

LAMBERT, JERRY
War Birds (1989)

LANDERS, TIM
Talking About Sex (1994)

LANE, ROB
Young Poisoner's Handbook, The (1995)
Girl With Brains in Her Feet, The (1997)

LANG, JIM
Love or Money (1990)
John Carpenter Presents Body Bags
(1993)
In the Mouth of Madness (1995)

LANG, JOHN
Rude (1995)

LANG, K.D.
Even Cowgirls Get the Blues (1993)

LANGHORNE, BRUCE
Upstairs Neighbor, The (1994)

LANOIS, DANIEL
Last of the Mohicans, The (1992)
Camilla (1993)
Lost in Mississippi (1996)
Sling Blade (1996)
Sweet Angel Mine (1996)

LANZ, DAVID
Daredreamer (1990)

LAPERIERRE, FREDERIC
 La Derniere Season (The Last Season)
  (1991)

LAROCHELLE, DENIS
 Angelo, Fredo and Romeo (1996)

LARRIVA, TITO
 Dream With the Fishes (1997)

LARSON, NATHAN
 First Love, Last Rites (1997)

LASAZIO, PAOLO
 Porami Via (Take Me Away) (1994)

LASS, JEFF
 American Born (1990)
 Killing Zone, The (1991)
 DaVinci's War (1992)
 Unbecoming Age (1992)
 Hard Vice (1994)
 Vegas Vice (1994)
 To the Limit (1995)
 Lay of the Land, The (1997)

LASS, JOHAN
 Armageddon: The Final Challenge
  (1994)

LAST, BOB
 Black and Blue (1992)
 Long Day Closes, The (1992)
 Orlando (1992)
 Backbeat (1993)

LASWELL, BILL
 Gravesend (1996)

LATHAM, JIM
 Just Friends (1996)

LATHAM-KOENIG, JAN
 Wittgenstein (1993)

LAURENCE, PAUL
 Def by Temptation (1990)

LAWRENCE, DAN & KRISTI
 Lift (1997)

LAWRENCE, DAVID
 Skeeter (1993)

Hits! (1994)
 Sleep With Me (1994)
 Great Mom Swap, The (1995)
 Encino Woman (1996)
 Dog's Best Friend (1997)

LAWRENCE, TREVOR
 Working Trash (1990)
 To Sir With Love II (1996)

LAWS, RONNIE
 Run for the Dream: The Gail Devers
  Story (1996)

LAWSON, DAVE
 Out of the Shadows (1988)

LAXTON, JULIAN
 Evil Below, The (1989)
 Purgatory (1989)
 Rising Storm (1989)
 Final Alliance, The (1990)
 Curse III: Blood Sacrifice, The (1991)

LAZAROV, SIMO
 Deathstalker IV: Match of Titans (1992)

LAZZARUS, Q
 Twisted (1996)

LE BRETON, JEAN-LOUIS
 Les Amants du Pont-Neuf (1991)

LEBARS, HUGUES
 Barjo (1993)

LEFORT, DICK
 Rugged Gold (1994)

LEE, BILL
 Do the Right Thing (1989)
 Mo' Better Blues (1990)

LEEDS, ERIC
 Giant Steps (1992)

LEESE, HOWARD
 L.A. Bounty (1989)

LEFDUP, DENIS
 Two Dads and a Mom (1996)

LEGER, ROBERT
  Love-Moi (1991)

LEGG, JAMES
  Wounded Heart (1995)
  Dirty Laundry (1996)
  Hearts Adrift (1996)
  Reasons of the Heart (1996)

LEGGETT, MARK
  Small Kill (1992)
  Me & My Matchmaker (1996)

LEGRAND, MICHEL
  Eternity (1990)
  Not a Penny More, Not a Penny Less
    (1990)
  Dingo (1991)
  Les Demoiselles ont eu 25 Ans (1993)
  Pickle, The (1993)
  Ready to Wear (Pret-a-Porter) (1994)
  Les Enfants de Lumiere (1995)
  Les Miserables (1995)
  World of Jacques Demy, The (1995)
  Danielle Steel's "The Ring" (1996)
  Aaron's Magic Village (1997)

LEIB, MITCHELL
  Empire Records (1995)

LEIBER, JED
  Love Potion No. 9 (1992)
  Blue Chips (1994)

LEITL, BRUCE
  Trip to Serendipity, A (1992)

LEMAIRE, EMMANUELLE
  Mina Tannenbaum (1993)

LEMETRE, JEAN-JACQUES
  Dieu Que les Femmes sont Amoureuses
    (1994)

LEMOTHE, CLAUDE
  Eldorado (1995)

LEMUSIER, ROBIN
  Inside the Goldmine (1994)

LENA, BATTISTA
  Ferie d'Agosto (August Vacation) (1993)

Con Gli Occhi Chiusi (With Closed
  Eyes) (1994)

LENNERTZ, CHRISTOPHER
  Suspect Device (1995)

LENOX, ANNIE
  Brother Minister: The Assassination of
    Malcolm X (1994)

LENOX, CARL
  Change of Place, A (1994)

LENZ, JACK
  Nutcracker Prince, The (1990)
  Due South (1994)

LEONARD, PATRICK
  Heart Condition (1990)
  Timebomb (1991)
  With Honors (1994)

LEPAGE, ROBERT MARCEL
  Clean Machine, The (1992)
  Cry in the Night, A (1996)
  Chile Obstinate Memory (1997)

LERIOS, CORY
  Night Angel (1990)
  To My Daughter (1990)
  Child's Play 3(1991)
  Entertainers, The (1991)
  Fixing the Shadow (aka Beyond the
    Law) (1992)
  Boiling Point (1993)
  Tower, The (1993)
  Baywatch the Movie: Forbidden Paradise
    (1994)
  Deadly Vows (1994)
  Angel Flight Down (1996)
  Fall Into Darkness (1996)
  Gone in a Heartbeat (1996)
  Assault on Devil's Island (1997)
  In the Line of Duty: Blaze of Glory
    (1997)
  Steel Chariots (1997)

LESTER, STEVEN
  Grinders (1996)

LEVAY, SYLVESTER
  Case Closed (1988)
  Cover Girl and the Cop, The (1989)

Courage Mountain (1989)
Manhunt: Search for the Night Stalker
   (1989)
Dark Avenger (1990)
Laker Girls (1990)
Navy SEALs (1990)
Snow Kill (1990)
Cry in the Wild: The Taking of Peggy
   Ann (1991)
False Arrest (1991)
Heroes of Desert Storm, The (1991)
Hot Shots! (1991)
Stone Cold (1991)
Condition Critical (1992)
In the Deep Woods (1992)
Dead Before Dawn (1993)
Donato and Daughter (1993)
Flashfire (1994)
I Can Make You Love Me (1993)

LEVI, ERIC
   Les Visiteurs (The Visitors) (1993)
   Why Is My Mother in My Bed? (1994)
   Les Anges Gardiens (Guardian Angels)
      (1995)
   Ma Femme Me Quitte (My Woman Is
      Leaving Me) (1996)
   Les Soeurs Soleil (The Sun Sisters)
      (1997)

LEVIN, GEOFF
   Personal Choice (1989)
   Price She Paid, The (1992)
   I'll Be Home for Christmas (1997)

LEVIN, STEWART
   Message From Holly, A (1992)
   Stay the Night (1992)
   Dad, the Angel and Me (1995)
   Past the Bleachers (1995)
   Our Son, the Matchmaker (1996)

LEVINSON, ROSS
   Nasty Hero (1990)
   Murder Without Motive: The Edmund
      Perry Story (1992)

LEVY, ADRIAN
   Never Say Die (1994)

LEVY, JAY
   Lady Avenger (1989)

Story of the Beach Boys: Summer
   Dreams, The (1990)

LEVY, KRISHNA
   Fast (1995)
   Ma vie sexuelle (1996)
   Artemisia (1997)
   Mordburo (1997)

LEVY, SHUKI
   Blind Vision (1992)
   Prey of the Chameleon (1992)
   Revenge on the Highway (1992)
   Christmas Reunion, A (1993)
   In the Shadows, Someone's Watching
      (1993)
   Blindfold: Acts of Obsession (1994)
   Honor Thy Father & Mother: The True
      Story of the Menendez Murders
      (1994)
   Turbo: A Power Rangers Movie (1997)

LEWIS, MICHAEL J.
   Rose and the Jackal, The (1990)
   She Stood Alone (1991)

LEWIS, TOM E.
   Nun and the Bandit, The (1992)

LEYH, BLAKE
   Star Time (1992)
   American Cyborg: Steel Warrior (1994)
   AstroCop (1994)
   Blood Runner (1994)
   Odile & Yvette at the Edge of the World
      (1994)
   Second Cousin, Once Removed (1994)
   Outside the Law (1995)
   Sick (The Life and Death of Bob
      Flanagan, Supermasochist) (1997)

LIBERATORI, FABIO
   Viaggi di Nozze (Honeymoon Trips)
      (1995)

LICHT, DANIEL
   Children of the Night (1991)
   Severed Ties (1991)
   Amityville 1992: It's About Time (1992)
   Where Are We?: Our Trip Through
      America (1992)
   Acting on Impulse (1993)
   Amityville: A New Generation (1993)

Children of the Corn II: The Final
  Sacrifice (1993)
Children of the Corn III: Urban Harvest
  (1993)
Necronomicon (1993)
Ticks (1993)
Final Embrace (1994)
Hard Truth, The (1994)
Zooman (1995)
Bad Moon (1996)
Hellraiser 4: Bloodline (1996)
Stephen King's "Thinner" (1996)
Woman Undone (1996)
Winner, The (1997)

LIEBMAN, MARTIN
  Let's Kill All the Lawyers (1992)

LIFTON, JIMMY
  Mirror, Mirror (1991)
  Mirror, Mirror 2: Raven Dance (1994)
  Takeover, The (1994)

LINCK, DANN
  Jitters, The (1989)

LINDES, HAL
  Born Kicking (1992)
  Don't Do It (1994)
  Infiltrator, The (1995)

LINDGREN, ALAN E.
  Thanksgiving Day (1990)

LINDHEIMER, JOEL
  Poco Loco (1995)

LINDON, HAL
  Bermuda Grace (1994)

LINDSEY, CHRISTOPHER
  Sioux City (1994)

LINN, MICHAEL
  Illicit Behavior (1992)
  Snapdragon (1993)

LIONELLI, GARY
  Wild Man (1989)

LISK, ALAN
  Maigret (1988)
  Secret Weapon (1990)

LLIBOURTY, OLIVIER
  Marie de Nazareth (1995)

LLOYD, MICHAEL
  Iron Triangle, The (1989)
  Swimsuit (1989)

LO DUCA, JOSEPH
  Lunatics: A Love Story (1991)
  Army of Darkness: Evil Dead 3 (1992)
  Dying to Love You (1993)
  Necronomicon (1993)
  River of Rage: The Taking of Maggie
    Keene (1993)
  Child's Cry for Help, A (1994)
  M.A.N.T.I.S. (1994)
  Messenger (1994)
  Fighting for My Daughter (1995)
  Running Time (1997)

LOCASCIULLI, MIMMO
  La Vera Vita di Antonio H. (1994)

LOCK, BRIAN
  Gambler, The (1997)

LOCKE, MATTHEW
  Baby of Macon, The (1993)

LOCKHART, JIM
  All Things Bright and Beautiful (1994)

LOCKHART, ROBERT
  Execution Protocol, The (1992)
  Long Day Closes, The (1992)
  Bullion Boys, The (1993)
  Cold Comfort Farm (1995)
  Neon Bible, The (1995)
  In Your Dreams (1996)

LOCKWOOD, DIDIER
  Lune Froide (Cold Moon) (1991)

LOCKWOOD, GEORGE
  Welcomes Says the Angel (1996)

LOEWY, RAYMOND
  Joint Adventure (1995)

LOFGREN, NILS
  Every Breath (1993)

LOLASHVILI, ENRI
   Confidences a un Inconnu (1995)

LOMBARDO, JOHN
   Hollywood Hot Tubs 2: Educating
     Crystal (1990)

LONDON, FRANK
   Everything Relative (1996)
   Murder and Murder (1996)
   Brother's Kiss, A (1997)

LOOMIS, PAUL
   Riverbend (1989)

LOPES, CARLOS
   Abraxas: Guardian of the Universe
     (1991)
   Dinner at Fred's (1997)

LORBER, JEFF
   Side Out (1990)

LORD, JUSTIN
   Eye of the Eagle II: Inside the Enemy
     (1989)
   Eyes of the Eagle 3 (1992)
   Field of Fire (1992)

LORENC, MICHAEL
   Blood and Wine (1996)

LOS LOBOS
   Wrong Man, The (1993)
   Desperado (1995)

LOUCHOURAN, BRUNO
   Cover Up (1991)

LOUSSIER, JACQUES
   Les Demoiselles ont eu 25 Ans (1993)

LOVANO, JOE
   Face Down (1997)

LOVY, STEVEN
   Weekend With Barbara und Ingrid, A
     (1992)

LOWE, BRUCE
   Evil Altar (1989)

LOWRY, RICHARD

   Mommy (1995)

LUBAT, BERNARD
   Love, Math and Sex (1997)

LUBBOCK, JEREMY
   Any Man's Death (1990)
   Dear God (1996)

LUBRAN, MARTIN
   True Love and Chaos (1997)

LUCANTONI, DAIO
   Le Mani Forti (The Gray Zone) (1997)

LUNDMARK, ERIK
   Hijacking Hollywood (1997)

LUNN, JOHN
   Cormorant (1992)

LURIE, EVAN
   Johnny Stecchino (1991)
   Night We Never Met, The (1993)
   Il Mostro (The Monster) (1994)
   Layin' Low (1996)
   Trees Lounge (1996)
   Office Killer (1997)

LURIE, JOHN
   Mystery Train (1989)
   John Lurie and the Lounge Lizards Live
     in Berlin (1992)
   Blue in the Face (1995)
   Get Shorty (1995)
   Box of Moonlight (1996)
   Excess Baggage (1997)
   Manny & Lo (1996)

LUSSIER, RENE
   Love Me, Love Me Not (1996)

LYNCH, RANDALL & ALLEN
   Rain Without Thunder (1992)
   Mosquito (1995)

LYNTON, ADAM
   Tempting a Married Man (1993)

LYONS, RICHARD
   Monster High (1990)
   Do or Die (1991)
   Hard Hunted (1992)

Cage II: Arena of Death (1994)

LYSDAL, JENS
Day in October, A (1992)

MacCAULEY, MATTHEW
Love & Murder (1990)

MacCORMACK, GEOFF
Wild Orchid (1990)

MacDONALD, BARRY
Sahara (1995)

MacDONALD, BRAD
Spenser: The Judas Goat (1994)
Spenser: A Savage Place (1995)

MacDONALD, DON
Kissed (1996)

MacGOWAN, SHANE
Informant, The (1997)

MACAR, RICH
Hell High (1989)

MACCHI, EGISTO
Rose Garden, The (1989)

MACCHI, LAMBERTO
Naufraghi Sotto Costa (Shipwrecks)
(1992)

MACERO, TEO
Walls & Bridges (1992)

MADER
Sons (1989)
Triple Bogey on a Par Five Hole (1991)
In the Soup (1992)
Xiyan (The Wedding Banquet) (1993)
Eat Drink Man Woman (1994)
Somebody to Love (1994)
Clockwatchers (1997)
Little City (1997)
National Lampoon's "The Don's
Analyst" (1997)

MAEBY, JACK
Belly Talkers (1996)

MAGNELLI, FRANCESCO

Escoriandoli (1996)

MAGNESS, CLIF
Body Shot (1993)
Taken Alive (1995)

MAI, VINCENT
Just One of the Girls (1993)

MAINETTI, STEFANO
Vendetta II: The New Mafia (1993)
Assassin Wore Yellow Shoes, The
(1995)
Shooter, The (1995)
Sub Down (1997)
Talos the Mummy (1997)

MALINA, AMY
Insomnia (1995)

MALKIN, GARY REMAL
Thousand Pieces of Gold (1990)
Victim of Love: The Shannon Mohr
Story (1993)
From the Files of "Unsolved Mysteries":
Voice From the Grave (1996)
Raising the Ashes (1997)
Sleepwalking Killer, The (1997)

MALLET, SAM
Holidays on the River Yarra (1991)

MALONE, VINCENT
Enfants de Salaud (1996)

MALOU, MANUEL
Gazon Maudit (French Twist) (1995)

MAMET, BOB
Necromancer (1989)

MAMEY, NORMAN
Satan's Princess (1990)
Round Numbers (1992)

MANCINA, MARK
Hell on the Battleground (1989)
Rage to Kill (1989)
Space Mutiny (1989)
Where Sleeping Dogs Lie (1991)
Lifepod (1993)
True Romance (1993)
Monkey Trouble (1994)

Speed (1994)
Assassins (1995)
Bad Boys (1995)
Fair Game (1995)
Man of the House (1995)
Money Train (1995)
Moll Flanders (1996)
Twister (1996)
Con Air (1997)
Speed 2: Cruise Control (1997)

MANCINA, MICHAEL
Outer Limits, The (1996)

MANCINI, HENRY
Peter Gunn (1989)
Physical Evidence (1989)
Welcome Home (1989)
Fear (1990)
Ghost Dad (1990)
Married to It (1991)
Never Forget (1991)
Switch (1991)
Tom and Jerry: The Movie (1992)
Son of the Pink Panther (1993)

MANDEL, ELLEN
Secretary, The (1992)

MANDEL, JOHNNY
Brenda Starr (1989)
Single Women, Married Men (1989)
Danielle Steel's "Kaleidoscope" (1990)

MANFREDINI, HARRY
Cameron's Closet (1989)
Deep Star Six (1989)
Horror Show, The (1989)
House IV: The Horror Show (1989)
Angel of Death (1990)
Double Revenge (1990)
Aces: Iron Eagle III (1992)
Kickboxer III: The Art of War (1992)
Jason Goes to Hell: The Final Friday
    (1993)
My Boyfriend's Back (1993)
Cries Unheard: The Donna Yaklich Story
    (1994)
Dead on Sight (1994)
TimeMaster (1995)
Follow Your Heart (1997)
Gun, a Car, a Blonde, A (1997)
Wishmaster (1997)

MANILOW, BARRY
Hans Christian Andersen's
    "Thumbelina" (1994)
Pebble and the Penguin, The (1995)

MANN, BARRY
Troll in Central Park, A (1994)
All Dogs Go to Heaven 2 (1996)
Muppet Treasure Island (1996)

MANN, HUMMIE
Box Office Bunny (1991)
In Gold We Trust (1992)
Year of the Comet (1992)
Benefit of the Doubt (1993)
Robin Hood: Men in Tights (1993)
Confessions of a Sorority Girl (1994)
Cool and the Crazy (1994)
Dragstrip Girl (1994)
Girls in Prison (1994)
Jailbreakers (1994)
Motorcycle Gang (1994)
Reform School Girl (1994)
Runaway Daughters (1994)
Dracula: Dead and Loving It (1995)
Fall Time (1995)
In Cold Blood (1996)
Sticks and Stones (1996)
. . . First Do No Harm (1997)
Rescuers: Stories of Courage: Two
    Women (1997)
Second Civil War, The (1997)

MANNIX, ERNIE
Men Lie (1994)
Cottonwood, The (1996)
Deli, The (1997)

MANOLAKAKIS, JOE
Cool Blue (1990)

MANSBRIDGE, MARK
Fire Down Below (1997)

MANSFIELD, DAVID
Miss Firecracker (1989)
Desperate Hours (1990)
Late for Dinner (1991)
Me and Veronica (1992)
Mrs. Cage (1992)
Ballad of Little Jo, The (1993)
David's Mother (1994)
Legend of O. B. Taggart, The (1994)

Dangerous Affair, A (1995)
Stranger Beside Me, The (1995)
Tennessee Williams' "A Streetcar
    Named Desire" (1995)
Truman (1995)
Deep Crimson (1996)
People Next Door, The (1996)
Radiant City (1996)
Suddenly (1996)
Advocate's Devil, The (1997)
Apostle, The (1997)
Floating (1997)
Road Ends (1997)

MANUEL, MARITA
Firing Line, The (1991)

MANUS, RON
Ricky Rosen's Bar Mitzvah (1995)

MANY, CHRIS
Price She Paid, The (1992)

MANZIE, JIM
Stepfather II: Make Room for Daddy
    (1989)
Leatherface: Texas Chainsaw Massacre
    III (1990)
Tales From the Darkside: The Movie
    (1990)
Dean R. Koontz's "Servants of Twilight"
    (1991)
Servants of Twilight, The (1991)
Sweet Poison (1991)
Fear of a Black Hat (1992)
My Grandpa Is a Vampire (1992)
Elvis Presley (1993)
Lurking Fear (1994)
Night of the Demons 2 (1994)
Pumpkinhead 2: Blood Wings (1994)
Night of the Scarecrow (1995)

MARCEL, LEONARD
Sexbomb (1989)
Street Asylum (1990)

MARCUCCI, STEFANO
Lo Zio Indegno (The Sleazy Uncle)
    (1989)

MARDER, MARC
True Identity (1991)

Les Gens de la Riziere (Rice People)
    (1994)

MARGOLIN, STUART
Vendetta: Secrets of a Mafia Bride
    (1991)

MARIANELLI, DARIO
I Went Down (1997)

MARIANO, DETTO
Striker (Combat Force) (1989)

MARICONDA, MIKE
Purgatory County (1997)

MARINE, SEBASTIAN
El Color de las Nubes (1997)

MARINELLI, ANTHONY
Spooner (1989)
Graveyard Shift (1990)
Internal Affairs (1990)
House of Secrets (1993)
Marked for Murder (1993)
My Forgotten Man (1993)
Reckless Kelly (1993)
There Was a Little Boy (1993)
Baby Brokers (1994)
Innocent, The (1994)
Fight for Justice: The Nancy Conn Story
    (1995)
2 Days in the Valley (1996)
Don King: Only in America (1997)
Hacks (1997)
Masterminds (1997)
Underworld (1997)

MARINI, GIOVANNA
Cronache del Terzo Millennio (1996)

MARINO, LEO
Absence, The (1992)

MARIS, STELLA
Under the Sun (1992)

MARIUN, RICHARD
Escape to Witch Mountain (1995)

MARKOWITZ, DONALD
On Seventh Avenue (1996)
North Shore Fish (1997)

MAROTTA, RICK
  Cover Girl Murders, The (1993)
  Painted Hero (1995)

MARRA, MICHAEL
  Ruffian Hearts (1995)

MARSALIS, BRANFORD
  Black to the Promised Land (1992)
  Music Tells You, The (1992)
  Sneakers (1992)
  To My Daughter With Love (1994)
  Mr. and Mrs. Loving (1996)

MARSALIS, WYNTON
  Shannon's Deal (1989)
  Tune in Tomorrow . . . (1990)

MARSHALL, PHIL
  Flying Blind (1990)
  Run (1991)
  Noises Off (1992)
  Revolver (1992)
  Endless Summer II, The (1994)
  Davy Jones' Locker (1995)
  Four Diamonds, The (1995)
  Kicking and Screaming (1995)
  Apollo 11 (1996)
  Beverly Hills Family Robinson (1997)
  Ditchdigger's Daughters, The (1997)
  Price of Kissing, The (1997)
  Trial and Error (1997)

MARSTON, STEPHEN C.
  Christmas Reunion, A (1993)

MARTEL, FERDNAND
  Mothers and Daughters (1992)

MARTIN, GEORGE PORTER
  White Girl, The (1990)

MARTIN, PETER
  Where the Heart Is (1990)

MARTINEZ, CLIFF
  sex, lies and videotape (1989)
  Kafka (1991)
  Black Magic (1992)
  King of the Hill (1993)
  Underneath, The (1995)
  Gray's Anatomy (1996)

MARTT, MIKE
  Slaves to the Underground (1997)

MARTYN, JOHN
  Il Verificatore (The Meter Reader)
    (1995)

MARVIN, MEL
  Cooperstown (1993)

MARVIN, RICK
  Flight of Black Angel (1991)
  3 Ninjas (1992)
  Interceptor (1992)
  Save Me (1993)
  When Love Kills: The Seduction of John
    Hearn (1993)
  3 Ninjas Kick Back (1994)
  Separated by Murder (1994)

MARVIN, RICHARD
  Trail of Tears (1995)
  Escape Clause (1996)

MAS, JEAN-PIERRE
  Mo' (1996)

MASCIS, J.
  Gas, Food, Lodging (1992)

MASEKELA, HUGH
  Sarafina! (1992)
  Mandela (1995)

MASON, HARVEY W.
  Only the Strong (1993)

MASON, JANETTE
  Paris Was a Woman (1995)

MASON, MOLLY
  Brother's Keeper (1992)

MASON, NICK
  Tank Malling (1989)

MASON, PAUL W.
  Insulted and the Humiliated, The (1996)

MASON, ROGER
  Love Crimes (1992)
  Crime Broker (1993)
  Seventh Floor, The (1993)

Gino (1994)
Joey (1997)

MASSARI, JOHN
Snake Eater (1990)
Steel & Lace (1990)
Big Sweat, The (1991)
Diplomatic Immunity (1991)
Snakeeater II: The Drug Pusher (1991)
Dog Bark Blue (1992)
Snakeeater III: His Law (1992)
Death Ring (1993)
Shooting Lily (1996)

MASSO, ALEJANDRO
Little Bird (1997)

MATHISON, TREVOR
Darker Side of Black (1994)

MATISON, JIM
Lisa Theory, The (1994)

MATSON, SASHA
Bloodfist (1989)
Lobster Man From Mars (1989)
Liberty & Bash (1990)
Red Surf (1990)
River of Death (1990)
Betrayal of the Dove (1991)
Total Exposure (1991)
Dead Center (aka Crazy Joe) (1992)

MATTHEWS, DAVID M.
Valhalla (1992)

MATTIOLI, MICHAEL
Kiss & Tell (1996)

MATZ, PETER
When We Were Young (1989)
Gumshoe Kid, The (1990)
10 Million Dollar Getaway, The (1991)
Stepping Out (1991)
This Can't Be Love (1994)

MAULUCCI, DYLAN
Are They Still Shooting? (1993)

MAXWELL, MARK
Pin Gods (1996)

MAY, BRIAN

Bloodmoon (1990)
Dead Sleep (1990)
Darlings of the Gods (1991)
Freddy's Dead: The Final Nightmare (1991)
Dr. Giggles (1992)
Hurricane Smith (1992)
Blind Side (1993)

MAY, DANIEL
Severance (1989)
Fatal Skies (1990)
Chopper Chicks in Zombie Town (1991)
Dead Space (1991)
Pizza Man (1991)

MAY, SCOTT
Meet the Parents (1992)

MAY, SIMON
Caught in the Act (1996)

MAYFIELD, CURTIS
Return of SuperFly, The (1990)

MAZZOCCHETTI, GERMANO
Finalmente Soli (1997)
Il Vaggio della Sposa (The Bride's Journey) (1997)

McBRIDE, JIM
Great Balls of Fire! (1989)

McCALLUM, JON
Soultaker (1990)
Little Heroes (1991)
Project Eliminator (1991)
Legend of Wolf Mountain, The (1992)
Grizzly Mountain (1997)

McCARTHY, DENNIS
Danielle Steel's "Kaleidoscope" (1990)
Leona Helmsley: The Queen of Mean (1990)
Love Boat: A Valentine Voyage, The (1990)
Danielle Steel's "Daddy" (1991)
Overkill: The Aileen Wuornos Story (1992)
Staying Afloat (1993)
Armed and Innocent (1994)
Star Trek Generations (1994)
Tonya & Nancy: The Inside Story (1994)

Colony, The (1995)
Inflammable (1995)
In the Name of Love: A Texas Tragedy
    (1995)
Care and Handling of Roses, The (1996)
Hidden in Silence (1996)
Lying Eyes (1996)
Any Place but Home (1997)
Breast Men (1997)
Get to the Heart: The Barbara Mandrell
    Story (1997)
Love's Deadly Triangle: The Texas
    Cadet Murder (1997)
McHale's Navy (1997)
When Innocence Is Lost (1997)

McCARTHY, JOHN
    Love and Human Remains (1993)
    Paris, France (1993)
    Due South (1994)
    Possession of Michael D, The (1995)
    Soul Survivor (1995)
    Sweet Angel Mine (1996)

McCLINTOCK, STEVE
    Hell on the Battleground (1989)
    Rage to Kill (1989)
    Final Sanction, The (1990)

McCOLL, NEIL
    Fever Pitch (1997)
    Pur Boy (1997)
    TwentyFourSeven (1997)

McCOLLOUGH, PAUL
    Night of the Living Dead (1990)

McCONNELL, PAGE
    Only in America (1996)

McCULLOCH, JOHN
    Careful (1992)
    Twilight of the Ice Nymphs, The (1997)

McDERMOTT, GALT
    Mistress (1992)

McDONALD, GARRY
    Flood: Who Will Save Our Children?,
        The (1993)
    Official Denial (1993)
    Thorn Birds: The Missing Years, The
        (1996)

McEUEN, JOHN
    Good Old Boys, The (1995)

McEVOY, MICHAEL
    Bearskin: An Urban Fairytale (1989)

McGARRIGLE, KATE and ANNE
    Deux Actrices (Two Can Play) (1993)

McGARRIGLE, KATE/ANNE/JANE
    Return of Tommy Tricker (1994)

McGEECHAN, PAUL
    Near Room, The (1995)

McHUGH, DAVID
    Dream Team, The (1989)
    Three Fugitives (1989)
    Casey's Gift: For Love of a Child (1990)
    Daddy's Dyin' . . . Who's Got the Will?
        (1990)
    Montana (1990)
    Chance of a Lifetime (1991)
    Dillinger (1991)
    Final Verdict (1991)
    Lies of the Twins (1991)
    Lonely Hearts (1991)
    Mannequin Two: On the Move (1991)
    Prisoners of the Sun (Blood Oath) (1991)
    Just My Imagination (1992)
    Over the Hill (1992)
    Shame (1992)
    Desperate Journey: The Allison Wilcox
        Story (1993)
    Counterfeit Contessa, The (1994)
    Dark Reflection (1994)
    Erotic Tales (1994)
    Hidden 2, The (1994)
    Justice in a Small Town (1994)
    Passion for Justice: The Hazel Brannon
        Smith Story (1994)
    Changing Habits (1996)

McHUGH, RICHARD
    Pumpkinhead 2: Blood Wings (1994)

McKEAN, MICHAEL
    Waiting for Guffman (1996)

McKENZIE, MARK
    To Die For 2: Son of Darkness (1991)
    Warlock: The Armagedon (1993)
    Mi Familia (My Family) (1994)

Dr. Jekyll and Ms. Hyde (1995)
Frank and Jesse (1995)
Death in Granada (1997)
Disappearance of Garcia Lorca, The
    (1997)

McKENZIE, PHILIPPE
La Postiere (The Postmistress) (1992)

McKEON, STEPHEN
Boy From Mercury, The (1996)

McKNIGHT, TRACY
Love God (1997)

McLAREN, MALCOLM
Catwalk (1995)

McLARY, DAVID
Talk to Me (1996)

McNABB, MURRAY
Once Were Warriors (1994)
Broken English (1996)

McNAUGHTON, ROBERT F.
Normal Life (1995)
Henry: Portrait of a Serial Killer 2 (1997)

McNEELY, JOEL
Parent Trap Hawaiian Honeymoon
    (1989)
Parent Trap III (1989)
Polly (1989)
Appearances (1990)
Hitler's Daughter (1990)
Polly--Comin' Home (1990)
Frankenstein: The College Years (1991)
Lady Against the Odds (1992)
Iron Will (1993)
Radioland Murders (1994)
Squanto: A Warrior's Tale (1994)
Terminal Velocity (1994)
Gold Diggers: The Secret of Bear
    Mountain (1995)
Flipper (1996)
Buffalo Soldiers (1997)
Vegas Vacation (1997)
Wild America (1997)

McNEILL, ANDY
Project: Genesis (1993)

McNICHOLAS, STEVE
Riot (1997)

McPHERSON, ANDREW
Omaha (The Movie) (1994)

McVAY, JAMES
Triumph of the Heart: The Ricky Bell
    Story, A (1991)
Charles & Diana: Unhappily Ever After
    (1992)
Diamond Fleece, The (1992)
Mother's Right: The Elizabeth Morgan
    Story, A (1992)
Gregory K (1993)
Not in My Family (1993)
Babymaker: The Dr. Cecil Jacobson
    Story (1994)
Cries From the Heart (1994)
Moment of Truth: Murder or Mercy?
    (1994)
Between Love and Honor (1995)
Dangerous Intentions (1995)
Desert Winds (1995)
Freaky Friday (1995)
Breaking Through (1996)
Co-Ed Call Girl (1996)
For My Daughter's Honor (1996)
In the Blink of an Eye (1996)
Mother's Instinct, A (1996)
Race Against Time: The Search for
    Sarah (1996)
Country Justice (1997)

MEACOCK, JIM
Let's Stick Together (1997)

MEDUSA
Switchblade Sisters (1996)

MEER, STEPHANE
Too Pure (1995)

MELLE, GIL
Taking of Flight 847: The Uli Derickson
    Story, The (1988)
Case of the Hillside Stranglers, The
    (1989)
From the Dead of Night (1989)
Good Cops, Bad Cops (1990)
So Proudly We Hail (1990)
Fire! Trapped on the 37th Floor (1991)
Night Owl (1993)

MELNICK, PETER RODGERS
  Get Smart, Again! (1989)
  Out of Sight, Out of Mind (1990)
  Bad Attitudes (1991)
  Convicts (1991)
  L.A. Story (1991)
  Running Mates (1992)
  12:01 (1993)
  Indictment: The McMartin Trial (1995)
  For Hope (1996)
  Grand Avenue (1996)
  Lily Dale (1996)
  No One Could Protect Her (1996)
  Two Mothers for Zachary (1996)
  Every 9 Seconds (1997)
  Jitters (1997)
  Only Thrill, The (1997)
  Time to Say Goodbye? (1997)

MELVOIN, WENDY
  Soul Food (1997)

MENKEN, ALAN
  Little Mermaid, The (1989)
  Beauty and the Beast (1991)
  Aladdin (1992)
  Newsies (1992)
  Life With Mikey (1993)
  Pocahontas (1995)
  Hunchback of Notre Dame, The (1996)
  Hercules (1997)

MENNONNA, JOEY
  Bad Blood (1989)
  Cleo/Leo (1989)
  Party Incorporated (1989)
  Woman Obsessed, A (1989)
  Enrapture (1990)
  Wildest Dreams (1990)
  Affairs of the Heart (1992)

MENTEN, DALE
  Keys, The (1992)

MENZER, KIM
  Mahabharata, The (1989)

MERTENS, WIM
  Fiesta (1995)

METALLICA
  Paradise Lost: The Child Murders of
    Robin Hood Hill (1996)

MEYERS, LENNY
  Bar Girls (1994)

MICHELINI, LUCHINO
  Opponent, The (1990)

MICHENAUD, JEAN-MICHEL
  Big Empty, The (1997)

MIDDLEBROOKS, HARRY
  Miracle at Beekman's Place (1988)

MILLER, BRUCE
  U.S. Marshals: Waco & Rhinehart
    (1987)
  Ski Patrol (1990)
  Mother of the Bride (1993)
  Bonanza: The Return (1993)
  Bonanza: Under Attack (1995)
  Stranger Beside Me, The (1995)
  No One Could Protect Her (1996)

MILLER, CYNTHIA
  Crazy in Love (1992)
  Foreign Affairs (1993)
  Portrait, The (1993)
  Voices From Within (1994)
  Run of the Country, The (1995)
  Three Wishes (1995)

MILLER, DOMINIC
  Wild West (1992)

MILLER, MARCUS
  House Party (1990)
  Boomerang (1992)
  Above the Rim (1994)
  Low Down Dirty Shame, A (1994)
  Great White Hype, The (1996)
  6th Man, The (1997)

MILLER, PETER
  Gumshoe (1992)

MILLER, RANDY
  Witchcraft (1988)
  And You Thought Your Parents Were
    Weird! (1991)
  Black Magic Woman (1991)
  Hellraiser III: Hell on Earth (1992)
  Into the Sun (1992)
  Case for Murder, A (1993)
  Indecent Behavior (1993)

Darkman II: The Return of Durant
  (1994)
Darkman 3: Die Darkman Die (1995)
Space Marines (1995)
Right to Remain Silent, The (1996)

MILLER, STEVEN
  Saints and Sinners (1995)

MILLO, MARIO
  Paws (1997)

MILLS, PAUL
  Still Breathing (1997)

MILLS, SIDNEY
  Fly by Night (1993)

MILROY, DAVID
  Day of the Dog (1993)
  Exile and the Kingdom (1993)

MINARD, MICHAEL
  Dead on the Money (1991)

MINDEL, DAVID
  Bob's Weekend (1996)

MINK, BEN
  Even Cowgirls Get the Blues (1993)

MIROWITZ, SHELDON
  Troublesome Creek: A Midwestern
    (1996)

MISHRA, SANJAY
  Port Djema (1997)

MITCHELL, RICHARD G.
  Bridge, The (1991)

MITHOFF, BOB
  Working Trash (1990)
  Class of Nuke 'Em High Part II (1991)
  Sgt. Kabukiman, N.Y.P.D. (1991)
  Dragonfight (1992)
  Landslide (1992)
  Seedpeople (1992)
  Cyborg Cop II (1994)

MIZZY, VIC
  Return to Green Acres (1990)

MOFFATT, MARK
  Rough Diamonds (1994)
  All Men Are Liars (1995)
  Back of Beyond (1995)

MOLE, CHARLIE
  Murder on Line One (Helpline) (1990)
  Othello (1995)

MOLINARI, ALESSANDRO
  Directors on Directors (1997)
  La Medaglia (The Medal) (1997)

MOLL, GUNTER
  Life Is a Bluff (1997)

MOLL, NORMAN
  Tarantella (1995)
  Green Plaid Shirt (1996)

MOLLIN, FRED
  Friday the 13th Part VIII: Jason Takes
    Manhattan (1989)
  Whispers (1990)
  In Advance of the Landing (1991)
  Amy Fisher: My Story (1992)
  Liar, Liar (1993)
  Survive the Night (1993)
  Abduction, The (1996)

MOLONEY, PADDY
  Three Wishes for Jamie (1987)
  Treasure Island (1990)
  I Dreamt I Woke Up (1991)
  Stolen Hearts (1996)
  Two If by Sea (1996)

MONFAREDZADEH, ESFANDIAR
  Face of the Enemy (1989)

MONTANARI, PIERO
  Ghosthouse (1989)

MONTES, MICHAEL
  Headhunter's Sister, The (1997)

MONTES, OSVALDO
  Lifeforce Experiment, The (1994)

MONTROSE, RONNIE
  Born to Ski (1992)

MOON, GUY
  Deadly Weapon (1989)
  Diving In (1989)
  Runnin' Kind, The (1989)
  Brady Bunch Movie, The (1995)
  Very Brady Sequel, A (1996)

MOONEY, KEVIN
  Mirror, Mirror (1996)

MOORE, GEOFFREY
  Glam (1997)

MOORE, THURSTON
  Heavy (1995)

MORALES, BEO
  Wax, or the Discovery of Television
    Among Bees (1993)

MORALES, MIO
  Next Step, The (1996)

MORGAN, MARK
  Where the Day Takes You (1992)

MORLEY, GLENN
  Drop Dead Gorgeous (1991)
  When the Vows Break (1995)
  Haunting of Lisa, The (1996)

MORODER, GIORGIO
  Let It Ride (1989)
  Neverending Story II: The Next Chapter,
    The (1990)
  Fair Game (1991)
  Cybereden (1993)

MORRICONE, ENNIO
  Blind Justice (1988)
  Casualties of War (1988)
  Cinema Paradiso (1989)
  Fat Man and Little Boy (1989)
  Human Factor (1989)
  Tempo Di Uccidere (The Short Cut)
    (1989)
  Dimenticare Palermo (1990)
  Endless Game, The (1990)
  Hamlet (1990)
  Maktub: The Law of the Desert (1990)
  State of Grace (1990)
  Tie Me Up! Tie Me Down! (1990)
  Time to Kill (1990)

Tutti Stanno Bene (Everybody's Fine)
    (1990)
  Voyage of Terror: The Achille Lauro
    Affair (1990)
  Bugsy (1991)
  City of Joy (1992)
  Husbands and Lovers (1992)
  L'Envers du Decor (Portrait of Pierre
    Guffroy) (1992)
  Rampage (1992)
  Il Lungo Silenzio (The Long Silence)
    (1993)
  In the Line of Fire (1993)
  Jonah Who Lived in the Whale (1993)
  La Scorta (The Bodyguards) (1993)
  Disclosure (1994)
  Genesi: La Creazione e il Diluvio (1994)
  Love Affair (1994)
  L'uomo delle Stelle (The Star Man)
    (1994)
  Night and the Moment, The (1994)
  Una Pura Formalita (A Pure Formality)
    (1994)
  Wolf (1994)
  Lo Schermo a Tre Punte (1995)
  Pasolini: An Italian Crime (1995)
  Sostiene Pereira (According to Pereira)
    (1995)
  L'uomo Proiettile (The Human
    Cannonball) (1995)
  I Magi Randagi (We Three Kings) (1996)
  La Lupa (She-Wolf) (1996)
  La Sindrome di Stendhal (1996)
  Ninfa Plebea (1996)
  Samson and Delilah (1996)
  Vitte Strozzate (Strangled Lives) (1996)
  Lolita (1997)
  U-Turn (1997)

MORRIS, JOHN
  Favorite Son (1988)
  Second Sight (1989)
  Last Best Year, The (1990)
  Stella (1990)
  Carolina Skeletons (1991)
  Last to Go, The (1991)
  Life Stinks (1991)
  Our Sons (1991)
  World War II: When Lions Roared
    (1994)
  Ellen Foster (1997)
  Scarlett (1994)

MORRIS, MICK
    Thousand Wonders of the Universe, The
        (1997)

MORRISON, VAN
    Beyond the Clouds (1995)

MORSE, FUZZBEE
    Dark Angel: The Ascent (1994)

MORSE, MATTHEW
    Silent Night, Deadly Night 5: The Toy
        Maker (1991)

MOSES, KATHRYN
    Skin Deep (1995)

MOSIER, MICHAEL
    100 Proof (1997)

MOTHERSBAUGH, BOB
    Love & Sex, etc. (1996)

MOTHERSBAUGH, MARK
    It's Pat (1994)
    New Age, The (1994)
    Shaggy Dog, The (1994)
    Courtyard, The (1995)
    Flesh Suitcase (1995)
    Last Supper, The (1995)
    Big Squeeze, The (1996)
    Bottle Rocket (1996)
    Happy Gilmore (1996)
    Best Men (1997)
    Breaking Up (1997)
    Quicksilver Highway (1997)
    Unwed Father (1997)

MOTION, DAVID
    Orlando (1992)

MOUNSEY, ROB
    Taken Away (1989)
    Dangerous Passion (1990)

MUHLER, ERIC
    Of Men and Angels (1989)

MULDOWNEY, DOMINIC
    Jane Austen's "Emma" (1996)

MULLIGAN, GERRY
    I'm Not Rappaport (1996)

MURPHY, JOHN
    Leon the Pig Farmer (1992)
    Dinner in Purgatory (1994)
    Clockwork Mice (1995)
    Feast at Midnight, A (1995)
    Proteus (1995)
    Solitaire for 2 (1995)
    Welcome II the Terrordome (1995)
    Continued Adventures of Reptile Man,
        The (1996)
    Darklands (1997)
    Stiff Upper Lips (1997)

MURPHY, WALTER
    Lady Forgets, The (1989)
    Wiseguy (1996)

MURPHY, WILLIAM
    Bound and Gagged: A Love Story (1992)

MURRAY, SEAN
    One Way Out (1996)
    Ocean Tribe (1997)

MURROW, FREDRIC
    Rubin and Ed (1991)

MUSKY, JANE
    Two Bits (1995)

MUSUMARRA, ROMAN
    Le Grand Pardon II (Day of Atonement)
        (1992)
    L'Orso du Peluche (The Teddy Bear)
        (1994)
    L'Eleve (The Pupil) (1996)

MUSY, JEAN
    Sweet Killing (1993)

MUZINGO, BOBBY
    Insomnia (1995)

MYERS, BILL
    All's Fair (1989)

MYERS, PETER
    Dynasty: The Reunion (1991)

MYERS, STANLEY
    Stones for Ibarra (1988)
    Age-Old Friends (1989)

Dark Obsession (1989)
Paperhouse (1989)
Roald Dahl's "Danny, The Champion of
     the World" (1989)
Scenes From the Class Struggle in
     Beverly Hills (1989)
Torrents of Spring (1990)
Witches, The (1990)
Iron Maze (1991)
Murder of Quality (1991)
Voyager (1991)
Claude (1992)
Clothes in the Wardrobe (1992)
Cold Heaven (1992)
Mrs. 'Arris Goes to Paris (1992)
Sarafina! (1992)
Summer House, The (1993)
Trusting Beatrice (1993)
Heart of Darkness (1994)
Middlemarch (1994)

MYROW, FRED
Hour of the Assassin (1987)
Survival Quest (1989)
Phantasm II: Lord of the Dead (1991)
Plan 10 From Outer Space (1996)

NACHON, ANGELIQUE
Tango (1993)

NACHON, JEAN-CLAUDE
Au Petit Marguery (1995)
Les Grands Ducs (The Grand Dukes)
     (1995)

NAIDOO, SEAN
Toughguy (1994)

NAMANWORTH, PHILLIP
Long Gone (1987)

NASH THE SLASH
Blood & Donuts (1995)

NATALE, LOUIS
Clarence (1990)
Girl From Mars, The (1991)
Deadly Betrayal: The Bruce Curtis Story
     (1992)
Partners 'n Love (1992)
Adrift (1993)
Model by Day (1994)

Snowbound: The Jim and Jennifer Stolpa
     Story (1994)
Sodbusters (1994)
Kurt Vonnegut's "Harrison Bergeron"
     (1995)
Man in the Attic, The (1995)
Deadly Current (1996)
To Brave Alaska (1996)

NATZSKE, PAUL
Terminal Force (1989)

NAVARRETE, JAVIER
Susanna (1996)

NAVAZIO, MIKI
All Over Me (1996)

NEAL, CHRIS
Celia (1989)
Emerald City (1989)
Trouble in Paradise (1989)
Turtle Beach (1992)
Jack Be Nimble (1993)
Nostradamus Kid, The (1993)

NEILL, ROGER
American Summer, An (1991)
Mercenary (1996)
Sea Wolf, The (1997)

NEUFELD, ROBERT
Creatures of Light (1992)

NEVILLE, CYRIL
Follow Me Home (1996)

NEWBORN, IRA
Cast the First Stone (1989)
Uncle Buck (1989)
Collision Course (1990)
My Blue Heaven (1990)
Short Time (1990)
Naked Gun 2-1/2: The Smell of Fear,
     The (1991)
Brain Donors (1992)
Innocent Blood (1992)
Opposite Sex . . . And How to Live With
     Them, The (1993)
Ace Ventura, Pet Detective (1994)
Naked Gun 33-1/3: The Final Insult
     (1994)
Jerky Boys, The (1995)

Mallrats (1995)
High School High (1996)
Late Shift, The (1996)
Bad Manners (1997)

NEWCASTLE, PAUL
Spice World (1997)

NEWMAN, DAVID
Bill & Ted's Excellent Adventure (1989)
Disorganized Crime (1989)
Gross Anatomy (1989)
Heathers (1989)
Little Monsters (1989)
War of the Roses, The (1989)
Duck Tales: The Movie--Treasure of the
    Lost Lamp (1990)
Fire Birds (1990)
Freshman, The (1990)
Madhouse (1990)
Mr. Destiny (1990)
Bill & Ted's Bogus Journey (1991)
Don't Tell Mom the Babysitter's Dead
    (1991)
Marrying Man, The (1991)
Other People's Money (1991)
Paradise (1991)
Rover Dangerfield (1991)
Talent for the Game (1991)
Hoffa (1992)
Honeymoon in Vegas (1992)
Mighty Ducks, The (1992)
Runestone, The (1992)
That Night (1992)
Coneheads (1993)
Sandlot, The (1993)
Undercover Blues (1993)
Air Up There, The (1994)
Cowboy Way, The (1994)
Flintstones, The (1994)
I Love Trouble (1994)
My Father, the Hero (1994)
Boys on the Side (1995)
Operation Dumbo Drop (1995)
Tommy Boy (1995)
Big Bully (1996)
Jingle All the Way (1996)
Matilda (1996)
Nutty Professor, The (1996)
Phantom, The (1996)
Anastasia (1997)
Out to Sea (1997)

NEWMAN, RANDY
Parenthood (1989)
Avalon (1990)
Awakenings (1990)
Maverick (1994)
Paper, The (1994)
Toy Story (1995)
James and the Giant Peach (1996)
Michael (1996)

NEWMAN, THOMAS
Cookie (1989)
Heat Wave (1990)
Men Don't Leave (1990)
Naked Tango (1990)
Welcome Home, Roxy Carmichael
    (1990)
Career Opportunities (1991)
Deceived (1991)
Fried Green Tomatoes (1991)
Linguini Incident, The (1992)
Rapture, The (1991)
Citizen Cohn (1992)
Player, The (1992)
Scent of a Woman (1992)
Those Secrets (1992)
Whispers in the Dark (1992)
Flesh and Bone (1993)
Josh and S.A.M. (1993)
Favor, The (1994)
Little Women (1994)
Shawshank Redemption, The (1994)
Threesome (1994)
War, The (1994)
How to Make an American Quilt (1995)
Unstrung Heroes (1995)
American Buffalo (1996)
People vs. Larry Flynt, The (1996)
Phenomenon (1996)
Up Close and Personal (1996)
Mad City (1997)
Oscar and Lucinda (1997)
Red Corner (1997)

NICHOLAS, GEORGE
100 Proof (1997)

NICHTERN, DAVID
Big Picture, The (1989)
Spirit of '76, The (1990)

NIEHAUS, LENNIE
Child Saver, The (1988)

Rookie, The (1990)
White Hunter, Black Heart (1990)
Unforgiven (1992)
Perfect World, A (1993)
Lush Life (1994)
Bridges of Madison County, The (1995)
Titanic (1996) [TV movie]
Absolute Power (1997)
Midnight in the Garden of Good and Evil
    (1997)

NIETO, JOSE
    Captain James Cook (1989)
    Amantes (Lovers) (1991)
    Beltenebros (Prince of Shadows) (1992)
    El Maestro de Esgrima (The Fencing
        Master) (1992)
    El Amante Bilingue (The Bilingual
        Lover) (1993)
    Intruso (Intruder) (1993)
    Of Love and Shadows (1994)
    Shortcut to Paradise (1994)
    Guantanamera (1995)
    La Passion Turca (Turkish Passion)
        (1995)
    Bwana (1996)
    Dog in the Manger, The (1996)
    Tu Nombre Envenena Mis Suenos
        (1996)
    Passion in the Desert (1997)

NINA, JOE
    Jump the Gun (1996)

NISSEN, GREGORY
    Capture the White Flag (1994)

NITZSCHE, JACK
    Next of Kin (1989)
    Hot Spot, The (1990)
    Last of the Finest, The (1990)
    Mermaids (1990)
    Revenge (1990)
    Indian Runner, The (1991)
    Blue Sky (1994)
    Crossing Guard, The (1995)

NOBLE, MATT
    Jason's Lyric (1994)

NORGAARD, PER
    Prince of Jutland (1994)

NORMAN, CLIFF
    Branwen (1994)

NORTH, ALEX
    Last Butterfly, The (1992)

NORTHEY, CRAIG
    Kids in the Hall Brain Candy (1996)

NOSSITER
    Sunday (1997)

NOTT, JULIAN
    Man of No Importance, A (1994)
    My Mother's Courage (1995)

NUMAN, GARY
    Unborn, The (1991)

NUNES, EMMANUEL
    Journey to the Beginning of the World
        (1997)

NUTI, GIOVANNI
    Occhiopinocchio (1994)

NYMAN, MICHAEL
    Cook, the Thief, His Wife & Her Lover,
        The (1989)
    Prospero's Books (1991)
    Hairdresser's Husband, The (1992)
    Piano, The (1993)
    A La Folie (Six Days, Six Nights) (1994)
    Mesmer (1994)
    Carrington (1995)
    Ogre, The (1996)
    Gattaca (1997)

O'BRIEN, JAMES
    Venice Bound (1995)

O'CONNOR, GREG
    Mona Must Die (1994)

O'CONNOR, SINEAD
    Hush-a-Bye Baby (1990)
    In the Name of the Father (1993)

O'DONNELL, MICHAEL
    October 32nd (1992)

O'HARA, MARY MARGARET
  Events Leading Up to My Death, The
    (1991)

O'HEARN, PATRICK
  Heaven Is a Playground (1991)
  White Sands (1992)
  Father Hood (1993)
  Silver Tongue (1993)
  As Good as Dead (1995)
  Crying Freeman (1995)

O'KENNEDY, JOHN
  Midwife's Tale, The (1995)

O'LOCHLAINN, OSCAR
  Girl With the Hungry Eyes, The (1995)

O'MARA, SHANE
  Everynight . . . Everynight (1994)

OBER, GENE
  Strike a Pose (1993)
  All's Fair in Love & War (1996)

ODLAND, BRUCE
  Top of the World (1993)

OLDFIELD, WENDY
  Never Say Die (1994)

OLDHAM, WILL
  Broken Giant, The (1996)

OLIVERIO, JAMES
  Sleepaway Camp 3: Teenage Wasteland
    (1989)

OLVIS, WILLIAM
  Evil in Clear River (1988)
  Babycakes (1989)
  Finish Line (1989)
  Kill Me Again (1989)
  El Diablo (1990)
  Framed (1990)
  Pair of Aces (1990)
  Secret Life of Archie's Wife, The (1990)
  29th Street (1991)
  Fourth Story (1991)
  To Save a Child (1991)
  Comrades of Summer, The (1992)
  In Sickness and In Health (1992)
  Red Rock West (1993)

  Woman Who Loved Elvis, The (1993)
  Separate Lives (1995)
  Steal Big, Steal Little (1995)

OMER, MICHAEL
  Little Lord Fauntleroy (1995)

ORENSTEIN, NORMAN
  Spike of Love (1995)

ORTOLANI, RIZ
  Season of Giants, A (1991)
  Story of Boys and Girls, The (1991)
  Vendetta: Secrets of a Mafia Bride
    (1991)
  Fratelli e Sorelle (Brothers and Sisters)
    (1992)
  L'Angelo con la Pistola (Angel of Death)
    (1992)
  Tuareg: The Desert Warrior (1992)
  Magnificat (1993)
  L'uomo che Guarda (The Voyeur)
    (1994)
  Fermo Posta Tinto Bass (P.O. Box Tinto
    Bass) (1995)

OSBORNE, CHRISTIAN
  Peephole (1992)

OTTMAN, JOHN
  Public Access (1993)
  Usual Suspects, The (1995)
  Cable Guy, The (1996)
  Incognito (1997)
  Snow White: A Tale of Terror (1997)

OTTO, BRIAN
  Next Step, The (1996)

OUIMET, DAVID
  Fortress of Amerikka (1989)

OUVRIER, ANTOINE
  Le Sourire (The Smile) (1994)

PAATA
  Undertow (1991)

PAGAN, JOSE MANUEL
  Amor de Hombre (Manly Love) (1997)

PAGANI, MAURO
  Puerto Escondido (1992)

Sarahsara (The Waterbaby) (1994)
In Barca a Verla Contromano (1997)
Nirvana (1997)

PAGE, CHRIS
Miracle at Beekman's Place (1988)

PAGE-PACTER, SCOTT
Bonnie & Clyde: The True Story (1992)

PALAZZO, UMBERTO
Jack Frusciante Left the Band (1996)

PALEY, ANDY
Shelf Life (1993)
Traveller (1997)

PALMER, CHRISTOPHER
Valmont (1989)

PALMER, NICK
Sacred Sex (1992)

PARKER, ALAN
Out of Time (1989)
Voice of the Heart (1990)
To Be the Best (1992)
What's Eating Gilbert Grape (1993)
Wild Justice (1993)
Phoenix and the Magic Carpet, The
(1995)
Rhodes (1997)
Up on the Roof (1997)

PARKER, JIM
Ex (1991)
House of Elliott, The (1992)
Final Cut, The (1995)

PARKS, VAN DYKE
Two Jakes, The (1990)
Out on a Limb (1992)
Next Door (1994)
Truman Capote's "One Christmas"
(1994)
Wild Bill (1995)
Bastard Out of Carolina (1996)
Summer of Ben Tyler, The (1996)
Oliver Twist (1997)
Private Parts (1997)

PARODI, STARR
Shame II: The Secret (1995)

Secret She Carried, The (1996)
Crowned and Dangerous (1997)
Little Girls in Pretty Boxes (1997)
Nightmare Come True, A (1997)

PARSONS, STEVE
Split Second (1992)
Beg! (1994)
Funny Man (1994)

PARSONS, STEPHEN
Another Nine & a Half Weeks (1997)

PARTON, DOLLY
Unlikely Angel (1996)

PARTOS, ANTHONY
Video Fool for Love (1995)

PATI, JOHN
Simple Justice (1989)

PATRICK, CAMERON
Magical World of Chuck Jones, The
(1992)

PATTERSON, SHAWN
Bible and Gun Club, The (1996)
Demolitionist, The (1996)

PATTISON, JOHN
Smoking/No Smoking (1993)
J'ai pas Sommiel (I Can't Sleep) (1994)

PATTON, ROBBIE
Human Shield, The (1992)

PAXTON, GLENN
Dream Breakers (1989)

PAYNE, BILL
Dirty Money (1994)

PEACH, EARLE
Kanada (1994)
House of Pain (1995)

PEAKE, DON
Modern Love (1990)
People Under the Stairs, The (1991)
Solar Force (1994)
Hard Justice (1995)

PEARSON, E.
Identity Crisis (1989)

PENN, MICHAEL
Boogie Nights (1997)

PEPIN, RAMON
Bernie (1996)

PERATHONER, SERGE
Apres l'amour (Love After Love) (1992)

PEREZ, DANILO
Hugo Pool (1997)

PERLMAN, LAURA
To Die For (1989)

PERRY, ROBERT
Nevada (1997)

PERSON, RICHARD
Switchblade Sisters (1996)

PETERSEN, JOHN
Keeper, The (1996)

PETERSEN, RANDY
Return of Jafar, The (1994)
Aladdin and the King of Thieves (1996)

PETIT, CAROLINE
L'Annee Juliette (1995)

PETIT, JEAN-CLAUDE
Return of the Musketeers, The (1989)
Cyrano de Bergerac (1990)
Mayrig (Mother) (1991)
Uranus (1991)
Coupable d'Innocence (Guilty of
Innocence) (1992)
Playboys, The (1992)
En Compagnie d'Antonin Artaud (1994)
Foreign Student (1994)
La Veritable Histoire d'Artaud le Momo
(1994)
Nobody's Children (1994)
Swallows Never Die in Jerusalem (1994)
Le Hussard sur le Toit (The Horseman
on the Roof) (1995)
Beaumarchais l'insolent (1996)
Desire (1996)

Messieurs Les Enfants (Men Will Be
Boys) (1997)
Saraka Bo (1997)

PETITGRAND, LAURENT
Faraway, So Close! (1993)
A Cran (On the Edge) (1995)
Beyond the Clouds (1995)

PETROV, ANDREI
La Prediction (1994)

PETTIS, CHARLES
If Lucy Fell (1996)

PETTY, TOM
She's the One (1996)

PEVSNER, MARK
Gate of Heavenly Peace, The (1995)

PHELOUNG, BARRINGTON
Closing Numbers (1993)
Wall of Silence (1993)
Cinder Path, The (1994)
Nostradamus (1994)
Shopping (1994)
Mangler, The (1995)
Politician's Wife, The (1996)
Saint-Ex (1996)

PHILLIPS, ART
Fatal Bond (1992)
Signal One (1994)

PHILLIPS, JOHN
Greenkeeping (1992)
That Eye, the Sky (1994)
River Street (1996)
What I Have Written (1996)
Myth of Fingerprints, The (1997)

PHILLIPS, STU
Highwayman, The (1987)
Road Raiders, The (1989)

PICCIONI, PIERO
Quo Vadis? (1987)
Assolto per Aver Commesso Il Fatto
(1992)
Nestore l'ultima Corsa (Nestor's Last
Trip) (1994)

PICCIRILLO, MICHAEL
Crack House (1989)

PICKARD, NIK
Road to Mecca, The (1992)

PIDGEON, REBECCA
Oleanna (1994)

PIERSANTI, FRANCO
Matilda (1991)
Il Ladro di Bambini (The Stolen
Children) (1992)
On My Own (1992)
Il Segreto del Bosch Vecchio (1993)
Mille Bolle Blu (1993)
Il Branco (The Pack) (1994)
Lamerica (1994)
La Seconda Volta (The Second Time)
(1995)
Without Evidence (1996)
Marianna Ucria (1997)
Tesstimone a Rischio (Witness in
Danger) (1997)

PIGOTT, JOHANNA
Daydream Believer (1991)

PIKE, NICHOLAS
Chud II: Bud the Chud (1989)
Cry for Help: The Tracey Thurman
Story, A (1989)
I'm Dangerous Tonight (1990)
Prince and the Pauper, The (1990)
Captain Ron (1992)
Perfect Family (1992)
Secret Passion of Robert Clayton, The
(1992)
Sleepwalkers (1992)
Attack of the 50 Ft. Woman (1993)
Blank Check (1994)
Child Is Missing, A (1995)
Fast Company (1995)
In the Shadow of Evil (1995)
Surrogate, The (1995)
W.E.I.R.D. World (1995)
Ghosts (1997)
Star Kid (1997)
Stephen King's "The Shining" (1997)
Telling Lies in America (1997)

PILHOFER, HERB
Home Fires Burning (1992)

PINDER, GARY
Project: Shadowchaser (1992)

PINE, TED
Late Bloomers (1996)

PINELL, CHUCK
Doc's Full Service (1994)

PIOVANI, NICOLA
Der Berg (The Mountain) (1990)
La Voce Della Luna (1990)
Hors la Vie (1991)
Jamon, Jamon (Salami, Salami) (1992)
Le Amiche Del Cuore (Close Friends)
(1992)
Utz (1992)
Amok (1993)
Caro Diario (Dear Diary) (1993)
De eso no se habla (We Don't Want to
Talk About It (1993)
Fiorile (1993)
I Giovane Mussolini (A Man Named
Mussolini) (1993)
Kim Novak Is on the Phone (1994)
La Teta I La Luna (1994)
Per Amore, Solo per Amore (1994)
De Vliegende Hollander (The Flying
Dutchman) (1995)
Month by the Lake, A (1995)
Nemici d'Infanzia (Childhood Enemies)
(1995)
Beyond the Garden (1997)
Camere da Letto (Bedrooms) (1997)
El Imposter (1997)
La Vita e Bella (Life Is Beautiful) (1997)
Santo Stefano (1997)

PIRNER, DAVID
Chasing Amy (1996)

PLESSNER, AMOTZ
Perfect Alibi, The (1994)
Rave Review (1994)
Shattered Image (1994)
Salvaged Lives (1995)

PLOWMAN, MICHAEL RICHARD
Trucks (1997)

PLUMERI, TERRY
Black Eagle (1988)
Body Chemistry (1990)

Rain Killer, The (1990)
Lower Level (1990)
Angel in Red (aka Uncaged) (1991)
Crackdown (1991)
Stephen King's "Sometimes They Come Back" (1991)
Terror Within II, The (1991)
Hit the Dutchman (1992)
Mad Dog Coll (1992)
Night Eyes 3 (1993)
Teenage Bonnie and Klepto Clyde (1993)
Breach of Conduct (1994)
Death Wish 5: The Face of Death (1994)
Relentless 4: Ashes to Ashes (1994)
Raging Angels (1995)

POLEDOURIS, BASIL
Prison for Children (1987)
Farewell to the King (1989)
Lonesome Dove (1989)
Nasty Boys (1989)
Split Decisions (1989)
Wired (1989)
Hunt for Red October, The (1990)
Quigley Down Under (1990)
Why Me? (1990)
Flight of the Intruder (1991)
Harley Davidson and the Marlboro Man (1991)
Return to the Blue Lagoon (1991)
White Fang (1991)
Ned Blessing: The True Story of My Life (1992)
Wind (1992)
Free Willy (1993)
Hot Shots! Part Deux (1993)
RoboCop 3 (1993)
Lassie (1994)
On Deadly Ground (1994)
Rudyard Kipling's The Jungle Book (1994)
Serial Mom (1994)
Free Willy 2: The Adventure Home (1995)
Under Siege 2: Dark Territory (1995)
Celtic Pride (1996)
It's My Party (1996)
War at Home, The (1996)
Breakdown (1997)
Starship Troopers (1997)
Switchback (1997)

POLLACK, MICHAEL
Redneck (1995)

POLLONI, CHRISTIAN
Macadam Tribu (Macadam Tribe) (1996)

PONGO, PETER
Death of a Schoolboy (1991)

POP, IGGY
Brave, The (1997)

POPE, CAROLE
Silencer, The (1992)

POPE, CONRAD
Project Metalbeast: DNA Overload (1994)
Set-Up, The (1995)
Butch Camp (1997)

POPOLI, TIZIANO
Nella Mischia (In the Thick of It) (1995)

PORCARO, STEVE
Metro (1997)

PORTAL, MICHEL
Children of Chaos (1989)
Docteur Petiot (1990)
Tale of the Wind, A (1991)
Les Couleurs du Diable (1997)

PORTMAN, RACHEL
Antonia and June (1991)
Flea Bites (1991)
Where Angels Fear to Tread (1991)
Elizabeth R: A Year in the Life of the Queen (1992)
Rebecca's Daughters (1992)
Used People (1992)
Benny and Joon (1993)
Ethan Frome (1993)
Friends (1993)
Joy Luck Club, The (1993)
Great Moments in Aviation (1994)
Only You (1994)
Road to Wellville, The (1994)
Sirens (1994)
War of the Buttons (1994)
Palookaville (1995)
Pyromaniac's Love Story, A (1995)
Smoke (1995)

To Wong Foo, Thanks for Everything!
  Julie Newmar (1995)
Adventures of Pinocchio, The (1996)
Emma (1996)
Marvin's Room (1996)
Addicted to Love (1997)

PORTNOY, ERICA
  Revenge of the Living Zombies (1989)

POST, MIKE
  Nashville Beat (1989)
  Ryan White Story, The (1989)
  Thunderboat Row (1989)
  Unspeakable Acts (1990)
  Without Her Consent (1990)
  Great Pretender, The (1991)
  Greyhounds (1994)
  Rockford Files: I Still Love L.A., The
    (1994)
  Jake Lassiter: Justice on the Bayou
    (1995)
  Rockford Files: A Blessing in Disguise,
    The (1995)
  Rockford Files: Friends and Foul Play,
    The (1996)
  Rockford Files: Godfather Knows Best,
    The (1996)
  Rockford Files: If the Frame Fits . . . ,
    The (1996)
  Rockford Files: Punishment and Crime,
    The (1996)
  Wiseguy (1996)
  Rockford Files: Murder and
    Misdemeanors, The (1997)

POSTEL, STEVE
  Jumpin' at the Boneyard (1991)

POSTER, RANDALL
  Bullet (1997)
  Kiss Me, Guido (1997)

POTTER, SALLY
  Orlando (1992)
  Tango Lesson, The (1997)

POTTS, ALBY
  Season of Change (1994)

POWELL, JOHN
  Face/Off (1997)

POWELL, REG
  California Casanova (1991)
  Test Tube Teens From the Year 2000
    (1993)
  Baja (1995)
  Alaska (1996)
  Forbidden Zone: Alien Abduction (1996)
  Pathfinder, The (1996)

PRAHI, KVARTETO MESTA
  La Fille Sueve (A Single Girl) (1995)

PRANOTO, STEVEN
  Shopping for Fangs (1997)

PRAY FOR RAIN
  Trust Me (1989)
  Zandalee (1990)
  Roadside Prophets (1992)
  Love, Cheat & Steal (1993)
  Car 54, Where Are You? (1994)
  Floundering (1994)
  White Water Mile (1994)
  Boy Called Hate, A (1995)
  She Fought Alone (1995)
  Her Last Chance (1996)
  Sweet Dreams (1996)
  Pretty Poison (1996)
  Winner, The (1996)
  Any Mother's Son (1997)
  Perfect Body (1997)
  Three Lives of Karen, The (1997)

PREISNER, ZBIGNIEW
  At Play in the Fields of the Lord (1991)
  Eminent Domain (1991)
  Europa, Europa (1991)
  La Double Vie de Veronique (1991)
  Damage (1992)
  Olivier, Olivier (1992)
  A Linha do Horizonte (The Line of the
    Horizon) (1993)
  Secret Garden, The (1993)
  Trois Couleurs: Blanc (1993)
  Trois Couleurs: Bleu (1993)
  Mouvements du Desir (Desire in Motion)
    (1994)
  Perez Family, The (1994)
  Trois Couleurs: Rouge (1994)
  When a Man Loves a Woman (1994)
  Elisa (1995)
  Feast of July (1995)
  Fairy Tale: A True Story (1997)

Island on Bird Street, The (1997)

PRESGURVIC, GERARD
La Verite si je Mens (1997)

PRESSER, GABOR
Storm and Sorrow (1990)

PRESTON, JAN
Footstep Man, The (1992)
Billal (1996)

PRICE, ALAN
Is That All There Is? (1993)

PRICE, JIM
Hangfire (1991)

PRICE, STEPHEN
Deadly Currents (1992)

PRINCE
Graffiti Bridge (1990)
Girl 6 (1996)

PRITCHARD, JOHN
Lost Language of Cranes, The (1991)

PRUDENTE, OSCAR
Poliziotti (Policemen) (1995)

PRUDHOMME, JEAN-CHRISTOPHE
Le Pari (The Bet) (1997)

PRUESS, CRAIG
Bhaji on the Beach (1993)

PUCCINI, GIACOMO
Madame Butterfly (1995)

PURCELL, REG
Dr. Alien (1989)

PUTTNAM, SASHA
Le Confessional (The Confessional)
(1995)

QD III
Menace II Society (1993)

QUINN, KEVIN
Return of Jafar, The (1994)
Aladdin and the King of Thieves (1996)

R.E.M.
Road Movie (1996)

RH FACTOR
Forever (1992)

RABIN, TREVOR
Glimmer Man, The (1996)
Con Air (1997)

RABJOHNS, PAUL
Cold Equations, The (1996)

RABOL, GEORGES
Peche Veniel . . . Peche Mortel . . .
(1994)

RACHTMAN, KARYN
Fear, Anxiety and Depression (1989)
Headless Body in Topless Bar (1995)
Feeling Minnesota (1996)

RAE, DOUGLAS STEPHEN
Mary (1994)
Traps (1994)
Blackwater Trail (1995)

RAE, STEPHEN
Well, The (1997)

RAFFAELLI, BENJAMIN
Les Truffes (Two Jerks and a Pig) (1995)
Bat Out of Hell (1997)

RAFFELLI, MICHEL
Nous Deux (The Two of Us) (1992)

RAGLAND, ROBERT O.
No Place to Hide (1993)
Raffle, The (1994)
Evil Obsession (1995)
Fear, The (1995)
Plato's Run (1995)
Top of the World (1997)

RAKSIN, DAVID
Lady in a Corner (1989)

RAMIN, RON
Mickey Spillane's Mike Hammer:
Murder Takes All (1989)
Menu for Murder (1990)

Posing: Inspired by Three Real Stories
(1991)
Sidney Sheldon's "Memories of
Midnight" (1991)
They've Taken Our Children: The
Chowchilla Kidnapping (1993)
Bionic Ever After? (1994)
Birds II: Land's End, The (1994)
Come Die With Me: A Mickey Spillane's
Mike Hammer Mystery (1994)
Cagney & Lacey: The View Through the
Glass Ceiling (1995)
Dare to Love (1995)
From the Mixed-Up Files of Mrs. Basil
E. Frankweiler (1995)
Rent-a-Kid (1995)
Cagney & Lacey IV: True Convictions
(1996)
My Son Is Innocent (1996)
Step Toward Tomorrow, A (1996)

RAMSEY, KENNARD
Without Air (1995)

RANDLES, ROBERT
Revenge of the Red Baron (1994)

RAPP, MICHAEL
Girlfriend From Hell (1990)
Kill Crazy (1990)

RARICK, KEN
In the Heat of Passion (1992)

RAVENSCROFT, RAF
Double X: The Name of the Game
(1992)

RAVIO, ROY J.
Desert Hawk (1992)

RAY, SATYAJIT
Agantuk (The Stranger) (1991)

RAYE, MICHAEL
Bittersweet (1992)

REA, CHRIS
Soft Top Hard Shoulder (1992)
La Passione (1996)
Parting Shots (1997)

REALE, ROBERT

Wigstock: The Movie (1995)

REALI, STEFANO
Quando Eravano Repressi (When We
Were Repressed) (1992)
Le Donne Non Vogliono Piu (1993)

REDBONE, LEON
Everybody Wins (1990)

REDFORD, J.A.C.
Dangerous Affection (1987)
Breaking Point (1988)
Save the Dog! (1989)
Son's Promise, A (1990)
Web of Deceit (1990)
Locked Up: A Mother's Rage (1991)
Louis L'Amour's "Conagher" (1991)
Stop at Nothing (1991)
For Their Own Good (1993)
Kiss of a Killer (1993)
And Then There Was One (1994)
D2: The Mighty Ducks (1994)
Is There Life Out There? (1994)
One More Mountain (1994)
Bye Bye, Love (1995)
Heavyweights (1995)
Kid in King Arthur's Court, A (1995)
Naomi & Wynonna: Love Can Build a
Bridge (1995)
D3: The Mighty Ducks (1996)
For the Future: The Irvine Fertility
Scandal (1996)
Wild America (1996)
Two Voices (1997)
What the Deaf Man Heard (1997)

REDMAN, JOSHUA
Vanya on 42nd Street (1994)

REDONDO, EMILIANO
Fistfighter (1989)

REEVES, ALAN
Bethune: The Making of a Hero (1990)
Natural Enemy (1996)
Rainbow (1996)
Jack London's "The Call of the Wild"
(1997)

REGAN, PAT
Stepfather II: Make Room for Daddy
(1989)

Leatherface: Texas Chainsaw Massacre
    III (1990)
Tales From the Darkside: The Movie
    (1990)

REGGIANI, CELIA
    De Force Avec d'Autres (Forced to Be
        With Others) (1993)

REGNIER, SEBASTIAN
    Nanook (1994)

REINHARDT, JUSTIN
    Swingers (1996)

REISER, NIKI
    I Was on Mars (1992)

REMY, TONY
    Career Girls (1997)

RENO, JOHNNY
    Roadracers (1994)

RENZETTI, JOE
    Basket Case 2 (1990)
    Frankenhooker (1990)
    Lisa (1990)
    Murderous Vision (1991)
    Basket Case 3: The Progeny (1992)
    South Beach (1992)
    Slaughter of the Innocents (1993)

RETTINO, ERNIE
    Original Intent (1989)

REVELL, GRAEME
    Dead Calm (1989)
    Bangkok Hilton (1990)
    Child's Play 2 (1990)
    Psycho IV: The Beginning (1990)
    Spontaneous Combustion (1990)
    Till There Was You (1990)
    Deadly (1991)
    Hand That Rocks the Cradle, The (1991)
    People Under the Stairs, The (1991)
    Until the End of the World (1991)
    Love Crimes (1992)
    Traces of Red (1992)
    Body of Evidence (1993)
    Boxing Helena (1993)
    Crush, The (1993)
    Ghost in the Machine (1993)

Hard Target (1993)
Hear No Evil (1993)
Crow, The (1994)
No Escape (1994)
S.F.W. (1994)
Street Fighter (1994)
Basketball Diaries, The (1995)
Down Came a Blackbird (1995)
Killer: A Journal of Murder (1995)
Mighty Morphin Power Rangers: The
    Movie (1995)
Strange Days (1995)
Tank Girl (1995)
Tie That Binds, The (1995)
Craft, The (1996)
Crow 2: City of Angels, The (1996)
Fled (1996
From Dusk Till Dawn (1996)
Race the Sun (1996)
Saint, The (1997)
Spawn (1997)
Chinese Box (1997)

REYNOLDS, DAVE
    Blue Skies Are a Life (1995)

REYNOLDS, DAVID
    George B. (1997)

REZNOR, TRENT
    Natural Born Killers (1994)

RHOADES, JEFF
    Challenge the Wind (1990)

RICCARDI, SAVIO
    Le Venere de Willendorf (1997)

RICE, TIM
    Aladdin (1992)
    Lion King, The (1994)

RICE, TODD
    Pledge Night (1991)

RICHARDSON, THOMAS
    Clownhouse (1989)

RICHMAN, LUCAS
    Judgment Day (1989)

RIDGEWAY, STAN
    Futurekick (1991)

RIDLEN, MARK
Among the Dead (1995)

RIDOLFI, MARCO
Il Giardino Dei Ciliegi (The Cherry
    Orchard) (1992)

RIFLE, NED
Surviving Desire (1989)
Ambition (1991)
Theory of Achievement (1991)
Simple Men (1992)
Amateur (1994)
Flirt (1995)

RINGER, CATHERINE
Foreign Body, A (Sinon, Oui) (1997)

RIPARETTI, TONY
Dollman vs. Demonic Toys (1991)
Knights (1992)
Brain Smasher (1993)
Adrenalin: Fear the Rush (1995)
Postmortem (1997)

RIVERA, NICHOLAS
Saturday Night Special (1992)

ROBB, PAUL
Orgazmo (1997)

ROBBINS, DAVID
Too Much Sun (1990)
Ted and Venus (1991)
Bob Roberts (1992)
Twenty Bucks (1993)
Fast Getaway II (1994)
Dead Man Walking (1995)

ROBBINS, RICHARD
Slaves of New York (1989)
Mr. & Mrs. Bridge (1990)
Ballad of the Sad Cafe, The (1991)
Howards End (1992)
Remains of the Day, The (1993)
Jefferson in Paris (1995)
Proprietor, The (1996)
Surviving Piccaso (1996)

ROBERTS, ANDY
Priest (1994)
Mad Love (1995)
Kidnapping in the Family, A (1996)

Face (1997)

ROBERTS, MICHAEL
Mad Bomber in Love (1992)

ROBERTSON, ERIC N.
Millennium (1989)
Love and Hate: A Marriage Made in Hell
    (1990)
On Thin Ice: The Tai Babilonia Story
    (1990)
Black Fox (1995)
Holiday to Remember, A (1995)
Captains Courageous (1996)
Waiting for Michelangelo (1996)

ROBERTSON, ROBBIE
Jimmy Hollywood (1994)

ROBINSON, J. PETER
Desert Rats (1988)
Blind Fury (1989)
Gifted One, The (1989)
Wizard, The (1989)
Cadillac Man (1990)
When You Remember Me (1990)
Deadly Intentions . . . Again? (1991)
Hell Hath No Fury (1991)
Lightning Field (1991)
Are You Lonesome Tonight (1992)
Encino Man, The (1992)
President's Child, The (1992)
Wayne's World (1992)
With a Vengeance (1992)
Day My Parents Ran Away, The (1993)
Highlander III: The Sorcerer (1994)
Wes Craven's New Nightmare (1994)
Vampire in Brooklyn (1995)
Wes Craven Presents Mind Ripper
    (1995)
Buried Secrets (1996)
Generation X (1996)
Primal Fear (1996)
Rumble in the Bronx (1996)
First Strike (1997)
Mr. Nice Guy (1997)
Runaway Car (1997)

ROBINSON, LARRY
Fear of a Black Hat (1992)

ROBINSON, PETER MANNING
Penthouse, The (1989)

Small Sacrifices (1989)
In the Best Interest of the Child (1990)
And the Sea Will Tell (1991)
. . . And Then She Was Gone (1991)
Deception: A Mother's Secret (1991)
Night of the Hunter (1991)
Whatever Happened to Baby Jane?
   (1991)
Critters 4 (1992)
Honor Thy Mother (1992)
Danger Island (1992)
Willing to Kill: The Texas Cheerleader
   Story (1992)
Darkness Before Dawn (1993)
Family of Strangers, A (1993)
Other Women's Children (1993)
Woman on the Run: The Lawrencia
   Bembenek Story (1993)
Beans of Egypt, Maine, The (1994)
Beyond Obsession (1994)
Christmas Romance, A (1994)
Green Dolphin Beat (1994)
Presence, The (1994)
Deadlocked: Escape From Zone 14
   (1995)
Family of Cops (1995)
Maddening, The (1995)
Other Woman, The (1995)
Every Woman's Dream (1996)
Hit Me (1996)
Once You Meet a Stranger (1996)
Princess in Love, A (1996)
Season in Purgatory, A (1996)
Talk to Me (1996)
To Face Her Past (1996)
All the Winters That Have Been (1997)
Breach of Faith: A Family of Cops II
   (1997)
Echo (1997)
Keeping the Promise (1997)
Stepsister, The (1997)

ROBY, JOHN
Hanging Garden, The (1997)

ROCHE, YVES
Tabu: Dernier Voyage (1996)

RODGERS, NILE
Beverly Hills Cop III (1994)

RODGERS, RICHARD

Rodgers and Hammerstein's
   "Cinderella" (1997)

ROESSINGEN, KAREL
In the Company of Men (1997)

ROEWE, SCOTT
Ministry of Vengeance (1989)
True Blood (1989)

ROFFE, PATRICK
Baxter (1989)

ROGER, NORMAND
Champagne Safari, The (1995)

ROGERS, AL
Trial at Fortitude Bay (1994)
Angel of Pennsylvania Avenue, The
   (1996)
Cold Heart of a Killer, The (1996)

ROGERS, SIMON
Preppie Murder, The (1989)

ROHATYN, MICHAEL
Angela (1995)
Delta, The (1996)

ROMANELLI, ROLAND
Voices in the Garden (1992)

ROMANO, JOE
Fear, Anxiety and Depression (1989)
When the Party's Over (1992)
Strapped (1993)
Niagaravation (1996)

RONA, JEFF
Death in Small Doses (1995)
White Squall (1996)
House of Yes, The (1997)

ROQUES, JEAN-LOUIS
Germinal (1993)

ROSE, EARL
Mad Dog Time (1996)

ROSEN, ARTHUR
Cracking Up (1994)

ROSENBAUM, JOEL
  U.S. Marshals: Waco & Rhinehart
    (1987)
  Littlest Victims, The (1989)

ROSENBERG, BRETT
  Hotel de Love (1996)
  Diana and Me (1997)

ROSENMAN, LEONARD
  Robocop 2 (1990)
  Where Pigeons Go to Die (1990)
  Aftermath: A Test of Love (1991)
  Ambition (1991)
  Keeper of the City (1992)
  Face on the Milk Carton, The (1995)
  Mrs. Munck (1995)
  Levitation (1997)

ROSENTHAL, LAURENCE
  Fight for Life (1987)
  Downpayment on Murder (1987)
  Stranger in My Bed (1987)
  Brotherhood of the Rose (1989)
  Forgotten, The (1989)
  Gore Vidal's Billy the Kid (1989)
  My Name Is Bill W. (1989)
  Twist of Fate (1989)
  Blind Faith (1990)
  Incident, The (1990)
  Kissing Place, The (1990)
  Plot to Kill Hitler, The (1990)
  Mark Twain and Me (1991)
  Grass Roots (1992)
  Young Indiana Jones Chronicles, The
    (1992)
  Fire Next Time, The (1993)
  Triumph Over Disaster: The Hurricane
    Andrew Story (1993)
  Man Who Captured Eichmann, The
    (1996)
  Member of the Wedding, The (1997)

ROSS, JOHN
  Easy Wheels (1989)
  Sherlock Holmes: The Case of the
    Temporal Nexus (1996)
  Visions (1996)

ROSS, MATTHEW
  Carnal Crimes (1991)

ROSS, WILLIAM

One Good Cop (1991)
Look Who's Talking Now (1993)
Cops and Robertsons (1994)
Hans Christian Andersen's
  "Thumbelina" (1994)
Little Rascals, The (1994)
Amazing Panda Adventure, The (1995)
Black Sheep (1996)
Evening Star, The (1996)
My Fellow Americans (1996)
Tin Cup (1996)
Smile Like Yours, A (1997)

ROSSI, PAOLO
  Camerieri (Waiters) (1995)

ROSTON, MILES
  Mr. Write (1994)
  Steaming Milk (1997)

ROTA, NINO
  Godfather Part III, The (1990)

ROTH, ADAM
  National Lampoon's Favorite Deadly
    Sins (1995)

ROTH, WALTER CHRISTIAN
  Finest Hour, The (1992)
  Warriors (1993)

ROTTER, PETER FRANCIS
  Brain Dead (1990)
  Stardumb (1990)
  Mind Twister (1993)

ROUSSET, CHRISTOPHER
  Farinelli il Castrato (1994)

ROVEN, GLEN
  Life in the Food Chain (1992)

ROWE, HAHN
  Clean, Shaven (1993)

ROWLAND, BRUCE
  Cheetah (1989)
  Gunsmoke: The Last Apache (1990)
  Weekend With Kate (1990)
  Fast Getaway (1991)
  Which Way Home (1991)
  Gross Misconduct (1993)
  Andre (1994)

Lightning Jack (1994)
Great Elephant Escape, The (1995)
North Star (1996)
Flash (1997)
Tidal Wave: No Escape (1997)
Zeus and Roxanne (1997)

ROYCROFT, MAURICE
Boxer, The (1997)

RUBIN, LANCE
Incredible Hulk Returns, The (1988)
Trial of the Incredible Hulk, The (1989)
Death of the Incredible Hulk, The (1990)
Hexed (1993)

RUBINI, MICHEL
Hands of a Stranger (1987)
Moving Target (1988)
Unholy Matrimony (1988)
Haunting of Sarah Hardy, The (1989)
Not Quite Human II (1989)
Silhouette (1990)
Stranger in the Family (1991)
Fear Inside, The (1992)
Nemesis (1992)
Indecent Behavior 2 (1994)
Ride With the Wind (1994)
Blood Knot (1995)

RUBINSTEIN, ARTHUR B.
Agatha Christie's "The Man in the
    Brown Suit" (1989)
Baywatch: Panic at Malibu Pier (1989)
Guts and Glory: The Rise and Fall of
    Oliver North (1989)
Heist, The (1989)
Hollywood Detective, The (1989)
Unconquered (1989)
Murder in Black and White (1990)
Murder Times Seven (1990)
Crazy from the Heart (1991)
Fatal Friendship (1991)
Hard Way, The (1991)
Line of Fire: The Morris Dees Story
    (1991)
Danielle Steel's "Secrets" (1992)
When No One Would Listen (1992)
Another Stakeout (1993)
Caught in the Act (1993)
Double Trouble (1993)
Hart to Hart Returns (1993)
Hart to Hart: Crimes of the Hart (1994)

Hart to Hart: Home Is Where the Heart Is
    (1994)
Hart to Hart: Old Friends Never Die
    (1994)
Hart to Hart: Secrets of the Hart (1995)
Nick of Time (1995)
Double Jeopardy (1996)

RUBINSTEIN, DAVID
Sword of Honor (1994)

RUBINSTEIN, DONALD A.
Tales From the Darkside: The Movie
    (1990)

RUBINSTEIN, JOHN
Walton Wedding, A (1995)

RUCKER, STEVE
976-Evil (1989)
Syngenor (1990)
Little Nemo: Adventures in Slumberland
    (1992)

RUDDEL, BRUCE
Vendetta: Secrets of a Mafia Bride
    (1991)

RUGOLO, PETE
This World, Then the Fireworks (1997)

RUNDGREN, TODD
Dumb and Dumber (1994)

RUSHEN, PATRICE
Without You I'm Nothing (1990)
America's Dream (1995)

RUSSELL, JULIAN DYLAN
Ballot Measure 9 (1995)

RUSSELL, RAY
Down Among the Big Boys (1993)

RUSSELL-PAVIER, NICHOLAS
Secret Friends (1991)
Look Me in the Eye (1994)

RUSSO, DAVID
Shaking the Tree (1990)
Spaced Invaders (1990)
Angus (1995)
Soulmates (1997)

Sparkler (1997)

RYDER, MARK
  Dark Side of the Moon, The (1989)
  Trancers II: Return of Jack Deth (1991)
  Society (1992)
  Trancers III: Deth Lives (1992)

SACKER, GRAHAM
  Double Vision (1992)

SADLER, ERIC
  Just Another Girl on the I.R.T. (1992)

SAFAN, CRAIG
  Shootdown (1988)
  Comeback, The (1989)
  Enid Is Sleeping (aka Over Her Dead
    Body) (1990)
  Revenge of Al Capone, The (1989)
  Inconvenient Woman, An (1991)
  Long Road Home (1991)
  Mission of the Shark (1991)
  Son of the Morning Star (1991)
  Breaking the Silence (1992)
  Burden of Proof, The (1992)
  Live Wire (1992)
  Terror on Track 9 (1992)
  Conviction of Kitty Dodds, The (1993)
  Judgment Day: The John List Story
    (1993)
  Miracle Child (1993)
  Money for Nothing (1993)
  Prophet of Evil: The Ervil LeBaron Story
    (1993)
  Rio Shannon (1993)
  Roseanne & Tom: Behind the Scenes
    (1994)
  Where Are My Children? (1994)
  Without Consent (1994)
  Degree of Guilt (1995)
  Major Payne (1995)
  Different Kind of Christmas, A (1996)
  Mr. Wong (1996)
  Seduced by Madness: The Diane
    Borchardt Story (1996)
  Their Second Chance (1997)

SAINTE MARIE, BUFFY
  Where the Spirits Live (1991)

SAKAMOTO, RYUICHI
  Handmaid's Tale, The (1990)

Sheltering Sky, The (1990)
Tacones Lejanos (High Heels) (1991)
Tokyo Decadence (1991)
Wuthering Heights (1992)
Little Buddha (1993)
Wild Palms (1993)

SALEM, PETER
  Indian Summer (1996)
  Alive & Kicking (1997)

SALESSES, GERARD
  L'enfant des Nieges (Child of the Wild)
    (1996)

SALVAY, BENNETT
  Winnie (1988)
  Burning Bridges (1990)
  Sand Trap (1997)

SAMPSON, CALEB
  Fast, Cheap & Out of Control (1997)

SAMPSON, JONATHAN
  Jo-Jo at the Gate of Lions (1992)
  Wadeck's Mother's Friend's Son (1992)
  Tempete dans un verre d'eau (1997)

SAMS, JEREMY
  Persuasion (1995)

SAMSON, CEDRIC
  Mandela (1995)

SANBORN, DAVID
  Lethal Weapon 2 (1989)
  Lethal Weapon 3 (1992)

SAND, JAMES
  Alien From L.A. (1988)

SANDERS, RICH
  Dead Boyz Can't Fly (1992)

SANDOVAL, ARTURO
  Perez Family, The (1994)

SANDOVAL, BERNARDO
  Western (1997)

SANKO, ANTON
  Women & Men 2: Three Short Stories
    (1991)

Cousin Bobby (1992)
Dead Beat (1994)
Party Girl (1994)
Captive (1995)
Girl in the Cadillac (1995)
Live Nude Girls (1995)
Love Always (1996)
Occasional Hell, An (1996)
Ripe (1996)
Before Women Had Wings (1997)

SANTA MARIA, CARMEN
I Crave Rock & Roll (1996)

SANVOISIN, MICHAEL
As You Like It (1992)

SARANEC, CHRIS
Huck and the King of Hearts (1993)
Hourglass (1995)

SARDE, PHILIPPE
Lost Angels (1989)
Music Box(1989)
Reunion (1989)
Chambre e Part (Separate Bedrooms)
  (1990)
La Baule--Les Pins (1990)
Lord of the Flies (1990)
Eve of Destruction (1991)
Iran: Days of Crisis (1991)
J'embrasse Pas (I Don't Kiss) (1991)
La Vieille qui marchait dans la mer
  (1991)
L.627 (1992)
La Voix (The Voice) (1992)
L'Envers du Decor (Portrait of Pierre
  Guffroy) (1992)
Max et Jeremie (Max and Jeremy) (1992)
Un Coeur en Hiver (A Heart of Stone)
  (1992)
La Petite Apocalypse (1993)
Le Jeune Werther (Young Werther)
  (1993)
Ma Saison Preferee (My Favorite
  Season) (1993)
La Fille de D'Artagnan (Daughter of
  D'Artagnan) (1994)
Le Fils Prefere (The Favorite Son)
  (1994)
Uncovered (1994)
Le Petit Garcon (1995)
Les Miserables (1995)

Nelly & Mr. Arnaud (1995)
Say Yes (1995)
Les Voleurs (Thieves) (1996)
Ponette (1996)
K (1997)
Le Bossu (On Guard!) (1997)
Lucie Aubrac (1997)
Un Frere (1997)

SARHANDI, SARAH
London Kills Me (1991)

SARNE, CLAUDIA
Punk and the Princess, The (1993)

SAUNDERS, TONY
Farmer & Chase (1995)

SAVALL, JORDI
Tous les Matins du Monde (1992)
Jeanne la Pucelle (Joan of Arc) (1994)
Marquise (1997)

SAWYER, PHIL
Twenty-One (1991)

SCHAFER, KARL-HEINZ
Street of No Return (1991)

SCHAMBERG, KIM
Lies of the Heart: The Story of Laurie
  Kellogg (1994)

SCHANKER, LARRY
Fakebook (1989)

SCHELL, JOHNNY LEE
Black Day Blue Night (1995)

SCHELLENBERG, GLENN
Zero Patience (1993)

SCHIFF, DON
Live! From Death Row (1992)
Pornographer, The (1994)

SCHIFF, STEVE
Lena's Holiday (1991)
Waxwork II: Lost in Time (1992)

SCHIFRIN, LALO
Little White Lies (1989)
Neon Empire, The (1989)

Original Sin (1989)
Face to Face (1990)
FX 2--The Deadly Art of Illusion (1991)
Woman Named Jackie, A (1991)
Beverly Hillbillies, The (1993)
Manhattan Merenge (1995)
Scorpion Spring (1995)
Mission: Impossible (1996)
Money Talks (1997)

SCHLOSS, ZANDOR
El Patrullero (Highway Patrolman)
(1991)
Winner, The (1996)

SCHLOSSBERG, BENOIT
L'Amour (Love) (1990)
Mes dix-sept Ans (I Was Seventeen)
(1996)

SCHMIDT, KENDALL
Chain, The (1996)

SCHMITT, JEFFREY
Backfire! (1994)

SCHNITTKE, ALFRED
Hantises (Hauntings) (1997)

SCHOEN, GAIL
Deja Vu (1997)

SCHOENBERG, ARNOLD
From Today Until Tomorrow (1997)

SCHOLES, PETER
Desperate Remedies (1993)

SCHULER, LEROY
True American, A (1996)

SCHULLER, GUNTHER
Face Down (1997)

SCHULTZ, CARL
Manufacturing Consent: Noam Chomsky
and the Media (1992)

SCHURMANN, GERARD
Gambler, The (1997)

SCHURTZ, CARL
Sweethearts (1997)

Morella (1997)

SCHUTZE, PAUL
Prisoner of St. Petersburg, The (1989)
Driving Force (1990)

SCHWARTZ, ALAN
Hotel Manor Inn, The (1996)

SCHWARTZ, DAVID
Dead Man's Revenge (1994)
Magic in the Water (1995)

SCHWARTZ, ISAAC
Young Catherine (1991)

SCHWARTZ, NAN
Spy (1989)
Take My Daughters, Please (1988)
Turn Back the Clock (1989)
Coins in the Fountain (1990)
Deadly Desire (1991)
Writer's Block (1991)

SCHWARTZ, PAUL
Ratchet (1996)

SCHWARTZ-MISHKIN, NAN
Complex of Fear (1993)
Cagney & Lacey: Together Again (1995)
Deadly Family Secrets (1995)
Color Me Perfect (1996)
Prison of Secrets (1997)
Something Borrowed, Something Blue
(1997)

SCHYMAN, GARRY
Hit List (1989)
Horseplayer, The (1990)
Last Hour, The (1991)
Revenge of the Nerds III: The Next
Generation (1992)
Lost in Africa (1993)
Day of Reckoning (1994)
Revenge of the Nerds IV: Nerds in Love
(1994)
Robin Cook's "Mortal Fear" (1994)
Deadly Invasion: The Killer Bee
Nightmare (1995)
Robin Cook's "Virus" (1995)
Robin Cook's "Terminal" (1996)
Tornado! (1996)
NightScream (1997)

SCHYZOMANIAC
Doberman (1997)

SCIACOLLA, DUANE
Roots of Evil (1991)

SCIAQUA, DUANE
Evil Spirits (1991)

SCIARRA, DANY
Undying Love (1991)

SCOTT, DANIEL
Bonjour Timothy (1995)
Whole in the Moon, The (1996)

SCOTT, GARY
Fulfillment of Mary Gray, The (1989)
Deceptions (1990)
Write to Kill (1991)

SCOTT, GARY STEVAN
3 Ninjas Knuckle Up (1995)

SCOTT, JOHN
Black Rainbow (1989)
Red King, White Knight (1989)
Winter People (1989)
Dog Tags (1990)
Journey of Honor (1990)
Becoming Colette (1992)
Ruby (1992)
Alistair MacLean's "Night Watch"
    (1995)
Far From Home: The Adventures of
    Yellow Dog (1995)
Deadly Voyage (1996)
Rudyard Kipling's "The Second Jungle
    Book" (1997)
Mill on the Floss, The (1997)
20,000 Leagues Under the Sea (1997)

SCOTT, ROBERT
Hayseed (1997)

SCOTT, TOM
Final Notice (1989)
Mothers, Daughters and Lovers (1989)
It's Nothing Personal (1993)
Percy and Thunder (1993)
Deconstructing Sarah (1994)
Mother's Prayer, A (1995)
Unexpected Family, An (1996)

SCOTTO, VINCENT
Le Roman de Renard (1929-1941)
    (1990)

SCULLION, MICHAEL
Jack Brown, Genius (1995)

SEARS, PETE
Fight in the Fields, The (1997)

SEEBER, ECKHART
To the Ends of Time (1996)

SEEGER, PETE
Harry Bridges: A Man and His Union
    (1992)

SEEZER, MAURICE
Boxer, The (1997)

SEGAL, MISHA
Phantom of the Opera, The (1989)
Men of Respect (1990)
Babies (1990)
Matters of the Heart (1990)
Body Language (1992)
Jersey Girl (1992)
Jonathan: The Boy Nobody Wanted
    (1992)
With Murder in Mind (1992)
Firestorm: 72 Hours in Oakland (1993)
Seventh Coin, The (1993)
She Led Two Lives (1994)
Colony, The (1996)
Have You Seen My Son? (1996)

SEKACZ, ILONA
Back Home (1990)
Common Pursuit (1991)
Countess Alice (1992)
Pin for the Butterfly, A (1994)
Antonia's Line (1995)
Mrs. Dalloway (1997)
Under the Skin (1997)

SELMECZI, GYORGY
Long Shadow, The (1992)

SEMBELLO, MICHAEL
Think Big (1990)

SEMKO, JAY
Due South (1994)

SENIA, JEAN-MARIE
 Elles n'oublient pas (Love in the
  Strangest Way) (1994)
 Diary of a Seducer (1995)
 Montana Blues (1996)
 Un Ete a la Goulette (1996)
 C'est Pour la Bonne Cause (1997)

SEPE, DANIELE
 Il Caricatore (The Reel) (1996)

SEPE, KEVIN
 Miami Hustle (1996)

SEREDA, JOHN
 Lotus Eaters, The (1993)

SERIO, RENATO
 Russicum (The Third Solution) (1989)

SERIOUS, YAHOO
 Reckless Kelly (1993)

SERRA, ERIC
 La Femme Nikita (1990)
 Atlantis (1991)
 Leon (The Professional) (1994)
 Goldeneye (1995)
 Professional, The (1995)
 Fifth Element, The (1997)

SERREAU, COLINE
 La Belle Verte (Visit to a Green Planet)
  (1996)

SEYMOUR, PATRICK
 No Worries (1993)
 Chantilly Lace (1993)
 Parallel Lives (1994)
 Night Eyes 4: Fatal Passion (1995)
 Critical Choices (1996)
 End of Summer (1997)
 Inspirations (1997)
 Northern Lights (1997)
 Tricks (1997)

SHAFER, KARL-HEINZ
 Vent d'Est (East Wind) (1992)

SHAIMAN, MARC
 When Harry Met Sally . . . (1989)
 Misery (1990)
 Addams Family, The (1991)

City Slickers (1991)
Scenes From a Mall (1991)
Few Good Men, A (1992)
Mr. Saturday Night (1992)
Sister Act (1992)
Addams Family Values (1993)
Heart and Souls (1993)
Sleepless in Seattle (1993)
City Slickers II: The Legend of Curly's
 Gold (1994)
North (1994)
Speechless (1994)
That's Entertainment III (1994)
American President, The (1995)
Forget Paris (1995)
Stuart Saves His Family (1995)
Bogus (1996)
First Wives Club, The (1996)
Ghosts of Mississippi (1996)
Mother (1996)
George of the Jungle (1997)
In & Out (1997)

SHAPIRO, COLIN
 Skeleton Coast (1988)

SHAPIRO, PAUL
 Watermelon Woman, The (1997)

SHAPIRO, THEODORE
 Hurricane Street (1997)
 Six Ways to Sunday (1997)

SHARAFI, JAMSHIED
 Harriet the Spy (1996)

SHARK
 I Shot a Man in Vegas (1995)

SHARPE, JENNIFER
 Go Fish (1994)

SHAW, JIM
 Goldy II: The Saga of the Golden Bear
  (1996)

SHEARER, HARRY
 Waiting for Guffman (1996)

SHEARMUR, EDWARD
 Cement Garden, The (1992)
 Tales From the Crypt Presents Demon
  Knight (1995)

Leading Man, The (1996)
Remember Me? (1996)
Hunchback, The (1997)
Wings of the Dove, The (1997)

SHEFFER, JONATHAN
  Bloodhounds of Broadway (1989)
  Dinner at Eight (1989)
  Intimate Stranger (1991)
  Pure Luck (1991)
  Omen IV: The Awakening (1991)

SHEHAN, STEVE
  Bye-Bye (1995)

SHELLER, WILLIAM
  Arlette (1997)

SHELSTAD, KIRBY
  Ernest Goes to Jail (1990)
  Ernest Rides Again (1993)

SHEPP, ARCHIE
  Foreign Body, A (Sinon, Oui) (1997)

SHERIFF, JAMIE
  Bad Jim (1990)
  Slumber Party Massacre 3 (1990)

SHERMAN, GARY
  Call Me Anna (1990)

SHERMAN, RICHARD M. & ROBERT B.
  Little Nemo: Adventures in Slumberland
    (1992)

SHIELDS, MARK
  American Beer (1996)

SHIRE, DAVID
  Mayflower Madam (1987)
  I Know My First Name Is Steven (1989)
  Women of Brewster Place, The (1989)
  Always Remember I Love You (1990)
  Big One: The Great Los Angeles
    Earthquake, The (1990)
  Common Ground (1990)
  Kennedys of Massachusetts, The (1990)
  Promise to Keep, A (1990)
  Boys, The (1991)
  Broadway Bound (1991)
  Paris Trout (1991)
  Sarah, Plain and Tall (1991)

Bed & Breakfast (1992)
Bed of Lies (1992)
Four Eyes and Six-Guns (1992)
Horton Foote's "The Habitation of
  Dragons" (1992)
Last Wish (1992)
Neil Simon's "Broadway Bound" (1992)
Nightmare in the Daylight (1992)
Something to Live For: The Alison Gertz
  Story (1992)
Barbara Taylor Bradford's "Remember"
  (1993)
Bloodlines: Murder in the Family (1993)
Danielle Steel's "Heartbeat" (1993)
Sidekicks (1993)
Skylark (1993)
Companion, The (1994)
Danielle Steel's "Once in a Lifetime"
  (1994)
Jane's House (1994)
Lily in Winter (1994)
Reunion (1994)
Almost Golden: The Jessica Savitch
  Story (1995)
Heidi Chronicles, The (1995)
Larry McMurtry's "Streets of Laredo"
  (1995)
Man Who Wouldn't Die, The (1995)
Murderous Intent (1995)
My Antonia (1995)
My Brother's Keeper (1995)
One Night Stand (1995)
Serving in Silence: The Margarethe
  Cammermeyer Story (1995)
Tecumseh: The Last Warrior (1995)
Neil Simon's "Jake's Women" (1996)
Horton Foote's "Alone" (1997)
Last Stand at Saber River (1997)
Ms. Scrooge (1997)
To Dance With Olivia (1997)

SHOCKLEE, HANK
  Juice (1992)

SHORE, HOWARD
  Innocent Man, An (1989)
  Lemon Sisters, The (1989)
  She-Devil (1989)
  Signs of Life (1989)
  Postcards From the Edge (1990)
  Quick Change (1990)
  Kiss Before Dying, A (1991)
  Naked Lunch (1991)

Silence of the Lambs, The (1991)
Prelude to a Kiss (1992)
Guilty as Sin (1993)
M. Butterfly (1993)
Mrs. Doubtfire (1993)
Philadelphia (1993)
Single White Female (1992)
Sliver (1993)
Client, The (1994)
Ed Wood (1994)
Nobody's Fool (1994)
Crash (1995)
Moonlight and Valentino (1995)
Seven (1995)
White Man's Burden (1995)
Before and After (1996)
Looking for Richard (1996)
Striptease (1996)
That Thing You Do (1996)
Truth About Cats and Dogs, The (1996)
Cop Land (1997)
Game, The (1997)

SHORE, RICHARD
Victim of Love (1991)

SHRAGGE, LAWRENCE
Smoke Screen (1988)
Beautiful Dreamers (1990)
Miracle on I-880 (1993)
Whose Child Is This?: The War for Baby
Jessica (1993)
For the Love of Aaron (1994)
Spoils of War (1994)
Star Struck (1994)
Blue River (1995)
Ebbie (1995)
Horse for Danny, A (1995)
Intimate Relations (1995)
Johnny's Girl (1995)
Ranger, the Cook and a Hole in the Sky,
The (1995)
Redwood Curtain (1995)
Secrets (1995)
Deliverance of Elaine, The (1996)
Her Desperate Choice (1996)
Maternal Instincts (1996)
Night of the Twisters (1996)
What Kind of Mother Are You? (1996)
All Lies End in Murder (1997)
Assistant, The (1997)
Barbara Taylor Bradford's "Love in
Another Town" (1997)

Clover (1997)
Sweetest Gift, The (1997)
William Faulkner's "Old Man" (1997)

SHREEVE, MARK
Honor Bound (1989)

SHRIEVE, MICHAEL
Take, The (1990)

SHTELEV, MITKO
Berlin Conspiracy, The (1990)

SHUTZE, PAUL
Siege of Firebase Gloria, The (1989)

SICILIANO, FABRIZIO
La Grande Quercia (The Wide Oak)
(1997)
Vacation in Hell (1997)

SIDRAN, BEN
Hoop Dreams (1994)

SILBERT, TONY
Vermont Is for Lovers (1992)
Scenes From the New World (1994)

SILIOTTO, CARLO
Di Ceria dell'Untore (The Plague Tower)
(1992)
La Corsa dell'Innocente (1992)
Fluke (1995)
Luna e l'Altra (1996)
Palla di Neve (Snowball) (1996)
David (1997)
Directors on Directors (1997)

SILL, GREGORY
For the Very First Time (1991)

SILL, JOEL
Hangin' With the Homeboys (1991)

SILVER, SHEILA
Alligator Eyes (1990)
Dead Funny (1995)

SILVERMAN, JEFFREY
Taxi Dancers (1993)

SILVESTRI, ALAN
Abyss, The (1989)

Back to the Future Part II (1989)
She's Out of Control (1989)
Back to the Future Part III (1990)
Downtown (1990)
Predator 2 (1990)
Young Guns II (1990)
Dutch (1991)
Father of the Bride (1991)
Ricochet (1991)
Shattered (1991)
Soapdish (1991)
Bodyguard, The (1992)
Death Becomes Her (1992)
Ferngully . . . The Last Rainforest (1992)
Stop! Or My Mom Will Shoot (1992)
And the Band Played On (1993)
Cop and a Half (1993)
Grumpy Old Men (1993)
Judgment Night (1993)
Sidekicks (1993)
Super Mario Bros. (1993)
Blown Away (1994)
Clean Slate (1994)
Forrest Gump (1994)
Perez Family, The (1994)
Richie Rich (1994)
Father of the Bride, Part II (1995)
Grumpier Old Men (1995)
Judge Dredd (1995)
Quick and the Dead, The (1995)
Eraser (1996)
Long Kiss Goodnight, The (1996)
Sgt. Bilko (1996)
Contact (1997)
Fools Rush In (1997)
Mouse Hunt (1997)
Volcano (1997)

SILVESTRI, DANIELE
  Couri al Verde (Penniless Hearts) (1996)

SILVESTRI, PAOLO
  Peggio di Cosi si Muore (1995)

SIMON, CARLY
  Postcards From the Edge (1990)
  This Is My Life (1992)

SIMON, LUCY
  Positively True Adventures of the
    Alleged Texas Cheerleader-Murdering
    Mom, The (1993)

SIMON, MARTY
  Eddie and the Cruisers II: Eddie Lives
    (1989)
  Squamish Fire, The (1989)
  Deadly Surveillance (1991)
  George's Island (1991)
  Scanners II: The New Order (1991)
  Quiet Killer (1992)
  Scanners III: The Takeover (1992)
  Paint Cans (1994)
  Relative Fear (1994)
  Wrong Woman, The (1996)

SIMON, YVES
  Apres l'Amour (Love After Love) (1992)

SIMONEC, TIM
  Suicide Kings (1997)

SINGER, RAY
  Tender Loving Care (1993)

SINGER, SCOTT
  Naked Obsession (1991)
  Midnight Confessions (1993)

SITRON, JOSHUA
  Strong Island Boys (1997)

SKIES, RONI
  Next Step, The (1996)

SKINNER, DAVID
  Roly Poly Man, The (1994)

SKLOFF, MICHAEL
  Here Come the Munsters (1995)
  Lovemaster, The (1997)

SKUBISZEWSKI, CEZARY
  Lilian's Story (1996)

SLANE, ROD
  All-American Murder (1992)

SLIDER, DAN
  Russian Roulette (1993)
  For the Love of Nancy (1994)
  Touched by Evil (1997)

SMALL, MICHAEL
  See You in the Morning (1988)
  Mountains of the Moon (1989)

American Dream (1990)
Mobsters (1991)
Consenting Adults (1992)
Alex Haley's "Queen" (1993)
Wagons East! (1994)

SMALLA, UMBERTO
Sognando la California (California
Dreaming) (1993)

SMALLEY, STEVEN SCOTT
Disturbed (1990)

SMART, CHRIS
Personal Choice (1989)

SMART, ROBERT
Time Runner (1992)
Ultimate Desires (1992)

SMILEY, NICHOLAS
Buffalo Jump (1992)

SMITH, BRADLEY
Summertime Switch (1994)

SMITH, DARDEN
Barbecue: A Love Story (1997)

SMITH, JOSEPH
Animal Behavior (1992)
Mirror Images (1992)
Other Woman, The (1992)

SMITH, MICHAEL R.
Unborn, The (1991)
Bikini Car Wash Company 2, The (1992)
Moondance (1992)
Cosmos (1996)

SMITH, PAUL ANTHONY
Violet's Visit (1997)

SMITH, REX TAYLOR
Gunrunner, The (1989)

SMITH, SCOTT THOMAS
November Men, The (1993)

SMOLAR, NEIL
Boys of St. Vincent, The (1993)
Captive Heart: The James Mink Story
(1996)

SNEDDON, GREG
Sword of Honour (1990)

SNOW, MARK
Murder by the Book (1987)
Roman Holiday (1987)
Goodbye, Miss 4th of July (1988)
Scandal in a Small Town (1988)
Everybody's Baby: The Rescue of
Jessica McClure (1989)
Settle the Score (1989)
Stuck With Each Other (1989)
Those She Left Behind (1989)
When He's Not a Stranger (1989)
Archie: To Riverdale and Back Again
(1990)
Child in the Night (1990)
Crash: The Mystery of Flight 1501 (1990)
Dead Reckoning (1990)
Follow Your Heart (1990)
Girl Who Came Between Them, The
(1990)
In the Line of Duty: A Cop for the
Killing (1990)
Little Kidnappers, The (1990)
Lost Capone, The (1990)
Miracle Landing (1990)
Opposites Attract (1990)
Dead and Alive: The Race for Gus
Farace (1991)
Gambler Returns: The Luck of the Draw,
The (1991)
In the Line of Duty: Manhunt in the
Dakotas (1991)
Living a Lie (1991)
Marla Hanson Story, The (1991)
Rape of Dr. Willis, The (1991)
White Hot: The Mysterious Murder of
Thelma Todd (1991)
Wife, Mother, Murderer: The Marie
Hilley Story (1991)
American Story, An (1992)
Battling for Baby (1992)
Danger of Love, The (1992)
Deliver Them From Evil: The Taking of
Alta View (1992)
Dolly Dearest (1992)
Her Final Fury: Betty Broderick The Last
Chapter (1992)
Highway Heartbreaker (1992)
In the Line of Duty: Street War (1992)
Taste for Killing, A (1992)

Woman Scorned: The Betty Broderick
  Story, A (1992)
Born Too Soon (1993)
Disappearance of Nora, The (1993)
Father & Son: Dangerous Relations
  (1993)
In the Line of Duty: Ambush at Waco
  (1993)
Last POW? The Bobby Garwood Story,
  The (1993)
Man With Three Wives, The (1993)
Precious Victims (1993)
Scattered Dreams (1993)
Telling Secrets (1993)
Caroline at Midnight (1994)
Following Her Heart (1994)
Heart of a Child (1994)
In the Line of Duty: The Price of
  Vengeance (1994)
Moment of Truth: Caught in the
  Crossfire (1994)
Moment of Truth: Cradle of Conspiracy
  (1994)
Murder Between Friends (1994)
Oldest Living Confederate Widow Tells
  All (1994)
Place for Annie, A (1994)
Playmaker (1994)
Shadows of Desire (1994)
Substitute Wife, The (1994)
Witness to the Execution (1994)
Born to Be Wild (1995)
Children of the Dust (aka A Good Day to
  Die) (1995)
Danielle Steel's "Mixed Blessings"
  (1995)
Down, Out & Dangerous (1995)
In the Line of Duty: Hunt for Justice
  (1995)
Other Mother, The: A Moment of Truth
  Movie (1995)
Seduced and Betrayed (1995)
Stranger in Town, A (1995)
Texas Justice (1995)
Trial by Fire (1995)
Unspoken Truth, The (1995)
Conundrum (1996)
Forgotten Sins (1996)
In the Line of Duty: Smoke Jumpers
  (1996)
Loss of Innocence, A (1996)
Project: ALF (1996)
Special Report: Journey to Mars (1996)

Summer of Fear (1996)
Sweet Temptation (1996)
Cloned (1997)
Jules Verne's "20,000 Leagues Under the
  Sea" (1997)
Night Sins (1997)
Payback (1997)
Perfect Mother, The (1997)
Price of Heaven, The (1997)

SNYDER, STEPHEN
  Victor's Big Score (1992)

SOBEL, CURT
  Cast a Deadly Spell (1991)
  Defenseless (1991)
  Treacherous Crossing (1992)
  Nurses on the Line: The Crash of Flight
    7 (1993)
  Betrayal of Trust (1994)
  Body Count (1997)

SOLAL, MARTIAL
  Jean Seberg, American Actress (1995)

SOLDATINI, MARIA
  Nerolio (1996)

SOLES, STEVE
  Silent Night, Deadly Night 3: Better
    Watch Out (1989)
  Destiny Turns on the Radio (1995)
  Georgia (1995)
  Tommy Boy (1995)
  Don't Look Back (1996)

SOLOMON, ELLIOT
  Black Roses (1988)
  Martial Law (1991)

SOLOMON, MARIBETH
  Blue Planet (1990)
  Hang Tough (1990)
  Women of Windsor, The (1992)
  Shattered Trust: The Shari Karney Story
    (1993)
  Trial & Error (1993)
  Destiny in Space (1994)
  I Know My Son Is Alive (1994)
  To Save the Children (1994)
  Treacherous Beauties (1994)
  Dancing in the Dark (1995)
  Deadly Love (1995)

Friends at Last (1995)
Lady Killer, The (1995)
Picture Perfect (1995)
Silence of Adultery, The (1995)
Visitors of the Night (1995)
Closer and Closer (1996)
Hostile Advances: The Kerry Ellison
   Story (1996)
Morrison Murders, The (1996)

SOLTI, SIR GEORG
Anna Karenina (1997)

SOMMER, MARC
La Sentinelle (The Sentinel) (1992)

SONDHEIM, STEPHEN
Dick Tracy (1990)

SONIS, DAN
Shot, The (1996)

SORRET, LODOVICO
What Happened Was . . . (1994)
Wife, The (1995)

SOUTHALL, GEOFF
Boy Meets Girl (1994)

SOUTHON, SONNY
Pleasure Principle, The (1991)

SPEAR, DAVID
No Return, No Surrender II (1989)

SPEER, PAUL
Daredreamer (1990)
To Cross the Rubicon (1991)

SPEKTOR, MIRA J.
Double Edge (1992)

SPILLANE, DAVY
Disappearance of Finbar, The (1996)

SPOTTS, ROGER HAMILTON
Importance of Being Earnest, The (1991)

SPRAYBERRY, ROBERT
Quick (1993)
Passion to Kill, A (1994)
Bodily Harm (1995)

SPRINGER, MARK
London Kills Me (1991)

SPRINGER, ODETTE
Me Myself and I (1992)
Raiders of the Sun (1992)

STACEY, PAUL
Dakota Road (1990)

STAFFORD, BILL
My Own Private Idaho (1991)

STAHL, MICHAEL
Roy Cohn/Jack Smith (1994)

STANDISH, JOHN
Laser Moon (1992)

STANK, ALEXANDRE
Malarek: A Street Kid Who Made It
   (1989)

STARK, LISA HARLOW
Freaky Friday (1995)

STEARNS, MICHAEL
Baraka (1992)
Temptress (1995)
Thrill Ride: The Science of Fun (1997)

STEELE, DAVID
Black & White & Red All Over (1997)

STEIN, DANIEL
Triplecross (1995)

STEINBERG, ADAM
North End, The (1997)

STEMPLE, JAMES WESLEY
Damned River (1990)
Adventures in Spying (1992)
Frank and Ollie (1995)

STERLING, JOHN
Under the Gun (1988)
L.A. Bounty (1989)

STERN, PHILIP
Understudy: Graveyard Shift II, The
   (1989)

STERN, STEVEN M.
    Sweet Nothing (1995)

STEVENS, MORTON
    Ladies, The (1987)
    Act of Piracy (1990)

STEVENS, STEVE
    Dogtown (1997)

STEWART, DAVID A.
    Rooftops (1989)
    No Worries (1993)
    Ref, The (1994)
    Showgirls (1995)
    Beautiful Girls (1996)

STEWART, GREG
    Freeway Maniac, The (1989)

STEWART, PAUL
    Phat Beach (1996)

STEYER, CHRISTIAN
    Das Lieben Ist Eine Baustelle (1997)

STINSON, HARRY
    XXX's & OOO's (1994)

STIRLING, NICHOLAS
    Last Supper, The (1994)

STOCKDALE, GARY
    Dance of the Damned (1989)
    Necromancer (1989)
    Savage Beach (1989)
    Stripped to Kill 2 (1989)
    Nothing Sacred (1997)

STONE, CHRISTOPHER
    Survival Quest (1989)
    Phantasm II: Lord of the Dead (1991)
    Munsters' Scary Little Christmas, The
        (1996)
    Special Effects (1996)
    Stupids, The (1996)

STONE, LAURIE
    Flood: Who Will Save Our Children?,
        The (1993)
    Official Denial (1993)

STONE, LAWRENCE

Sahara (1995)
Thorn Birds: The Missing Years, The
    (1996)

STONE, RICHARD
    Never on Tuesday (1989)
    No Holds Barred (1989)
    Sundown: The Vampire in Retreat
        (1990)
    Vietnam, Texas (1990)
    In a Child's Name (1991)

STORA, JEAN-PIERRE
    Peche Veniel . . . Peche Mortel . . .
        (1994)

STOREY, MICHAEL
    Just Like a Woman (1992)
    Losing Track (1992)
    Wavelength (1996)

STORM, YALE
    Life Apart: Hasidism in America, A
        (1997)

STRANGIO, FRANK
    Encounters (1994)
    Lex and Rory (1994)
    Sex Is a Four-Letter Word (1995)

STRAUSS, JOHN
    Impromptu (1991)

STRAVINSKY, IGOR
    La Belle Noiseuse (1991)

STREISAND, BARBRA
    Mirror Has Two Faces, The (1996)

STRIMPLE, NICK
    Iron Triangle, The (1989)

STROBEL, FRANK
    Young Poisoner's Handbook, The (1995)

STROMBERG, WILLIAM T.
    Order of the Eagle (1989)
    Deadly Dancer (1990)
    Edge of Honor (1991)
    Silent Victim (1992)
    Minotaur (1994)
    Trinity and Beyond (1995)

STRONG, PHILLIP
Skull: A Night of Terror (1989)

STROUSE, CHARLES
All Dogs Go to Heaven (1989)
Bye Bye Birdie (1995)

STRUBLE, EDGAR
Gambler V: Playing for Keeps, The
(1994)
MacShayne: Final Roll of the Dice
(1994)
MacShayne: Winner Takes All (1994)
Big Dreams & Broken Hearts: The
Dottie West Story (1995)
Joe & Joe (1995)

STRUMMER, JOE
When Pigs Fly (1993)
Grosse Pointe Blank (1997)

STRUNZ, JORGE
Drug Wars: The Camarena Story (1990)

STYLES, MARK
Night Owl (1993)

STYNE, JULE
Gypsy (1993)

SUBRAMANIAM, L.
Mississippi Masala (1991)

SUEIRO, JUAN
Going Ballistic (1997)

SUMMERS, ANDY
Weekend at Bernie's (1989)
Motorama (1991)

SUMMERS, BOB
Goin' to Chicago (1990)
Murder by Numbers (1990)
Frame Up (1991)
Frame-up II: The Cover-up (1992)

SUOZZO, MARC
Metropolitan (1990)
Barcelona (1994)
Nick and Jane (1997)

SURES, RON
Silencer, The (1992)

I Love a Man in Uniform (1993)
Long Day's Journey Into Night (1996)
Joe's so Mean to Josephine (1997)

SUSSMAN, BRUCE
Hans Christian Andersen's
"Thumbelina" (1994)
Pebble and the Penguin, The (1995)

SUTEU, ANTON
Unforgettable Summer, An (1994)

SWADOS, ELIZABETH
Under Heat (1994)

SWINDLER, WILLIAM
Prisoners of Inertia (1989)

SWINGHAMMER, KURT
Cockroach That Ate Cincinnati, The
(1996)

SYREWICZ, STANISLAS
Adventures of William Tell, The (1989)
Stalin (1992)
Paper Marriage (1993)
Kidnapped (1995)
True Blue (1996)
Shooting Fish (1997)

SZMADZINSKI, JAMII
Street Justice (1989)

TABACCHI, GIAN ANDREA
Growing Artichokes in Mimongo (1996)

TABRIZI, DAVOOD
Resistance (1992)
Floating Life (1996)

TAFAR, JORGE
Eight Hundred Leagues Down the
Amazon (1993)

TAJ MAHAL
Zebrahead (1992)

TAKEMITSU, TORU
Kuroi Ame (Black Rain) (1989)
Rising Sun (1993)

TALBOT, BILLY
Confessions of a Hit Man (1994)

TALGORN, FREDERIC
  Edge of Sanity (1989)
  Buried Alive (1990)
  Delta Force 2 (1990)
  Robot Jox (1991)
  Fortress (1993)
  Temp, The (1993)
  Angels in the Endzone (1997)

TALLMAN, ROGER
  Hail Caesar (1994)

TANGERINE DREAM
  Catch Me If You Can (1989)
  Miracle Mile (1989)
  Rainbow Drive (1990)
  Highway to Hell (1992)
  Switch, The (1993)

TARDIF, GRAHAM
  Bad Boy Bubby (1993)
  Quiet Room, The (1997)

TATGENHORST, JOHN
  Demon Possessed (1993)

TATRO, DUANE
  Deadly Deception (1987)

TAVERA, MICHAEL
  Frozen Assets (1992)
  Bitter Harvest (1993)
  Honey, We Shrunk Ourselves! (1996)
  No One Would Tell (1996)
  Dying to Belong (1997)
  Holiday in Your Heart (1997)
  Mr. Magoo (1997)
  Rocketman (1997)
  Two Came Back (1997)

TAYLOR, JEFFREY
  Amateur (1994)
  Flirt (1995)

TAYLOR, JOHN
  Mi Vida Loca (1993)

TAYLOR, STEPHEN JAMES
  To Sleep With Anger (1990)
  Giving, The (1991)
  Glass Shield, The (1994)
  Divas (1995)
  Piano Lesson, The (1995)

Nightjohn (1996)

TCHAIKOVSKY, PYOTR ILYICH
  George Balanchine's "The Nutcracker"
    (1993)
  Imax Nutcracker, The (1997)

TEETSEL, FREDRIC
  Haunting of Morella, The (1990)
  Adventures in Dinosaur City (1992)

TEJADA-FLORES, MIGUEL
  House in the Hills, A (1993)

TELSON, BOB
  Rosalie Goes Shopping (1989)
  Salmonberries (1991)

TEMPLE, TIM
  Blood Savage (1990)

TENAS, GERMINAL
  Justinien Trouve, ou le Bastard de Dieu
    (1993)

TENBROEK, NICHOLAS
  American Ninja 4: The Annihilation
    (1991)

TENNEY, DENNIS MICHAEL
  Witchtrap (1989)
  Witchboard 2: The Devil's Doorway
    (1993)

TERMINI, RICHARD
  Mac (1992)
  States of Control (1997)

TESH, JOHN
  Limit Up (1990)

TEXIER, HENRI
  Le Cri du Coeur (The Heart's Cry)
    (1994)

THERIAULT, MICHAEL
  Pale Saints (1997)

THIRIET, BEATRICE
  L'age des Possibles (The Age of
    Potential) (1996)
  Still Waters Run Deep (1996)
  L'autre Cote de la Mer (1997)

THOMAS, CHRISTOPHER
There's Nothing Out There (1992)

THOMAS, IAN
Oh, What a Night (1992)
Ghost Mom (1993)
Boulevard (1994)
Hostage for a Day (1994)
Soft Deceit (1994)
Bloodknot (1995)
Falling From the Sky! Flight 174 (1995)
Hijacked: Flight 285 (1996)
Pale Saints (1997)

THOMAS, JOE
Perfect Model, The (1989)

THOMAS, MARK
One Full Moon (1991)
Wild Justice (1994)
Daisies in December (1995)
Making of Maps, The (1995)
Cameleon (1997)
Twin Town (1997)
Up 'n' Under (1997)

THOMPSON, BILL
Shoemaker (1996)

THOMPSON, LINDA
Little Rascals, The (1994)

THOMPSON, RICHARD
Sweet Talker (1991)

THORNE, KEN
If It's Tuesday, This Still Must Be
Belgium (1987)
Great Expectations (1989)
Bejewelled (1991)
Diana: Her True Story (1993)
Lethal Exposure (1993)
Return to Lonesome Dove (1993)
Liz: The Elizabeth Taylor Story (1995)
Season of Hope, A (1995)
Escape Clause (1996)
Robert Ludlum's "The Apocalypse
Watch" (1997)

THORP, GARY
Morgan's Cake (1989)

THORPE, BILLY

Eight Is Enough Wedding, An (1989)

TIBBS, BRIAN
Combination Platter (1993)

TIMMINS, MICHAEL
House (1995)
Boys Club, The (1996)
Niagara Niagara (1997)

TINDERSTICKS
Nenette et Boni (1996)

TIROMANCYNO
Body Moves (1991)

TOLLAR, ERNIE
Eclipse (1994)

TOMANDANDY
Killing Zoe (1993)
Mr. Stitch (1996)
Going All the Way (1997)

TOMASHEK, PETER
Destination Vegas (1995)

TOMNEY, ED
Liquid Dreams (1991)
Night of the Warrior (1991)
Guncrazy (1992)
Ultraviolet (1992)
Dracula Rising (1993)
Safe (1995)

TOONEY, MICHAEL
Too Much Sleep (1997)

TORIKIAN, GERARD
Aux Yeux du Monde (Autobus) (1991)
Love Without Pity (1991)
Les Patriotes (The Patriots) (1994)
Time Is Money (1994)

TORRANCE, TIM
Mutant on the Bounty (1989)

TORRES, ISRAEL
Deathmaster and the Warriors From Hell
(1989)

TOWNS, COLIN
Getting It Right (1989)

Daughter of Darkness (1990)
Fellow Traveller (1990)
Hands of a Murderer (1990)
Only One Survived (1990)
Curacao (1993)
Wide Eyed and Legless (1993)
Cadafel (1994)
Captives (1994)
Puppet Masters, The (1994)
Sin Bin (1994)
Body Language (1995)
Buccaneers, The (1995)
Space Truckers (1996)
Wind in the Willow, The (1996)

TOZER, GEOFFREY LEIGH
9 ½ Ninjas (1990)

TOZER, SHAUN
Hard Core Logo (1996)
Kitchen Party (1997)

TRAGESSAR, BILLY
Rover Dangerfield (1991)

TRAVEL, AVION
Hotel Paura (1996)

TRAVIS, RANDY
Legend of O. B. Taggart, The (1994)

TREFOUSSE, ROGER
Elliot Fauman, Ph.D. (1990)

TRENCHARD-SMITH, BRIAN
Doomsday Rock (1997)

TREPANIER, GUY
Silencing the Guns (1996)

TRESTER, FRANCINE
Liability Crisis (1995)

TROIANO, DOMENIC
Remember Me (1995)
Let Me Call You Sweetheart (1997)
While My Pretty One Sleeps (1997)

TROOB, DANNY
Boys Life 2 (1997)

TROOST, ERNEST
Tremors (1990)

Follow the River (1995)
Calm at Sunset (1996)
Canterville Ghost, The (1996)
Miracle in the Woods (1997)

TROUT, KILGORE
One Dog Day (1997)

TROUTMAN, ROGER
Thin Line Between Love and Hate, A
(1996)

TROVAJOLI, ARMANDO
Two Women (aka Running Away)
(1989)
Cinecitta . . . Cinecitta (1992)
Gangsters (1992)
Mario, Maria e Mario (1994)
Romanzo du un Giovane Povero (1995)
Marcello Mastroianni: I Remember, Yes
I Remember (1997)

TRUDELL, JOHN
Incident at Oglala (1992)

TRUMAN, TIM
Double Your Pleasure (aka The
Reluctant Angel) (1989)
L.A. Takedown (1989)
Dead Silence (1991)
Deadly Game (1991)
South Central (1992)
In the Company of Darkness (1993)
Price of Love, The (1995)
Sketch Artist II: Hands That See (1995)
Good Luck (1996)
Kiss and Tell (1996)
Marshal Law (1996)
Retroactive (1997)

TSCHANZ, MARC
Fun (1994)

TSUCHITORI, TOSHI
Mahabharata, The (1989)

TUCCIARONE, TOM & MATTHEW
Hardcase and Fist (1989)

TUNICK, JONATHAN
You Ruined My Life (1987)
Last Good Time, The (1994)
Birdcage, The (1996)

TURKEL, ERIC
Simple Justice (1989)

TURMAN, GLYNN
Stickin' Together (1992)

TURNER, GREG
Blood Games (1991)
Cop-Out (1991)
Raw Nerve (1991)
Center of the Web (1992)
Eyes of the Beholder (1992)

TURNER, SIMON FISHER
Garden, The (1990)
Edward II (1991)
Elenya (1992)
Blue (1993)
Loaded (1994)
Nadja (1994)
All Men Are Mortal (1995)

TURRE, STEVE
Anna Oz (1996)

TYCHO, TOMMY
Reckless Kelly (1993)

TYNG, CHRISTOPHER
Delta Heat (1992)
Across the Moon (1994)
Evolver (1994)
Unveiled (1994)
Crosscut (1995)
National Lampoon's Favorite Deadly
Sins (1995)
Slave of Dreams (1995)
Associate, The (1996)
Cadillac Ranch (1996)
Kazaam (1996)
Mr. Sprechman's Boat (1996)
Bring Me the Head of Mavis Davis
(1997)

TYRELL, STEVE
Getting It Right (1989)
Captive (1991)
Love and Curses . . . and All That Jazz
(1991)
Pink Lightning (1991)
Reason for Living: The Jill Ireland Story
(1991)
T Bone N Weasel (1992)

Family Prayers (1993)
Out of Sync (1995)
Once Upon a Time . . . When We Were
Colored (1996)

TYSON-CHEW, NERIDA
Hotel Sorrento (1995)
Under the Lighthouse Dancing (1997)

U2
Beyond the Clouds (1995)

ULMAN, VLADIMIR
Motel (1995)

UNCLE TUPELO
Puddle Crusier (1996)

UNGER, JAY
Brother's Keeper (1992)

URBANIAK, MICHAEL
Misplaced (1989)

VACHE, WARREN
Luckiest Man in the World, The (1989)

VAI, STEVE
PCU (1994)

VALENTINO, JOHN
Bonnie & Clyde: The True Story (1992)

VALLE, JAIME
Love Always (1996)

VAN BEETHOVEN, LUDWIG
Immortal Beloved (1994)

VAN BLERK, PATRIC
Curse III: Blood Sacrifice, The (1991)

VAN DORMAEL, PIERRE
Le Huitieme Jour (The Eighth Day)
(1995)

VAN KAMPEN, CLAIRE
Thin Ice (1995)

VAN ORDEN, FRITZ
Little Noises (1991)

VAN PEEBLES, MELVIN
  Erotic Tales (1994)

VAN TIEGHEM, DAVID
  My Father Is Coming (1991)
  Eye of God (1997)

VANASSE, JEAN
  Mistaken Identity (1996)

VANCE, KENNY
  Long Gone (1987)
  Heart of Dixie (1989)
  Hard Promises (1991)
  Murderous Affair: The Carolyn Warmus
    Story, A (1992)

VANGELIS
  Francesco (1989)
  Third Solution (1989)
  1492: Conquest of Paradise (1992)
  Bitter Moon (1992)
  Lune de Fiel (Bitter Moon) (1992)
  Cavafy (1996)

VANNELLI, ROSS
  Final Cut, The (1995)
  Wounded (1997)

VANNIER, JEAN-CLAUDE
  Comedie d'Ete (Summer Interlude)
    (1989)
  Je M'Appelle Victor (My Name Is
    Victor) (1993)

VARNER, TOM
  Saints and Sinners (1995)

VAROUJE
  Back in Action (1994)
  Fearless Tiger (1994)
  Expect No Mercy (1995)
  Jungleground (1995)
  Undertaker's Wedding, The (1997)

VASCONCELOS, NANA
  Amazon (1992)

VASSEUR, DIDIER
  Sweet Revenge (1990)
  Stroke of Midnight (1991)
  La Contre-Allee (Both Sides of the
    Street) (1992)

Business Affair, A (1994)

VAUGHAN, LES
  Strange Blues of Cowboy Red, The
    (1996)

VAUGHN, BEN
  Lewis & Clark & George (1997)

VEDELSMAN, RENE
  Woman of Desire (1993)

VEGA, SUZANNE
  Women & Men 2: Three Short Stories
    (1991)

VELLA, RICHARD
  Parklands (1996)

VENKOV, SIMEON
  Electric Moon (1991)

VENOSTA, GIOVANNI
  Tutti Gli Anni, Una Volta l'Anno (1994)
  Le Acrobate (The Acrobats) (1997)

VENTIMIGLIA, PAUL
  Up Your Alley (1989)

VERBOORT, JAMES
  Vanishing Point (1997)

VERHOEVEN, SIMON
  My Mother's Courage (1995)

VERLAINE, TOM
  Love and a .45 (1994)

VESPERINI, EDITH
  Van Gogh (1992)

VETTESSE, PETER JOHN
  Never Ever (1996)

VILALONGA, ALFONSO
  Things I Never Told You (1996)

VILLALTA, MANUEL
  Excuse Me, Darling, but Lucas Loved
    Me (1997)

VINCENT, ROLAND
  De Sueur et du Sang (Wonderboy)
    (1994)

VINE, CARL
  Bedevil (1993)
  40,000 Years of Dreaming (1996)

VITALE, JOE
  Uncle From Brooklyn, The (1995)

VITARELLI, JOSEPH
  Big Man on Campus (1989)
  How I Got Into College (1989)
  Last Seduction, The (1994)
  Crossing Guard, The (1995)
  Invaders, The (1995)
  Nothing But the Truth (1995)
  Tall, Dark and Deadly (1995)
  Evil Has a Face (1996)
  Substance of Fire, The (1996)
  Bella Mafia (1997)
  Commandments (1997)
  First Time Felon (1997)
  She's So Lovely (1997)

VITIER, JOSE MARIA
  Fresa y Chocolate (Strawberry and
    Chocolate) (1993)

VITTORINI, TOMASO
  Bidoni (Cheats) (1995)

VIVALDI, PAOLO
  Banditi (Bandits) (1995)
  Facciamo Fiesta (Let's Fiesta) (1997)

VIVRES, JOAN
  De Que Se Rien Las Mujeres? (1997)

VLAD, ALESSIO
  Sparrow (1993)
  Follow Your Heart (1996)
  Jane Eyre (1996)

VOLLACK, LIA
  Longtime Companion (1990)

VUSTIN, ALEXANDER
  Anna Karamazova (1991)

WAIT, ROBERT
  Breakaway (1995)

WAITS, TOM
  Night on Earth (1991)
  American Heart (1992)

WAKEMAN, RICK
  Len Deighton's "Bullet to Beijing"
    (1995)

WALDEN, CHRIS
  Tangled Web, A (1996)
  Deadly Vision, A (1997)

WALDEN, DANA
  My Mom's a Werewolf (1989)
  Whisper to a Scream, A (1989)
  Street Hunter (1990)
  Molly & Gina (1994)

WALDEN, W.G. SNUFFY
  Winnie (1988)
  Roe vs. Wade (1989)
  Burning Bridges (1990)
  Guess Who's Coming for Christmas?
    (1990)
  Chase, The (1991)
  I'll Fly Away (1991)
  Shoot First: A Cop's Vengeance (1991)
  Good Fight, The (1992)
  Leaving Normal (1992)
  Wild Card (1992)
  Place to Be Loved, A (1993)
  Rise and Walk: The Dennis Byrd Story
    (1994)
  Friend's Betrayal, A (1996)
  Homage (1995)
  Homecoming (1996)

WALDMAN, PETER
  Assault on Dome 4 (1997)

WALKER, RUSSELL
  Famine Within, The (1990)

WALKER, SHIRLEY
  Chicago Joe and the Showgirl (1990)
  Strike It Rich (1990)
  Majority Rule (1992)
  Memoirs of an Invisible Man (1992)
  Sexual Advances (1992)
  Batman: Mask of the Phantasm (1993)
  Crying Child, The (1996)
  It Came From Outer Space II (1996)

John Carpenter's Escape From L.A.
  (1996)
Turbulence (1996)
Asteroid (1997)
Love Bug, The (1997)

WALL OF NOISE
  God Drives a Pontiac (1995)

WALLACE, BENNIE
  Blaze (1989)
  White Men Can't Jump (1992)

WALLENSTEIN, BRUCE
  Demon Wind (1990)

WALLINGER, KARL
  Reality Bites (1994)

WALSH, ROBERT J.
  Number One Fan (1994)

WALSTALL, JULIAN
  Lost Language of Cranes, The (1991)

WALTERS, MARK
  Aladdin and the King of Thieves (1996)

WALTON, JEFFREY
  Fatal Justice (1993)
  Prey of the Jaguar (1996)

WANG, NATHAN
  Screwball Hotel (1989)
  Natural Causes (1994)

WANNBERG, KEN
  Fatal Memories (1992)

WARBECK, STEPHEN
  Prime Suspect (1991)
  Prime Suspect II (1992)
  You, Me & Marley (1992)
  Prime Suspect III (1993)
  Bambino Mio (1994)
  O Mary This London (1994)
  Sister My Sister (1994)
  Skallarigg (1994)
  Brothers in Trouble (1995)
  Nervous Energy (1995)
  Different for Girls (1996)
  Mrs. Brown (1997)

WARINER, STEVE
  Dukes of Hazzard, The: Reunion! (1997)

WARREN, MERVYN
  Wharf Rat, The (1995)
  Steel (1997)

WAS, DON
  Backbeat (1993)

WASHINGTON, GROVER JR.
  Percy and Thunder (1993)

WATERS, DAVID
  Rescue Me (1993)

WATKINS, MARY
  Black Is . . . Black Ain't (1995)

WATTERS, MARK
  Return of Jafar, The (1994)
  Pebble and the Penguin, The (1995)
  All Dogs Go to Heaven 2 (1996)
  Mrs. Winterbourne (1996)

WAY, DARRYL
  Rage and Honor (1992)

WAYNE, HAYDEN
  Tainted (1989)

WEBB, CHUCK
  How U Like Me Now (1993)

WEBBER, ANDREW LLOYD
  Evita (1996)

WEBBER, STEPHEN
  Knowing Lisa (1992)

WEBER, ALAIN
  Mondo (1996)

WECKER, KONSTANTIN
  Sunday's Child (1989)

WEILL, CYNTHIA
  All Dogs Go to Heaven 2 (1996)
  Muppet Treasure Island (1996)

WEILL, KURT
  Mack the Knife (1989)
  Shadows and Fog (1992)

September Songs: The Music of Kurt
   Weill (1995)

WEINBERG, FRED
   Tommy & the Ghost (1995)

WEINSTEIN, JIMMY
   Under the Bridge (1996)

WEISMAN, BEN
   Crossroads at Laredo (1995)

WEISMAN, JOHN
   Lantern Hill (1990)
   Prisoner of Zenda Inc., The (1996)
   Robin of Locksley (1996)
   Borrowed Hearts (1997)
   In His Father's Shoes (1997)
   Joe Torre: Curveballs Along the Way
      (1997)

WEISS, RONALD J.
   Scorned (1994)
   Donor, The (1995)

WELDREN, CRAIG
   First Love, Last Rites (1997)

WENDY & LISA
   Dangerous Minds (1995)

WENGER, BRAHM
   Absolute Truth, The (1997)
   Air Bud (1997)
   Christmas List, The (1997)

WENTWORTH, RICK
   How to Get Ahead in Advertising (1989)

WENTZEL, STAN
   Goodbye, Paradise (1992)

WERZOWA, WALTER
   Sweet Jane (1997)

WEST, JIM
   Angel of Fury (1993)
   Lady Dragon 2 (1993)

WEST, JOCELYN
   Two Nudes Bathing (1995)

WESTERBERG, PAUL

Singles (1992)

WESTLAKE, NIGEL
   Backsliding (1991)
   Babe (1995)
   Children of the Revolution (1996)

WETHERWAX, MICHAEL
   Cage (1989)
   Midnight (1989)

WETTON, JOHN
   Chasing the River (1994)

WHALEN, MICHAEL
   Perfect Moment (1997)

WHEATLEY, DAVID
   China O'Brien II (1989)
   Out of the Dark (1989)
   Speed Zone (1989)
   JFK Assassination, The (1992)

WHEELER, HAROLD
   Straight Out of Brooklyn (1991)
   Stompin' at the Savoy (1992)
   You Must Remember This (1992)
   There Are No Children Here (1993)
   Silent Witness: What a Child Saw (1994)
   Tears and Laughter: The Joan and
      Melissa Rivers Story (1994)
   Love! Valour! Compassion! (1997)

WHELAN, BILL
   Some Mother's Son (1996)

WHITE, BARRY
   Mon Homme (My Man) (1996)

WHITE, DAVID
   Ricky Rosen's Bar Mitzvah (1995)

WHITE, JOHN CLIFFORD
   Romper Stomper (1992)
   Heartbreak Kid, The (1993)
   Metal Skin (1994)
   Talk (1994)
   Angel Baby (1995)
   Life (1996)

WIDELITZ, STACY
   Dark Tower (1988)

Phantom of the Mall: Eric's Revenge
     (1989)
Megaville (1991)
Prayer of the Rollerboys (1991)
Deceived by Trust: A Moment of Truth
     Movie (1995)
Eye of the Stalker: A Moment of Truth
     Movie (1995)
Abduction of Innocence (1996)
Deadly Web (1996)
Justice for Annie: A Moment of Truth
     Movie (1996)
Secret Between Friends, A: A Moment
     of Truth Movie (1996)
She Woke Up Pregnant (1996)
Stand Against Fear: A Moment of Truth
     Movie (1996)
Accident, The: A Moment of Truth
     Movie (1997)
Badge of Betrayal (1997)
Child's Wish, A (1997)
Into the Arms of Danger: A Moment of
     Truth Movie (1997)

WIEDERHORN, KEN
   House in the Hills, A (1993)

WIEGEL, JAY
   St. Tammany Miracle, The (1994)

WILBORN, BEN
   Ties to Rachel (1997)

WILD, CHUCK
   Panama Deception, The (1992)

WILK, SCOTT
   Bare Essentials (1991)

WILKINSON, K. ALEXANDER
   Street Corner Justice (1996)

WILLIAMS, ALAN
   Asylum (1996)

WILLIAMS, BROOKS
   Wax, or the Discovery of Television
      Among Bees (1993)

WILLIAMS, DAVID
   After School (1989)
   Dead Men Don't Lie (1990)
   God's Army (1995)

Prophecy, The (1995)
No Way Back (1996)

WILLIAMS, H. SHEP
   Lillian (1993)

WILLIAMS, JAKE
   Blackout (1994)

WILLIAMS, JOHN
   Always (1989)
   Born on the Fourth of July (1989)
   Indiana Jones and the Last Crusade
      (1989)
   Home Alone (1990)
   Presumed Innocent (1990)
   Stanley & Iris (1990)
   Hook (1991)
   JFK (1991)
   Home Alone 2: Lost in New York (1992)
   Jurassic Park (1993)
   Schindler's List (1993)
   Nixon (1995)
   Sabrina (1995)
   Sleepers (1996)
   Amistad (1997)
   Lost World: Jurassic Park, The (1997)
   Rosewood (1997)
   Seven Years in Tibet (1997)

WILLIAMS, JOSEPH
   Embrace of the Vampire (1995)
   Last Gasp (1995)
   Poison Ivy 2: Lily (1995)
   Kissing a Fool (1997)

WILLIAMS, KENNY
   Secret Sins of the Father (1994)

WILLIAMS, KEN
   In the Company of Men (1997)

WILLIAMS, PATRICK
   Laguna Heat (1987)
   Night Walk (1989)
   Worth Winning (1989)
   Cry-Baby (1990)
   Decoration Day (1990)
   Good Night Sweet Wife: A Murder in
      Boston (1990)
   In the Spirit (1990)
   Love and Lies (1990)
   Daughters of Privilege (1991)

In Broad Daylight (1991)
Keeping Secrets (1991)
Whereabouts of Jenny, The (1991)
Back to the Streets of San Francisco (1992)
Big Girls Don't Cry... They Get Even (1992)
Cutting Edge, The (1992)
Danielle Steel's "Jewels" (1992)
Grave Secrets: The Legacy of Hilltop Drive (1992)
Legacy of Lies (1992)
Stepkids (1992)
Blind Spot (1993)
Geronimo (1993)
Mercy Mission: The Rescue of Flight 771 (1993)
Murder in the Heartland (1993)
Taking the Heat (1993)
Zelda (1993)
Accidental Meeting (1994)
Because Mommy Works (1994)
Corpse Had a Familiar Face, The (1994)
French Silk (1994)
Getting Gotti (1994)
Gift of Love, The (1994)
Take Me Home Again (1994)
Twilight Zone: Rod Serling's Lost Classics (1994)
Betrayed: A Story of Three Women (1995)
Deadline for Murder: From the Files of Edna Buchanan (1995)
Grass Harp, The (1995)
Her Hidden Truth (1995)
Tom Clancy's "Op Center" (1995)
Kingfish: A Story of Huey P. Long (1995)
Journey (1995)
Saved by the Light (1995)
Weekend in the Country, A (1995)
West Side Waltz, The (1995)
After Jimmy (1996)
Brother's Promise: The Dan Jansen Story, A (1996)
My Very Best Friend (1996)
Never Give Up: The Jimmy V Story (1996)
Ruby Ridge: An American Tragedy (1996)
Childhood Sweetheart? (1997)
Ed McBain's 87th Precinct: Heatwave (1997)

Heart Full of Rain (1997)
Home Invasion (1997)
Julian Po (1997)
Mother Knows Best (1997)
Sisters and Other Strangers (1997)
That Old Feeling (1997)
Walton Easter, A (1997)

WILLIAMS, PAUL
Muppet Christmas Carol, The (1992)

WILLIE, SWEET DICK
Live Boat (1995)

WILLIS, RANDALL
Always Say Goodbye (1997)

WILNER, HAL
Theremin: An Electronic Odyssey (1996)

WILSON, JULIA
Game, The (1989)

WILSON, NANCY
Say Anything (1989)
Jerry McGuire (1996)

WINANS, SAM
Dr. Alien (1989)
California Casanova (1991)
Call to Remember, A (1997)

WINBORNE, HUGHES
Sling Blade (1996)

WINFIELD, CHRIS
Feelin' Screwy (1991)

WINFIELD, TULLY
Live! From Death Row (1992)

WINKLESS, JEFF
Corporate Affairs (1990)

WINNER, MARK
Fatal Mission (1990)

WINSTON, LESLIE
Masala (1993)

WINTER, EDGAR
Netherworld (1990)

WISE, ARI
  Tokyo Cowboy (1994)

WISEMAN, DEBBIE
  Tom & Viv (1994)
  Haunted (1995)
  Female Perversions (1996)
  Wilde (1997)

WISOFF, JILL
  Welcome to the Dollhouse (1995)

WITER, OLEH
  Love and Other Catastrophes (1996)

WOLF, PETER
  Weekend at Bernie's II (1992)
  Neverending Story III, The (1994)
  Father's Day (1997)

WOLFF, LARRY
  Silk Degrees (1994)
  Caged Hearts (1995)

WOLFF, MICHAEL
  Who's the Man (1993)
  Dark Angel (1996)

WOLFSON, JON
  "M" Word, The (1997)

WOLINSKI, DAVID
  Season of Fear (1989)

WOOD, ART
  In the Heat of Passion (1992)

WOODRUFF, CHRISTINE
  Hotel de Love (1996)

WOOLF, WOLUM
  Saigon Baby (1995)

WORKMAN, GLENN
  Sarah's Child (1996)

WORRELL, BERNIE
  Car 54, Where Are You? (1994)

WORTMAN, KURT
  Shattered Mind (1996)

WURMAN, ALEX

Crew, The (1994)
  Dominion (1994)
  Student Body (1995)
  Grave, The (1996)

WURST, DAVID & ERIC
  Blackbelt (1992)
  Bloodfist IV: Die Trying (1992)
  Human Target: Bloodfist V (1994)
  Liar's Club, The (1994)
  Dillinger and Capone (1995)
  Where Truth Lies (1996)

YALTKAYA, CENGIZ
  Out of the Rain (1991)

YAMAGUCHI, MOTOFUMI
  Hunted, The (1995)

YANNI
  Nitti (1988)
  Steal the Sky (1988)
  Heart of Midnight (1989)
  I Love You Perfect (1989)
  Children of the Bride (1990)
  I'll Take Romance (1990)

YARED, GABRIEL
  Camille Claudel (1989)
  Romero (1989)
  Jeanne, Putain du Roi (The King's
    Whore) (1990)
  Vincent and Theo (1990)
  I.P.5: L'Ile aux Pachydermes (1992)
  L'Amant (The Lover) (1992)
  La Fille de l'Air (The Girl in the Air)
    (1992)
  Map of the Human Heart (1992)
  Les Marmottes (The Groundhogs) (1993)
  Black Water (1994)
  Des Feux Mal Eteints (Poorly
    Extinguished Fires) (1994)
  Fall From Grace (1994)
  Arthur Rimbaud (1996)
  Black for Remembrance (1996)
  English Patient, The (1996)
  Tonka (1997)
  Wings of the Dove, The (1997)

YAROL
  Freres: La Roulette Roge (1994)
  L'incruste (Infiltrate) (1994)

YATES, CARMEN
  Ice House (1989)

YELLO
  Adventures of Ford Fairlane, The (1990)
  Nuns on the Run (1990)

YENCKEN, ANDREW
  Seeing Red (1992)

YOAKAM, DWIGHT
  Chasers (1994)

YOUNG, CHRISTOPHER
  Fly II, The (1989)
  Hider in the House (1989)
  Last Flight Out (1990)
  Max and Helen (1990)
  Bright Angel (1991)
  Hellraiser III: Hell on Earth (1992)
  Jennifer Eight (1992)
  Rapid Fire (1992)
  Vagrant, The (1992)
  Dark Half, The (1993)
  Dream Lover (1993)
  Judicial Consent (1994)
  Copycat (1995)
  Murder in the First (1995)
  Species (1995)
  Tales From the Hood (1995)
  Virtuosity (1995)
  Head Above Water (1996)
  Norma Jean and Marilyn (1996)
  Set It Off (1996)
  Unforgettable (1996)
  Man Who Knew Too Little, The (1997)
  Murder at 1600 (1997)

YOUNG, JIM
  Bottom Land (1992)

YOUNG, NEIL
  Dead Man (1995)

YOUNG, RUSSELL
  Run of the House (1992)

YUILL, JIMMY
  In the Bleak Midwinter (1995)

ZAMBRINI, BRUNO
  La Comiche 2 (The Comics 2) (1992)
  Italians (1996)

ZAVOD, ALLAN
  Communion (1989)
  Full Fathom Five (1990)
  Martians Go Home (1990)
  Project: Alien (1991)
  Shotgun Wedding (1993)
  Snide & Prejudice (1997)

ZAZA, PAUL
  Ford: The Man and the Machine (1987)
  Murder by Night (1989)
  Loose Cannons (1990)
  Prom Night III: The Last Kiss (1990)
  Liar's Edge (1991)
  No Contest (1991)
  Popcorn (1991)
  White Light (1991)
  Blown Away (1992)
  To Catch a Killer (1992)
  Arthur Miller's "The American Clock"
    (1993)
  Cold Sweat (1993)
  Spenser: Ceremony (1993)
  Club, The (1994)
  Fudge-a-Mania (1994)
  My Summer Story (aka It Runs in the
    Family) (1994)
  Spenser: Pale Kings and Princes (1994)
  Derby (1995)
  Iron Eagle IV (1995)
  Saltwater Moose (1995)
  Ex, The (1996)
  Rage, The (1996)
  Red Blooded 2 (1996)
  Stolen Memories: Secrets From the Rose
    Garden (1996)
  Brooklyn State of Mind, A (1997)
  Married to a Stranger (1997)
  Misbegotten (1997)
  Stag (1997)

ZERAFA, GUY
  Vivid (1996)

ZEVON, WARREN
  Drug Wars: The Camarena Story (1990)

ZIMMER, HANS
  Black Rain (1989)
  Dark Obsession (1989)
  Diamond Skulls (1989)
  Double Exposure (1989)
  Driving Miss Daisy (1989)

Twister (1989)
Bird on a Wire (1990)
Chicago Joe and the Showgirl (1990)
Dakota Road (1990)
Days of Thunder (1990)
Fools of Fortune (1990)
Green Card (1990)
Pacific Heights (1990)
Backdraft (1991)
Regarding Henry (1991)
Thelma & Louise (1991)
Where Sleeping Dogs Lie (1991)
Code Name: Chaos (1992)
K2 (1992)
League of Their Own, A (1992)
Millennium: Shock of the Other (1992)
Power of One, The (1992)
Radio Flyer (1992)
Toys (1992)
Calendar Girl (1993)
Cool Runnings (1993)
House of the Spirits, The (1993)
Point of No Return (The Assassin)
    (1993)
True Romance (1993)
Younger and Younger (1993)
Drop Zone (1994)
I'll Do Anything (1994)
Lion King, The (1994)
Renaissance Man (1994)
Beyond Rangoon (1995)
Crimson Tide (1995)
Nine Months (1995)
Something to Talk About (1995)
Two Deaths (1995)
Broken Arrow (1996)
Fan, The (1996)
Muppet Treasure Island (1996)
Preacher's Wife, The (1996
Rock, The (1996)
White Squall (1996)
As Good As It Gets (1997)
Peacemaker, The (1997)
Smilla's Sense of Snow (1997)

ZIPPEL, DAVID
    Swan Princess, The (1994)

ZIVKOVIC, BRANE
    That Summer of White Roses (1989)

ZORN, JOHN
    Distribution of Lead, The (1989)
    Thieves Quartet (1994)
    Zigrail (1995)
    Art of Remembrance: Simon Wiesenthal,
        The (1996)
    Latin Boys Go to Hell (1997)

ZURZULO, ANGELO
    Le Fils de Gascone (The Son of
        Gascone) (1995)

FILM TITLE INDEX

Adventures of Priscilla, Queen of the
Desert, The (1994)
Adventures of William Tell, The (1989)
Advocate's Devil, The (1997)
Affair, The (1995)
Affairs of the Heart (1992)
Affliction (1997)
Afraid of the Dark (1991)
After Dark, My Sweet (1990)
After Jimmy (1996)
After Midnight (1989)
After School (1989)
After the Promise (1987)
Afterburn (1992)
AfterGlow (1997)
Aftermath: A Test of Love (1991)
Against Her Will: An Incident in Baltimore
(1992)
Against Her Will: The Carrie Buck Story
(1994)
Against Their Will: Women in Prison
(1994)
Against the Wall (1994)
Agantuk (The Stranger) (1991)
Agatha Christie's "The Man in the Brown
Suit" (1989)
Age of Innocence, The (1993)
Age-Old Friends (1989)
Aileen Wuornos: The Selling of a Serial
Killer (1992)
Air America (1990)
Air Bud (1997)
Air Force One (1997)
Air Up There, The (1994)
Airborne (1993)
Airheads (1994)
Akira Kurosawa's Dream (1990)
Al Limite (To the Limit) (1997)
Aladdin (1992)
Aladdin and the King of Thieves (1996)
Alan & Naomi (1992)
Alaska (1996)
Albino Alligator (1996)
Alchemy (1995)
Alex (1993)
Alex Haley's "Queen" (1993)
Alexa (1989)
Alibi (1997)
Alien From L.A. (1988)
Alien Intruder (1993)
Alien Resurrection (1997)
Alien Space Avenger (1991)
Alien 3 (1992)
Alienator (1990)

Alistair MacLean's "Death Train" (1993)
Alistair MacLean's "Night Watch" (1995)
Alive (1992)
Alive--20 Years Later (1994)
Alive & Kicking (1997)
All Dogs Go to Heaven (1989)
All Dogs Go to Heaven 2 (1996)
All I Want for Christmas (1991)
All Lies End in Murder (1997)
All Men Are Liars (1995)
All Men Are Mortal (1995)
All My Husbands (1992)
All Over Me (1996)
All She Ever Wanted (1996)
All Things Bright and Beautiful (1994)
All Tied Up (1992)
All of Them Witches (1996)
All the Vermeers in New York (1990)
All the Winters That Have Been (1997)
All's Fair (1989)
All's Fair in Love & War (1996)
All-American Murder (1992)
Allie & Me (1997)
Alligator Eyes (1990)
Almost an Angel (1990)
Almost Blue (1992)
Almost Golden: The Jessica Savitch Story
(1995)
Altri Domini (Other Men) (1997)
Always (1989)
Always Remember I Love You (1990)
Always Say Goodbye (1997)
Amantes (Lovers) (1991)
Amateur (1994)
Amazing Panda Adventure, The (1995)
Amazon (1992)
Ambition (1991)
Ambulance, The (1993)
Ambush of Ghosts, An (1993)
Amelia Earhart: The Final Flight (1994)
America's Dream (1995)
American Angels: Baptism of Blood, The
(1990)
American Beer (1996)
American Born (1990)
American Buffalo (1996)
American Cyborg: Steel Warrior (1994)
American Dream (1990)
American Dreamers (1992)
American Friends (1991)
American Harvest (1987)
American Heart (1992)
American Kickboxer I (1991)
American Me (1992)

Beyond Rangoon (1995)
Beyond Suspicion (1993)
Beyond the Call (1996)
Beyond the Clouds (1995)
Beyond the Garden (1997)
Bhaji on the Beach (1993)
Bible and Gun Club, The (1996)
Bidoni (Cheats) (1995)
Big Bully (1996)
Big Dreams & Broken Hearts: The Dottie
  West Story (1995)
Big Empty, The (1997)
Big Girls Don't Cry . . . They Get Even
  (1992)
Big Green, The (1995)
Big Man on Campus (1989)
Big Night (1995)
Big One: The Great Los Angeles
  Earthquake, The (1990)
Big Picture, The (1989)
Big Slice, The (1990)
Big Squeeze, The (1996)
Big Swap, The (1997))
Big Sweat, The (1991)
Bigfoot: The Unforgettable Encounter
  (1994)
Bikini Car Wash Company 2, The (1992)
Bikini Island (1991)
Bikini Summer (1991)
Bikini Summer 2 (1992)
Bill & Ted's Bogus Journey (1991)
Bill & Ted's Excellent Adventure (1989)
Billal (1996)
Billy Bathgate (1991)
Billy Madison (1995)
Billy's Holiday (1995)
Bingo (1991)
Bio-Dome (1996)
Bionic Ever After? (1994)
Bionic Showdown: The Six Million Dollar
  Man and The Bionic Woman(1989)
Bird of Prey (1995)
Bird on a Wire (1990)
Birdcage, The (1996)
Birds II: Land's End, The (1994)
Bishop's Story, The (1995)
Bit of Scarlet, A (1996)
Bitter End, The (1997)
Bitter Harvest (1993)
Bitter Herbs and Honey (1996)
Bitter Moon (1992)
Bitter Vengeance (1994)
Bittersweet (1992)
Bix (1991)

Black & White & Red All Over (1997)
Black and Blue (1992)
Black Beauty (1994)
Black Day Blue Night (1995)
Black Eagle (1988)
Black for Remembrance (1996)
Black Fox (1995)
Black Ice (1992)
Black Is . . . Black Ain't (1995)
Black Magic (1992)
Black Magic Woman (1991)
Black Rain (1989)
Black Rainbow (1989)
Black Robe (1991)
Black Roses (1988)
Black Sheep (1996)
Black to the Promised Land (1992)
Black Velvet Gown, The (1992)
Black Water (1994)
Black Widow Murders: The Blanche
  Taylor Moore Story (1993)
Blackbelt (1992)
Blackmail (1991)
Blackout (1994)
Blackout, The (1997)
Blackrock (1997)
Blackwater Trail (1995)
Blame It on the Bellboy (1992)
Blank Check (1994)
Blankman (1994)
Blast 'Em (1992)
Blaze (1989)
Bleeding Hearts (1995)
Blessing (1994)
Blind Faith (1990)
Blind Fury (1989)
Blind Justice (1988)
Blind Justice (1994)
Blind Man's Bluff (1992)
Blind Side (1993)
Blind Spot (1993)
Blind Vengeance (1990)
Blind Vision (1992)
Blind Witness (1989)
Blindfold: Acts of Obsession (1994)
Blindsided (1993)
Blink (1994)
Bliss (1997)
Blonde Fist (1991)
Blood & Donuts (1995)
Blood and Concrete (1991)
Blood and Sand (1989)
Blood and Wine (1996)
Blood for Blood (1995)

Boys Club, The (1996)
Boys Life 2 (1997)
Boys Next Door, The (1996)
Boys of St. Vincent, The (1993)
Boys on the Side (1995)
Boys, The (1991)
Boyz N the Hood (1991)
Brady Bunch Movie, The (1995)
Brain Dead (1990)
Brain Donors (1992)
Brain Smasher (1993)
Braindead (1992)
Brainscan (1994)
Bram Stoker's Dracula (1992)
Branwen (1994)
Brassed Off (1996)
Brave, The (1997)
Braveheart (1995)
Breach of Conduct (1994)
Breach of Faith: A Family of Cops II
  (1997)
Breach of Trust (1995)
Breakaway (1995)
Breakdown (1997)
Breakfast of Aliens (1989)
Breaking In (1989)
Breaking Point (1989)
Breaking Point (1994)
Breaking the Rules (1992)
Breaking the Silence (1992)
Breaking the Surface (1997)
Breaking the Waves (1995)
Breaking Through (1996)
Breaking Up (1997)
Breast Men (1997)
Breathing Lessons (1994)
Breathing Room (1996)
Breathing Under Water (1991)
Brenda Starr (1989)
Bride in Black, The (1990)
Bride of Re-Animator (1991)
Bridesmaids (1989)
Bridge of Time (1997)
Bridge to Silence (1989)
Bridge, The (1991)
Bridges of Madison County, The (1995)
Brief History of Time, A (1992)
Bright Angel (1991)
Brilliant Disguise, A (1994)
Bring Me the Head of Mavis Davis (1997)
Broadway Bound (1991)
Broken Arrow (1996)
Broken Chain, The (1993)
Broken Cord, The (1992)

Broken English (1996)
Broken Giant, The (1996)
Broken Harvest (1994)
Broken Highway (1993)
Broken Lullaby (1994)
Broken Promises: Taking Emily Back
  (1993)
Broken Trust (1995)
Brokers (1997)
Bronx Tale, A (1993)
Brooklyn State of Mind, A (1997)
Brother Minister: The Assassination of
  Malcolm X (1994)
Brother's Keeper (1992)
Brother's Kiss, A (1997)
Brother's Promise: The Dan Jansen Story,
  A (1996)
Brotherhood of the Gun (1991)
Brotherhood of the Rose (1989)
Brothers in Arms (1989)
Brothers in Trouble (1995)
Brothers McMullen, The (1995)
Brothers of the Frontier (1996)
Browning Version, The (1994)
Bruno's Waiting in the Car (1996)
Brutal Glory (1990)
Brylcreem Boys, The (1996)
Buccaneers, The (1995)
Bucchi Neri (Black Holes) (1995)
Buckminster Fuller: Thinking Out Loud
  (1996)
Buddy (1997)
Buddy Factor, The (1994)
Buffalo Girls (1995)
Buffalo Jump (1992)
Buffalo Soldiers (1997)
Buffy the Vampire Slayer (1992)
Bugsy (1991)
Bullet (1997)
Bulletproof (1996)
Bulletproof Heart (1995)
Bullion Boys, The (1993)
Bullseye! (1990)
Bump in the Night (1991)
Bumping the Odds (1997)
'burbs, The (1989)
Burden of Proof, The (1992)
Buried Alive (1990)
Buried Alive II (1997)
Buried Secrets (1996)
Burning Bridges (1990)
Burning Passion: The Margaret Mitchell
  Story, A (1994)
Burning Season, The (1994)

Castle Freak (1995)
Castle, The (1997)
Casualties of Love: The "Long Island
   Lolita" Story (1993)
Casualties of War (1989)
Casualty of War, A (1990)
Cat Chaser (1989)
Catacombs (1989)
Catch Me If You Can (1989)
Cats Don't Dance (1997)
Catwalk (1995)
Caught (1996)
Caught in the Act (1993)
Caught in the Act (1996)
Cavafy (1996)
CB4 (1993)
Ce Que Femme Veut . . . (What a Woman
   Wants) (1993)
Celia (1989)
Celluloid Closet, The (1995)
Celluloide (1996)
Celtic Pride (1996)
Cement Garden, The (1992)
Cemetery Club, The (1993)
Center of the Web (1992)
Century (1993)
Chain of Desire (1992)
Chain Reaction (1996)
Chain, The (1996)
Chaindance (1991)
Chained Heat II (1993)
Chains of Gold (1989)
Challenge the Wind (1990)
Challenger (1990)
Chamane (1996)
Chamber, The (1996)
Chambre e Part (Separate Bedrooms)
   (1990)
Chameleon (1995)
Chameleons (1989)
Champagne Charlie (1989)
Champagne Safari, The (1995)
Chance of a Lifetime (1991)
Chances Are (1989)
Change of Place, A (1994)
Changing Habits (1996)
Chantilly Lace (1993)
Chaplin (1992)
Charles & Diana: Unhappily Ever After
   (1992)
Charlie's Ear (1992)
Chase, The (1991)
Chase, The (1994)
Chasers (1994)

Chasing Amy (1996)
Chasing the Dragon (1996)
Chasing the River (1994)
Chattahoochee (1989)
Cheap Shots (1991)
Checking Out (1989)
Cheetah (1989)
Chef in Love, A (1996)
Chernobyl: The Final Warning (1991)
Cherokee Kid, The (1996)
Cheyenne Warrior (1994)
Chicago Joe and the Showgirl (1990)
Chiedi la Luna (Ask for the Moon) (1991)
Child in the Night (1990)
Child Is Missing, A (1995)
Child Lost Forever, A (1992)
Child of Darkness, Child of Light (1991)
Child of Rage (1992)
Child's Cry for Help, A (1994)
Child's Play 2 (1990)
Child's Play 3 (1991)
Child's Wish, A (1997)
Childhood Sweetheart? (1997)
Children of Chaos (1989)
Children of the Bride (1990)
Children of the Corn II: The Final Sacrifice
   (1993)
Children of the Corn III: Urban Harvest
   (1993)
Children of the Dark (1994)
Children of the Dragon (1992)
Children of the Dust (aka A Good Day to
   Die) (1995)
Children of the Night (1991)
Children of the Revolution (1996)
Chile Obstinate Memory (1997)
Chili's Blues (1994)
China Cry (1990)
China Lake Murders, The (1990)
China Moon (1991)
China O'Brien II (1989)
Chinese Box (1997)
Chips, the War Dog (1990)
Choices of the Heart: The Margaret Sanger
   Story (1995)
Chopper Chicks in Zombie Town (1991)
Chorus of Disapproval, A (1989)
Christian (1989)
Christmas Box, The (1995)
Christmas Every Day (1996)
Christmas in Connecticut (1992)
Christmas in My Hometown (1996)
Christmas on Division Street (1991)
Christmas List, The (1997)

Comincio Tutto per Caso (It Started by
Chance) (1993)
Commandments (1997)
Common Bonds (1991)
Common Ground (1990)
Common Pursuit (1991)
Communion (1989)
Como Agua Para Chocolat (Like Water for
Chocolate) (1992)
Companion, The (1994)
Company Business (1991)
Complex of Fear (1993)
Computer Wore Tennis Shoes, The (1995)
Comrades of Summer, The (1992)
Con Air (1997)
Con Gli Occhi Chiusi (With Closed Eyes)
(1994)
Condannato a Nozze (Condemned to Wed)
(1993)
Condition Critical (1992)
Coneheads (1993)
Confessional (1990)
Confessions of a Hit Man (1994)
Confessions of a Sorority Girl (1994)
Confessions of a Suburban Girl (1992)
Confessions: Two Faces of Evil (1994)
Confidences a un Inconnu (1995)
Congo (1995)
Connecticut Yankee in King Arthur's
Court, A (1989)
Consenting Adults (1992)
Conspiracy of Love (1987)
Conspiracy of Silence (1992)
Conspiracy Theory (1997)
Contact (1997)
Contagious (1997)
Conte d'Ete (A Summer's Tale) (1996)
Conte d'Hiver (A Winter's Tale) (1992)
Continued Adventures of Reptile Man, The
(1996)
Contre l'Oubli (Against Oblivion) (1992)
Conundrum (1996)
Convict Cowboy (1995)
Conviction of Kitty Dodds, The (1993)
Convictions (1997)
Convicts (1991)
Cook, the Thief, His Wife & Her Lover,
The (1989)
Cookie (1989)
Cool and the Crazy (1994)
Cool as Ice (1991)
Cool Blue (1990)
Cool Runnings (1993)
Cool Surface, The (1992)

Cool World (1992)
Coopersmith: Sweet Scent of Murder
(1992)
Cooperstown (1993)
Cop Land (1997)
Cop and a Half (1993)
Cop-Out (1991)
Cops and Robertsons (1994)
Copycat (1995)
Cormorant (1992)
Corporate Affairs (1990)
Corpse Had a Familiar Face, The (1994)
Corrina, Corrina (1994)
Cosby Mysteries, The (1994)
Cosi (1996)
Cosmos (1996)
Cottonwood, The (1996)
Count of Solar, The (1991)
Counterfeit Contessa, The (1994)
Counterforce (1988)
Countess Alice (1992)
Country Justice (1997)
Country Life (1994)
Coupable d'Innocence (Guilty of
Innocence) (1992)
Coupe de Ville (1990)
Couples et Amants (Couples and Lovers)
(1993)
Courage Mountain (1989)
Courage Under Fire (1996)
Couri al Verde (Penniless Hearts) (1996)
Court-Martial of Jackie Robinson, The
(1990)
Courting Courtney (1997)
Courtyard, The (1995)
Cousin Bobby (1992)
Cousins (1989)
Cover Girl and the Cop, The (1989)
Cover Girl Murders, The (1993)
Cover Me (1995)
Cover Up (1991)
Cowboy Way, The (1994)
Crack House (1989)
Crack Me Up (1993)
Crackdown (1991)
Crackerjack (1994)
Cracking Up (1994)
Craft, The (1996)
Crash (1995)
Crash and Burn (1990)
Crash Landing: The Rescue of Flight 232
(1992)
Crash: The Mystery of Flight 1501 (1990)
Crazy From the Heart (1991)

Dangerous Heart (1994)
Dangerous Indiscretion (1994)
Dangerous Intentions (1995)
Dangerous Minds (1995)
Dangerous Obsession (Mortal Sins) (1990)
Dangerous Passion (1990)
Dangerous Pursuit (1990)
Dangerous Woman, A (1993)
Danielle Steel's "A Perfect Stranger"
   (1994)
Danielle Steel's "Changes" (1991)
Danielle Steel's "Daddy" (1991)
Danielle Steel's "Family Album" (1994)
Danielle Steel's "Fine Things" (1990)
Danielle Steel's "Full Circle" (1996)
Danielle Steel's "Heartbeat" (1993)
Danielle Steel's "Jewels" (1992)
Danielle Steel's "Kaleidoscope" (1990)
Danielle Steel's "Message From Nam"
   (1993)
Danielle Steel's "Mixed Blessings" (1995)
Danielle Steel's "No Greater Love" (1996)
Danielle Steel's "Once in a Lifetime"
   (1994)
Danielle Steel's "Palomino" (1991)
Danielle Steel's "Remembrance" (1996)
Danielle Steel's "Secrets" (1992)
Danielle Steel's "Star" (1993)
Danielle Steel's "The Ring" (1996)
Danielle Steel's "Vanished" (1995)
Danielle Steel's "Zoya" (1995)
Dante's Peak (1997)
Dare to Love (1995)
Daredreamer (1990)
Darien Gap, The (1996)
Dark Angel (1996)
Dark Angel: The Ascent (1994)
Dark Avenger (1990)
Dark Backward, The (1991)
Dark Breed (1996)
Dark City (1997)
Dark Half, The (1993)
Dark Holiday (1989)
Dark Horse (1992)
Dark Obsession (1989)
Dark Reflection (1994)
Dark Rider (1991)
Dark River (1989)
Dark Side of Genius (1994)
Dark Side of the Moon, The (1989)
Dark Summer (1994)
Dark Tower (1988)
Dark Wind, The (1991)
Darker Side of Black (1994)

Darklands (1997)
Darkman (1990)
Darkman 3: Die Darkman Die (1995)
Darkman II: The Return of Durant (1994)
Darkness Before Dawn (1993)
Darling Family, The (1994)
Darlings of the Gods (1991)
Das Lieben Ist Eine Baustelle (1997)
Dating the Enemy (1996)
Daughter of Darkness (1990)
Daughter of the Streets (1990)
Daughters of Privilege (1991)
Daughters of the Dust (1991)
Dave (1993)
David (1997)
David's Mother (1994)
DaVinci's War (1992)
Davy Jones' Locker (1995)
Day My Parents Ran Away, The (1993)
Day in October, A (1992)
Day of Reckoning (1994)
Day of the Dog (1993)
Day One (1989)
Day-O (1992)
Daybreak (1993)
Daydream Believer (1991)
Daylight (1996)
Days of Thunder (1990)
De Force Avec d'Autres (Forced to Be
   With Others) (1993)
De Que Se Rien Las Mujeres? (1997)
De Sueur et du Sang (Wonderboy) (1994)
De Vliegende Hollander (The Flying
   Dutchman) (1995)
De eso no se habla (We Don't Want to Talk
   About It (1993)
Dead Again (1991)
Dead Ahead (1996)
Dead Ahead: The Exxon Valdez Disaster
   (1992)
Dead Air (1994)
Dead and Alive: The Race for Gus Farace
   (1991)
Dead Alive (1992)
Dead Bang (1989)
Dead Beat (1994)
Dead Before Dawn (1993)
Dead Boyz Can't Fly (1992)
Dead by Midnight (1997)
Dead by Sunset (1995)
Dead Calm (1989)
Dead Center (aka Crazy Joe) (1992)
Dead Connection (1994)
Dead End City (1989)

Delinquent (1995)
Delinquents, The (1989)
Delirious (1991)
Deliver Them From Evil: The Taking of
   Alta View (1992)
Deliverance of Elaine, The (1996)
Dellamorte Delamore (Cemetery Man)
   (1994)
Delphine 1--Yvan 0 (1996)
Delta Force 2 (1990)
Delta Heat (1992)
Delta of Venus (1995)
Delta, The (1996)
Delusion (1991)
Demolition High (1996)
Demolition Man (1993)
Demolitionist, The (1996)
Demon in My View, A (1992)
Demon Keeper (1994)
Demon Possessed (1993)
Demon Wind (1990)
Demonic Toys (1992)
Denise Calls Up (1995)
Dennis the Menace (1993)
Dennis the Menace: The Live-Action
   Movie (1987)
Dentist, The (1996)
Der Berg (The Mountain) (1990)
Der Unfisch (The Unfish) (1997)
Derby (1995)
Des Feux Mal Eteints (Poorly Extinguished
   Fires) (1994)
Descending Angel (1990)
Desert Hawk (1992)
Desert Rats (1988)
Desert Steel (1994)
Desert Winds (1995)
Designated Mourner, The (1997)
Desire (1996)
Desire and Hell at Sunset Motel (1992)
Desperado (1995)
Desperado: Badlands Justice (1989)
Desperado: The Outlaw Wars (1989)
Desperate (1987)
Desperate Choices: To Save My Child
   (1992)
Desperate for Love (1989)
Desperate Hours (1990)
Desperate Journey: The Allison Wilcox
   Story (1993)
Desperate Motive (1993)
Desperate Remedies (1993)
Desperate Rescue: The Cathy Malone Story
   (1993)

Desperate Trail, The (1995)
Destination Vegas (1995)
Destiny in Space (1994)
Destiny Turns on the Radio (1995)
Detention: Siege at Johnson High (1997)
Detour (1992)
Deuce Coupe (1992)
Deux Actrices (Two Can Play) (1993)
Devil in a Blue Dress (1995)
Devil's Advocate, The (1997)
Devil's Child, The (1997)
Devil's Daughter, The (1991)
Devil's Food (1996)
Devil's Own, The (1997)
Devlin (1992)
Di Ceria dell'Untore (The Plague Tower)
   (1992)
Diabolique (1996)
Diagnosis of Murder (1992)
Diamond Fleece, The (1992)
Diamond Skulls (1989)
Diana and Me (1997)
Diana: Her True Story (1993)
Diario du un Vizio (Diary of a Maniac)
   (1993)
Diary of a Hit Man (1992)
Diary of a Rapist (1995)
Diary of a Seducer (1995)
Dichiarazioni d'Amore (Declarations of
   Love) (1994)
Dick Tracy (1990)
Didier (1997)
Die Hard 2 (1990)
Die Hard With a Vengeance (1995)
Dien Bien Phu (1992)
Dieu Que les Femmes sont Amoureuses
   (1994)
Different Affair, A (1987)
Different for Girls (1996)
Different Kind of Christmas, A (1996)
Digger (1993)
Diggstown (1992)
Dillinger (1991)
Dillinger and Capone (1995)
Dimenticare Palermo (1990)
Ding et Dong: Le Film (1991)
Dingo (1991)
Dinner at Eight (1989)
Dinner at Fred's (1997)
Dinner in Purgatory (1994)
Dinner, The (1997)
Dinosaur Island (1994)
Diplomatic Immunity (1991)
Directors on Directors (1997)

Exquisite Tenderness (1995)
Extreme Close-Up (1990)
Extreme Justice (1993)
Extreme Measures (1996)
Eye for an Eye (1995)
Eye of God (1997)
Eye of the Eagle II: Inside the Enemy (1989)
Eye of the Stalker: A Moment of Truth Movie (1995)
Eye of the Storm (1992)
Eye of the Stranger (1993)
Eyes of a Witness (1991)
Eyes of Asia (1996)
Eyes of Terror (1994)
Eyes of the Beholder (1992)
Eyes of the Eagle 3 (1992)
Eyes of the Prey (1993)

F.T.W. (1994)
Fabulous Baker Boys, The (1989)
Facciamo Fiesta (Let's Fiesta) (1997)
Face (1997)
Face Down (1997)
Face of a Stranger (1991)
Face of Evil (1996)
Face of Fear, The (1990)
Face of the Enemy (1989)
Face on the Milk Carton, The (1995)
Face to Die For, A (1996)
Face to Face (1990)
Face/Off (1997)
Fade to Black (1993)
Fair Game (1991)
Fair Game (1995)
Fairy Tale: A True Story (1997)
Faithful (1996)
Fakebook (1989)
Fakin' Da Funk (1997)
Fall (1997)
Fall From Grace (1990)
Fall From Grace (1994)
Fall Into Darkness (1996)
Fall Time (1995)
Fall and Spring (1996)
Fall of Saigon, The (1995)
Fallen Angels (1993)
Falling Down (1992)
Falling for You (1995)
Falling From the Sky! Flight 174 (1995)
Falling Over Backwards (1990)
Fallout (1996)
False Arrest (1991)

False Witness (1989)
Familia (Family) (1996)
Family (1994)
Family Affair (1995)
Family Business (1989)
Family Divided, A (1995)
Family for Joe, A (1990)
Family of Cops (1995)
Family of Spies (1990)
Family of Strangers, A (1993)
Family Pictures (1993)
Family Prayers (1993)
Family Reunion: A Relative Nightmare (1995)
Family Sins (1987)
Family Thing, A (1996)
Family Torn Apart, A (1993)
Famine Within, The (1990)
Fan, The (1996)
Fanfan (1993)
Fantome avec Chauffeur (1996)
Far From Home (1989)
Far From Home: The Adventures of Yellow Dog (1995)
Far Off Place, A (1993)
Far Out Man (1990)
Faraway, So Close! (1993)
Farewell to the King (1989)
Fargo (1996)
Farinelli il Castrato (1994)
Farmer & Chase (1995)
Fast (1995)
Fast Company (1995)
Fast Food (1989)
Fast Getaway (1991)
Fast Getaway II (1994)
Fast, Cheap & Out of Control (1997)
Fat Man and Little Boy (1989)
Fatal Bond (1992)
Fatal Charm (1992)
Fatal Exposure (1991)
Fatal Friendship (1991)
Fatal Image, The (1990)
Fatal Instinct (1993)
Fatal Justice (1993)
Fatal Memories (1992)
Fatal Mission (1990)
Fatal Skies (1990)
Fatal Vows: The Alexandra O'Hara Story (1994)
Father & Son: Dangerous Relations (1993)
Father and Scout (1994)
Father Hood (1993)
Father of the Bride (1991)

Flash (1997)
Flash, The (1990)
Flashback (1990)
Flashfire (1994)
Flatliners (1990)
Flea Bites (1991)
Fled (1996)
Flesh and Bone (1993)
Flesh Suitcase (1995)
Fletch Lives (1989)
Flight of Black Angel (1991)
Flight of the Intruder (1991)
Flintstones, The (1994)
Flipper (1996)
Flirt (1995)
Flirting With Disaster (1996)
Floating (1997)
Floating Life (1996)
Flood: A River's Rampage (1997)
Flood: Who Will Save Our Children?, The (1993)
Floundering (1994)
Flubber (1997)
Fluke (1995)
Fly Away Home (1996)
Fly II, The (1989)
Fly by Night (1993)
Flying Blind (1990)
Folks! (1992)
Follow Me Home (1996)
Follow the Bitch (1997)
Follow the River (1995)
Follow Your Heart (1990)
Follow Your Heart (1996)
Following Her Heart (1994)
Food of Love (1997)
Fool's Fire (1992)
Fools Die Fast (1996)
Fools of Fortune (1990)
Fools Rush In (1997)
Footstep Man, The (1992)
For Hope (1996)
For Love and Glory (1993)
For Love or Money (aka Concierge, The) (1993)
For My Daughter's Honor (1996)
For Richer or Poorer (1997)
For Richer, For Poorer (1992)
For the Boys (1991)
For the Future: The Irvine Fertility Scandal (1996)
For the Love of Aaron (1994)
For the Love of My Child (1993)
For the Love of Nancy (1994)

For the Moment (1994)
For the Very First Time (1991)
For Their Own Good (1993)
Forbidden Dance, The (1990)
Forbidden Nights (1990)
Forbidden Territory: Stanley's Search for Livingstone (1997)
Forbidden Zone: Alien Abduction (1996)
Forced to Kill (1993)
Ford: The Man and the Machine (1987)
Foreign Affairs (1993)
Foreign Body, A (Sinon, Oui) (1997)
Foreign Field, A (1993)
Foreign Student (1994)
Forever (1992)
Forever Young (1992)
Forget Paris (1995)
Forget-Me-Not Murders, The (1994)
Forgotten Prisoners: The Amnesty Files (1990)
Forgotten Silver (1996)
Forgotten Sins (1996)
Forgotten, The (1989)
Forrest Gump (1994)
Fortress (1993)
Fortress of Amerika (1989)
Four Diamonds, The (1995)
Four Eyes and Six-Guns (1992)
Four Rooms (1995)
Four Weddings and a Funeral (1994)
Fourth Story (1991)
Fourth War, The (1990)
Foxfire (1996)
Frame Up (1991)
Frame-up II: The Cover-up (1992)
Framed (1990)
Framed (1993)
Francesco (1989)
Frank and Jesse (1995)
Frank and Ollie (1995)
Frank Capra's American Dream (1997)
Frankenhooker (1990)
Frankenstein (1993)
Frankenstein Unbound (1990)
Frankenstein and Me (1996)
Frankenstein: The College Years (1991)
Frankie and Johnny (1991)
Frankie Starlight (1995)
Fratelli Coltelli (Knife Brothers) (1997)
Fratelli e Sorelle (Brothers and Sisters) (1992)
Frauds (1992)
Freaked (1993)
Freaky Friday (1995)

Freddie as F.R.O.7 (1992)
Freddy's Dead: The Final Nightmare
  (1991)
Free Willy (1993)
Free Willy 2: The Adventure Home (1995)
Free Willy 3: The Rescue (1997)
Freefall (1993)
Freejack (1992)
Freeway (1996)
Freeway Maniac, The (1989)
French Kiss (1995)
French Silk (1994)
Frequent Flyer (1996)
Freres: La Roulette Roge (1994)
Fresa y Chocolate (Strawberry and
  Chocolate) (1993)
Fresh (1994)
Freshman, The (1990)
Friday (1995)
Friday the 13th Part VIII: Jason Takes
  Manhattan (1989)
Fried Green Tomatoes (1991)
Friend to Die For, A (1994)
Friend's Betrayal, A (1996)
Friends (1993)
Friends and Enemies (1992)
Friends at Last (1995)
Friends 'Til the End (1997)
Friendship in Vienna, A (1988)
Fright Night--Part 2 (1989)
Frighteners, The (1996)
From Dusk Till Dawn (1996)
From the Dead of Night (1989)
From the Files of "Unsolved Mysteries":
  Voice From the Grave (1996)
From the Files of Joseph Wambaugh: A
  Jury of One (1992)
From the Mixed-Up Files of Mrs Basil E.
  Frankweiler (1995)
From Today Until Tomorrow (1997)
Frozen Assets (1992)
Fudge-a-Mania (1994)
Fugitive Among Us, The (1992)
Fugitive Nights: Danger in the Desert
  (1993)
Fugitive X (1996)
Fugitive, The (1993)
Fulfillment of Mary Gray, The (1989)
Full Body Massage (1995)
Full Eclipse (1993)
Full Exposure: The Sex Tapes Scandal
  (1989)
Full Fathom Five (1990)
Full Monty, The (1997)

Full Tilt Boogie (1997)
Fun (1994)
Fun Down There (1989)
Funeral, The (1996)
Funny About Love (1990)
Funny Bones (1995)
Funny Man (1994)
Further Gesture, A (1997)
Futurekick (1991)
FX2: The Deadly Art of Illusion (1991)

G.I. Jane (1997)
Gadael Lenin (Leaving Lenin) (1993)
Galaxies Are Colliding (1992)
Gallivant (1996)
Gambler Returns: The Luck of the Draw,
  The (1991)
Gambler V: Playing for Keeps, The (1994)
Gambler, The (1997)
Game, The (1989)
Game, The (1997)
Gang Related (1997)
Gangs in Blue (1996)
Gangsters (1992)
Garden of Redemption, The (1997)
Garden, The (1990)
Gas Food Lodging (1992)
Gate II (1992)
Gate of Heavenly Peace, The (1995)
Gattaca (1997)
Gazon Maudit (French Twist) (1995)
Genealogies d'un Crime (1997)
Generation X (1996)
Genesi: La Creazione e il Diluvio (1994)
Genghis Cohn (1993)
Genuine Risk (1990)
George B. (1997)
George Balanchine's "The Nutcracker"
  (1993)
George of the Jungle (1997)
George Wallace (1997)
George's Island (1991)
Georgia (1995)
Germinal (1993)
Geronimo (1993)
Geronimo: An American Legend (1993)
Gerrie & Louise (1997)
Get on the Bus (1996)
Get Shorty (1995)
Get Smart, Again! (1989)
Get to the Heart: The Barbara Mandrell
  Story (1997)
Getaway, The (1994)

Hero (1992)
Hero's Life, A (1994)
Heroes Stand Alone (1989)
Heroes of Desert Storm, The (1991)
Hexed (1993)
Hi Honey I'm Dead (1991)
Hidden 2, The (1994)
Hidden Agenda (1990)
Hidden in America (1996)
Hidden in Silence (1996)
Hideaway (1995)
Hider in the House (1989)
High Desert Kill (1989)
High School High (1996)
High Stakes (1997)
High Voltage (1997)
Higher Learning (1994)
Highlander III: The Sorcerer (1994)
Highway Heartbreaker (1992)
Highway of Heartache (1994)
Highway to Hell (1992)
Highwayman, The (1987)
Hijacked: Flight 285 (1996)
Hijacking Hollywood (1997)
Hijacking of the Achille Lauro, The (1989)
Hired Heart, The (1997)
Hiroshima: Out of the Ashes (1990)
Histoires D'Amerique (1989)
Hit List (1989)
Hit List, The (1993)
Hit Man, The (1991)
Hit Me (1996)
Hit the Dutchman (1992)
Hitler's Daughter (1990)
Hitman, The (1991)
Hits! (1994)
Hitting the Ground (1996)
Hitwoman: The Double Edge (1993)
Hocus Pocus (1993)
Hoffa (1992)
Hold Me, Thrill Me, Kiss Me (1992)
Holiday Affair (1996)
Holiday in Your Heart (1997)
Holiday to Remember, A (1995)
Holidays on the River Yarra (1991)
Hollow Reed (1996)
Hollywood Boulevard II (1991)
Hollywood Detective, The (1989)
Hollywood Hot Tubs 2: Educating Crystal
  (1990)
Hologram Man (1995)
Holy Matrimony (1994)
Homage (1995)
Home Alone (1990)

Home Alone 2: Lost in New York (1992)
Home Alone 3 (1997)
Home Before Dark (1997)
Home Fires (1987)
Home Fires Burning (1989)
Home Fires Burning (1992)
Home for Christmas: Little Miss Millions
  (1993)
Home for the Holidays (1995)
Home Invasion (1997)
Home of Our Own, A (1993)
Homecoming (1996)
Homer and Eddie (1989)
Homeward Bound II: Lost in San Francisco
  (1996)
Homeward Bound: The Incredible Journey
  (1993)
Homewrecker (1992)
Homicide (1991)
Hommes Femmes: Mode d'Emploi (1996)
Honey, I Blew Up the Kid (1992)
Honey, I Shrunk the Kids (1989)
Honey, We Shrunk Ourselves! (1996)
Honeymoon Academy (1990)
Honeymoon in Vegas (1992)
Honor Bound (1989)
Honor Thy Father & Mother: The True
  Story of the Menendez Murders (1994)
Honor Thy Mother (1992)
Hoodlum (1997)
Hook (1991)
Hoop Dreams (1994)
Hoover vs. The Kennedys: The Second
  Civil War (1987)
Hope (1997)
Hope in the Year Two (1994)
Horror Show, The (1989)
Hors la Vie (1991)
Horse for Danny, A (1995)
Horseplayer, The (1990)
Horsey (1997)
Horton Foote's "Alone" (1997)
Horton Foote's "The Habitation of
  Dragons" (1992)
Hostage for a Day (1994)
Hostages (1993)
Hostile Advances: The Kerry Ellison Story
  (1996)
Hostile Waters (1997)
Hot Shots! (1991)
Hot Shots! Part Deux (1993)
Hot Spot, The (1990)
Hotel de Love (1996)
Hotel Manor Inn, The (1996)

Hotel Oklahoma (1991)
Hotel Paura (1996)
Hotel Sorrento (1995)
Hour of the Assassin (1987)
Hour of the Pig, The (1993)
Hourglass (1995)
House (1995)
House Arrest (1996)
House IV: The Horror Show (1989)
House in the Hills, A (1993)
House of America (1997)
House of Cards (1993)
House of Elliott, The (1992)
House of Frankenstein (1997)
House of Pain (1995)
House of Secrets (1993)
House of Secrets and Lies, A (1992)
House of the Spirits, The (1993)
House of Usher, The (1990)
House of Yes, The (1997)
House on Sycamore Street, The (1992)
House Party (1990)
House Party 2: The Pajama Jam (1991)
House Party 3 (1994)
HouseSitter (1992)
Houseguest (1994)
Household Saints (1993)
How I Got Into College (1989)
How I Spent My Summer Vacation (1997)
How U Like Me Now (1993)
How the West Was Fun (1994)
How to Get Ahead in Advertising (1989)
How to Make an American Quilt (1995)
How to Murder a Millionaire (1990)
Howard Beach: Making the Case for
    Murder (1989)
Howards End (1992)
Howling V: The Rebirth (1989)
Howling VI: The Freaks (1991)
Huck and the King of Hearts (1993)
Hudson Hawk (1991)
Hudson River Blues (1997)
Hudsucker Proxy, The (1994)
Hugo Pool (1997)
Human Factor (1989)
Human Shield, The (1992)
Human Target: Bloodfist V (1994)
Hummingbird Tree, The (1992)
Hunchback of Notre Dame, The (1996)
Hunchback, The (1997)
Hunt for Red October, The (1990)
Hunted, The (1995)
Hunting (1991)
Hurricane Smith (1992)

Hurricane Street (1997)
Husband, A Wife, and a Lover, A (1996)
Husbands and Lovers (1992)
Hush Little Baby (1994)
Hush-a-Bye Baby (1990)

I Can Make You Love Me (1993)
I Come in Peace (1990)
I Crave Rock & Roll (1996)
I Don't Buy Kisses Anymore (1992)
I Dreamt I Woke Up (1991)
I Giovane Mussolini (A Man Named
    Mussolini) (1993)
I Know My First Name Is Steven (1989)
I Know My Son Is Alive (1994)
I Know What You Did Last Summer
    (1997)
I Like It Like That (1994)
I Love a Man in Uniform (1993)
I Love Trouble (1994)
I Love You Perfect (1989)
I Love You to Death (1990)
I Love You, I Love You Not (1997)
I Love You . . . Don't Touch Me! (1997)
I Magi Randaci (We Three Kings) (1996)
I Shot a Man in Vegas (1995)
I Shot Andy Warhol (1996)
I Spy Returns (1994)
I Still Dream of Jeannie (1991)
I Want to Go Home (1989)
I Was on Mars (1992)
I Went Down (1997)
I Went to the Dance (1989)
I'll Be Home for Christmas (1988)
I'll Be Home for Christmas (1997)
I'll Do Anything (1994)
I'll Fly Away (1991)
I'll Love You Forever . . . Tonight (1993)
I'll Take Romance (1990)
I'm Dangerous Tonight (1990)
I'm Not Rappaport (1996)
I, Madman (1989)
i.d. (1994)
I.P.5: L'Ile aux Pachydermes (1992)
I.Q. (1994)
Ice (1994)
Ice House (1989)
Ice Runner, The (1992)
Ice Runner, The (1993)
Ice Storm, The (1997)
Identity Crisis (1989)
If It's Tuesday, This Still Must Be Belgium
    (1987)

J'ai pas Sommiel (I Can't Sleep) (1994)
J'embrasse Pas (I Don't Kiss) (1991)
Jack (1996)
Jack & Sarah (1995)
Jack Be Nimble (1993)
Jack Brown, Genius (1995)
Jack Frusciante Left the Band (1996)
Jack Higgins' "On Dangerous Grounds" (1996)
Jack London's "The Call of the Wild" (1997)
Jack Reed: A Killer Amongst Us (1996)
Jack Reed: A Search for Justice (1994)
Jack Reed: Badge of Honor (1993)
Jack Reed: Death and Vengeance (1996)
Jack the Bear (1993)
Jackal, The (1997)
Jackie Collins' "Lady Boss" (1992)
Jackie Collins' "Lucky/Chances" (1990)
Jacknife (1989)
Jacob (1994)
Jacob's Ladder (1990)
Jacquot de Nantes (1991)
Jade (1995)
Jailbirds (1991)
Jailbreakers (1994)
Jake Lassiter: Justice on the Bayou (1995)
Jake Spanner, Private Eye (1989)
James A. Michener's "Texas" (1995)
James Gang, The (1997)
James and the Giant Peach (1996)
Jamon, Jamon (Salami, Salami) (1992)
Jane Austen's "Emma" (1996)
Jane Austen's "Pride and Prejudice" (1995)
Jane Eyre (1996)
Jane Street (1996)
Jane's House (1994)
January Man, The (1989)
Jason Goes to Hell: The Final Friday (1993)
Jason's Lyric (1994)
Je M'Appelle Victor (My Name Is Victor) (1993)
Jean Seberg, American Actress (1995)
Jeanne la Pucelle (Joan of Arc) (1994)
Jeanne, Putain du Roi (The King's Whore) (1990)
Jefferson in Paris (1995)
Jeffrey (1995)
Jekyll & Hyde (1990)
Jeniapo (1995)
Jennifer Eight (1992)
Jericho Fever (1993)
Jerky Boys, The (1995)

Jerry McGuire (1996)
Jersey Girl (1992)
Jesus De Montreal (1989)
Jetsons: The Movie (1990)
Jezebel's Kiss (1990)
JFK (1991)
JFK Assassination, The (1992)
JFK: Reckless Youth (1993)
Jimmy Hollywood (1994)
Jingle All the Way (1996)
Jitters (1997)
Jitters, The (1989)
Jo-Jo at the Gate of Lions (1992)
Jobman (1990)
Joe & Joe (1995)
Joe Torre: Curveballs Along the Way (1997)
Joe Versus the Volcano (1990)
Joe's Apartment (1996)
Joe's Rotten World (1995)
Joe's So Mean to Josephine (1997)
Joe's Wedding (1997)
Joey (1997)
John Carpenter Presents Body Bags (1993)
John Carpenter's Escape From L.A. (1996)
John Grisham's "The Rainmaker" (1997)
John Henrik Clarke: A Great and Mighty Walk (1996)
John Jakes' "Heaven & Hell: North & South Book 3" (1994)
John Lurie and the Lounge Lizards Live in Berlin (1992)
John Woo's "Once a Thief" (1996)
Johnny Handsome (1989)
Johnny Mnemonic (1995)
Johnny Ryan (1990)
Johnny Stecchino (1991)
Johnny Suede (1991)
Johnny's Girl (1995)
Johns (1995)
Joint Adventure (1995)
Jonah Who Lived in the Whale (1993)
Jonathan Stone: Threat of Innocence (1994)
Jonathan: The Boy Nobody Wanted (1992)
Joseph (1995)
Joseph Conrad's "The Secret Agent" (1996)
Josephine Baker Story, The (1991)
Josh and S.A.M. (1993)
Joshua's Heart (1990)
Journey (1995)
Journey of August King, The (1995)
Journey of Honor (1990)
Journey of the Heart (1997)

Lost in Mississippi (1996)
Lost in Yonkers (1993)
Lost Language of Cranes, The (1991)
Lost Treasure of Dos Santos (1997)
Lost World: Jurassic Park, The (1997)
Lottery, The (1996)
Lotto Land (1995)
Lotus Eaters, The (1993)
Louis L'Amour's "Conagher" (1991)
Louis, Enfant Roi (Louis, the Child King)
   (1993)
Louisa May Alcott's "The Inheritance"
   (1997)
Love & Greed (1991)
Love & Murder (1990)
Love & Sex, etc. (1996)
Love Affair (1994)
Love Always (1996)
Love Boat: A Valentine Voyage, The
   (1990)
Love Bug, The (1997)
Love Can Be Murder (1992)
Love Crimes (1992)
Love Field (1992)
Love God (1997)
Love Hurts (1990)
Love Is All There Is (1996)
Love Jones (1997)
Love Kills (1991)
Love Matters (1993)
Love Me, Love Me Not (1996)
Love Potion No. 9 (1992)
Love She Sought, The (1990)
Love Without Pity (1991)
Love Ya Tomorrow (1991)
Love and Betrayal (1989)
Love and Betrayal: The Mia Farrow Story
   (1995)
Love and Curses . . . and All That Jazz
   (1991)
Love and Death on Long Island (1997)
Love and Happiness (1995)
Love and Hate: A Marriage Made in Hell
   (1990)
Love and Human Remains (1993)
Love and Lies (1990)
Love and Other Catastrophes (1996)
Love and a .45 (1994)
Love at Large (1990)
Love etc. (1996)
Love in Limbo (1993)
Love or Money (1990)
Love! Valour! Compassion! (1997)

Love's Deadly Triangle: The Texas Cadet
   Murder (1997)
Love, Cheat & Steal (1993)
Love, Honor & Obey: The Last Mafia
   Marriage (1993)
Love, Lies and Murder (1991)
Love, Math and Sex (1997)
Love-Moi (1991)
Love-Struck (1997)
Loved (1997)
Lovelife (1997)
Lovemaster, The (1997)
Lover Girl (1997)
Lover's Knot (1996)
Loverboy (1989)
Loving (1995)
Loving Lulu (1992)
Low Down Dirty Shame, A (1994)
Low Life, The (1995)
Lower Level (1990)
Lucie Aubrac (1997)
Luckiest Man in the World, The (1989)
Lucky Break (1994)
Lucky Day (1991)
Lucy & Desi: Before the Laughter (1991)
Luna e l'Altra (1996)
Lunatic, The (1992)
Lunatics: A Love Story (1991)
Lune Froide (Cold Moon) (1991)
Lune de Fiel (Bitter Moon) (1992)
Lurking Fear (1994)
Lush Life (1994)
Lust and Revenge (1996)
Lying Eyes (1996)

"M" Word, The (1997)
M. Butterfly (1993)
M.A.N.T.I.S. (1994)
Ma Femme Me Quitte (My Woman Is
   Leaving Me) (1996)
Ma Saison Preferee (My Favorite Season)
   (1993)
Ma vie en rose (1997)
Ma vie sexuelle (1996)
Mac (1992)
MacGyver: Lost Treasure of Atlantis
   (1994)
MacGyver: Trail to Doomsday (1994)
MacShayne: Final Roll of the Dice (1994)
MacShayne: Winner Takes All (1994)
Macadam Tribu (Macadam Tribe) (1996)
Macbeth (1997)
Mack the Knife (1989)

Mad Bomber in Love (1992)
Mad City (1997)
Mad Dog Coll (1992)
Mad Dog Time (1996)
Mad Dog and Glory (1993)
Mad Dogs and Englishmen (1995)
Mad Love (1995)
Mad at the Moon (1992)
Madame Bovary (1991)
Madame Butterfly (1995)
Maddening, The (1995)
Made in America (1993)
Made Men (1997)
Madhouse (1990)
Madness of King George, The (1994)
Magdalene (1990)
Magic in the Water (1995)
Magic Island (1996)
Magic Kid (aka Ninja Dragons) (1992)
Magic Moments (1989)
Magic Riddle, The (1991)
Magical World of Chuck Jones, The (1992)
Magicians of the Earth (1990)
Magnificat (1993)
Mahabharata, The (1989)
Maid for Each Other (1992)
Maigret (1988)
Major Crime (1997)
Major League (1989)
Major League II (1994)
Major Payne (1995)
Majority Rule (1992)
Maker, The (1997)
Making of Maps, The (1995)
Maktub: The Law of the Desert (1990)
Malarek: A Street Kid Who Made It (1989)
Malcolm X (1992)
Malena Is a Name From a Tango (1996)
Malice (1993)
Malicious (1995)
Malik le Maudit (Calamity Malik) (1996)
Mallrats (1995)
Mambo Kings, The (1992)
Man Against the Mob (1988)
Man Against the Mob: The Chinatown
   Murders (1989)
Man Called Serge, A (1990)
Man From Left Field, The (1993)
Man in the Attic, The (1995)
Man in the Moon, The (1991)
Man Next Door, The (1996)
Man of No Importance, A (1994)
Man of the House (1995)
Man of the Year (1995)

Man to Man (1992)
Man Trouble (1992)
Man Upstairs, The (1992)
Man Who Captured Eichmann, The (1996)
Man Who Knew Too Little, The (1997)
Man Who Lived in the Ritz (1988)
Man Who Wouldn't Die, The (1995)
Man With Three Wives, The (1993)
Man With a Gun (1995)
Man With the Perfect Swing, The (1995)
Man Without a Face, The (1993)
Man Without a World, The (1992)
Man's Best Friend (1993)
Mandela (1987)
Mandela (1995)
Mandela and deKlerk (1997)
Mangler, The (1995)
Manhattan Merenge (1995)
Manhunt: Search for the Night Stalker
   (1989)
Maniac Cop 2 (1990)
Maniac Cop 3: Badge of Silence (1993)
Maniaci Sentimentali (Sentimental
   Maniacs) (1994)
Mannequin Two: On the Move (1991)
Manny & Lo (1996)
Manufacturing Consent: Noam Chomsky
   and the Media (1992)
Map of the Human Heart (1992)
Marcello Mastroianni: I Remember, Yes I
   Remember (1997)
March, The (1991)
Marcindo nel Buio (Marching in the Dark)
   (1995)
Mardi Gras for the Devil (1993)
Margaret Bourke-White (1989)
Margaret's Museum (1995)
Maria's Child (1992)
Marianna Ucria (1997)
Marie Baie des Anges (1997)
Marie de Nazareth (1995)
Marie-Louise (1995)
Marilyn & Bobby: Her Final Affair (1993)
Marilyn and Me (1991)
Mario and the Mob (1992)
Mario Puzo's "The Last Don" (1997)
Mario, Maria e Mario (1994)
Marion (1997)
Mark Twain and Me (1991)
Marked for Death (1990)
Marked for Murder (1993)
Marla Hanson Story, The (1991)
Marquise (1997)
Married to It (1991)

Midnight Clear, A (1992)
Midnight Confessions (1993)
Midnight Cop (1989)
Midnight Edition (1993)
Midnight Fear (1992)
Midnight in the Garden of Good and Evil
  (1997)
Midnight Kiss (1993)
Midnight Movie (1994)
Midnight Ride (1992)
Midnight Witness (1993)
Midnight's Child (1992)
Midsummer Night's Dream, A (1996)
Midwife's Tale, A (1997)
Mighty Ducks, The (1992)
Mighty Morphin Power Rangers: The
  Movie (1995)
Mighty Quinn, The (1989)
Miles From Nowhere (1992)
Milk Money (1994)
Mill on the Floss, The (1997)
Mille Bolle Blu (1993)
Millennium (1989)
Millennium: Shock of the Other (1992)
Miller's Crossing (1990)
Million Dollar Babies (1994)
Million to Juan, A (1994)
Milou en Mai (May Fools) (1990)
Mimic (1997)
Mina Tannenbaum (1993)
Mind Games (1989)
Mind Twister (1993)
Mind, Body & Soul (1992)
Mindwalk (1990)
Mindwarp (1992)
Miniskirted Dynamo, The (1996)
Minister's Wife, The (1992)
Ministry of Vengeance (1989)
Minotaur (1994)
Miracle at Beekman's Place (1988)
Miracle Child (1993)
Miracle in the Wilderness (1991)
Miracle in the Woods (1997)
Miracle Landing (1990)
Miracle Mile (1989)
Miracle on 34th Street (1994)
Miracle on I-880 (1993)
Miracle, The (1991)
Mirada Liquida (Liquid Gaze) (1996)
Mirage (1995)
Mirror Has Two Faces, The (1996)
Mirror Images (1992)
Mirror, Mirror (1991)
Mirror, Mirror (1996)

Mirror, Mirror 2: Raven Dance (1994)
Misadventures of Mr. Wilt, The (1990)
Misery (1990)
Misbegotten (1997)
Misery Brothers, The (1996)
Misfit Brigade, The (1988)
Misplaced (1989)
Miss America: Behind the Crown (1992)
Miss Evers' Boys (1997)
Miss Firecracker (1989)
Miss Rose White (1992)
Missing Pieces (1991)
Mission of the Shark (1991)
Mission: Impossible (1996)
Mississippi Masala (1991)
Mistaken Identity (1996)
Mistress (1992)
Mistrial (1996)
Mixed Nuts (1994)
Mo' (1996)
Mo' Better Blues (1990)
Mo' Money (1992)
Mob Boss (1990)
Mobsters (1991)
Model by Day (1994)
Modern Affair, A (1995)
Modern Love (1990)
Mojave Moon (1996)
Mojo (1997)
Moll Flanders (1996)
Molly & Gina (1994)
Mom and Dad Save the World (1992)
Mom for Christmas, A (1990)
Moment of Truth: A Child Too Many
  (1993)
Moment of Truth: A Mother's Deception
  (1994)
Moment of Truth: Broken Pledges (1994)
Moment of Truth: Caught in the Crossfire
  (1994)
Moment of Truth: Cradle of Conspiracy
  (1994)
Moment of Truth: Murder or Mercy?
  (1994)
Moment of Truth: Stalking Back (1993)
Moment of Truth: To Walk Again (1994)
Moment of Truth: Why My Daughter?
  (1993)
Mommy (1995)
Mon Homme (My Man) (1996)
Mon Pere, ce Heros (1991)
Mona Must Die (1994)
Mondo (1996)
Money Talks (1997)

National Lampoon's Favorite Deadly Sins (1995)
National Lampoon's Loaded Weapon I (1993)
National Lampoon's Senior Trip (1995)
Natural Born Killers (1994)
Natural Causes (1994)
Natural Enemy (1996)
Naufraghi Sotto Costa (Shipwrecks) (1992)
Navy SEALs (1990)
Near Room, The (1995)
Necessary Roughness (1991)
Necessity (1988)
Necromancer (1989)
Necronomicon (1993)
Ned Blessing: The True Story of My Life (1992)
Needful Things (1993)
Neil Simon's "Broadway Bound" (1992)
Neil Simon's "Jake's Women" (1996)
Neil Simon's "London Suite" (1996)
Neil Simon's "The Sunshine Boys" (1997)
Nell (1994)
Nella Mischia (In the Thick of It) (1995)
Nelly & Mr. Arnaud (1995)
Nemesis (1992)
Nemici d'Infanzia (Childhood Enemies) (1995)
Nenette et Boni (1996)
Neon Bible, The (1995)
Neon Empire, The (1989)
Nerolio (1996)
Nervous Energy (1995)
Nervous Ticks (1992)
Nestore L'ultima Corsa (Nestor's Last Trip) (1994)
Net, The (1995)
Netherworld (1990)
Neuf Mois (Nine Months) (1994)
Nevada (1997)
Never Ever (1996)
Never Forget (1991)
Never Give Up: The Jimmy V Story (1996)
Never Leave Nevada (1991)
Never Met Picasso (1996)
Never on Tuesday (1989)
Never Say Die (1994)
Never Say Never: The Deidre Hall Story (1995)
Never Talk to Strangers (1995)
Never Too Late (1996)
Neverending Story II: The Next Chapter, The (1990)
Neverending Story III, The (1994)

New Age, The (1994)
New Jack City (1991)
New Jersey Drive (1995)
New York Stories (1989)
Newsies (1992)
Next Door (1994)
Next Karate Kid, The (1994)
Next of Kin (1989)
Next Step, The (1996)
Next Year . . . We'll Go to Bed by Ten (1996)
Niagara Niagara (1997)
Niagaravation (1996)
Nick & Rachel (1997)
Nick and Jane (1997)
Nick Knight (1989)
Nick of Time (1995)
Nickel & Dime (1992)
Night and the City (1992)
Night and the Moment, The (1994)
Night Angel (1990)
Night Eyes (aka Hidden Vision) (1990)
Night Eyes 3 (1993)
Night Eyes 4: Fatal Passion (1995)
Night Falls on Manhattan (1997)
Night Game (1989)
Night Life (1990)
Night of the Demons 2 (1994)
Night of the Fox (1990)
Night of the Hunter (1991)
Night of the Living Dead (1990)
Night of the Scarecrow (1995)
Night of the Twisters (1996)
Night of the Warrior (1991)
Night on Earth (1991)
Night Orchid (1997)
Night Owl (1993)
Night Rhythms (1992)
Night Siege: Project Shadowchaser II (1994)
Night Sins (1997)
Night Train to Venice (1993)
Night Trap (1993)
Night Visions (1990)
Night Visitor (1989)
Night Visitors (1996)
Night Walk (1989)
Night We Never Met, The (1993)
Nightbreaker (1989)
Nightbreed (1990)
Nightfire (1994)
Nightjohn (1996)
Nightlife (1989)
Nightman, The (1992)

Perfect Man, The (1993)
Perfect Model, The (1989)
Perfect Moment (1997)
Perfect Mother, The (1997)
Perfect Profile (1991)
Perfect Tribute, The (1991)
Perfect Weapon, The (1991)
Perfect Witness (1989)
Perfect World, A (1993)
Perfectly Normal (1991)
Perry Mason Mystery: The Case of the
  Grimacing Governor (1994)
Perry Mason Mystery: The Case of the
  Jealous Jokester (1995)
Perry Mason Mystery: The Case of the
  Lethal Lifestyle (1994)
Perry Mason Mystery: The Case of the
  Wicked Wives (1993)
Perry Mason: The Case of the All-Star
  Assassin (1989)
Perry Mason: The Case of the Avenging
  Ace (1988)
Perry Mason: The Case of the Defiant
  Daughter (1990)
Perry Mason: The Case of the Desperate
  Deception (1990)
Perry Mason: The Case of the Fatal Fashion
  (1991)
Perry Mason: The Case of the Fatal
  Framing (1992)
Perry Mason: The Case of the Glass Coffin
  (1991)
Perry Mason: The Case of the Heartbroken
  Bride (1992)
Perry Mason: The Case of the Killer Kiss
  (1993)
Perry Mason: The Case of the Lady in the
  Lake (1988)
Perry Mason: The Case of the Lethal
  Lesson (1989)
Perry Mason: The Case of the Lost Love
  (1987)
Perry Mason: The Case of the Maligned
  Mobster (1991)
Perry Mason: The Case of the Murdered
  Madam (1987)
Perry Mason: The Case of the Musical
  Murder (1989)
Perry Mason: The Case of the Poisoned Pen
  (1990)
Perry Mason: The Case of the Reckless
  Romeo (1992)
Perry Mason: The Case of the Ruthless
  Reporter (1991)

Perry Mason: The Case of the Scandalous
  Scoundrel (1987)
Perry Mason: The Case of the Silenced
  Singer (1990)
Perry Mason: The Case of the Sinister
  Spirit (1987)
Perry Mason: The Case of the Skin-Deep
  Scandal (1993)
Perry Mason: The Case of the Telltale Talk
  Show Host (1993)
Personal Choice (1989)
Personal Journey With Martin Scorsese, A
  (1995)
Persuasion (1995)
Pest, The (1997)
Pet Semetary (1989)
Pet Semetary Two (1992)
Petain (1993)
Peter Benchley's "The Beast" (1996)
Peter Gunn (1989)
Phantasm II: Lord of the Dead (1991)
Phantom of the Mall: Eric's Revenge
  (1989)
Phantom of the Opera, The (1989)
Phantom of the Opera, The (1990)
Phantom, The (1996)
Pharaoh's Army (1995)
Phat Beach (1996)
Phenomenon (1996)
Philadelphia (1993)
Philadelphia Experiment 2, The (1993)
Philosophy in the Bedroom (1995)
Phoenix and the Magic Carpet, The (1995)
Photographing Fairies (1997)
Physical Evidence (1989)
Pianese Nunzio, 14 Anni a Maggio (1996)
Pianist, The (1991)
Piano Lesson, The (1995)
Piano, The (1993)
Piccoli Orrori (Little Horrors) (1994)
Piccolo Grande Amore (Pretty Princess)
  (1993)
Pickle, The (1993)
Picture Bride (1994)
Picture Perfect (1997)
Pie in the Sky (1995)
Pin for the Butterfly, A (1994)
Pin Gods (1996)
Pink Cadillac (1989)
Pink Lightning (1991)
Pippi Longstocking (1997)
Pistol: The Birth of a Legend, The (1991)
Pit and the Pendulum, The (1991)
Pizza Man (1991)

Radiant City (1996)
Radio Flyer (1992)
Radio Inside (1994)
Radioland Murders (1994)
Raffle, The (1994)
Rage and Honor (1992)
Rage in Harlem, A (1991)
Rage to Kill (1989)
Rage, The (1996)
Raging Angels (1995)
Raiders of the Sun (1992)
Railway Station Man, The (1992)
Rain Killer, The (1990)
Rain Without Thunder (1992)
Rainbow (1996)
Rainbow Drive (1990)
Rainbow, The (1989)
Raining Stones (1993)
Raising Cain (1992)
Raising the Ashes (1997)
Rambling Rose (1991)
Rampage (1992)
Ranger, the Cook and a Hole in the Sky,
 The (1995)
Ransom (1996)
Rapa Nui (1994)
Rape of Dr. Willis, The (1991)
Rapid Fire (1992)
Rapture, The (1991)
Rasputin (1996)
Ratchet (1996)
Rattled (1996)
Rave--Dancing to a Different Beat (1993)
Rave Review (1994)
Raw Nerve (1991)
Ray Alexander: A Menu for Murder (1995)
Ray Alexander: A Taste for Justice (1994)
Ready to Wear (Pret-a-Porter) (1994)
Real Blonde, The (1997)
Real McCoy, The (1993)
Reality Bites (1994)
Reason for Living: The Jill Ireland Story
 (1991)
Reasons of the Heart (1996)
Rebecca's Daughters (1992)
Rebound: The Legend of Earl "The Goat"
 Manigault (1996)
Reckless (1995)
Reckless Kelly (1993)
Rector's Wife (1994)
Red Blooded 2 (1996)
Red Corner (1997)
Red Earth, White Earth (1989)
Red King, White Knight (1989)

Red Ribbon Blues (1995)
Red Rock West (1993)
Red Scorpion (1989)
Red Scorpion 2 (1994)
Red Surf (1990)
Red Wind (1991)
Redheads (1992)
Redneck (1995)
Redwood Curtain (1995)
Ref, The (1994)
Reflecting Skin, The (1991)
Reflections on a Crime (1994)
Reform School Girl (1994)
Regarde les hommes tomber (See How
 They Fall) (1993)
Regarding Henry (1991)
Regeneration (1997)
Relative Fear (1994)
Relentless (1989)
Relentless 3 (1993)
Relentless 4: Ashes to Ashes (1994)
Relentless: Mind of a Killer (1993)
Relic, The (1997)
Reluctant Angel (1997)
Remains of the Day, The (1993)
Remember Me (1995)
Remote (1993)
Renaissance Man (1994)
Renegades (1989)
Rent-a-Kid (1995)
Repo Jake (1990)
Repossessed (1990)
Requiem for a Handsome Bastard (1993)
Rescue Me (1993)
Rescuers Down Under, The (1990)
Rescuers: Stories of Courage: Two Women
 (1997)
Rescuing Desire (1996)
Resistance (1992)
Restoration (1995)
Resurrected, The (1992)
Resurrection Man (1997)
Retroactive (1997)
Return of Eliot Ness, The (1991)
Return of Hunter: Everyone Walks in L.A.,
 The (1995)
Return of Ironside, The (1993)
Return of Jafar, The (1994)
Return of Sam McCloud, The (1989)
Return of SuperFly, The (1990)
Return of the Borrowers, The (1996)
Return of the Living Dead 3 (1993)
Return of the Musketeers, The (1989)
Return of the Native, The (1994)

Secretary, The (1992)
Secretary, The (1995)
Secrets (1992)
Secrets (1995)
Secrets & Lies (1995)
Seduced and Betrayed (1995)
Seduced by Evil (1994)
Seduced by Madness: The Diane Borchardt
 Story (1996)
Seduction in a Small Town (1997)
Seduction in Travis County, A (1991)
Seduction: Three Tales From the Inner
 Sanctum (1992)
See Jane Run (1995)
See No Evil, Hear No Evil (1989)
See You in the Morning (1988)
Seedpeople (1992)
Seeds of Tragedy (1991)
Seeing Red (1992)
Seeking the Cafe Bob (1996)
Segreto di Stato (State Secret) (1995)
Select Hotel (1996)
Selena (1997)
Selvaggi (Savages) (1995)
Sensation (1994)
Sense and Sensibility (1995)
Separate but Equal (1991)
Separate Lives (1995)
Separated by Murder (1994)
September Songs: The Music of Kurt Weill
 (1995)
Serial Mom (1994)
Serpent's Kiss, The (1997)
Serpent's Lair (1995)
Servants of Twilight, The (1991)
Serving in Silence: The Margarethe
 Cammermeyer Story (1995)
Set It Off (1996)
Set-Up, The (1995)
Setting Son, The (1997)
Settle the Score (1989)
Seven (1995)
Seven Years in Tibet (1997)
Seventh Coin, The (1993)
Seventh Floor, The (1993)
Severance (1989)
Severed Ties (1991)
Sex Is a Four-Letter Word (1995)
sex, lies and videotape (1989)
Sex, Love and Cold Hard Cash (1993)
Sexbomb (1989)
Sexual Advances (1992)
Sexual Outlaws (1994)
Sexual Response (1992)

Sgt. Bilko (1996)
Sgt. Kabukiman, N.Y.P.D. (1991)
Shadow Conspiracy (1997)
Shadow of a Doubt (1991)
Shadow of a Doubt (1995)
Shadow of a Stranger (1992)
Shadow of Obsession (1994)
Shadow of the Wolf (1993)
Shadow, The (1994)
Shadowlands (1993)
Shadows and Fog (1992)
Shadows of Desire (1994)
Shadowzone (1990)
Shaggy Dog, The (1994)
Shake, Rattle and Rock! (1994)
Shaking the Tree (1990)
Shallow Grave (1994)
Shame (1992)
Shame II: The Secret (1995)
Shameful Secrets (1993)
Shampoo Horns (1997)
Shamrock Conspiracy, The (1995)
Shannon's Deal (1989)
Sharon's Secret (1995)
Shattered (1991)
Shattered Dreams (1990)
Shattered Image (1994)
Shattered Mind (1996)
Shattered Trust: The Shari Karney Story
 (1993)
Shawshank Redemption, The (1994)
She Cried No (1996)
She Fought Alone (1995)
She Knows Too Much (1989)
She Led Two Lives (1994)
She Said No (1990)
She Says She's Innocent (1991)
She Stood Alone (1991)
She Stood Alone: The Tailhook Scandal
 (1995)
She Woke Up (1992)
She Woke Up Pregnant (1996)
She's Back (1989)
She's Been Away (1989)
She's Out of Control (1989)
She's So Lovely (1997)
She's the One (1996)
She-Devil (1989)
Shelf Life (1993)
Shell Seekers, The (1989)
Sheltering Sky, The (1990)
Sherlock Holmes: The Case of the
 Temporal Nexus (1996)
Shiloh (1996)

Skeeter (1993)
Skeleton Coast (1988)
Sketch Artist (1992)
Sketch Artist II: Hands That See (1995)
Ski Patrol (1990)
Skin Deep (1995)
Skin White Mask (1996)
Skull: A Night of Terror (1989)
Sky High (1990)
Skylark (1993)
Slab Boys, The (1997)
Slam Dunk Ernest (1995)
Slash Dance (1989)
Slaughter of the Innocents (1993)
Slave of Dreams (1995)
Slaves of New York (1989)
Slaves to the Underground (1997)
Sleep With Me (1994)
Sleep, Baby, Sleep (1995)
Sleepaway Camp 3: Teenage Wasteland
   (1989)
Sleepers (1991)
Sleepers (1996)
Sleeping Car, The (1990)
Sleeping With the Enemy (1991)
Sleeping With the Devil (1997)
Sleepless in Seattle (1993)
Sleepwalkers (1992)
Sleepwalking Killer, The (1997)
Sliding Doors (1997)
Sling Blade (1996)
Slipstream (1989)
Sliver (1993)
Slumber Party Massacre 3 (1990)
Small Dance, A (1991)
Small Faces (1995)
Small Hours, The (1997)
Small Kill (1992)
Small Sacrifices (1989)
Small Time (1991)
Smalltime (1996)
Smile Like Yours, A (1997)
Smilla's Sense of Snow (1997)
Smoke (1995)
Smoke Screen (1988)
Smoking/No Smoking (1993)
Snake Eater (1990)
Snake Eyes (1993)
Snake Skin Jacket (1997)
Snakeeater II: The Drug Pusher (1991)
Snakeeater III: His Law (1992)
Snapdragon (1993)
Sneakers (1992)
Snide & Prejudice (1997)

Sniper (1993)
Snow Kill (1990)
Snow White: A Tale of Terror (1997)
Snowbound: The Jim and Jennifer Stolpa
   Story (1994)
So I Married an Axe Murderer (1993)
So Proudly We Hail (1990)
Soapdish (1991)
Social Suicide (1991)
Society (1992)
Sodbusters (1994)
Soft Deceit (1994)
Soft Top Hard Shoulder (1992)
Sognando la California (California
   Dreaming) (1993)
Solar Crisis (1990)
Solar Force (1994)
Soldier's Fortune (1992)
Soldier's Tale, A (1991)
Soleil (Sun) (1997)
Solitaire (1992)
Solitaire for 2 (1995)
Solo (1996)
Solomon and Sheba (1995)
Some Kind of Life (1995)
Some Mother's Son (1996)
Somebody Has to Shoot the Picture (1990)
Somebody Is Waiting (1996)
Somebody to Love (1994)
Somebody's Daughter (1992)
Someone Else's America (1994)
Someone Else's Child (1994)
Someone She Knows (1994)
Something Borrowed, Something Blue
   (1997)
Something to Live For: The Alison Gertz
   Story (1992)
Something to Talk About (1995)
Somewhere in the City (1997)
Sommersby (1993)
Son of the Morning Star (1991)
Son of the Pink Panther (1993)
Son's Promise, A (1990)
Son-in-Law (1993)
Sonny Boy (1990)
Sons (1989)
Sophie and the Moonhanger (1996)
Sorry Wrong Number (1989)
Sortez des Rangs (Fall Out) (1996)
Sostiene Pereira (According to Pereira)
   (1995)
Soul Food (1997)
Soul Survivor (1995)
Soul of the Game (1996)

Stephen King's "It" (1990)
Stephen King's "Sometimes They Come
  Back" (1991)
Stephen King's "The Langoliers" (1995)
Stephen King's "The Shining" (1997)
Stephen King's "The Tommyknockers"
  (1993)
Stephen King's "Thinner" (1996)
Stepkids (1992)
Stepping Out (1991)
Stepsister, The (1997)
Steve Martini's "Undue Influence" (1996)
Stickin' Together (1992)
Sticks and Stones (1996)
Stiff Upper Lips (1997)
Still Breathing (1997)
Still Not Quite Human (1992)
Still Waters Run Deep (1996)
Stir (1997)
Stolen Babies (1993)
Stolen Hearts (1996)
Stolen Innocence (1995)
Stolen Memories: Secrets From the Rose
  Garden (1996)
Stolen Women (1997)
Stolen: One Husband! (1990)
Stompin' at the Savoy (1992)
Stone Cold (1991)
Stones for Ibarra (1988)
Stonewall (1995)
Stop at Nothing (1991)
Stop! Or My Mom Will Shoot (1992)
Storia d'Amore con i Crampi (1996)
Storm and Sorrow (1990)
Stormy Weathers (1992)
Story Lady, The (1991)
Story of Boys and Girls, The (1991)
Story of the Beach Boys: Summer Dreams,
  The (1990)
Storyville (1992)
Straight Out of Brooklyn (1991)
Straight Talk (1992)
Strange Blues of Cowboy Red, The (1996)
Strange Days (1995)
Stranger Among Us, A (1992)
Stranger at My Door (1991)
Stranger Beside Me, The (1995)
Stranger in My Bed (1987)
Stranger in My Home (1997)
Stranger in the Family (1991)
Stranger in Town, A (1995)
Stranger to Love, A (1996)
Stranger Within, The (1990)
Strangers by Night (1994)

Strangers in Good Company (1991)
Strapless (1989)
Strapped (1993)
Strays (1991)
Street Asylum (1990)
Street Corner Justice (1996)
Street Crimes (1991)
Street Fighter (1994)
Street Hunter (1990)
Street Justice (1989)
Street Knight (1993)
Street Wars (1992)
Street of No Return (1991)
Streetlife (1995)
Streets (1990)
Strictly Ballroom (1992)
Strictly Business (1991)
Strike a Pose (1993)
Strike It Rich (1990)
Striker (Combat Force) (1989)
Striking Distance (1993)
Strip Jack Naked: Nighthawks II (1991)
Stripped to Kill 2 (1989)
Striptease (1996)
Stroke of Midnight (1991)
Strong Island Boys (1997)
Stuart Saves His Family (1995)
Stuck With Each Other (1989)
Student Body (1995)
Stupids, The (1996)
Sub Down (1997)
Substance of Fire, The (1996)
Substitute Wife, The (1994)
Substitute, The (1993)
Substitute, The (1996)
Suburban Commando (1991)
Subway Stories (1997)
Sudden Death (1995)
Sudden Terror: The Hijacking of School
  Bus 17 (1996)
Suddenly (1996)
Sudie and Simpson (1990)
Suffering Bastards (1989)
Sugar Hill (1993)
Sugartime (1995)
Suicide Kings (1997)
Suite 16 (1994)
Sum of Us, The (1994)
Summer House, The (1993)
Summer My Father Grew Up, The (1991)
Summer of Ben Tyler, The (1996)
Summer of Fear (1996)
Summertime Switch (1994)
Sun the Moon and the Stars, The (1996)

Tout Ca . . . Pour Ca! (All That . . . for
  This?) (1993)
Tower of Terror (1997)
Tower, The (1993)
Town Torn Apart, A (1992)
Toxic Avenger Part II, The (1989)
Toxic Avenger Part III: The Last
  Temptation of Toxie, The (1989)
Toy Soldiers (1991)
Toy Story (1995)
Toys (1992)
Traces of Red (1992)
Tracks of a Killer (1995)
Trading Mom (1994)
Tragedy of Flight 103: The Inside Story,
  The (1990)
Trail of Tears (1995)
Tram a la Malvarrosa (1997)
Trancers II: Return of Jack Deth (1991)
Trancers III: Deth Lives (1992)
Trancers IV: Jack of Swords (1994)
Trancers V: Sudden Death (1995)
Transatlantique (1997)
Transylvania Twist (1990)
Trapped (1989)
Trapped in Paradise (1994)
Trapped in Space (1995)
Traps (1994)
Trauma (1993)
Traveling Man (1989)
Traveller (1997)
Treacherous Beauties (1994)
Treacherous Crossing (1992)
Treasure Island (1990)
Trees Lounge (1996)
Tremors (1990)
Tremors II: Aftershocks (1992)
Trenchcoat in Paradise (1989)
Trespass (1992)
Trial & Error (1993)
Trial and Error (1997)
Trial at Fortitude Bay (1994)
Trial by Fire (1995)
Trial by Jury (1994)
Trial of the Incredible Hulk, The (1989)
Trial, The (1992)
Trial: The Price of Passion (1992)
Trick of the Eye (1994)
Tricks (1997)
Trigger Effect, The (1996)
Trilogy of Terror II (1996)
Trinity and Beyond (1995)
Trip to Serendipity, A (1992)
Triple Bogey on a Par Five Hole (1991)

Triplecross (1995)
Triumph of the Heart: The Ricky Bell
  Story, A (1991)
Triumph of the Spirit (1989)
Triumph Over Disaster: The Hurricane
  Andrew Story (1993)
Trois Couleurs: Blanc (1993)
Trois Couleurs: Bleu (1993)
Trois Couleurs: Rouge (1994)
Trois Vies et un Suele Mort (1996)
Trojan Eddie (1996)
Troll in Central Park, A (1994)
Troop Beverly Hills (1989)
Tropical Heat (1993)
Trouble Bound (1993)
Trouble in Paradise (1989)
Trouble on the Corner (1997)
Trouble Shooters: Trapped Beneath the
  Earth (1993)
Troublesome Creek: A Midwestern (1996)
Trucks (1997)
True American, A (1996)
True Believer (1989)
True Blood (1989)
True Blue (1996)
True Colors (1991)
True Identity (1991)
True Lies (1994)
True Love and Chaos (1997)
True Romance (1993)
True Women (1997)
Truman (1995)
Truman Capote's "One Christmas" (1994)
Trust Me (1989)
Trust, The (1993)
Trusting Beatrice (1993)
Truth About Cats and Dogs, The (1996)
Truth or Consequences, N.M. (1997)
Tryst (1994)
Tu Nombre Envenena Mis Suenos (1996)
Tuareg: The Desert Warrior (1992)
Tune in Tomorrow . . . (1990)
Tunnel Vision (1995)
Turbo: A Power Rangers Movie (1997)
Turbulence (1996)
Turn Back the Clock (1989)
Turn of the Screw, The (1992)
Turner & Hooch (1989)
Turning April (1996)
Turtle Beach (1992)
Tuskegee Airmen, The (1995)
Tusks (aka Fire in Eden) (1990)
Tutti Gli Anni, Una Volta l'Anno (1994)

Film Title Index

FILM AND TELEVISION SOUNDTRACKS AND SCORES

Absolute Power (1997)
Lennie Niehaus
Varese Sarabande VSD-5808

Abyss, The (1989)
Alan Silvestri
Varese Sarabande VSD-5235

Addams Family Values (1993)
Artie Kane
Varese Sarabande VSD-5485

Adventures of Huck Finn, The (1993)
Bill Conti
Varese Sarabande VSD-5418

Adventures of the Great Mouse Detective,
  The (1986)
Henry Mancini
Varese Sarabande VSD-5359

Age of Innocence, The (1993)
Elmer Bernstein
Epic Soundtrax 57451

Air Force One (1997)
Jerry Goldsmith
Varese Sarabande VSD-5825

Alien 3 (1992)
Elliot Goldenthal
MCA 10629

Alien Nation (Music from the television
  scores)
Steve Dorff, Larry Herbstritt, David Kurtz
GNP Crescendo 8024

Alien Resurrection (1997)
John Frizzell
RCA Victor 68955

American President, The (1995)
Artie Kane
MCA 11380

Amistad (1997)
John Williams
Dreamworks 50035

Anastasia (1997)
David Newman
Atlantic 83053

Anaconda (1997)
Randy Edelman
Edel America 0036852

And the Band Played On (1993)
Carter Burwell
Varese Sarabande VSD-5449

Andre (1994)
Bruce Rowland
Milan 35682

Angel at My Table, An (1990)
Don McGlashen
DRG 12603

Angels in the Outfield (1994)
Randy Edelman
Hollywood Records 61608

Angie (1994)
Jerry Goldsmith
Varese Sarabande VSD-5469

Anna Karenina (1997)
Tchakiovsky (conducted by Solti)
Icon America 92752

Anne (from "Anne of Green Gables")
Hagood Hardy
Channel Productions 2203

Arctic Blue
Peter Rodgers Melnick
Narada Records 63030

Army of Darkness (1992)
Joseph Lo Duca
Varese Sarabande VSD-5411

Arrival, The (1991)
Richard Band
Intrada Records MAF-7032

Arrival, The (1996)
Arthur Kempel
Silva America 1071

At Play in the Fields of the Lord (1991)
Zbigniew Preisner
Fantasy 21007

Awfully Big Adventure, An (1995)
Richard Hartley
Silva America 2001

Babylon 5 (TV soundtrack) (1994)
Christopher Franke
Sonic Images 8502

Back to the Future Part II (1989)
Alan Silvestri
MCA 6361

Back to the Future Part III (1990)
Alan Silvestri
Varese Sarabande VSD-5272

Ballad of Little Jo, The (1993)
David Mansfield
Intrada Records MAF-7053

Balto (1995)
James Horner
MCA 11388

Batman (1989)
Danny Elfman
Warner Bros. 25977

Batman & Robin (1997)
Elliot Goldenthal
Warner Bros. 46260

Batman Forever (1995)
Elliot Goldenthal
Altantic Records 82776

Batman Returns (1992)
Danny Elman
Warner Bros. 26972

Beast, The (1988)
Don Davis
Varese Sarabande VSD-5731

Beethoven (1992)
Randy Edelman
MCA 10593

Before and After (1996)
Howard Shore
Hollywood Records 62039

Before the Rain (1994)
Anastasia
London 314-526407

Being Human (1994)
Michael Gibbs
Varese Sarabande VSD-5479

Betty Blue (1986)
Gabriel Yared
Virgin Movie Music 86054

Beyond Rangoon (1995)
Hans Zimmer
Milan 35725

Big Blue, The (1988)
Eric Serra
Virgin Movie Music 86078

Blink (1994)
Brad Fiedel
Milan 35659

Blue (1993)
Zbigniew Preisner
Virgin Records America 39027

Body Bags (TV soundtrack)
John Carpenter/Jim Lang
Varese Sarabande VSD-5448

Bram Stoker's "Dracula" (1992)
Wojciech Kilar
Columbia 53165

Brassed Off (1997)
Trevor Jones
RCA Victor 68757

Braveheart (1995)
James Horner
London 448295

Breaking the Rules (1992)
Hidden Faces
Varese Sarabande VSD-5386

Broken Arrow (1996)
Hans Zimmer
Milan 35744

Brothers McMullen, The (1995)
Seamus Egan
Arista 18803

Buddy (1997)
Elmer Bernstein
Varese Sarabande VSD-5829

Carrington (1995)
Michael Nyman
Argo Records 444-873

Castle Freak (1995)
Richard Band
Intrada MAF-7068

Caught (1996)
Chris Botti
Verve/Forecast 314-533095

Cemetery Club, The (1992)
Elmer Bernstein
Varese Sarabande VSD-5412

Chain Reaction (1996)
Jerry Goldsmith
Varese Sarabande VSD-5746

Chaplin (1992)
John Barry
Epic Soundtrax 52986

Christopher Columbus--The Discovery
   (1992)
Cliff Eidelman
Varese Sarabande VSD-5389

Cinema Paradiso (1988)
Ennio Morricone/Andrea Morricone
DRG CDSBL-12598

Citizen X (TV Soundtrack) (1995)
Randy Edelman
Varese Sarabande VSD-5601

City Hall (1996)
Jerry Goldsmith
Varese Sarabande VSD-5699

City of Joy (1992)
Ennio Morricone
Epic Soundtrax 52750

City Slickers (1991)
Hummie Mann/Mark McKenzie
Varese Sarabande VSD-5321

City Slickers II: The Legend of Curly's
   Gold (1994)
Artie Kane
Chaos Records 66183

Clear and Present Danger (1994)
James Horner
Milan 35679

Client, The (1994)
Howard Shore
Elektra 61686

Cliffhanger (1993)
Trevor Jones
Scotti Bros. Records 75417

Clockers (1995)
Terence Blanchard
Columbia 67440

Cobb (1994)
Elliot Goldenthal
Sony Classical 66923

Columbus and the Age of Discovery
(TV soundtrack)
Sheldon Mirowitz
Narada 66002

Commitments, The (1991)
The Commitments
MCA 10286

Commitments, The (Vol. 2)
The Commitments
MCA 10506

Con Air (1997)
Mark Mancina/Trevor Rabin
Hollywood Records 162099

Congo (1995)
Jerry Goldsmith
Epic Soundtrax 67266

Contact (1997)
Alan Silvestri
Warner Bros. 46811

Courage Under Fire (1996)
James Horner
Angel 53105

Cousins (1989)
Angelo Badalamenti
Warner Bros. 25901

Craft, The (1996)
Graeme Revell
Varese Sarabande VSD-5732

Crash (1996)
Howard Shore
Milan 35774

Crash and Burn (1990)
Richard Band
Intrada MAF-7033

Crimson Tide (1995)
Hans Zimmer
Hollywood Records 62025

Criss Cross (1992)
Trevor Jones
Intrada MAF-7021

Critters 2: The Main Course (1988)
Nicholas Pike
Intrada MAF-7045

Crow: City of Angels, The (1996)
Graeme Revell
Varese Sarabande VSD-5499

Cure, The (1995)
Dave Grusin
GRP Records 9828

Cutthroat Island (1995)
John Debney
Nu.Millennia Records 00009-4

Cyrano de Bergerac (1990)
Jean-Claude Petit
DRG Records 12602

Dad (1989)
James Horner
MSP Records 6359

Damage (1992)
Wojciech Michniewski
Varese Sarabande VSD 5406

Dances With Wolves (1990)
John Barry
Epic Soundtrax 46982

Dangerous Liaisons (1988)
George Fenton
Virgin Movie Music 86102

Dante's Peak (1997)
John Frizzell/James Newton Howard
Varese Sarabande VSD-5793

Dark Half, The (1993)
Christopher Young
Varese Sarabande VSD-5340

Darkman (1990)
Danny Elfman
MCA 10094

Dave (1993)
James Newton Howard
Big Screen Records 24510

Daylight (1996)
Randy Edelman
Universal Records 53024

Dead Again (1991)
Patrick Doyle
Varese Sarabande VSD-5339

Dead Poets Society (1989)
Maurice Jarre
Milan 35761

Dead Zone, The (1983)
Michael Kamen
Milan 35694

Death Becomes Her (1992)
Alan Silvestri
Varese Sarabande VSD-5375

DeepStar Six (1989)
Harry Manfredini
Intrada MAF-7004

Demolition Man (1993)
Jonathan Sheffer
Varese Sarabande VSD-5447

Desperate Remedies (1993)
Carmel Carroll
Milan 35673

Dingo (1991)
Miles Davis/Michel Legrand
Warner Bros. 26438

Disclosure (1994)
Ennio Morricone
Virgin Movie Music 40162

Distinguished Gentleman, The (1992)
Randy Edelman
Varese Sarabande VSD-5402

Do the Right Thing (1989)
Branford Marsalis
Columbia 45406

Doc Hollywood (1991)
Carter Burwell
Varese Sarabande VSD-5332

Doctor Mordrid (1990)/Demonic Toys
  (1991)
Richard Band
Moonstone Records 12985

Dolores Claiborne (1995)
Danny Elfman
Varese Sarabande VSD-5602

Dr. Giggles (1992)
Brian May
Intrada MAF-7043

Dr. Jekyll & Ms. Hyde (1995)
Mark McKenzie
Intrada MAF-7063

Dragon: The Bruce Lee Story (1993)
Randy Edelman
MCA 10627

Dragonheart (1996)
Randy Edelman
MCA 11449

Dream Lover (1994)
Christopher Young
Koch International Classic 8700

Drop Squad (1994)
Michael Bearden
GRP 4028

Eat Drink Man Woman (1994)
Mader
Varese Sarabande VSD-5528

Ed Wood (1994)
Howard Shore
Hollywood Records 82002

Eddie & The Cruisers II (Eddie Lives!)
  (1989)
John Cafferty
Scotti Bros. Records 15203

Edward Scissorhands (1990)
Danny Elfman
MCA 10133

English Patient, The (1996)
Gabriel Yared
Fantasy 16001

Englishman Who Went Up a Hill but Came
  Down a Mountain, The (1995)
Stephen Endelman
Epic Soundtrax 67151

Eraser (1996)
Alan Silvestri
Atlantic 82957

Escape From L.A. (1996)
John Carpenter/Shirley Walker
Milan 35773

Even Cowgirls Get the Blues (1994)
k.d. lang
Sire Records 45433

Evita (1996)
Andrew Lloyd Webber/Tim Rice
Warner Bros. 46348

Exit to Eden (1994)
Patrick Doyle
Varese Sarabande VSD-5553

Exotica (1994)
Mychael Danna
Varese Sarabande VSD-5543

Family Thing, A (1996)
Charles Gross
Edel America 2970

Far and Away (1992)
John Williams
MCA 10628

Fargo (1996)/Barton Fink (1991)
Carter Burwell
TVT Records 8010

Father of the Bride (1991)
Alan Silvestri
Varese Sarabande VSD-5348

Fearless (1993)
Maurice Jarre
Nonesuch 79334

Feast of July (1995)
Zbigniew Preisner
Angel 55357

Ferngully . . . The Last Rainforest (1992)
Alan Silvestri
MCA 10619

Fierce Creatures (1997)
Jerry Goldsmith
Varese Sarabande 5792

Fifth Element, The (1997)
Eric Serra
Virgin Movie Music 44203

Fire in the Sky (1993)
Mark Isham
Varese Sarabande VSD-5417

First Knight (1995)
Jerry Goldsmith
Epic Soundtrax 67270

First Wives Club, The (1996)
Marc Shaiman
Varese Sarabande VSD-5781

Fluke (1995)
Carlo Siliotto
Milan 35720

For Roseanna (1997)
Trevor Jones
RCA Victor 68836

Forever Young (1992)
Jerry Goldsmith
Big Screen Records 24482

Forrest Gump (1994)
Alan Silvestri
Epic Soundtrax 66430

1492: Conquest of Paradise (1992)
Vangelis
Atlantic 82432

Frank & Jesse (1995)
Mark McKenzie
Intrada MAF-7059

Frankenstein (1993)
Patrick Doyle
Epic Soundtrax 66631

Frankie Starlight (1995)
Elmer Bernstein
Varese Sarabande VSD-5679

Freddy's Dead: The Final Nightmare
   (1991)
Brian May
Varese Sarabande VSD-5333

Fried Green Tomatoes (1991)
Thomas Newman
MCA 10634

Frighteners, The (1996)
Danny Elfman
MCA 11469

Fugitive, The (1993)
James Newton Howard
Elektra 61592

Gettysburg (1993)
Randy Edelman
Milan 35654

Gold Diggers: The Secret of Bear Mountain
 (1995)
Joel McNeely
Varese Sarabande VSD-5633

Golden Gate (1993)
Elliot Goldenthal
Varese Sarabande VSD-5470

GoldenEye (1995)
Eric Serra
Virgin Movie Music 41048

Gorillas in the Mist (1988)
Maurice Jarre
MCA 6255

Green Card (1990)
Hans Zimmer
Varese Sarabande VSD-5309

Gremlins 2: The New Batch (1990)
Jerry Goldsmith
Varese Sarabande VSD-5269

Guarding Tess (1994)
Michael Convertino
TriStar Records 64353

Gulliver's Travels (TV soundtrack) (1996)
Trevor Jones
RCA Victor 68475

Halloween IV: The Return of Michael
 Myers (1988)
John Carpenter/Alan Howarth
Varese Sarabande VSD-5205

Halloween: The Curse of Michael Myers
 (1995)
Alan Howarth
Varese Sarabande VSD-5678

Hamlet (1990)
Ennio Morricone
Virgin Record America 86206

Hamlet (1996)
Patrick Doyle
Sony Classical 62857

Hand That Rocks the Cradle, The (1992)
Graeme Revell
Hollywood Records 61304

Handmaid's Tale, The (1990)
Ryuichi Sakamoto
GNP Crescendo 8020

Hard Target (1993)
Graeme Revell/Kodo
Varese Sarabande VSD-5445

Heart of Midnight (1988)
Yanni
Silva America 1003

Heathers (1989)
David Newman
Varese Sarabande VSD-5223

Heaven & Earth (1993)
Kitaro
Geffen 24814

Henry V (1989)
Patrick Doyle
Angel 49919

Her Majesty, Mrs. Brown (1997)
Stephen Warbeck
Milan 35821

Hercules: The Legendary Journey (1995)
(TV soundtrack)
Joseph Lo Duca
Varese Sarabande VSD-5660

Hero and the Terror (1988)
David Michael Frank
Cinedisc 1007

High Heels (1991)
Ryuichi Sakamoto
Antilles Records 510855

High Spirits (1988)
George Fenton
GNP Crescendo 8016

Home Alone 2: Lost in New York (1992)
John Williams
Fox 1002

Homeward Bound: The Incredible Journey
(1993)
Bruce Broughton
Intrada MAF-7041

Homeward Bound: Lost in San Francisco
(1996)
Bruce Broughton
 Disney 60903

Honey, I Blew Up the Kid (1992)
Bruce Broughton
Intrada MAF-7030

Hook (1991)
John Williams
Epic Soundtrax 48888

Hot Shots! Part Deux (1993)
Basil Poledouris
Varesee Sarabande VSD-5426

House of the Spirits, The (1993)
Hans Zimmer
Virgin Records America 39219

House on Sorority Row, The (1983)/The
 Alchemist (1986)
Richard Band
Intrada MAF-7046

Howards End (1992)
Richard Robbins
Nimbus Records 5339

Hudson Hawk (1991)
Michael Kamen/Robert Kraft
Varese Sarabande VSD-5323

Hudsucker Proxy, The (1994)
Carter Burwell
Varese Sarabande VSD-5477

Human Quest, The
Jim Latham
Laserlight Records 12564

Hunt for Red October, The (1990)
Basil Poledouris
MCA 6428

Hunted, The (1995)
Kodo
TriStar Records 67202

I Love Trouble (1994)
David Newman
Varese Sarabande VSD-5510

I'll Do Anything (1994)
Hans Zimmer
Varese Sarabande VSD-5474

Immortal Beloved (1994)
Beethoven (Sir Georg Solti, cond.)
Sony Classical 66301

In Love and War (1996)
George Fenton
RCA Victor 68725

In the Army Now (1994)
Robert Folk
Intrada MAF-7058

In the Line of Duty (TV scores)
Mark Snow
Intrada MAF-7034

In the Mouth of Madness (1995)
John Carpenter/Jim Lang
DRG 12611

Independence Day (1996)
David Arnold
RCA Victor 68564

Indian in the Cupboard, The (1995)
Randy Edelman
Sony Classical 68475

Indiana Jones and the Last Crusade (1989)
John Williams
Warner Bros. 25883

Indochine (1992)
William Kraft
Varese Sarabande VSD-5397

Infinity (1996)
Bruce Broughton
Intrada MFS-7072

Interview With the Vampire (1994)
Elliot Goldenthal
Geffen 24719

Iron Will (1994)
Joel McNeely
Varese Sarabande VSD-5467

It's My Party (1996)
Basil Poledouris
Varese Sarabande VSD-5701

Jack (1996)
Michael Kamen
Hollywood Records 62063

Jeanne La Pucelle (1994)
Jordi Savall/Guillaume DuFay
Harmonia Mundi USA 1006

Jefferson in Paris (1995)
Richard Robbins
Angel 55311

Josh and S.A.M. (1993)
Thomas Newman
Varese Sarabande VSD-5432

Joy Luck Club, The (1993)
Rachel Portman
Hollywood Records 61561

Judicial Consent (1994)
Christopher Young
Intrada MAF-7062

Jumanji (1995)
James Horner
Epic Records 67424

Junior (1994)
James Newton Howard
Varese Sarabande VSD-5558

Jurassic Park (1993)
John Williams
MCA 10859

Just Cause (1995)
James Newton Howard
Varese Sarabande VSD-5596

K2 (1992)
Hans Zimmer
Varese Sarabande VSD-5354

Kid in King Arthur's Court, A (1995)
J.A.C. Redford
Disney Records 60885

Killing Zoe (1993)
Tomandandy
Milan 35696

Kindergarten Cop (1990)
Randy Edelman
Varese Sarabande VSD-5305

King of the Hill (1993)
Cliff Martinez
Varese Sarabande VSD-5425

King of the Olympics (TV soundtrack)
   (1988)
Paul Chihara
Sonic Atmospheres 80021

Kiss of Death (1995)
Trevor Jones
Milan 35715

Kung Fu: The Legend Continues
(TV soundtrack)
Jeff Danna
Narada Records 66008

La Belle et la Bete
Philip Glass
Nonesuch 79347

La Femme Nikita (1990)
Eric Serra
Varese Sarabande VSD-5314

La Fille de d'Artagnan (1994)
Philippe Sarde
TriStar Records 36639

Land and Freedom (1995)
George Fenton
DRG 12613

Lassie (1994)
Basil Poledouris
Sony Wonder 66414

Last Action Hero (1993)
Michael Kamen
Columbia 57393

Last Dance (1996)
Mark Isham
Hollywood Records 62005

Last Exit to Brooklyn (1989)
Mark Knopfler
Warner Bros. 25986

Last of the Dogmen (1995)
David Arnold
Atlantic 82859

Last of the Mohicans, The (1992)
Randy Edelman/Trevor Jones
Morgan Creek Records 20015

Last Seduction, The (1994)
Joseph Vitarelli
Pure Records 2240

Late Shift, The (TV soundtrack) (1996)
Ira Newborn
Silva America 1070

Lawnmower Man 2: Beyond Cyberspace
    (1996)
Robert Folk
Varese Sarabande VSD-5698

Legends of the Fall (1994)
James Horner
Epic Soundtrax 66462

Leprechauun (1993)
Kevin Kiner
Intrada MAF-7050

Leprechaun 2 (1994)
Jonathan Elias
Varese Sarabande VSD-5495

Leviathan (1989)
Jerry Goldsmith
Varese Sarabande VSD-5226

Like Water for Chocolate (1992)
Leo Brower
Milan 35760

Lincoln (TV soundtrack)
Alan Menken
Angel 54751

Lion King, The (1994)
Hans Zimmer/Elton John/Tim Rice
Disney 60858

Lionheart (1991)
John Scott
Intrada MAF-7011

Little Buddha (1993)
Ryuichi Sakamoto
Milan 35676

Little Man Tate (1991)
Mark Isham
Varese Sarabande VSD-5343

Little Princess, A (1995)
Patrick Doyle
Varese Sarabande VSD-5628

Little Women (1994)
Thomas Newman
Sony Classical 66922

Losing Isaiah (1995)
Mark Isham
Columbia 67087

Lost in Yonkers (1993)
Elmer Bernstein
Varese Sarabande VSD-5419

Love Affair (1994)
Ennio Morricone
Reprise Records 45810

Love Field (1992)
Jerry Goldsmith
Varese Sarabande VSD-5316

Lover, The (1992)
Gabriel Yared
Varese Sarabande VSD-5394

M. Butterfly (1993)
Howard Shore
Varese Sarabande VSD-5435

Mad Dog & Glory (1993)
Elmer Bernstein
Varese Sarabande VSD-5415

Magdalene (1988)
Cliff Eidelman
Intrada MAF-7029

Magic in the Water (1995)
David Schwartz
Varese Sarabande VSD-5659

Malcolm X (1992)
Terence Blanchard
40 Acres & a Mule Musicworks 53190

Malice (1993)
Jerry Goldsmith
Varese Sarabande VSD-5442

Man Without a Face, The (1993)
James Horner
Philips Records 518244

Mandela (1996)
Cedric Gradus-Samson
Island 524305

Mandela and deKlerk (TV soundtrack)
  (1997)
Cedric Gradus-Samson
Rhino 72766

Map of the Human Heart (1993)
Gabriel Yared
Verve 514900

Marvin's Room (1996)
Rachel Portman
Pangaea Records 10002

Mary Reilly (1996)
George Fenton
Sony Classical 62259

Mask, The (1994)
Gregg Edelman
TriStar 66646

Matinee (1993)
Jerry Goldsmith
Varese Sarabande VSD-5408

Maverick (1994)
Randy Newman
Warner Bros. 45816

Medicine Man (1992)
Jerry Goldsmith
Varese Sarabande VSD-5350

Michael Collins (1996)
Elliot Goldenthal
Atlantic 82960

Midnight Run (1988)
Danny Elfman
MCA Special Products 6250

Mission: Impossible (1996)
Danny Elfman
Philips Classic 454525

Moderns, The (1988)
Mark Isham
Virgin Movie Music 86059

Moll Flanders (1996)
Mark Mancina
London 452485

Mom and Dad Saved the World (1992)
Jerry Goldsmith
Varese Sarabande VSD-5385

Mortal Kombat (1995)
George S. Clinton
TVT 6410

Mother Night (1996)
Michael Convertino
Varese Sarabande VSD-5780

Mr. Baseball (1992)
Jerry Goldsmith
Varese Sarabande VSD-5383

Mr. Holland's Opus (1995)
Michael Kamen
London 452965

Mrs. Doubtfire (1993)
Howard Shore
Fox 11015

Mrs. Parker and the Vicious Circle (1994)
Mark Isham
Varese Sarabande VSD-5471

Mrs. Winterbourne (1996)
Mark Watters
Varese Sarabande VSD-5720

Much Ado About Nothing (1993)
Patrick Doyle
Epic Soundtrax 54009

Mulholland Falls (1996)
Dave Grusin
Edel America Records 29732

Muppet Christmas Carol, The (1992)
Miles Goodman
Jim Henson Records 30017

Muppet Treasure Island (1996)
Hans Zimmer
Jim Henson Records 30019

Mute Witness (1995)
Wilbert Hirsch
TriStar Records 35052

My Cousin Vinny (1992)
Randy Edelman
Varese Sarabande VSD-5364

My Father's Glory/My Mother's Castle
  (1990)
Vladimir Cosma
DRG 12604

My Life (1993)
John Barry
Epic Soundtrax 57663

Mystery of Rampo, The (1994)
Vaclav Neumann
Discovery Records DCO-77029

Nails (1992)
Bill Conti
Varese Sarabande VSD-5384

Naked Gun 2-1/2: The Smell of Fear (1991)
Ira Newborn
Varese Sarabande VSD-5331

Needful Things (1993)
Patrick Doyle
Varese Sarabande VSD-5438

Nell (1994)
Mark Isham
Fox 11023

Nemesis (1993)
Michel Rubini
Beachwood Records 2510

Never Talk to Strangers (1995)
Pino Donaggio
Scotti Bros. Records 75495

New Nightmare (1994)
J. Peter Robinson
Milan 35890

Newsies (1992)
Alan Menken/Jack Feldman
Disney 60832

Nick of Time (1995)
Arthur B. Rubinstein
Milan 35737

Night on Earth (1991)
Tom Waits
Island 510725

Nightbreed (1990)
Danny Elfman
MCA 8037

Nightmare Before Christmas, The (1993)
Danny Elfman
Disney 60855

Nightmare on Elm Street 4, A:
The Dream Master (1988)
Craig Safan
Varese Sarabande VSD-5203

Nightmare on Elm Street 5, A:
The Dream Child (1989)
Jay Ferguson
Varese Sarabande VSD-5238

Nine Months (1995)
Hans Zimmer
Milan 35726

Nixon (1995)
John Williams
Hollywood Records 62043

No Escape (1994)
Graeme Revell
Varese Sarabande VSD-5483

Nobody's Fool (1994)
Howard Shore
Milan 35689

Norma Jean and Marilyn (TV soundtrack)
  (1996)
Christopher Young
Intrada MAF-7070

Not Without My Daughter (1991)
Jerry Goldsmith
Intrada MAK-7012

Now and Then (1995)
Cliff Eidelman
Varese Sarabande VSD-5675

Nutcracker, The (1993)
Tchaikovsky
Nonesuch 79294

O Pioneers! (TV soundtrack) (1992)
Bruce Broughton
Intrada MAF-7023

Of Mice and Men (1992)
Mark Isham
Varese Sarabande VSD-5371

Oldest Living Confederate Widow Tells All
(TV soundtrack)
Lee Holdridge
GNP Crescendo 8017

On Deadly Ground (1994)
Basil Poledouris
Varese Sarabande VSD-5468

One Against the Wind (TV soundtrack)
  (1991)
Lee Holdridge
Intrada MAF-7039

101 Dalmations (1996)
Michael Kamen
Disney 60911

Only You (1994)
Rachel Portman
Columbia 66182

Operation Dumbo Drop (1995)
David Newman
Hollywood Records 62032

Othello (1995)
Charlie Mole
Varese Sarabande VSD-5689

Outbreak (1995)
James Newton Howard
Varese Sarabande VSD-5599

Pagemaster, The (1994)
James Horner
Fox 11019

Paper, The (1994)
Randy Newman
Reprise 45616

Paradise Road (1997)
Ross Edwards
Sony Classical 63026

Park Is Mine, The (TV soundtrack) (1985)
Tangerine Dream
Silva America 1004

Passenger 57 (1992)
Stanley Clarke
Epic Soundtrax 53232

Patriot Games (1992)
James Horner
Milan 66051

Peacemaker, The (1997)
Hans Zimmer
Dreamworks 50027

Peter the Great (TV soundtrack) (1986)
Laurence Rosenthal
Southern Cross Records 1011

Phantom, The (1996)
David Newman
Milan 35756

Philadelphia (1993)
Howard Shore
Epic Soundtrax 57823

Piano, The (1993)
Michael Nyman
Virgin Records America 88274

Picasso
Roman Vlad
Smithsonian/Folkways 3860

Picture Bride (1994)
Mark Adler
Virgin Movie Music 40413

Pit and the Pendulum, The (1991)
Richard Band
Moonstone Records 9903

Platoon Leader (1988)
George S. Clinton
GNP Crescendo 8013

Player, The (1992)
Thomas Newman
Varese Sarabande VSD-5366

Pocahontas (1995)
Alan Menken/Stephen Schwartz
Disney 60874

Point of No Return (1993)
Hans Zimmer
Milan 66225

Powder (1995)
Jerry Goldsmith
Hollywood Records 62038

Power of One, The (1992)
Hans Zimmer
Elektra 61335

Predator II (1990)
Alan Silvestri
Varese Sarabande VSD-5302

Prelude to a Kiss (1992)
James Newton Howard
Milan 66076

Presumed Innocent (1990)
John Williams
Varese Sarabande VSD-5280

Pride and Prejudice (TV soundtrack) (1997)
Carl Davis
Angel 36090

Primal Fear (1996)
James Newton Howard
Milan 35716

Prince of Tides, The (1991)
Barbra Streisand/James Newton Howard
Columbia 48627

Princess Caraboo (1994)
Richard Hartley
Varese Sarabande VSD-5544

Professional, The (1994)
Eric Serra
TriStar Records 67201

Proprietor, The (1996)
Richard Robbins
TriStar Records 36797

Prospero's Books (1991)
Michael Nyman
London 425224

Public Eye, The (1992)
Ken Kugler
Varese Sarabande VSD-5374

Puppet Master I and II (1989 and 1990)
Richard Band
Moonstone Records 9902

Pure Country (1992)
George Strait
MCA 10651

Pure Formality, A (1994)
Ennio Morricone
Sony Classical 67166

Pyromaniac's Love Story, A (1995)
Rachel Portman
Varese Sarabande VSD-5620

Quest, The (1996)
Randy Newman
Varese Sarabande VSD-5718

Quick and the Dead, The (1995)
Alan Silvestri
Varese Sarabande VSD-5595

Quigley Down Under (1990)
Basil Poledouris
Intrada MAF-7006

Quiz Show (1994)
Mark Isham
Hollywood Records 61604

Rapa Nui (1994)
Stewart Copeland
Milan 35681

Rapid Fire (1992)
Christopher Young
Varese Sarabande VSD-5388

Real McCoy, The (1993)
Brad Fidel
Varese Sarabande VSD-5450

Red (1994)
Zbigniew Preisner
Virgin Movie Music 39860

Remains of the Day, The (1993)
Richard Robbins
Angel 55029

Renaissance Man (1994)
Hans Zimmer
Varese Sarabande VSD-5502

Rent-a-Cop (1988)
Jerry Goldsmith
Intrada MAF-7002

Restoration (1995)
James Newton Howard
Milan 35707

Resurrected, The 1992)
Richard Band
Intrada MAF-7036

Return to Snowy River (1988)
Bruce Rowland
Varese Sarabande VSD-70451

Rich in Love (1993)
Georges Delerue
Varese Sarabande VSD-5370

Richard III (1995)
Trevor Jones
London 828719

Richie Rich (1994)
Alan Silvestri
Varese Sarabande VSD-5582

River Runs Through It, A (1992)
Mark Isham
Milan 35631

Road to Wellville, The (1994)
Rachel Portman
Varese Sarabande VSD-5512

Rob Roy (1995)
Carter Burwell
Virgin Movie Music 40351

Robin Hood: Prince of Thieves (1991)
Michael Kamen
Morgan Creek Records 20004

RoboCop 2 (1990)
Leonard Rosenman
Varese Sarabande VSD-5271

RoboCop 3 (1993)
Basil Poledouris
Varese Sarabande VSD-5416

Robot Wars (1993)
David Arkenstone
Moonstone Records 5102

Romeo Is Bleeding (1993)
Mark Isham
Verve 521231

Roommates (1995)
Elmer Bernstein
Hollywood Records 62003

Rosewood (1997)
John Williams
Sony Classical 63031

Ruby (1992)
John Scott
Intrada MAF-7026

Rudy (1993)
Jerry Goldsmith
Varese Sarabande VSD-5446

Rush (1991)
Eric Clapton
Reprise 26794

Russia House, The (1990)
Jerry Goldsmith
MCA 10136

Sabrina (1995)
John Williams
A&M Records 540456

Saint, The (1997)
Graeme Revell
Angel 56446

Saint of Fort Washington, The (1993)
James Newton Howard
Varese Sarabande VSD-5444

Santa Clause, The (1994)
Michael Convertino
Milan 35713

Saved by the Bell (TV soundtrack) (1990)
Scott Gale/Rich Eames
Rhino Records 71880

Scarlet Letter, The (1995)
John Barry
Epic Soundtrax 67431

Scent of a Woman (1992)
Thomas Newman
MCA 10759

Schindler's List (1993)
John Williams
MCA 10969

Sea of Love (1989)
Trevor Jones
Polydor 842170

SeaQuest DSV (TV soundtrack) (1993)
John Debney
Varese Sarabande VSD-5565

Searching for Bobby Fischer (1993)
James Horner
Big Screen Records 24532

Secret Agent, The (1996)
Philip Glass
Nonesuch 79442

Secret Garden, The (1993)
Zbigniew Preisner
Varese Sarabande VSD-5443

Secret of Roan Inish, The (1994)
Mason Daring
Daring Records DR-3015

Sense and Sensibility (1995)
Patrick Doyle
Sony Classical 62258

Seventh Sign, The (1988)
Jack Nitzsche
Cinedisc 1006

Shadow Conspiracy (1997)
Bruce Broughton
Intrada MAF-7073

Shaka Zulu (TV soundtrack)
Dave Pollecutt
Cinedisc 1002

Shawshank Redemption, The (1994)
Thomas Newman
Epic Soundtrax 66621

Sheltering Sky, The (1990)
Ryuichi Sakamoto
Virgin Records America 86204

She's the One (1996)
Tom Petty & the Heartbreakers
Warner Bros. 46285

Shock to the System, A (1990)
Gary Chang
Windham Hill 0123

Silence of the Lambs, The (1991)
Howard Shore
MCA 10194

Silent Fall (1994)
Stewart Copeland
Morgan Creek Records 20029

Simple Twist of Fate (1994)
Cliff Eidelman
Varese Sarabande VSD-5538

Sirens (1994)
Rachel Portman
Milan 35669

Six Days and Six Nights
Michael Nyman
Virgin Movie Music 39882

Six Degrees of Separation (1993)
Jerry Goldsmith
Elektra 61623

Sleeping With the Enemy (1991)
Jerry Goldsmith
Columbia 47380

Sleepwalkers (1992)
Nicholas Pike
Milan 35616

Sneakers (1992)
James Horner/Branford Marsalis
Columbia 53146

Soapdish (1991)
Alan Silvestri
Varese Sarabande VSD-5322

Some Mother's Son (1996)
Bill Whelan
Celtic Heartbeat 82956

Something to Talk About (1995)
Hans Zimmer
Varese Sarabande VSD-5664

Sommersby (1993)
Danny Elfman
Elektra 61491

Son of the Morning Star (TV soundtrack)
   (1991)
Craig Safan
Intrada MAF-7037

Space Jam (1996)
James Newton Howard
Warner Sunset 82979

Specialist, The (1994)
John Barry
Epic Soundtrax 70799

Speed (1994)
Mark Mancina
Fox 1020

Speed 2: Cruise Control (1997)
Mark Mancina
Virgin Movie Music 44204

Spitfire Grill, The (1996)
James Horner
Sony Classical 62776

Stand, The
W.G. Snuffy Walden
Varese Sarabande VSD-5496

Stanley & Iris (1990)
John Williams
Varese Sarabande VSD-5255

Star Maker, The (1995)
Ennio Morricone
Hollywood Records 62056

Star Trek Generations (1994)
Dennis McCarthy
GNP Crescendo 8040

Star Trek V: The Final Frontier (1989)
Jerry Goldsmith
Epic 45267

Star Trek 6: The Undiscovered Country
  (1991)
Cliff Edelman
MCA 10512

Star Trek: Deep Space Nine (TV
  soundtrack) (1993)
Dennis McCarthy
GNP Crescendo 8034

Start Trek: First Contact (1996)
Jerry Goldsmith/Joel Goldsmith
GNP Crescendo 8052

Star Trek: Voyager (TV soundtrack) (1995)
Jay Chattaway
GNP Crescendo 8041

Stargate (1994)
David Arnold
Milan 35697

Stars Fell on Henrietta, The (1995)
David Benoit
Varese Sarabande VSD-5667

State of Grace (1990)
Ennio Morricone
MCA 10119

Steal Big, Steal Little (1995)
William Olvis
Milan 35729

Stealing Home (1988)
David Foster
Atco 81885

Storyville (1992)
Carter Burwell
Varese Sarabande VSD-5347

Straight Talk (1992)
Dolly Parton
Hollywood Records 61303

Strawberry and Chocolate (1994)
Jose Maria Vitier
Milan 35710

Street Fighter (1994)
Graeme Revell
Varese Sarabande VSD-5560

Strictly Ballroom (1991)
David Hirschfelder
Columbia 53079

Stuart Saves His Family (1995)
Marc Shaiman
Milan 35709

Stupids, The (1996)
Christopher Young
Intrada MFA-7071

Sudden Death (1995)
John Debney
Varese Sarabande VSD-5663

Sweet Hereafter, The (1997)
Mychael Danna
Virgin Movie Music 44955

Swing Kids (1993)
James Horner
Hollywood Records 61357

Tales From the Crypt: Bordello of Blood
  (1996)
Chris Boardman
Varese Sarabande VSD-5728

Tales From the Darkside: The Movie
  (1990)
Donald A. Rubinstein
GNP Crescendo 8021

Tall Tales: The Unbelievable Adventures
of Pecos Bill (1995)
Randy Edelman
Disney 60867

Temp, The (1993)
Frederic Talgorn
Varese Sarabande VSD-5410

Terminal Velocity (1994)
Joel McNeely
Varese Sarabande VSD-5546

Terminator 2: Judgment Day (1991)
Brad Fiedel
Varese Sarabande VSD-5335

Thin Blue Line, The (1988)
Philip Glass
Nonesuch 79209

Thirtysomething (TV soundtrack) (1988)
W.G. Snuffy Walden
Geffen 24413

This Is My Life (1992)
Carly Simon
Qwest 26901

Thorn Birds II: The Missing Years, The
  (1996)
Garry McDonald/Laurie Stone
Varese Sarabande VSD-5712

Three Musketeers, The (1993)
Michael Kamen
Hollywood Records 61581

Thumbelina (1994)
Barry Manilow
SBK Records 29126

Thunderheart (1992)
James Horner
Intrada MAF-7027

Time to Kill, A (1996)
Elliot Goldenthal
Atlantic 82959

Timecop (1994)
Mark Isham
Varese Sarabande VSD-5532

Titanic (1997)
James Horner
Sony Classical 63213

To Die For (1995)
Danny Elfman
Varese Sarabande VSD-5648

Tom & Huck (1995)
Stephen Endelman
Disney 60892

Tom & Jerry: The Movie (1992)
Henry Mancini
MCA 10721

Tom & Viv (1994)
Debbie Wiseman
Sony Classical 64381

Tombstone (1993)
Bruce Broughton
Intrada MAF-7038

Toy Story (1995)
Randy Newman
Disney 60883

Toys (1992)
Hans Zimmer
Geffen 24505

Trapped in Paradise (1994)
Robert Folk
Varese Sarabande VSD-5555

True Lies (1994)
Brad Fiedel
Epic Soundtrax 64437

Trusting Beatrice (1991)
Stanley Meyers
Intrada MAF-7048

Tune in Tomorrow (1990)
Wynton Marsalis
Columbia 47044

12 Monkeys (1995)
Paul Buckmaster
MCA 11392

Twin Peaks: Fire Walk With Me (1992)
Angelo Badalamenti
Warner Bros. 45019

Twin Peaks: Music from the TV Series
  (1990)
Angelo Badalamenti
Warner Bros. 26316

Two-Moon Junction (1988)
Jonathan Elias
Varese Sarabande VSD-5518

Two Much (1996)
Michel Camilo
Verve 529852

Unbearable Lightness of Being, The (1988)
Various classical composers
Fantasy 21006

Under Siege (1992)
Gary Chang
Varese Sarabande VSD-5409

Under Siege 2: Dark Territory (1995)
Basil Poledouris
Varese Sarabande VSD-5648

Underneath (1994)
Cliff Martinez
Varese Sarabande VSD-5587

Unforgiven (1992)
Lennie Niehaus
Varese Sarabande VSD-5380

Universal Soldier (1992)
Christopher Franke
Varese Sarabande VSD-5373

Unlawful Entry (1992)
James Horner
Intrada MAF-7031

Unstrung Heroes (1995)
Thomas Newman
Hollywood Records 62305

Untamed Heart (1993)
Cliff Eidelman
Varese Sarabande VSD-5404

Up Close and Personal (1996)
Thomas Newman
Hollywood Records 62053

Usual Suspects, The (1995)
John Ottman
Milan 35721

VR.5
John Frizzell
Zoo Entertainment 11109

Vagrant, The (1992)
Christopher Young
Intrada MAF-7028

Village of the Damned (1995)
John Carpenter
Varese Sarabande VSD-5629

Volcano (1997)
Alan Silvestri
Varese Sarabande VSD-5833

Wagons East (1994)
Michael Small
Varese Sarabande VSD-5533

Walk in the Clouds, A (1995
Maurice Jarre
Milan 35719

War of the Buttons (1994)
Rachel Portman
Varese Sarabande VSD-5554

Warlock (1991)
Jerry Goldsmith
Intrada MAF-7003

Warlock: The Armageddon (1993)
Mark McKenzie/Kevin Benson
Intrada MAF-7049

Waterworld (1995)
James Newton Howard
MCA 11282

Wedding Banquet, The (1993)
Mader
Varese Sarabande VSD-5457

Welcome Home, Roxy Carmichael (1990)
Thomas Newman
Varese Sarabande VSD-5300

We're Back--A Dinosaur's Story (1993)
James Horner
MCA 10988

When a Man Loves a Woman (1994)
Zbigniew Preisner
Hollywood Records 61606

While You Were Sleeping (1995)
Randy Edelman
Varese Sarabande VSD-5627

White (1993)
Zbigniew Preisner
Virgin Movie Music 39662

White Palace (1990)
George Fenton
Varese Sarabande VSD-5289

White Squall (1996)
Jeff Rona
Hollywood Records 62040

Widow's Peak (1994)
Carl Davis
Varese Sarabande VSD-5487

Winds of War, The (TV soundtrack)
  (1988)
Bob Cobert
Varese Sarabande VSD-4718

Wings of Courage (1995)
Harry Rabinowitz
Sony Classical 68350

Wings of the Dove (1997)
Edward Shearmur
Milan 35833

Winter in Lisbon, The (1990)
Dizzy Gillespie
Milan 35600

Wolf (1994)
Ennio Morricone
Columbia 64231

Working Girl (1988)
Carly Simon
Arista 8593

World Apart, A (1988)
Hans Zimmer
Milan 35763

Wrestling Ernest Hemingway (1993)
Michael Convertino
Mercury 518897

Wyatt Earp (1994)
James Newton Howard
Warner Bros. 45660

Year of the Comet (1992)
Hummie Mann
Varese Sarabande VSD-5365

Young Indiana Jones Chronicles, The,
  Vol. 1
Laurence Rosenthal
Varese Sarabande VSD-5381

Young Indiana Jones Chronicles, The,
  Vol. II
Laurence Rosenthal
Varese Sarabande VSD-5391

Young Indiana Jones Chronicles, The,
  Vol. III
Laurence Rosenthal/Joel McNeely
Varese Sarabande VSD-5401

Young Indiana Jones Chronicles, The,
  Vol. IV
Laurence Rosenthal/Joel McNeely
Varese Sarabande VSD-5421

Younger and Younger (1993)
Hans Zimmer
Varese Sarabande VSD-5456

Zero Patience (1993)
Glenn Schellenberg
Milan 35675

FILM AND TELEVISION MUSIC AWARDS

ACADEMY AWARD NOMINATIONS (winner indicated by asterisk)

1988
Original Score
George Fenton, *Dangerous Liaisons*
*David Grusin, *The Milagro Beanfield War*
Maurice Jarre, *Gorillas in the Mist*
John Williams, *The Accidental Tourist*
Hans Zimmer, *Rain Man*

Original Song
Lamont Dozier (Phil Collins, lyrics), "Two Hearts," from *Buster*
*Carly Simon (music and lyrics), "Let the River Run," from *Working Girl*
Bob Telson (music and lyrics), "Calling You," from *Bagdad Cafe*

1989
Original Score
David Grusin, *The Fabulous Baker Boys*
James Horner, *Field of Dreams*
*Alan Menken, *The Little Mermaid*
John Williams, *Born on the Fourth of July*
John Williams, *Indiana Jones and the Last Crusade*

Original Song
Marvin Hamlisch (Marilyn & Alan Bergman, lyrics), "The Girl Who Used to Be Me,"
    from *Shirley Valentine*
Alan Menken (Howard Ashman, lyrics), "Kiss the Girl," from *The Little Mermaid*
*Alan Menken (Howard Ashman, lyrics), "Under the Sea," from *The Little Mermaid*
Randy Newman (music and lyrics), "I Love to See You Smile," from *Parenthood*
Tom Snow (Dean Pitchford, lyrics), "After All," from *Chances Are*

1990
Original Score
*John Barry, *Dances With Wolves*
David Grusin, *Havana*
Maurice Jarre, *Ghost*
Randy Newman, *Avalon*
John Williams, *Home Alone*

Original Song
Carmine Coppola (John Bettis, lyrics), "Promise Me You'll Remember," from *The Godfather
    Part III*
Jon Bon Jovi (music and lyrics), "Blaze of Glory," from *Young Guns II*
Shel Silverstein (music and lyrics), "I'm Checkin' Out," from *Postcards From the Edge*
*Stephen Sondheim (music and lyrics), "Sooner or Later (I Always Get My Man)," from *Dick Tracy*
John Williams (Leslie Bricusse, lyrics), "Somewhere in My Memory," from *Home Alone*

1991
Original Score
George Fenton, *The Fisher King*
James Newton Howard, *The Prince of Tides*
*Alan Menken, *Beauty and the Beast*
Ennio Morricone, *Bugsy*
John Williams, *JFK*

Original Song
Michael Kamen (Bryan Adams and Robert John Lange, lyrics), "(Everything I Do) I Do It for You,"
    from *Robin Hood: Prince of Thieves*
*Alan Menken (Howard Ashman, lyrics), "Beauty and the Beast," from *Beauty and the Beast*
Alan Menken (Howard Ashman, lyrics), "Belle," from *Beauty and the Beast*
Alan Menken (Howard Ashman, lyrics), "Be Our Guest," from *Beauty and the Beast*
John Williams (Leslie Bricusse, lyrics), "When You're Alone," from *Hook*

1992
Original Score
John Barry, *Chaplin*
Jerry Goldsmith, *Basic Instinct*
Mark Isham, *A River Runs Through It*
*Alan Menken, *Aladdin*
Richard Robbins, *Howards End*

Original Song
David Foster (Linda Thompson, lyrics), "I Have Nothing," from *The Bodyguard*
Jud J. Friedman (Allan Rich, lyrics), "Run to You," from *The Bodyguard*
Robert Kraft (Arne Glimcher, lyrics), "Beautiful Maria of My Soul," from *The Mambo Kings*
Alan Menken (Howard Ashman, lyrics), "Friends Like Me," from *Aladdin*
*Alan Menken (Tim Rice, lyrics), "Whole New World," from *Aladdin*

1993
Original Score
Elmer Bernstein, *The Age of Innocence*
David Grusin, *The Firm*
James Newton Howard, *The Fugitive*
Richard Robbins, *The Remains of the Day*
*John Williams, *Schindler's List*

Original Song
Janet Jackson, James Harris III, and Terry Lewis (music and lyrics), "Again," from *Poetic Justice*
Carol Bayer Sager, James Ingram, and Clif Magness (music and lyrics), "The Day I Fell in Love,"
    from *Beethoven's 2nd*
*Bruce Springsteen (music and lyrics), "Streets of Philadelphia," from *Philadelphia*
Marc Shaiman (Ramsey McLean, lyrics), "A Wink and a Smile," from *Sleepless in Seattle*
Neil Young (music and lyrics), "Philadelphia," from *Philadelphia*

1994
Original Score
Elliot Goldenthal, *Interview With the Vampire*
Thomas Newman, *Little Women*
Thomas Newman, *The Shawshank Redemption*
Alan Silvestri, *Forrest Gump*
*Hans Zimmer, *The Lion King*

Original Song
*Elton John (Tim Rice, lyrics), "Can You Feel the Love Tonight," from *The Lion King*
Elton John (Tim Rice, lyrics), "Circle of Life," from *The Lion King*
Elton John (Tim Rice, lyrics), "Hakuna Matata," from *The Lion King*
Randy Newman (music and lyrics), "Make Up Your Mind," from *The Paper*
Carol Bayer Sager, John Newton Howard, James Ingram, Patty Smyth (music and lyrics),
  "Look What Love Had Done," from *Junior*

1995
Original Musical or Comedy Score
*Alan Menken, *Pocahontas*
Randy Newman, *Toy Story*
Thomas Newman, *Unstrung Heroes*
Marc Shaiman, *The American President*
John Williams, *Sabrina*

Original Dramatic Score
*Luis Bacalov, *Il Postino (The Postman)*
Patrick Doyle, *Sense and Sensibility*
James Horner, *Apollo 13*
James Horner, *Braveheart*
John Williams, *Nixon*

Original Song
Michael Kamen, Bryan Adams, Robert John Lange (music and lyrics), "Have You Ever
  Really Loved a Woman," from *Don Juan DeMarco*
*Alan Menken (Stephen Schwartz, lyrics), "Colors of the Wind," from *Pocahontas*
Randy Newman (music and lyrics), "You've Got a Friend," from *Toy Story*
Bruce Springsteen (music and lyrics), "Dead Man Walking," from *Dead Man Walking*
John Williams (Marilyn & Alan Bergman, lyrics), "Moonlight," from *Sabrina*

1996
Original Musical or Comedy Score
Alan Menken, *The Hunchback of Notre Dame*
Randy Newman, *James and the Giant Peach*
*Rachel Portman, *Emma*
Marc Shaiman, *The First Wives Club*
Hans Zimmer, *The Preacher's Wife*

Original Dramatic Score
Patrick Doyle, *Hamlet*
Elliot Goldenthal, *Michael Collins*
David Hirschfelder, *Shine*
John Williams, *Sleepers*
*Gabriel Yared, *The English Patient*

Original Song
James Newton Howard, Jud J. Friedman, Allan Dennis Rich (music and lyrics), "For the
  First Time," from *One Fine Day*
Barbra Streisand, Marvin Hamlisch, Bryan Adams, Robert "Mutt" Lange (music and lyrics),
  "I Finally Found Someone," from *The Mirror Has Two Faces*
Adam Schlesinger (music and lyrics), "That Thing You Do!" from *That Thing You Do!*
Diane Warren (music and lyrics), "Because You Loved Me," from *Up Close and Personal*
*Andrew Lloyd Webber (Tim Rice, lyrics), "You Must Love Me," from *Evita*

1997

Original Musical or Comedy Score
*Anne Dudley, *The Full Monty*
Danny Elfman, *Men in Black*
James Newton Howard, *My Best Friend's Wedding*
David Newman; songs: Stephen Flaherty (music) and Lynn Ahrens (lyrics), *Anastasia*
Hans Zimmer, *As Good As It Gets*

Original Dramatic Score
Danny Elfman, *Good Will Hunting*
Philip Glass, *Kundun*
Jerry Goldsmith, *L.A. Confidential*
*James Horner, *Titanic*
John Williams, *Amistad*

Original Song
Stephen Flaherty (Lynn Ahrens, lyrics), "Journey to the Past," from *Anastasia*
*James Horner (Will Jennings, lyrics), "My Heart Will Go On," from *Titanic*
Alan Menken (David Zippel, lyrics), "Go the Distance," from *Hercules*
Elliott Smith (music and lyrics), "Miss Misery," from *Good Will Hunting*
Diane Warren (music and lyrics), "How Do I Live," from *Con Air*

EMMY NOMINATIONS FOR MUSIC COMPOSITION (winner indicated by asterisk)

1987-88
[Miniseries or Special: Dramatic Underscore]
Dick DeBenedictis, *Perry Mason: The Case of the Avenging Ace* (NBC)
Allyn Ferguson, *Hallmark Hall of Fame: April Morning* (CBS)
Gerald Fried, *Napoleon and Josephine: A Love Story* (part 3) (ABC)
Johnny Mandel, *Hallmark Hall of Fame: Foxfire* (CBS)
*Laurence Rosenthal, *The Bourne Identity* (part 1) (ABC)

[Main Title Theme Music]
John Corigliano, *Great Performances* (PBS)
*Lee Holdridge, *Beauty and the Beast* (CBS)
Stewart Levin and W.G. Snuffy Walden, *thirtysomething* (ABC)
Richard Markowitz, *The Law and Harry McGraw* (CBS)

1988-89
[Miniseries or Special: Dramatic Underscore]
Chris Boardman, *The Hijacking of the Achille Lauro* (NBC)
Bob Cobert, *War and Remembrance* (part 11) (ABC)
Allyn Ferguson, *Pancho Barnes* (CBS)
Fred Karlin, *Bridge to Silence* (CBS)
*Basil Poledouris, *Lonesome Dove* (part 4) (CBS)

[Main Title Theme Music]
Stanley Clarke, *Knightwatch* (ABC)
James Newton Howard, *Men* (CBS)
Jerrold Immel, *Paradise* (CBS)
Mike Post, *Unsub* (NBC)
Jonathan Tunick, *Tattinger's* (NBC)

1989-90

[Miniseries or Special: Dramatic Underscore]
John Addison, *The Phantom of the Opera* (part 2) (NBC)
Bruce Broughton, *The Old Man and the Sea* (NBC)
*James DiPasquale, *Hallmark Hall of Fame: The Shell Seekers* (CBS)
Billy Goldenberg, *People Like Us* (part 2) (NBC)
Lee Holdridge, *Do You Know the Muffin Man?* (CBS)
David Shire, *The Kennedys of Massachusetts* (ABC)
Christopher Young, *Last Flight Out* (NBC)

[Main Title Theme Music]
Angelo Badalamenti and David Lynch, *Twin Peaks* (ABC)
John Debney, *The Young Riders* (ABC)
Danny Elfman, *The Simpsons* (Fox)
Dan Foliart and Howard Pearl, *Carol & Company* (NBC)
Patrick Williams, *FM* (NBC)

1990-91

[Miniseries or Special: Dramatic Underscore]
*Richard Bellis, *Stephen King's "It"* (part 1) (ABC)
Chris Boardman, *Johnny Ryan* (NBC)
Don Davis, *Lies Before Kisses* (CBS)
James DiPasquale, *The Killing Mind* (Lifetime)
Patrick Williams, *Hallmark Hall of Fame: Decoration Day* (CBS)

[Main Title Theme Music]
Stanley Clarke (Lawrence Edwards, lyrics), *Hull High* (NBC)
Ray Colcord, *Singer and Son* (NBC)
Lee Holdridge, *ABC World of Discovery* (ABC)
Thomas Newman, *Against the Law* (Fox)
Michael Skloff, *Dream On* (HBO)

1991-92

[Miniseries or Special: Dramatic Underscore]
Richard Bellis, *Doublecrossed* (HBO)
*Bruce Broughton, *Hallmark Hall of Fame: O Pioneers* (CBS)
Don Davis, *A Little Piece of Heaven* (NBC)
Fred Karlin, *Survive the Savage Sea* (ABC)
Arthur Kempel, *Fire in the Dark* (CBS)

[Main Title Theme Music]
Steve Dorff, *Major Dad* (CBS)
Marvin Hamlisch (Alan & Marilyn Bergman, lyrics), *Brooklyn Bridge* (CBS)
Mike Post, *Silk Stalkings* (USA)
*Laurence Rosenthal, *The Young Indiana Jones Chronicles* (ABC)
W.G. Snuffy Walden, *I'll Fly Away* (NBC)

1992-93

[Miniseries or Special: Dramatic Underscore]
Charles Bernstein, *The Sea Wolf* (TNT)
Joseph Conlan, *Mortal Sins* (USA)
Lee Holdridge, *Call of the Wild* (CBS)
Mark Snow, *Hallmark Hall of Fame: An American Story* (CBS)
*Patrick Williams, *Danielle Steel's "Jewels"* (part 1) (NBC)

[Main Title Theme Music]
Carl Davis, *Covington Cross* (ABC)
Lee Holdridge, *Bob* (CBS)
Chris Klatman, *Bodies of Evidence* (CBS)
Stewart Levin, *Picket Fences* (CBS)
*Dennis McCarthy, *Star Trek: Deep Space Nine* (Syn)
Jonathan Tunick, *Love & War* (CBS)

1993-94
[Miniseries or Special: Dramatic Underscore]
Richard Bellis, *Double, Double, Toil and Trouble* (ABC)
*Lennie Niehaus, *Lush Life* (Showtime)
Mark Snow, *Oldest Living Confederate Widow Tells All* (part 2) (CBS)
W.G. Snuffy Walden, *Stephen King's "The Stand"* (part 4) (ABC)
Patrick Williams, *Geronimo* (TNT)

[Main Title Theme Music]
*John Debney, *seaQuest DSV* (NBC)
Jay Gruska, *Lois & Clark: The New Adventures of Superman* (ABC)
Bruce Miller (Darryl Phinnesse, lyrics), *Frasier* (NBC)
Mike Post, *NYPD Blue* (ABC)
Mark Snow, *The X-Files* (Fox)

1994-95
[Miniseries or Special: Dramatic Underscore]
Jay Chattaway, *30 Years of National Geographic Specials* (NBC)
Lee Holdridge, *Buffalo Girls* (part 1) (CBS)
*Laurence Rosenthal, *Young Indiana Jones and the Hollywood Follies* (Fam Ch)
Mark Snow, *Children of the Dust* (part 1) (CBS)
Patrick Williams, *Kingfish: A Story of Huey P. Long* (TNT)

[Main Title Theme Music]
*Jerry Goldsmith, *Star Trek: Voyager* (UPN)
James Newton Howard, *ER* (NBC)
Mark Isham, *Chicago Hope* (CBS)
Michael Skloff (Allee Willis, lyrics), *Friends* (NBC)
W.G. Snuffy Walden, *My So-Called Life* (ABC)

1995-96
[Miniseries or Special: Dramatic Underscore]
David Bell, *Larry McMurtry's "Dead Man's Walk"* (part 1) ABC
David Michael Frank, *Annie: A Royal Adventure* (ABC)
Lee Holdridge, *Tuskegee Airmen* (HBO)
*Ernest Troost, *The Canterville Ghost* (ABC)
Christopher Young, *Norma Jean and Marilyn* (HBO)

[Main Title Theme Music]
Bruce Broughton, *JAG* (NBC)
Mark Isham, *Chicago Hope* (CBS)
*Mike Post, *Murder One* (ABC)
Mark Snow, *Nowhere Man* (UPN)
Tim Truman, *Central Park West* (CBS)

1996-97
[Miniseries or Special: Dramatic Underscore]
Bruce Boughton, *True Women* (CBS)
Mark Mothersbaugh, *Quicksilver Highway* (Fox)
*Laurence Rosenthal, *The Young Indiana Jones Chronicles: Travels With Father* (Fam Ch)
Ernest Troost, *Hallmark Hall of Fame: Calm at Sunset* (CBS)
Patrick Williams, *After Jimmy* (CBS)

[Main Title Theme Music]
*John Debney, *The Cape* (pilot) (Syndicated)
Michael Hoenig, *Dark Skies* (NBC)
Mark Isham, *EZ Streets* ("A Terrible Beauty") (CBS)
Danny Lux, *Crisis Center* (pilot) (NBC)
W.G. Snuffy Walden, *Early Edition* (CBS)

ACE AWARDS NOMINATIONS FOR ORIGINAL SCOPE IN A MADE-FOR-CABLE MOVIE OR SPECIAL (CableAce from 1992 to 1997, after which awards were disbanded) (winner indicated by asterisk)

1987
Michel Colombier, *Florida Straits* (HBO)
*Hagood Hardy, *Anne of Avonlea* (Disney Channel)
Georges Delerue, *Sword of Gideon* (HBO)
Lucio Morricone, *Control* (HBO)
Lee Holdridge, *16 Days of Glory II* (Disney Channel)

1988
*Richard Hartley, *The Impossible Spy* (HBO)
Charles Bernstein, *The Man Who Broke 1,000 Chains* (HBO)
Richard Hartley, *Mandela* (HBO)
Lee Holdridge, *A Friendship in Vienna* (Disney Channel)
David Newman, *The Brave Little Toaster* (Disney Channel)

1989
Peter Bernstein, *Nightbreaker* (TNT)
Cliff Eidelman, *Dead Man Out* (HBO)
Jay Ferguson, *Tales From the Crypt: Only Skin Deep* (HBO)
Brian May, *A Dangerous Life* (HBO)
*Alan Silvestri, *Tales From the Crypt: And All Through the House* (HBO)

1990
Michael J. Lewis, *The Rose and the Jackal* (TNT)
Thomas Newman, *Heat Wave* (TNT)
John Scott, *Red King, White Knight* (HBO)
*Lalo Schifrin, *The Neon Empire* (Showtime)
Stanley Myers, *Ivory Wars* (Discovery Channel)

1991
*Georges Delerue, *The Josephine Baker Story* (HBO)
James Di Pasquale, *The Killing Mind* (Lifetime)
Nicholas Pike, *Tales From the Crypt: Mournin' Mess* (HBO)

1992
Michael Bacon, *The Man Who Loves Sharks* (Discovery)
Bill Conti, *Tales From the Crypt: Maniac at Large* (HBO)
*Stewart Copeland, *Afterburn* (HBO)
Jennie Muskett, *People of the Forest: The Chimps of Gombe* (Discovery)
Curt Sobel, *Cast a Deadly Spell* (HBO)

1993
Todd Boekelheide, *Earth and the American Dream* (HBO)
Lee Holdridge, *Heidi* (Disney Channel)
Michael Kamen, *Blue Ice* (HBO)
*Stanislas Syrewicz, *Stalin* (HBO)
Shirley Walker, *Majority Rule* (Lifetime)

1994
Marco Frisina and Ennio Morricone, *Abraham* (TNT)
Gerald Gouriet, *The Substitute* (USA)
Richard Harvey, *Doomsday Gun* (HBO)
*Patrick Williams, *Geronimo* (TNT)
Patrick Williams, *Zelda* (TNT)

1995
*Marco Frisina, *Joseph* (TNT)
Marco Frisina, *Jacob* (TNT)
Mark Mancina and John Van Tongeren, *The Outer Limits* (Showtime)
David Shire, *My Antonia* (USA)
Patrick Williams, *Kingfish: A Story of Huey P. Long* (TNT)

1996
Meir Finkelstein, *Survivors of the Holocaust* (TBS Superstation)
Lee Holdridge, *The Tuskegee Airmen* (HBO)
Arthur Kempel, *Riders of the Purple Sage* (TNT)
*Ron Ramin, *Rent-a-Kid* (Disney Channel)
Laurence Rosenthal, *Young Indiana Jones and Travels With Father* (Fam Ch)

1997
*Dave Grusin, *In the Gloaming* (HBO)
Laurence Rosenthal, *The Man Who Captured Eichmann* (TNT)
Laurence Rosenthal, *Member of the Wedding* (USA)
John Van Tongeren, *Poltergeist: The Legacy* (Showtime)
Nathan Wang, *The Lost Children of Berlin* (A&E)

GOLDEN GLOBE NOMINATIONS (winner indicated by asterisk)

1991
Original Score
Zbigniew Preisner, *At Home in the Fields of the Lord*
*Alan Menken, *Beauty and the Beast*
Ennio Morricone, *Bugsy*
Patrick Doyle, *Dead Again*
Dave Grusin, *For the Boys*
Michael Kamen, *Robin Hood: Prince of Thieves*

Original Song
Eric Clapton (Will Jennings, lyrics), "Tears in Heaven," from *Rush*
James Horner and Will Jennings (music and lyrics), "Dreams to Dream," from *An American Tail: Fievel Goes West*
Michael Kamen, Bryan Adams, Robert John Lange (music and lyrics), "(Everything I Do) I Do It for You," from *Robin Hood: Prince of Thieves*
Alan Menken (Howard Ashman, lyrics), "Be Our Guest," from *Beauty and the Beast*
*Alan Menken (Howard Ashman, lyrics), "Beauty and the Beast," from *Beauty and the Beast*

1992
Original Score
John Barry, *Chaplin*
Jerry Goldsmith, *Basic Instinct*
*Alan Menken, *Aladdin*
Trevor Jones and Randy Edelman, *The Last of the Mohicans*
Vangelis, *1492: Conquest of Paradise*

Original Song
Madonna Ciccone and Shep Pettibone (music and lyrics), "This Used to Be My Playground," from *A League of Their Own*
Robert Kraft (Arne Glimcher, lyrics), "Beautiful Maria of My Soul," from *The Mambo Kings*
Alan Menken (Howard Ashman, lyrics), "Friend Like Me," from *Aladdin*
Alan Menken (Howard Ashman, lyrics), "Prince Ali," from *Aladdin*
*Alan Menken (Tim Rice, lyrics), "A Whole New World," from *Aladdin*

1993
Original Score
Danny Elfman, *The Nightmare Before Christmas*
*Kitaro, *Heaven and Earth*
Michael Nyman, *The Piano*
Zbigniew Preisner, *Blue*
John Williams, *Schindler's List*

Original Song
Bono, Gavin Friday, Maurice Seezer (music and lyrics), "(You Made Me the) Thief of Your Heart," from *In the Name of the Father*
Janet Jackson, James Harris III, Terry Lewis (music and lyrics), "Again," from *Poetic Justice*
Carole Bayer Sager, James Ingram, Clif Magness (music and lyrics), "The Day I Fall in Love," from *Beethoven's 2nd*
*Bruce Springsteen (music and lyrics), "Streets of Philadelphia," from *Philadelphia*
U2 (Bono, lyrics), "Stay," from *Faraway So Close*

1994
Original Score
Elliot Goldenthal, *Interview With the Vampire*
James Horner, *Legends of the Fall*
Mark Isham, *Nell*
Alan Silvestri, *Forrest Gump*
*Hans Zimmer, *The Lion King*

Original Song
Lex De Azevedo (David Zippel, lyrics), "Far Longer Than Forever," from *The Swan Princess*
Jud J. Friedman, Lauren Christy, Dominic Frontiere (music and lyrics), "The Color of the Night," from *Color of Night*

*Elton John (Tim Rice, lyrics), "Can You Feel the Love Tonight," from *The Lion King*
Elton John (Tim Rice, lyrics), "Circle of Life," from *The Lion King*
Madonna, Patrick Leonard, Richard Page (music and lyrics), "I'll Remember," from *With Honors*
Carol Bayer Sager, James Ingram, James Newton Howard, Patty Smyth (music and lyrics), "Look What Love Has Done," from *Junior*

1995
Original Score
Patrick Doyle, *Sense and Sensibility*
James Horner, *Braveheart*
*Maurice Jarre, *A Walk in the Clouds*
Michael Kamen, *Don Juan DeMarco*
Alan Menken, *Pocahontas*

Original Song
Bryan Adams, Michael Kamen, Robert "Mutt" Lange (music and lyrics), "Have You Ever Really Loved a Woman?" from *Don Juan DeMarco*
*Alan Menken (Stephen Schwartz, lyrics), "Color of the Wind," from *Pocahontas*
Randy Newman (music and lyrics), "You Got a Friend in Me" from *Toy Story*
U2 (Bono, lyrics), "Hold Me, Thrill Me, Kiss Me, Kill Me," from *Batman Forever*
John Williams (Alan and Marilyn Bergman, lyrics), "Moonlight," from *Sabrina*

1996
Original Score
Elliot Goldenthal, *Michael Collins*
Marvin Hamlisch, *The Mirror Has Two Faces*
David Hirschfelder, *Shine*
Alan Menken, *The Hunchback of Notre Dame*
*Gabriel Yared, *The English Patient*

Original Song
James Newton Howard, Jud L. Friedman, Allan Dennis Rich (music and lyrics), "For the First Time," from *One Fine Day*
Barbra Streisand, Marvin Hamlisch, Bryan Adams, Robert "Mutt" Lange (music and lyrics), "I've Finally Found Someone," from *The Mirror Has Two Faces*
Adam Schlesinger (music and lyrics), "That Thing You Do!" from *That Thing You Do!*
*Andrew Lloyd Weber (Tim Rice, lyrics), "You Must Love Me," from *Evita*
Diane Warren (music and lyrics), "Because You Loved Me," from *Up Close and Personal*

1997
Original Score
Philip Glass, *Kundun*
Jerry Goldsmith, *L.A. Confidential*
*James Horner, *Titanic*
Michael Nyman, *Gattaca*
John Williams, *Seven Years in Tibet*

Original Song
Sheryl Crow and Mitchell Froom (music and lyrics), "Tomorrow Never Dies," from *Tomorrow Never Dies*
Stephen Flaherty (Lynn Ahrens, lyrics), "Journey to the Past," from *Anastasia*
Stephen Flaherty (Lynn Ahrens, lyrics), "Once Upon a December," from *Anastasia*
*James Horner (Will Jennings, lyrics), "My Heart Will Go On," from *Titanic*
Alan Menken (David Zippel, lyrics), "Go the Distance," from *Hercules*

About the Author

Longtime film and TV-movie authority ALVIN H. MARILL is the author of many books in the field and consultant and editor on many others. Among his works are *Movies Made for Television* (and its several updates), *More Theatre: Stage to Screen to Television* (Scarecrow Press), *Blockbuster Entertainment's Guide to Television on Video*, and personality books such as *The Films of Tommy Lee Jones, The Complete Films of Edward G. Robinson, The Ultimate John Wayne Trivia Book, Samuel Goldwyn Presents*, and *Robert Mitchum on the Screen*. He also is associate editor of Leonard Maltin's annual *Movie & Video Guide*, an editor of the mystery/horror film magazine *Scarlet Street*, and annotator of dozens of albums and CDs dealing with pop music and the stage and screen. He lives in New Jersey.

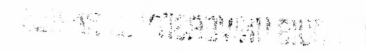